A BIG HISTORY OF NORTH AMERICA

A BIG HISTORY OF
NORTH AMERICA

From Montezuma to Monroe

Kevin Jon Fernlund

UNIVERSITY OF MISSOURI PRESS

Columbia

Library of Congress Cataloging-in-Publication Data

Names: Fernlund, Kevin J., author.
Title: A big history of North America : from Montezuma to Monroe / Kevin
 Jon Fernlund.
Description: Columbia : The University of Missouri Press, [2022] | Includes
 bibliographical references and index.
Identifiers: LCCN 2022013713 (print) | LCCN 2022013714 (ebook) | ISBN
 9780826222657 (hardcover) | ISBN 9780826222749 (paperback) | ISBN
 9780826274779 (ebook)
Subjects: LCSH: Power (Social sciences)--North America. | North
 America--History. | North America--Civilization. | North
 America--Discovery and exploration. | North America--Historical
 geography.
Classification: LCC E45 .F47 2022 (print) | LCC E45 (ebook) | DDC
 970--dc23/eng/20220805
LC record available at https://lccn.loc.gov/2022013713
LC ebook record available at https://lccn.loc.gov/2022013714

Typeface: Aktiv Grotesque and Minion Pro

Cover image: Frans Floris, *Geometry* (allegory and personification of Geometry holding a
compass above a globe), 1557. Oil on canvas, 59 ¼ x 68 1/8 in. (150.5 x 173 cm; originally 125 x 173 cm). Private collection, Genoa.

To Sharon
the Best in the West

and

To Richard W. Etulain
a Moderate in an Immoderate Time

No man is an island, entire of itself; every man is a piece of

the continent,

a part of the main.

JOHN DONNE

Devotions

Contents

PART III: THE ANGLOSPHERE

EPILOGUE

Acknowledgments

MOST HISTORIES OF NORTH AMERICA either explicitly or implicitly divide the continent by geography and culture between British North America, i.e., Canada and the United States, on the one hand, and Mexico or Mexico and Latin America, on the other. As I have tried to demonstrate with this book, there are any number of reasons for integrating the histories of these two North Americas into a single narrative, even if doing so runs sharply counter to older Anglo and Hispanic historiographical traditions.

For support in undertaking this admittedly unorthodox endeavor, as well as expertise and sage advice, I would very much like to salute the University of Missouri Press, especially Andrew J. Davidson, the Editor in Chief, and his colleagues Mary Conley, Drew Griffith, Rosie Williamson, Deanna M. Davis, Tracy Tritschler, and Robin Rennison. I would also like to thank Miranda Ottewell. Her copyediting and queries sharpened my writing and saved me from numerous errors.

I would also like to express my gratitude to the historians, editors, and peer reviewers who helped guide me through the various stages of this project. These individuals include John R. Gillingham, Maris Gillette, Richard W. Etulain, Andrew J. Davidson, Samuel Brunk, Barry Rodrigue, Liping Zhu, Nikolaos Poulopoulos, Steve W. Rowan, Carlos A. Schwantes, Mark Burkholder, Priscilla A. Dowden-White, Minsoo Kang, and David Christian. I would also like to thank Molly Holz, the former editor of *Montana The Magazine of Western History*, Durwood Ball, the editor of the *New Mexico Historical Review*, and David Blanks, the editor of the *Journal of Big History*, for their support and encouragement in publishing exploratory articles on this subject. Of course, any mistakes or questionable interpretations are entirely my responsibility and mine alone.

Many ideas that appear in this book were originally classroom-tested in lectures and PowerPoint presentations. I appreciate my students who offered critical but always cheerful feedback on my related propositions, theses, and arguments. Finally, I would like to thank the History Department and the College of Arts and Sciences at the University of Missouri–St. Louis, for providing support for research and travel. This funding and time allowed me to see the book to completion.

Kevin Jon Fernlund
Des Peres, Missouri 2022

A BIG HISTORY OF NORTH AMERICA

Prologue

The Athenians to the Melians

Since you know as well as we do the right, as the world goes, is only in question between equals in power, while the strong do what they can and the weak suffer what they must.

> "The Melian Dialogue" in Thucydides,
> *The Peloponnesian War*, 411 BC

As Geography without History seemeth a carkasse without motion, so History without Geography wandereth as a vagrant without certain habitation.

> Captain John Smith, *Generall Historie*

CHAPTER 1

On Method

"It is the fear of great history which has killed great history."

—Edmond Faral

The Monroe Doctrine 1.0 and 2.0

THE MONROE DOCTRINE 1.0 OF 1823, named after President James Monroe, proclaimed a United States sphere of influence. This notice applied to the western hemisphere, primarily North America, and was intended primarily for Europe, specifically Spain. With perhaps the exception of Great Britain, which at one point united the British Isles, no power has ever before been able to dominate so thoroughly its own region as the United States. And with safe borders and security at home, the United States was free to extend its power throughout the world. Still, "she did not go abroad," in the words of John Quincy Adams, President Monroe's secretary of state, "in search of monsters to destroy." But as the Pax Britannica gave way to the Pax Americana, America became a slayer of monsters, if an often ambivalent one.

Now fast forward to the end of 1991, when the implosion of the Soviet Union allowed the United States to emerge from the Cold War as the world's sole superpower. Less than two years later, in November 1993, Europe would form a new United States—the European Union. At the same time, the original United States created in the North American Free Trade Agreement (NAFTA) a continent-size free trade zone with its two North American neighbors, Canada and Mexico, and issued a sweeping post–Cold War policy statement, the Defense Planning Guidance of 1992, which globalized the Monroe Doctrine. In this Monroe Doctrine 2.0, the United States proclaimed that it would not brook the emergence of any new rival or threat anywhere in the world—Asia, Africa, Europe, or the Americas. What followed was a period of unprecedented peace and prosperity—a globalization of the world's economy and culture within an American-led, rules-based order. But this order has not gone unchallenged; since 1992 an increasingly reckless Russia, a declining power, and a steadily less cautious China, a rising power, both filled with revanchist ambitions and deep-seated grievances, have sought to challenge America's unique unipolarity. Effectively confronting this dual threat will require the West's best minds, political resolve, and sacrifice.[1]

To put this moment and challenge into perspective, this book looks at America's initial rise to power and considers what made its relatively short path to hemispheric dominance possible. Since it does this within a conti-nental context, it begins with the conquest of the Aztec Empire of Mexico by Spain's Hernán Cortés. But unlike a typical historical survey, this book tracks over time the sources of social power—the abilities of a particular society "to get things done," in the archaeologist and historian Ian Morris's apt formulation, including the projection of military force—by placing America's rise in a continental as well as a transatlantic context. I end this study with James Monroe's proclamation of hemispheric hegemony. The result is a not another national narrative of the early US republic, of which there are many, but a new North American history, one inclusive of Mexico, of which there are very few.[2]

For two centuries beginning in 1607 British North America was a theater of European rivalry and warfare, whereas Mexico, after its initial conquest by Spain in the early sixteenth century, enjoyed a nearly three-century-long Pax Hispanica. In both, North America's relationship with Europe was determinative. I argue that after the wars of independence in the late eigh-teenth and early nineteenth centuries, this transatlantic relationship, or its absence in Mexico's case, was if anything even more significant. In upper North America, Canada remained in and prospered as part of the British Empire. In middle North America, however, the emergent United States tried—first during the War of American Independence and again during the War of 1812, the so-called second war of independence—to dislodge Great Britain from the continent. It failed to do so, and there would be no third attempt to realize this important if elusive revolutionary goal. Instead the two nations—one an established power, the other a rising power—agreed to share the continent and its wealth, and the United States went on to flourish under the Pax Britannica. In short, the two nations avoided the Thucydides trap and effected instead a Thucydides escape. According to political scientist Graham T. Allison, a Thucydides trap snaps shut when an established power like Sparta, feeling threatened by a rising power like Athens, goes to war with it before, as it believes, it is too late. This concept is based on Thucydides's thesis that Sparta's fear of Athens's growing power was the cause of the Peloponnesian War. Allison found that in the vast majority of cases in which a rising power has threatened a ruling power, the result has been war.[3]

The special relationship between the United Kingdom and the United States that originated in North America would later shape the entire Atlantic world. In lower North America, by contrast, Mexico succeeded in driving Spain out of the continent, a victory formalized by the Treaty of Córdoba on August 24, 1821. But in its triumph Mexico had incurred the enmity of a sullen and vindictive declining power. As Sparta had with Athens, Spain chose to suppress Mexico's rise to power. Tragically, it succeeded, leaving North America deeply divided into Anglo- and Hispanospheres with different levels of social development, despite the continent's shared civilization, geography, and Indigenous past. Mexico had traded security and subordination for isolation and vulnerability, and political turmoil, strife, and foreign invasion marked the century that followed its independence. These changing relationships and reversals of fortune reveal a rich as well as a tragic North American history, one largely hidden from view by the separate national and conventional histories of Mexico, Canada, and the United States.

While numerous histories of the continent of Europe exist, the continent of North America has largely failed to capture the historian's imagination. The patrician scholars Francis Parkman and William H. Prescott are notable but qualified exceptions. Parkman charted the fall of New France and Prescott the rise of New Spain, both against a vast continental setting. Their contemporary George Bancroft also stressed the importance of the colonial period in his ten-volume history of the United States, which he framed in transatlantic as well as continental terms. The present volume, then, is a rare thing: a linear history of North America's social development in both the Hispanosphere and Anglosphere viewed in toto, establishing a baseline in the continent's prehistory before turning to the period from 1521 to 1823. More space is given to the Hispanosphere, since New Spain's history was significantly longer than that of its colonial neighbors to the north.

What, then, is the main argument of this book? The story of the United States, in particular the story of the origins of the nation's social power, cannot be told without that of its two continental neighbors, Canada and Mexico. These three countries form a whole—if a poorly understood whole—that is indeed greater than the sum of its parts. It is true that the United States would eventually dominate the continent—militarily, economically, and otherwise—and later the world, so much so that the stories of its two next-door neighbors have been all but lost in the shadow of the US colossus. But North America's early rise as a regional power was very much conditioned by transcontinental, transpacific, and above all transatlantic factors. And while the United States profoundly shaped the history of Canada and Mexico, so too did Canada and Mexico—to say nothing of the influences of Europe and Asia on North America—shape US history. Any society's social development is directly related to either its own social power or, just as crucially, the protective extension or destructive intrusion of the social power of other societies. This three-century narrative and analysis of the interrelationship of the three countries that make up North America, then, is organized around the concepts of social power and cultural evolution as well as the theme of exploration, a partly political, partly scientific cultural activity that is a prime example of social power and was the unique modus operandi of Europe's territorial expansion.

Big History, or A Map of Time

This is a Big History—a history that seeks to unite natural and human history, geography and culture, from the Big Bang to this morning's breakfast. Our *place* of interest, however, is much more modest: namely, the continent of North America. Our *period* is no less limited, confined as it is to the interval between the beginning of Europe's military conquest of North America in 1521 and North America's rise to parity with Europe in 1823, when the United States asserted a hemispheric hegemony in concert with Great Britain, which remained very much ensconced in Canada.[4] Unlike its two continental neighbors, which fought for national independence, Canada sought its autonomy gradually and largely peacefully. Moreover, the postcolonial history of Anglo-American amity contrasts sharply with the postcolonial hostility between Spain and Mexico. These international relations would have profound implications for the continent. And while historians have sliced and diced humanity into any number of categories—race, class, gender, and so on—for analysis, the category of analysis here is humanity itself: a single species but one differentiated by social development or cultural evolution (not to be confused with organic evolution, a very different thing!). I contend here that these differences in development are the principal drivers of modern history. And during our period, as we shall see, the North Atlantic world would experience not one but two major phases of sociocultural development: the Renaissance, when Europe recovered its classical inheritance and discovered a new world, and the Enlightenment, a transatlantic period of material and intellectual reform, which produced democratic revolutions in America and France.

Geography and Culture

The Spanish divided the Americas into an América Septentrional (North America) and an América Meridional (South America). The North America discussed as a historical entity here coincides with the geological definition of North America: that is, the North American tectonic plate, which notably does not include the countries of Central America or the islands of the Caribbean (the Greater and Lesser Antilles). What this place of our study does include is Mexico (along with the Yucatán Peninsula), the United States—the lower forty-eight adjoining states, plus the Alaska Peninsula and far northeastern Asia, across the Bering Strait—as well as mainland Canada and the Arctic islands. The North American plate also includes half of Iceland, a good part of Cuba, the Lucayan Archipelago, and all of Greenland, but this book will focus primarily on the three large, contiguous North American nations: Canada, the United States, and Mexico, each of which originated as a former settler colony of Europe but went on to become, and remain, fully sovereign. As a constitutional monarchy, Canada does possess the Westminster form of government and therefore retains a significant formal tie with the United Kingdom of Great Britain and Northern Ireland, as well as the other Commonwealth realms, but it is otherwise entirely free and independent.

There exists an invidious view of the United States (and by extension Canada and Mexico), often expressed with a certain supercilious disdain, that it is a young country, fresh, as it were, off the turnip truck. "China's civilization has been around far longer," as Chinese ambassador to the United States Cui Tiankai recently took pains to point out. The United States, like the nations of Canada and Mexico, may have been a recent creation, if not nearly as recent as Cui's People's Republic of China, which was founded in 1949. Still, the ambassador was right in one respect. China's Confucian roots are very old and predate by millennia the current Communist regime. But they are no older than the roots of Western civilization. The Spanish, the English, the French, the Dutch, and the Russians who came to North America all shared, to a greater or lesser extent, this ancient and underlying cultural unity or civilization—one based on three broad and very old traditions, which may be thought of as the three legs of a stool: the Greco-Roman, the Germanic, and the Judeo-Christian. And what was true of Europe was no less true of the civilization that Europeans transplanted to North America. Geographer Donald W. Meinig adds this insight: the Atlantic world was the "scene of a vast interaction rather than merely the transfer of Europeans onto American shores. Instead of a European discovery of a new world, we might better consider it as a sudden and harsh encounter between two old worlds that transformed both and integrated them into a single New World."[5]

One might argue that in North America's social development, the cultural factors that underlaid New England, New France, and New Netherland as well as New Spain basically canceled one another out, making geography all the more significant. There is no question that the very different geographies of Mexico, Canada, and the United States have a great deal of explanatory power.

The great extent to which Mexico is mountainous, for example, is key to understanding the nation's infrastructural and socioeconomic development. In fact, if Mexico were flattened out, its square mileage would exceed that of Asia. But due to its highly mountainous terrain, it has neither large swaths of land suitable for extensive railroad and highway networks nor long, navigable rivers like the St. Lawrence, Mississippi, Ohio, and Columbia. Mexico's longest river, the Rio Grande—known in Spanish as the Río Bravo del Norte or simply Río Bravo ("Wild River")—is indeed long, at 1,896 miles. But it is so shallow in most places as to be unnavigable, so of no use for the transportation of goods and peoples. The Sierra Madre Oriental, the Sierra Madre del Sur, and the Sierra Madre Occidental run diagonally, north to southeast, while the Sierra Nevada—the volcano belt—transverses south-central Mexico. Together, these ranges wall off the Altiplanicie Mexicana (the central Mexican plateau) separating a great many of Mexico's cities, towns, and villages from the coasts. The large Yucatán Peninsula to the east and the long, skinny peninsula of Baja (lower) California to the west are in effect islands unto themselves, separated from Mexico proper by the gulfs of Campeche and California, respectively. Mexican history is incomprehensible without reference to this broken geography.[6]

In Canada geography is if anything even more important to the nation's infrastructural and socioeconomic development. Only Russia has a larger area, and Canada faces three oceans—the Atlantic, the Arctic, and the Pacific—giving it the world's longest coastline. Yet its population is comparatively small: only 38 million, roughly 10 percent that of its southern neighbor, the United States. And three-quarters of this population is huddled within the nation's habitable zone, a narrow band along the Canadian-US border, scarcely one hundred miles wide. Above this zone lies the great white and largely empty north.

Northwestern Canada is drained by the Mackenzie River, which flows into the Beaufort Sea and forms North America's second largest river system, after that of the Mississippi. The Mackenzie drains an area almost the size of Mexico. To the west of the Mackenzie Mountains lies the source of the Yukon River, at Lakes Atlin and Tagish in northern British Columbia. The Yukon then crosses the US-Canadian border, drains central Alaska, and finally empties into the Bering Sea, south of Norton Sound. On the southern end of British Columbia, the Columbia River originates at Columbia Lake, between the Canadian Rockies and the Selkirk Mountains; from there it flows south to the US Pacific Northwest, where it is joined by the Snake River before turning and rolling westward, forming the border between the US states of Washington and Oregon. The Columbia, which is 1,243 miles long, finally empties into the Pacific Ocean.

The significance of the great Laurentian Shield to Canadian history cannot be overstated. This vast cap of Precambrian rock, centered under the frigid waters of Hudson Bay, covers the eastern half of the country from the Great Lakes to the Arctic Ocean. Canada is rich in timber, fish—the Grand Banks off Newfoundland was once the richest cod fishery in the world—furs, and minerals, but relative to the United States it can boast of few farms because of the thin soils on this vast eroded plain. Canada's fertile prairie provinces—Manitoba, Saskatchewan, and Alberta—lie between the rocky shield to the east and the Rocky Mountains to the west.

The French found arable land to the east and south of the country in the St. Lawrence Valley, between the cities of Quebec (founded in 1608 by Samuel de Champlain) on the Gulf of St. Lawrence and Montreal in the continent's interior. Montreal (from *mont réal*, "the royal mount," the hill at

the city's heart) was established in 1642 on a riparian island. The French seigneurs, or lords, sensibly divided their seigneuries (feudal territories) into
long, narrow lots, a Norman practice. Each strip of land, which was worked
by a farm family, ran down to the river, thereby offering many more points
of riverfront access than would have been afforded by square or rectilinear
lots. In this case, an adherence to Old World manorialism brought economy
and efficiency to New World land use.[7]

The United States of America, or simply America, encompasses the
rich midsection of the North American continent, stretching from Cape
Hatteras in North Carolina to Cape Mendocino in California. Its two
very long coastlines—one fronting the Atlantic and the other the Pacific
Ocean—are both crenulated by numerous harbors and bays, the eastern
coast much more so than the western. The largest and most useful (for shipping) of these indentations include Cook Inlet, Puget Sound, San Francisco
Bay, Massachusetts Bay, New York Harbor, and Chesapeake Bay.

The United States and Canada share the Great Lakes, a series of huge
freshwater seas (Lakes Superior, Michigan, Huron, Erie, and Ontario), except for Lake Michigan, which is entirely in the United States. Other great
North American bodies of fresh water are, in the United States, the Great
Salt Lake in Utah and Lake Okeechobee in Florida, and in Canada, Great
Bear Lake and Great Slave Lake, as well as Lakes Athabasca, Reindeer, and
Winnipeg. In the early colonial era, it should be noted, Mexico possessed
its own remarkable, if shallow, lakes, high up in the Valley of Mexico, the
largest being Lake Texcoco. These lakes were endorheic—that is, like the
Humboldt Sink in Nevada or the Dead Sea in the Jordan Valley, they had
no surface outlets to the sea—so flooding could follow heavy rains. To solve
this chronic problem, the Spanish drained most of these bodies of water,
at great human cost and expense, during the seventeenth and eighteenth
centuries. They accomplished this impressive and environmentally transformative feat by connecting the waters of the Valley of Mexico to the Río
Tula basin and thence to the Gulf of Mexico by means of a massive and
labor-consuming hydraulic drainage system, the Desagüe de Huehuetoca.[8]

The US National Aeronautics and Space Administration (NASA) has
released satellite composite and cloud-free images of the United States at
night, revealing a country clearly bisected along the hundredth meridian
into two distinct patterns of illumination—a proxy measure of American
adaptation to the continent's environmental and climatic patterns. In 1878
John Wesley Powell, at the time one of the government's foremost scientists,

warned Congress that the western half of the nation, outside of the Pacific Northwest, received less than twenty inches of rain a year.[9] This amount was insufficient to support traditional rain-fed agriculture, as practiced in western Europe and transplanted to eastern North America. Powell's inconvenient truth was angrily ignored by growth-minded western politicians who insisted that the westward movement could proceed on the old business-as-usual basis, provided the federal government agreed to fund irrigation projects in the nation's arid lands, which covered some twenty states. In 1902 US president Theodore Roosevelt created a federal bureaucracy in Washington, DC, to reclaim the American West. These policies and projects, such as the Salt River Project in Arizona, profoundly altered the nation's settlement and agricultural patterns.

What developed was what historian Gerald D. Nash has described as an "oasis civilization," a region of large, isolated urban and population centers and corridors like Utah's Wasatch Front, Colorado's Front Range, or the Los Angeles–to–San Diego conurbation, separated by vast tracts of irrigated or empty lands. This pattern stands in strong contrast to those of the eastern half of the United States, as depicted by NASA's cameras. (The current megadrought is testing the hydraulic basis of this oasis civilization.) While the night lights of the western United States stand in strong contrast to the thickly webbed illumination of the eastern half, they form a pattern very like that created by the scattered, relatively dimly lit human-built environments of western Canada and northern Mexico.[10]

America shares long borders with Canada and Mexico. According to the US Geological Survey, which Powell helped to establish in 1879, the international boundary between America and its northern neighbor runs 3,987 miles from east to west. The Alaska-Canada border, which runs north to south, adds another 1,538 miles, making it the world's longest international border at 5,525 miles. The US-Mexican border, which also runs east to west, is shorter, but still an impressive 1,933 miles. America shares with its northern and southern neighbors not only these long borders but also the surrounding borderland geography. The lines dividing the US grassland state of North Dakota and the Canadian grassland province of Manitoba, for example, and the US desert state of Arizona and the Mexican desert state of Sonora are clearly not natural but cultural—the products of diplomacy, purchase, or war.

As important as geography is, as Jared Diamond reminds us, it does not explain all the differences in social development. The gap in social development between Ciudad Juárez—formerly known as the Paso del Norte, "Pass of the North"—in Chihuahua and its Texas neighbor El Paso, for example, is shockingly wide, the former poor and in recent times plagued by violent drug gangs, while the latter is rich, safe, and full of opportunity and promise. Yet they are separated by a single physical barrier, a thin line on the map: the Rio Grande, a ribbon of muddy brown water, for most of the year shallow enough in places for a human to wade across. Otherwise these two cities' geographies are identical. They share the same mountain pass and highway, the old Camino Real (Royal Road) through the Sierra de Juárez to the south and east and the Franklin Mountains to the north and west. (In colonial times the Camino Real linked Mexico City and Chihuahua with Santa Fe and Taos.) Here culture, as the economic historian David Landes would have said, has made all the difference.[11]

Within Western civilization there is a remarkable amount of cultural diversity, a fact that holds true on both sides of the Atlantic. This is also true not only in terms of the respective differences that exist on either side of the Tortilla Curtain, as the Mexican novelist and essayist Carlos Fuentes called it,[12] between largely Catholic Mexico and the Protestant United States (not until the late nineteenth century did the United States start to become religiously and culturally diverse), but also in the dynamic interplay of these two cultures over time. Neither Mexico nor the United States has ever existed in a vacuum, and the same dynamic applies to Canada, although the material differences on each side of the United States' northern border have been far less stark.

Unity versus Diversity

Much of the scholarship on the history of North America stresses the continent's divisions. By contrast, this book will emphasize the unity of the continent and its peoples—*Homo sapiens* all. Mexico, Canada, and the United States have far more than a vast, varied, and resource-rich continent in common. Each nation enjoys an incredibly rich Indigenous history and heritage as well as sharing the alien, if dynamic, European culture that was transplanted, often with great violence and brutality, to North America from Europe, principally from Spain and England but also from France (in Quebec), the Netherlands (in New York), Russia (in Alaska), and Denmark (in Greenland). While the Indigenous heritage of North America is most evident in the far north and far south, Europe's influence may be found in every corner of the continent. In contrast to that of North America, the "continent" of Europe is a maddeningly ambiguous geographical expression. Still, the same civilization that unites the history of Europe unites the national histories of Mexico, Canada, and the United States, all of which have traditionally been considered separate and distinct.

An important subtheme in this history of North America is the slavery, concentration, exclusion, segregation, or control of non-European peoples, a crucial factor that impeded or retarded the continent's social development. In 2020 Indigenous peoples numbered 34 million (25.7 million in Mexico, 6.7 million in the United States, and 1.6 million in Canada), approximately 7 percent of North America's total population of 493.4 million, while the number of peoples of African descent stood at 45.7 million (42 million in the United States, 2.5 million in Mexico, and 1.2 million in Canada), or 9 percent of the continent's total. Mexico has the largest Indigenous population, at 25.7 million, while the United States has by far and away the largest African or Black population, at 42 million. (These estimates are based on the latest figures available from Mexico's Nacional de Estadística y Geografía, Statistics Greenland, Statistics Canada, and the US Census Bureau.) Today the African or Black population of Mexico stands at 1.38 million, which is slightly larger than Canada's African population of nearly 1.2 million. Mexico's African population is concentrated in the southern states of Veracruz, Guerrero, and Oaxaca, while Canada's is distributed widely throughout the country.

Given the pervasive dominance of European culture in North America and the similarity of the two continents' environments, it is hardly an exaggeration to describe the three nations of North America as "Neo-Europes." The European connection to North America is not only important in explaining the continent's initial development, beginning with the conquest of Mexico in 1521, but remains a crucial point of reference throughout the entire period under study. In fact, transatlantic ties and reciprocal and mutually reinforcing relationships between the two continents have increased in importance over time. In the sixteenth century the West's core (as defined by wealth, military power, technology, social development, and influence) resided in Iberia, or southwestern Europe. During the eighteenth century the core shifted to northwestern Europe. And by the mid-twentieth century, between the signings of the Atlantic Charter and the North Atlantic Treaty, the core had shifted yet again, this time to eastern North America, where it remains today—for now. (I am indebted to Alfred Crosby for the concept of Neo-Europe, though I use the term in a political and cultural sense and do not necessarily accept Crosby's environmental scheme; and I have found Ian Morris's idea of "shifting cores" within a civilization to be very useful.[13])

In short, I contend that the history of North America cannot be told except in relation to Asia, Oceania, Latin America, Africa, and above all North America's sister continent, Europe—a point that becomes immediately obvious when the histories of Mexico, Canada, and the United States are considered together. Yet over the centuries historians, especially those who study the United States, have for the most part treated the histories of North America's individual nations separately, both from one another and, as a group, from that of Europe, all but ignoring the significance of a larger North American history.

The Significance of Social Power

Theories of social development or histories based on nonorganic evolutionary typologies such as savagery, barbarism, and civilization, which classify and rank societies and cultures, date back at least to the Age of Enlightenment, with those postulated by thinkers such as Adam Ferguson and Adam Smith. In the nineteenth century the idea of cultural evolution or social development was central to the historical and socioeconomic theories of scholars as different as Karl Marx, who stressed the role of class struggle and oppression in world history; Herbert Spencer, for whom social evolution was the story of increasing complexity and differentiation of function; and Frederick Jackson Turner, who emphasized the significance of an expanding frontier, and the opportunity that expansion offered, in shaping America's development.[14] The Gini coefficient, developed before World War I by Corrado Gini, an Italian statistician interested in the demographic evolution of nations, could test the ideas of a Marx or a Turner to determine whether a society was advancing toward, or sliding away from, equality by measuring the dispersion of wealth in a society. One could also use it to evaluate the efficacy of national policies and programs.

Later, social development would prove to be central to the great ideological, political, and military struggles of the latter half of the twentieth century. In the West, modernizationists like C. P. Snow in Britain or Walt Rostow in the United States argued that the key to social progress or development for underdeveloped "Third World" countries was adherence to free markets, democratic practice, the rule of law, individual liberties, respect for property, and the sanctity of contracts.[15] Marxists in the East, on the other hand, and not a few in the West, believed that socioeconomic advancement could be best achieved by supporting dictatorships of the proletariat and creating command (state-controlled) economies. Through central planning, five-year plans, and great leaps forward, Communist governments sought to accelerate their countries' social development, in the process catching up with and eventually surpassing—or "burying," as Soviet premier Nikita Khrushchev put it in the midst of the Cold War—the West.

Since that time the idea of social development has thrived. In 1990, one year after the fall of the Berlin Wall, an event that marked the liberation of Eastern Europe, and one year before the implosion of the Soviet Union and the start of decommunization in Russia, the United Nations adopted the Human Development Index (HDI), the work of Mahbub ul Haq, a Pakistani international development theorist. Every year since then, the UN has graded nations on the basis of three traits: longevity, per capita income, and education, calling to mind Benjamin Franklin's celebrated admonition to be "healthy, wealthy, and wise." HDI scores are based on a scale of 0 to 1, with 1 being the highest. According to the UN Human Development Report for 2020, Norway, with a score of 0.957, tops the list. At the very bottom, entry 189, is Niger, with a score of 0.394. The economic historian Leandro Prados de la Escosura, incidentally, has extended Haq's index as far back as 1870.

In 1934 Simon Kuznets, a Russian immigrant to the United States, formulated a way to measure a nation's gross domestic product (GDP), creating an index widely adopted after the 1944 meeting of the UN Monetary and Financial Conference, better known as the Bretton Woods Conference. In contrast to the HDI, GDP measures not whether a society is getting healthier, wealthier, and wiser but rather its total output of goods and services, and, notably, the *rate* of economic activity, although GDP per capita remains an important measure of a country's standard of living.

GDP provides a lot of useful information. And no comparative history would be complete without reference to Angus Maddison's historical statistics, in which GDP per capita is measured across time and space, going all the way back to the birth of Christ. The problem is that such comparisons can be very misleading.[16] A country may export a great deal of silver, as did colonial Mexico, and as a result have a high GDP, but if the benefits of those sales are not shared widely among the populace of the producing country, it can still be a desperately poor one. Indeed, as Kuznets brilliantly hypothesized, in poor countries increased economic activity *increases* inequality, whereas in developed countries increased economic activity *decreases* inequality. Kuznets graphed his hypothesis, which creates an arc (the y axis measures inequality; the x axis measures income per capita). The HDI provides a corrective to GDP because it measures a country's well-being or happiness (quality of life and degree of contentedness) relative to that of other countries, rather than merely its overall economic output and activity. The HDI, we might say is more Jeffersonian in its attempt to attach real metrics to the otherwise subjective pursuit of happiness. GDP, on the other hand, as a measure of raw economic power, is purely Hamiltonian. Although the HDI is newer than GDP, its philosophical basis is ancient, dating back to Aristotle, who believed that well-being or happiness should be measured by what a man does rather than by what he owns.[17]

For the historian, all three of these indexes—Gini, GDP, and HDI—pose problems. This is because these snapshots in time do not tell us very much about the *why*: Why are some countries more developed than others? Why are some countries rich and some poor? Why are some countries democratic or free and others totalitarian? And why are some countries able to influence or even dominate other countries? It is also notoriously difficult to make cross-country comparisons, even in this day and age, and even though GDP and the HDI were designed precisely with this specific problem in mind. How much more difficult to try to project these measurements backward in time, especially back five centuries! And yet by endeavoring to combine social science with history, we can try to bridge the divide that C. P. Snow argued existed between the sciences and the humanities.

Ian Morris is an example of a scholar who has succeeded in crossing Snow's cultural divide. An archaeologist from Stanford University who has built on the work of many others, including Earl Cook, Raoul Naroll, Kenneth Pomeranz, and Leslie White, Morris attempts to answer the timely question suggested by the title of his book *Why the West Rules—For Now*.[18] His social development (SD) index measures four traits—energy capture, social organization (city size), information technology, and war-making capacity. For Morris, energy capture is based on the average number of kilocalories of food/nonfood energy consumed by humans in any given period. The size of cities serves as a rough proxy for a society's organizational complexity. Information technology, or the ability to store and share information, is divided into the level and rate of literacy and numeracy as well as the speed and reach of communication. And finally, a society's capacity to project power, or to defend itself from belligerents, is based on the size, firepower, efficiency, and reach of its armed forces. In short, it takes a lot more SD to build a skyscraper than it does a log cabin.[19]

Covering a period that stretches back to the Ice Age, Morris uses his simple but, as he insists, not *too* simple index to assign points for each trait. He then adds up the scores to compare the respective social development of the East (the core of which lay in eastern China) and the West (the core of which has shifted back and forth between the eastern Mediterranean and western Europe), starting ten thousand years ago. Morris concludes that while the West has been in the lead for much of that time, it has no locked-in advantage. Like Jared Diamond, Morris favors geographical ("location, location, location") over cultural explanations.

Between the fall of Rome and the rise of the modern West, medieval Europe (AD 500–1500) fell well behind the high point reached by the Roman Empire at its zenith, as well as behind China during the Song dynasty (AD 960–1279), when China's social development easily matched that of Rome. But by the eighteenth century, with the start of the fossil fuel revolution, Europe caught up with and finally surpassed Rome at its height; by the nineteenth century it had surpassed the rest of the world.[20] And while the West may rule now, as it has since some point in the nineteenth century, there are indications that in perhaps as little as a century the East will again overtake it, if for no other reason than the growing size and number of its cities. Of course climate change may quash this business of making predictions. Morris uses the term *social development*, but a far more apt term, I would argue, is *social power*, since he is measuring not just a society's ability to get things done but also, critically, its ability to influence other societies—a point of keen interest in the history of North America.

The advantage of using Morris's index, in conjunction with other indexes, traits, and observations, to measure relative success is that it helps explain why, for instance, Norway, which ranks consistently at the top of HDI reports—ahead of the United States as well as China and Russia—is not otherwise considered a world power, or even a regional one. Certainly the policies of Norway's government in particular, and Norway's culture in general, are key factors in its high social development. But while Norway's social development is higher than that of the United States, Norway's social power is much lower. In fact the Scandinavian country's high social development is due in no small part to the fact that it enjoys the very real security that the United States and its military allies, which include Norway, provide the entire North Atlantic region. (Norway is a member of the North Atlantic Treaty Organization, or NATO, founded in 1949; the US military dwarfs the other militaries in the alliance in terms of its size, firepower, reach, and efficiency.) In other words, the story of social development is incomplete without context—that is, without considering that story in regard to social power, as Morris's history makes abundantly clear. This is true of each of the world's regions: Europe, Asia, Africa, and the Americas. It is especially true of North America, where the West's core and leadership ultimately shifted from western Europe to eastern North America during the mid-twentieth century. In short, the argument I make here is that a society's well-being is related either to its own social power or to the social power of other societies. This insight is fundamental to the explanation of North American history and why the United States came first to dominate the continent and later the world. One effect of Morris's index is the enormous magnification of the importance of the nineteenth and especially twentieth centuries, which loom very large. Indeed, the last two centuries could be likened to the Himalayas, while all the rest of human history is nothing more than the Indo-Gangetic Plain below, almost flat and featureless.

In these pages, the term *social development* generally refers to what occurs *within* a society, while *social power* is used to define the relationship that exists *between* societies—and clearly a society's social development will have a bearing on the level of its social power.[21] A society's social power may either facilitate or hinder the social development of other societies. Or, because of its lack thereof, a society may find itself on the wrong end of another society's stick, or within another society's "sphere of interest." The narrative arc of this book is framed with this very consideration in mind. It begins with the European conquest of North America—that is, the Spanish conquest of the Aztecs in 1521, the point at which North America began to fall within Europe's growing sphere of interest or spread of empire. And it ends with the Monroe Doctrine, North America's declaration of defiance against Europe, when the United States not only formally asserted its independence from Europe's sphere of influence but also proclaimed its own, namely that of the Western Hemisphere.

Central to any history of North America is how the United States, formerly a small collection of British colonies confined to a narrow strip of the Atlantic coast almost until the end of the eighteenth century, emerged to become a continent-girdling federation, the world's sole superpower, and leader of the free world by the 1990s. Indeed, the United States was the major driver of change on the continent as well as in the rest of the world. And if we want to know why the United States rules North America, at least for now, then the utility of Morris's index—his measurement of social power over time—is at once apparent.

But charting the growth of social power can do much more than inform yet another narrative about America's meteoric rise from colony to regional hegemon, and ultimately superpower. It can also be used to integrate, as this book tries to demonstrate, the various histories of the entire continent, whether these histories are of high social development or low, into a single narrative. To put it another way, Native, Mexican, American, and Canadian histories did not develop in isolation; they have developed together, if unevenly, within a continental as well as transatlantic context. The purpose of this book, then, is to explain the significance of the disparities or asymmetries in levels of social development, which have changed over time, between western Europe and Native North America, and later between Anglo and Hispanic North America. The use of traits, whether those of Haq or Morris, allows scholars of global history to compare apples to apples rather than apples to oranges. And to avoid confusion, depending on the context, the terms *Mexico*, *pre-federal* and *federal United States*, and *Canada* are not historical entities or regions. They are standardized national accounts that allow for comparison and analysis and refer to the territories that either become or are the nations of Mexico, Canada, and the United States.

Using social and comparative development and other evolutionary approaches to interpret history was once commonplace. In fact Turner, who invented the professional study of American history in 1893 by using the frontier to distinguish European from United States history, was very much a disciple of Darwin. As Turner grandly stated:

> The United States lies like a huge page in the history of society. Line by line as we read this continental page from West to East we find the record of social evolution. It begins with the Indian and the hunter; it goes on to tell of the disintegration of savagery by the entrance of the trader, the pathfinder of civilization; we read the annals of the pastoral stage in ranch life; the exploitation of the soil by the raising of unrotated crops of corn and wheat in sparsely settled farming communities; the intensive culture of the denser farm settlement; and finally the manufacturing organization with city and factory system.[22]

But by 1943, fifty years later and in the midst of World War II and all the ugly nationalism and racism associated with it, Margaret Mead, who had written the classic study *Coming of Age in Samoa* (1928), fleshed out the Boasian creed in "The Role of Small South Sea Cultures in the Post War World," an article that appeared in *American Anthropologist*. Franz Boas, her mentor, had been a major proponent of cultural relativism and opponent of cultural evolutionism. "As anthropologists," Mead wrote,

> our contribution has been a recognition of the co-equal value of human cultures seen as wholes. . . . We have stood out against any grading of cultures in hierarchical systems which would place our own culture at the top and placed the other cultures of the world in a descending scale according to the extent that they differ from ours. Refusing to admit that one culture could be said to be better than another. . . , we have stood out for a sort of democracy of cultures, a concept which would naturally take its place beside the other great democratic beliefs in the equal potentiality of all races of men, and in the inherent dignity and right to opportunity of each human being.[23]

And in 1946, in her study of Japan, Ruth Benedict, also a Boas student, declared that the goal of anthropology was "to make the world safe for human differences." In 1952 Alfred L. Kroeber (yet another Boas student) and Clyde Kluckhohn further disentangled the concept of culture and its study from race by clearly and very usefully delineating culture as a "set of attributes and products of society, and therewith of mankind, which are extra-somatic and transmissible by mechanisms other than biological heredity." Since these statements were made, the Boasian creed has gone on to be widely accepted by the disciplines of anthropology and history.[24] These views are certainly shared here. But while it is true that "all men are created" equal, to quote a signal proposition of the Enlightenment, they are not necessarily born into equal societies, as the United Nations' HDI index makes abundantly clear, year after year. Moreover, these differences are some of the major drivers of history. They clearly drove, as we shall see, the history of North America.

The terms *Mexican, American, Canadian,* and *Native,* I should add here, are abstractions or composites that refer to collections of different and very diverse peoples from Europe, Africa, the Americas, and elsewhere. The formation of national identity in North America was a slow and complex process, one that occurred at different times, in different places, among different groups, and even among different subgroups inside other groups. To complicate the matter further, national self-identification of one group was not necessarily accepted by the others. For European Americans in the United States, for instance, who largely came to accept each other as "White," despite their centuries-old rivalries, enmities, and fratricidal conflicts in the Old World, their skin color served as at least one common denominator, and became the basis for the invention of a new people. This newfound national identity, however, was slow to be extended to non-European peoples. Indeed, these European Americans were notoriously reluctant to accept African or Black Americans as fellow citizens and countrymen.

But the more enlightened—for instance, the French American author J. Hector St. John de Crèvecoeur who condemned American slavery—thought the new nation was based less on ethnic, cultural, or racial backgrounds than on conditions of equality. As he put it, America society was not "composed, as in Europe, of great lords who possess everything, and of a herd of people who have nothing. Here are no aristocratical families, no courts, no kings, no bishops, no ecclesiastical dominion, no invisible power giving to a few a very visible one; no great refinements of luxury. The rich and the poor are not so far removed from each other as they are in Europe. Some few towns excepted, we are all tillers of the earth, from Nova Scotia to West Florida."[25]

On the other hand, similar-looking English-speaking and French-speaking European Canadians may have coexisted within a single state, but they nevertheless lived in separate linguistic "solitudes." And having segregated African or Black Americans, whether well-established or newcomers, White Americans on the same principle went on to discriminate against Chinese laborers who made their way to the United States, and in 1882 they legally barred Chinese from the United States altogether. Canada would follow suit in 1923. European Americans also discriminated against Mexican Americans on the basis, in part, of skin color. In contrast Mormons, who were overwhelmingly drawn from European American *stock*, to use an old-fashioned term, regarded themselves as a chosen people. And they long remained cautious toward, and slow to identify with, their fellow European Americans and former persecutors. The formation of national identities and dual or even poly identities among the continent's Native peoples adds yet another layer of interest and complexity, especially in Mexico, which imagined a new cultural identity, *la raza cósmica*, "the cosmic race," a mixture of Indigenous and Iberian elements.

The history of national identity in Europe was of course also layered, and if anything even more complicated, as Brexit Britain and the persistence of

Scottish and Catalonian independence movements remind everyone today. But there exists one big difference between Europe and North America. Europeans managed to form a relatively clear continental identity, which finally was given formal economic and political expression by the founding of the European Union in 1992. On February 6, 2018, as reported in the *Wall Street Journal*, the European Union announced its plans to expand its borders to include the Western Balkans. Federica Mogherini, the EU's foreign policy chief, explained the criteria for EU membership: this region, although relatively poor, shares "the same history as the members of the European Union, the same cultural heritage, the same challenges."

However, as British prime minister Boris Johnson declared on October 17, 2019, while Britain was leaving the European Union, it was not leaving Europe, for Britain was a "quintessentially European country." North Americans, on the other hand, have failed to produce even a rudimentary North American identity. We speak of Europeans, but not of North Americans. In fact, in Mexico the term *norteamericano* is used to distinguish non-Spanish-speaking Americans and Canadians from Spanish-speaking Mexicans or, more generally, Latin Americans. More recently, when US president Donald Trump renegotiated the North American Free Trade Agreement, he excised the words "North American" altogether from the new agreement's title, dubbing it the United States–Mexico–Canada Agreement (USMCA). In 1974 Gary Snyder, the poet laureate of deep ecology, did suggest calling North America by an all-embracing term, Turtle Island. This exception only proved the rule, and nothing came of it. In short, North America may not possess a shared identity or sense of itself, but as we shall see, the continent very much has a shared history.

CHAPTER 2

On Asymmetry

THE PROFOUNDLY DIFFERENT LEVELS OF social development that existed between North America and western Europe—between the Postclassic civilizations of Mexico or lower North America and the the Archaic hunter-gatherers in middle and upper North America—are keys to understanding much of the history, deeply tragic and otherwise, that followed. These developmental differences, while largely obscured by the anthropological and historical scholarship of cultural relativism, were nevertheless strongly determinative.

The idea that societies or cultures can evolve and therefore can be compared and graded has been central to modern history and, in particular, to big history, which seeks to unite natural and human history, biology and culture. However, while extremely useful, this notion is not without significant moral and ethical challenges, which have been noted by scholars. Elsewhere I have traced the intellectual history of the idea of cultural evolution and its critics, the cultural relativists, from the Age of Enlightenment—what David Deutsch called the "beginning of infinity"—to the neo-Hegelianism of Francis Fukuyama. With the emphasis on Europe and the Americas, I argue that the universal evolutionism of the Enlightenment ultimately prevailed over historical particularism, as once-profound global disparities in social development narrowed or even disappeared altogether.[1]

On Prehistory: North America versus South America

The question of when humans first arrived in the Americas is as old as the founding of the American anthropology profession in the late nineteenth century. The question was initially dominated by the Smithsonian Institution's foremost expert on American antiquity, a cultural evolutionist named William Henry Holmes, and his close associate, the Czech-born

Figure 1. The two towers of the Mission San Xavier del Bac in Southern Arizona form
a perfect illustration of the idea of asymmetry. This architectural jewel, known to
Tucsonans as "The White Dove of the Desert," is located on the cultural divide between
Latin America and British North America. Detroit Photographic Co. *San Xavier
Mission, Tucson, Arizona* (opened in 1797), United States, Tucson, Arizona, circa 1902.
Photograph. https://www.loc.gov/item/2008679603/.

Aleš Hrdlička. In 1902 Holmes succeeded John Wesley Powell—the one-
armed explorer of the Grand Canyon of the Colorado River—as chief
of the Bureau of American Ethnology, and as such Holmes was the US
government's leading authority on the American Indian. To answer the
antiquity question, he insisted that his fellow archaeologists—and by this,
he meant professionals as opposed to amateurs and enthusiasts—use multiple lines of evidence and adhere to the strictest evidentiary standards.
As he wrote in 1919 in the *Handbook of Aboriginal American Antiquities*,
these experts should subject their claims of an early American antiquity to
"the severest tests that science can devise." As a consequence, the claims of
an American Paleolithic or an American Old Stone Age were initially met
with skepticism and doubt.[2]

This situation changed abruptly in 1927, when an important find came to the attention of Jesse Figgins, the director of the Colorado Museum of Natural History in Denver. In a bone bed at Wild Horse Arroyo near Folsom, New Mexico, a man-made point was discovered in situ with the ribs of an extinct Pleistocene animal, namely, a large Ice Age bison or buffalo. (George McJunkin, a Black cowboy, former slave, and amateur naturalist, had first grasped the site's significance as early as 1908.) This time Figgins made sure that the artifact found at the site passed science's "severest tests," and thus became the first American archaeologist to break the Pleistocene time barrier.[3] After Folsom, the prevailing view was that Upper Pleistocene hunters had in fact entered North America from Siberia, after crossing a land bridge—Beringia—connecting the Old and New Worlds, and then following a pathway down between North America's Cordilleran and Laurentide ice sheets. Since the land bridge became crossable only when the ice sheets expanded and sea levels thus fell, and the pathway, conversely, became passable only when the ice sheets contracted, this migration involved some careful geological choreography.[4] Once through, however, these first Americans, accompanied by their Old World dogs—the earliest domesticated animals in the Old and New Worlds—found rich virgin hunting grounds teeming with Pleistocene megafauna such as bison, mastodon, and sloths. And once they found these game-rich lands, these hunter-gatherers, or Paleo-Indians, thrived and ranged widely.

Evidence abounds of an Upper Paleolithic or, in the distinctive nomenclature adopted by Americanists, an early "lithic" or Clovis culture.[5] This culture's signature fluted projectile or spear point was first discovered in 1932 near Clovis, New Mexico, by Edgar B. Howard of the Penn Museum and the Academy of Natural Sciences in Philadelphia. From 1933 to 1937 Howard unearthed more artifacts from the dry lake beds of the Llano Estacado, "Staked Plains," a large, featureless mesa or tableland shared by New Mexico and Texas. Howard's finds were unique to North America and have long been hailed as the continent's first technological invention. Moreover, these stone projectile points—like the Folsom projectile point discovered five years earlier and over two hundred miles to the north— were found in association with the skeletal remains of mammoths.[6] Indeed, Clovis was a late Ice Age kill site, its artifacts more than two thousand years older than the projectile point found at Folsom. Thus multiple lines of geological, paleontological, and archaeological evidence agreed, forming a deep timeline and pointing to an Upper Paleolithic as well as to a very late Pleistocene colonization of the North American continent.[7]

But while evidence of Clovis culture was found all over North and Central America as far south as the Isthmus of Darién (in Panama), it did not extend to the continent of South America. According to Thomas D. Dillehay, an expert on South American prehistory at Vanderbilt University, "South America [was] very different archaeologically from North America because no single culture dominated the continent the way Clovis culture, with its representative spear points, had North America."[8] David J. Meltzer, a professor of prehistory at Southern Methodist University who specializes in North American archaeology, agrees. "The archaeological records" of the two continents, he wrote, are "dissimilar," just as "Pleistocene glaciation, climates, and environments play out in very different ways in the Northern and Southern hemispheres." Indeed, the archaeological sites near Clovis, New Mexico, Kimmswick, Missouri, and elsewhere in North America all point to a land-bridge crossing, an ice-free corridor, Paleolithic big game hunters, and a late Pleistocene colonization.

But in 1997, exactly seventy years after Figgins's discovery at Folsom— well south of the equator in an ancient encampment at Monte Verde, southern Chile, thirty-one miles inland from the Pacific coast near Puerto Montt and fifty-five hundred miles from Clovis, New Mexico—a very different picture of American antiquity emerged. The revolutionary finds at Folsom and Monte Verde enjoy near universal acceptance because in both cases, outside investigators were brought in to certify the validity and authenticity of the site and the science.

At Monte Verde, Dillehay and his team of eighty scientists dated evidence unearthed beside Chinchihuapi Creek, a small tributary of the Maullín River, and found that humans had occupied the area around 12,500 years ago. The Chilean site, which was not a butchery but an encampment of people who hunted *and* gathered, had been buried under a layer of wet peat. As a consequence the artifacts excavated there—stone and wooden tools, the bones and even hides of extinct animals, plant foodstuffs, fire pits, and residential structures—were remarkably well preserved. Monte Verde was older than Clovis by almost one thousand years, and thus Dillehay's findings broke the Clovis time barrier and complicated the Clovis-first narrative. Monte Verde and other archaeological sites in South America suggest an earlier coastal migration or series of migrations—maybe by foot, maybe by boat—along the nutritionally rich "kelp highway" that runs along the Pacific Rim from the Asian to the Andean coasts, except for a break in the tropics, where mangrove forests and coral reefs would have provided other suites of abundant marine foods. Migrating peoples could thus have tapped into marine as well as terrestrial sources of nutrition. Of the two possible routes—the ice-free corridor and the kelp highway—the latter has the virtue of being the simplest, applying the principle of Occam's razor.[9]

Still, there is no consensus on exactly when humans first arrived in the Americas. The claims made for the earliest pre-Clovis sites, such as the Meadowcroft Rockshelter in southwestern Pennsylvania, do not enjoy the same level of acceptance as do those made for the earliest sites in Europe, Africa, and Australia. Indeed, the debate over American antiquity remains as unsettled as it did a century ago, when William Henry Holmes starchily dismissed an American Paleolithic as a "phantom." Holmes was wrong about that, but his own phantom, his fierce skepticism, hovers like a specter over the field to this day.[10] Meltzer puts it this way: "No matter how vigorously claims for a pre-Clovis site are promoted, they will never be compelling unless the site's artifacts, stratigraphy, and ages are unimpeachable. . . . It has to be utterly unimpeachable in all respects: one that can withstand withering criticism and meet the criteria with room to spare." Holmes had raised the evidentiary bar very high, and there it remains.[11]

Dillehay's pre-Clovis claim has, however, been generally accepted, and given the location of Monte Verde, it has proved as paradigm-shifting as Folsom. Indeed, Dillehay draws five startling conclusions from his research in austral Chile: first, that "people were in South America at least 12,500 years ago, implying they must have been in North America by at least 15,000 to 20,000 years ago, if we accept migration into the Americas by way of land;" second, that "there were multiple early migrations into the Americas, probably from different points within Asia and possibly elsewhere;" third, that "although late Pleistocene South American cultures are historically related to North American ones, they are also distinct, characterized by different technologies and generalized hunting and gathering lifeways;" fourth, that "much cultural diversity existed throughout the Americas, but especially in South America, by 11,000 years ago;" and fifth, that "there is some (though scant) evidence from human skeleton and genetic comparisons that regional populations were physically more different from one another than we once believed, suggesting not only early cultural but biological diversity."[12]

Since the Monte Verde discovery, American prehistory has become even more complicated. In 2009 David Bustos, the resource program manager at White Sands National Park in New Mexico, discovered human and animal footprints near what had been an ancient lake during the Last Glacial Maximum. Subsequently an international team of scientists dated the carbon in ancient seeds of ditch grass, found in the same strata as human and mammoth footprints. If the White Sands find holds up under scrutiny, this would suggest that humans arrived in North America twenty-three rather than thireeen thousand years ago, ten thousand years earlier than has been thought.[13]

As we learn more about pre-Clovis North America, it does seem clear that the Clovis culture itself, once established late in the Pleistocene epoch, continued as long as there were Pleistocene megafauna to hunt. We can surmise that this makes the late Pleistocene the only time when the entire continent of North America—at least in regions where megafauna hunting occurred, such as the High Plains—was marked throughout by roughly the same level of social development. This situation did not last, of course. With the extinction of the megafauna, due possibly to human hunters but more probably to changes in climate at the closing of the Pleistocene, post-Clovis North Americans began to settle in, and adapt to, different areas of the continent and its varied biomes—woodlands, deserts, plains, riversides, and coasts.[14] Not surprisingly, in time they began to diverge from each other. Moreover, linguistic and genetic evidence suggests at least two subsequent waves of migration from Asia to North America, separated by thousands of years. The first was made up of the Na-Diné, who occupied parts of Alaska, Canada (the Slave or Slavey Indians), and later the American Southwest (the Navajo and Apache); the second wave carried the Eskimo-Aleut, who exploited the marine environments of the Far North (Alaska, the Aleutian Islands, Arctic Canada, and the west coast of Greenland).[15]

For all of these reasons a multiplicity of different lifeways gradually replaced the cultural uniformity of late Paleolithic or early Lithic North America. Thus when Renaissance Europe encountered North America, it found a social landscape that was richly varied but cleaved into two large regions. The development of Upper North America (north of the Rio Grande and Gila River) stood in clear contrast to that of lower North America (sometimes referred to as Mesoamerica), which included Mexico and adjacent parts of Central America, like Guatemala and Belize. This divergent prehistory, and the social asymmetry it represented, profoundly affected the course of North American history.

The social development of North America was closely related to the continent's geographical differences. North America, when it was the home of Pleistocene megafauna, was also then home, as we have seen, to a single continentwide big-game hunting culture, the Clovis. With the extinction of the megafauna and the end of the last Ice Age, this late Paleolithic and continental unity slowly gave way to a bewildering diversity of regional cultures. But for all of the continent's cultural and linguistic variety, there was an unmistakable downward slope of social development, one that started in the more complex south, below Mexico's twenty-first parallel, and extended northward as far as the Arctic Circle. In 1519 lower North America encompassed the high point or summit of North America's cultural evolution. We can find evidence there of all five stages of cultural change, after Gordon R. Willey and Philip Phillips's influential Lithic, Archaic, Formative, Classic, and Postclassic typology, a scheme that dates back to 1955 (as anthropologists R. Lee Lyman and Michael J. O'Brien have pointed out, although dated, the stages of Willey and Phillips are "still in use today, with minimal modification, by most American archaeologists, and the model that provided the framework for the cultural evolutionary stages is stronger today than it was in the 1950s or early 1960s"[16]). In the far upper reaches of North America (above the forty-ninth parallel in what is now Canada), on the other hand, there is evidence of the existence of but two of these cultural stages: the first and second, the Lithic and the Archaic. In middle North America (within the present-day boundaries of the United States), we find evidence of the Lithic and Archaic as well as the Formative.

The chief characteristics of the Lithic stage, which lasted from the end of the Ice Age to 5000 BC, were, first, small and thinly scattered populations; second, the use of stone tools and weapons; and third, the hunting and gathering of wild food. The notable achievement of the Lithic peoples was that they colonized the entire continent of North America. During the Lithic stage, subsistence was based on the hunting and gathering of wild food. Tools and weapons were made of chipped stone. By the end of this stage, human populations, though small and thinly scattered, nevertheless reached into every corner of the New World. In fact the first great colonization of the Americas was completed during this stage.

The Archaic stage was marked by sophisticated hunting and gathering techniques, supplemented by horticulture. The principal distinction between horticulture and agriculture, as modern anthropologists would have it, is that horticulture involved technologies of plant cultivation that did not involve the use of plows or draft animals. However, in the Americas these definitions are complicated by the fact that there were no beasts of burden such as horses or oxen prior to the arrival of Europeans. Fieldwork was accomplished solely by means of human sweat and muscle.

For many tribes in the resource-rich areas of the Eastern Woodlands, California, and the Pacific Northwest, where there were exploitable terrestrial as well as marine environments, the Archaic stage, from around 5000 BC to the late 1800s of the Christian era, represented a cultural climax. If not for the invasion of Europeans, these tribes might never have awoken from this splendid Archaic Dreamtime. And for good reason. It made little sense at the time for the peoples of North America to adopt more risky food-production strategies, as had occurred in lower North America. The Formative societies in the Mississippi Valley and in the desert Southwest, such as the Cahokian, Chacoan, Hohokam, and Mogollon, that tried to make the shift from food gathering to food production had all crashed, probably into a Malthusian wall, long before 1492. Vestiges of the Mississippian culture, however, survived into the historic period. This said, hunters and gatherers throughout North America to a greater or lesser extent practiced horticulture, which was a significant food production strategy but one sans the critically important secondary products revolution, of which more later.[17]

The Classic and Postclassic stages were reached, according to Willey and Phillips, only in a region comprised of "the Valley of Mexico, and its environs, Oaxaca, the Guatemalan highlands, the Petén-Usumacinta-Motagua lowlands, and coastal Veracruz." The Classic cultures—which in North America included the Teotihuacán in the Valley of Mexico, the Zapotec at Monte Albán in the Valley of Oaxaca, and the Maya on the Yucatán Peninsula—rose during the first millennium of the Christian era. This stage is important, Willey and Phillips contend, because it "marks the beginning of the urban life in native America," and because the cities of the New World were built around ceremonial centers characterized by temples, pyramids, and palaces, which were of "great size and elaboration, attesting to the planning, skill, and labor organization of the builders."[18] In the Classic stage, society was highly stratified, and the arts and craftsmanship were well developed. The subsequent Postclassic, which spanned the period from roughly AD 1000 to the Conquest in 1521, was characterized by three basic patterns: urbanism, militarism, and secularism. The term *Postclassic* should not connote a decline from the high culture achieved during the Classic, though Maya civilization had broken down completely before the arrival of the Spanish.

These different levels of social development would shape the European conquests and the history of Europe's empires in lower (Mexico), middle (the United States), and upper (Canada) North America. The Spanish would swiftly conquer the peoples of Mesoamerica, forcibly erecting an early modern civilization on top of the remains of an unwilling Postclassic society. War and conquest are as old as history itself, of course, but nothing quite as dramatic and shocking as this had ever occurred before, although the Mongols' 1258 sacking of Baghdad, the capital of the Abbasid Caliphate, might be a close second. In contrast, it would take not two years but three centuries for the English, French, Dutch, Russians, and later the Anglo-Americans to confront and subjugate the thinly scattered Archaic peoples in the lands north of the Rio Grande.

As the Atlantic historian John H. Elliott observes, "Where Montezuma's empire in central America had a population estimated at anything from five to twenty-five million when [Hernán] Cortés first set foot on Mexican soil, that of Powhatan [in Virginia] consisted in 1607 of some thirteen to fifteen thousand. The difference in size and density of the Indigenous populations would profoundly affect the subsequent character of the [British and Spanish] colonial worlds."[19] The implications of this point for North American history simply cannot be overstated. The encounter between Europe's intensive-use, population-heavy societies and the extensive-use, population-light societies of Middle and Upper America produced a violent and tragic situation. It also produced a revolution in the use of the continent's land and resources as hunters and gatherers, despite the sophistication of their horticulture or subsistence agriculture in many cases, nevertheless gave way to the vastly more numerous and powerful European or European American agriculturalists and later industrialists. In North America thousands of years of cultural evolution were compressed into a few short centuries. In 1500 the continent's precontact economy could support a mere ten million persons; today it supports nearly half a billion.

Yet though Europe's social development, as well as its social power, was vastly greater than that found anywhere in North America, the latter's impact on Europe, paradoxically, was far greater than the other way around. The large influx of American silver and gold during and after the sixteenth century, for example, inflated prices not just in Seville (and later Cádiz), the point of entry of New World bullion, but throughout Europe, with profound short- and long-term economic and social effects. (Significant silver deposits were also discovered in sixteenth-century Europe, forming the basis for the Bohemian and other thalers.) Meanwhile, vast parts of the interior of Archaic North America remained isolated from—indeed untouched by—the outside world until well into the 1800s, over three centuries after the arrival of Castile's plumed knights in shining armor. The brilliant nineteenth-century artists George Catlin, Karl Bodmer, and Alfred Jacob Miller captured on their canvases the ethnology, as they imagined it, of this pristine and primitive world in a romantic vision that moved their European American audiences, and even today glows with a warm, suffused light.

To put it another way, the Columbian exchange conceptualized by Alfred Crosby was, at least at first, anything but a two-way street.[20] This worldwide exchange of peoples, ideas, goods, plants, animals, and microbes was determined by levels of social development, and therefore it had a more immediate and disproportionate impact on Europe, whose voyages of discovery had made the global transfer possible in the first place. Even as imported diseases caused Mexico's Native populations to plunge downward, further widening the gap between the two continents, the Columbian exchange fueled Europe's social development. Europe's largest impact on North America, not surprisingly, was precisely where North America's pre-Hispanic social development was the highest, namely, in Mexico—the central tableland south of the Pánuco and Santiago Rivers. (According to the great Prussian sage Alexander von Humboldt, the line between the mouths of these two rivers was a frontier of social development: to the south of it, civilization and agriculture; to the north, barbarism.) In gross terms, however, the New World was the real beneficiary of the great exchange. Out of 247 plants that would be cultivated in the Americas, 199 originated in the Old World, 45 in the Americas, and 1 in Australia.[21]

On Population

In light of the dramatic population loss experienced by lower North America and Mexico in the decades following the Conquest, it might seem more than perverse to discuss social development. Hard numbers are difficult to come by in the extant literature of the sixteenth century, making population estimates difficult at best. The historical record is far from complete, and what figures do exist may have over the years been inflated or reduced to serve various ends and political agendas. Fortunately, archaeology has helped in some cases to correct or corroborate the written evidence. After decades of sorting out all of the historical and archaeological evidence, what does seem clear is the catastrophic population decline in Mexico following the

European invasion. Estimates of the scale of these losses range from less than 25 percent to as high as 90 percent.[22] Disease, rather than war or famine, was the principal cause for this population collapse. Yet there is also little doubt that the shock of conquest and the subsequent stress of colonization further weakened Native populations, making them even more susceptible to foreign pathogens as well as to the continent's own lethal diseases, such as the hemorrhagic fever *cocoliztli* or *matlazáhuatl*.[23]

If North American archaeology has been largely an argument between the late and early daters, North American demography has been a battleground between scholars who, like James Mooney and Alfred Kroeber, thought the North American population at the time of contact was low versus postwar high counters such as the influential Woodrow Borah, Sherburne F. Cook, and Henry F. Dobyns, who reached quite different conclusions based on what appear to be grossly inflated numbers. Dobyns, the high priest of the high counters, estimated the precontact Native population of the New World at ninety million, with eighteen million in North America.[24] The high counters contended that Mexico's pre-Hispanic population was no less than "twenty-five million" and that it did not fully recover until 1947, instead of 1850, as Angus Maddison would maintain (Alexander von Humboldt thought New Spain's population had more than recovered by the late eighteenth century).[25] This would mean that a full demographic recovery was not achieved in Mexico until 428 years after Cortés landed in Veracruz in 1519! As a point of comparison, it took Europe's population two hundred years to recover from the devastation of the Black Death, the first wave of which broke out in 1347. Today, the pendulum has swung back. Modern scholars now accept much lower population figures for the continent, in general, and for Hispaniola, the cradle of Spain's American empire, in particular. For Hispaniola, these figures range between 250,000 and 1 million.

On December 23, 2020, however, the science journal *Nature* published a landmark paper by lead author Daniel M. Fernandes, "A Genetic History of the Pre-contact Caribbean." The *New York Times* immediately recognized the article's significance, reporting in an article entitled "Ancient DNA Is Changing How We Think about the Caribbean" that we now know, based on genomic evidence, that the precontact population of the island of Hispaniola was very small—no more than a few tens of thousands of people. Needless to say, this new research and its implications suggest that a historiographical revolution is on the way, as new science replaces older scholarship.[26]

In contrast to these new low numbers, Christopher Columbus and his brother Bartholomew estimated the island's population at 1.1 million—an enormous exaggeration, to say the very least, but one in keeping with the estimates of modern scholarship. Such a large population suggested enormous wealth, a fact that would have impressed potential investors back in Europe. And that was precisely the point the Columbus brothers wanted to make. The contemporary Bartolomé de las Casas, on the other hand, had a very different agenda. He was the prime instigator of the *leyenda negra* or black legend, which cast the Spanish conqueror as a man as malicious as he was perfidious, whose cruelty and greed brought death and destruction to the peoples of the Indies. Las Casas arrived in the New World ten years after Columbus's first voyage, first as an encomendero in Hispaniola and later, after he had seen the error of his ways, as a bishop of Chiapas, then part of Guatemala. Like the Columbus brothers, Las Casas saw what he wanted to see: in his case, a peopled paradise turned into an empty desert by Spanish greed. Las Casas, who saw Hispaniola with his own eyes, claimed that its original precontact population stood somewhere around three or four *million*, as opposed to a few tens of thousands, or actually less than that by the time he arrived on the island.[27]

Thus, to underscore his excoriation of the Ugly Spaniard, Las Casas enlarged the holocaust by greatly magnifying the loss of life. According to a census taken in 1540, the number of Natives on Hispaniola had dwindled to a mere 250 hapless souls. The real death rate, which was bad enough, was a drop from tens of thousands—not millions—to a couple of hundred. But the wild exaggerations of Las Casas put the sixteenth-century Spaniard, who had one foot in the Middle Ages, in the same league as the twentieth century's mass murderers, Germany's National Socialists and Russia and China's Communists, who could kill in the name of racial purity or class struggle on an industrial scale.

In light of the new genomic evidence provided by Fernandes and his coauthors, we now know that Las Casas was prone to wild exaggeration. The population figures of the Columbus brothers were no less pure fiction. But at least these two men sincerely believed that Hispaniola, Cuba, and the Bahamas were near Asia and its immense population centers, which is why they called the region's Native peoples Indians. For Las Casas, on the other hand, facts were not stubborn things but rather things to be pulled from the thinnest of air and then crassly used to serve the cause of social justice, as he proved in his fiery polemic *The Very Brief Relation of the Destruction of the Indies* (1542).

Four centuries later Woodrow Borah, Berkeley's high counter, concurred with Las Casas that a massive depopulation had occurred in the Caribbean as well as in the rest of the Americas, provocatively suggesting that New Spain's pre-Hispanic population had been as high as twenty-five million. For Borah, however, the real killer was disease rather than Spanish sadism and cupidity. This was a powerful insight, creating a controversial new paradigm for thinking about pre-Columbian and postcontact American demography. And unlike Las Casas, Borah allowed that the Spanish brought benefits to the New World's Native peoples, such as the suppression of intertribal military conflict as well as the introduction of new technologies and domesticated animals. For his labors, Borah was accused of—depending on one's perspective—blackening the black legend or whitening the white legend by blaming the demographic collapse of the sixteenth century largely on the unwitting spread of disease rather than on Spanish genocidal fury or systemic "structural violence," as some modern scholars would have it.[28] His work nevertheless resurrected the essential thesis, or rather moral indictment, of Las Casas: that the Spanish had wantonly killed millions of Indians—four million in New Spain, three million on Hispaniola.[29] Spain's enemies used Las Casas's writings as propaganda, as would academic and antiwar critics of Western civilization later, in the 1960s and 1970s. (During the Vietnam War, the United States would be portrayed as the new Spain, and the Vietnamese people as the new Indians.) Borah's more nuanced views were lost to view, as the black legend was broadened to impugn all of Western civilization, not just the Spanish Empire.

Throughout this study I have avoided the hyperbole of the high counters, the work of whom unfortunately has made its way into the popular imagination, and refer instead primarily to the much-welcomed empiricism of the late macroeconomic historian Angus Maddison, a leader in the field. Maddison based his work, in part, on the numbers provided by Mexico's National Institute of Statistics and Geography. "Despite methodological differences and continuing debates over particular cases," according to the leading Latin Americanist John H. Coatsworth, "the Maddison estimates appear to embody an emerging consensus on long term trends."[30] Moreover, Maddison's research has been dramatically vindicated by recent genomic research.[31]

Since Maddison's death in 2010, his work has been continued by the Maddison Project at the University of Groningen in the Netherlands. For the year 1500, Maddison estimates a population of 7.5 million for pre-Hispanic

Mexico (Spain's population was comparable, standing at 6.8 million in the same year), probably close to 250,000 for what became Canada, and 2 million for what became the United States. Maddison's total for all of precontact North America, then, is 9.75 million, closer to the estimates of the original low counters than to those of the later high counters.

In 1518 Indigenous peoples made up 100 percent of the North American population, as opposed to approximately 7 percent today. With Maddison's estimates in mind, the Indigenous population of North America in absolute terms increased, then, from an estimated nearly 10 million in 1518, prior to the arrival of the Spanish, to nearly 34 million today—nearly half a millennium later. In other words, the Indigenous population of North America has more than tripled since the time of contact.

As encouraging as these figures and trends appear in the long view, they conceal the very real and devastating population loss or contraction experienced by the Indigenous peoples of North America after contact with the peoples of Eurasia and Africa. In central Mexico, at that time the most densely populated region of North America, the population may have declined from 7.5 million in 1518 to 1 million in 1603. The gradient of decline in populations elsewhere on the continent and at later times, as the European and European American frontier advanced across the continent from the sixteenth to the nineteenth century, was not always nearly so steep as in central Mexico, to say nothing of the earlier initial holocaust in Hispaniola (a drop in population from tens of thousands—rather than millions—to 250 still constitutes a shocking loss). But regardless of the differences in the severity of individual epidemics, taken all together these tragic and massive die-offs throughout the Americas are comparable to the impact of the bubonic plague or Black Death on fourteenth-century Europe, and go far in helping to explain North America's subsequent social development .

The historian and geographer Alfred W. Crosby summed up the matter in this way: "There is no doubt that Euro- and Afro-Americans carried diseases deadly to Indians, but said diseases did not rain down uniformly and all at once on all the original peoples of the New World. The differences enabled some peoples to survive, and some, eventually, to return to their pre-Columbian densities. Other disappeared forever with a swiftness that must chill our spines if we are capable of any empathy at all for our fellow creatures."[32]

The Conquest of Mexico: A Great Dying?

Bartolomé de las Casas was Spain's official "Protector of the Indians," fierce champion of social justice, and biting critic of empire. He was a passionate advocate, evangelist, polemicist (he used gross distortions of facts to make points), reporter, and historian whose works included the 1542 *A Short Account of the Destruction of the Indies*. He was also a direct participant in the conquest and colonization of the Indies.

Las Casas's allegations, however, strain credulity. As we have already seen, his estimate of the population of Hispaniola as three to four million was wildly out of line with current scientific evidence, which puts the real number closer to tens of thousands. According to Las Casas, the population of central Mexico, like Hispaniola, "veritably teemed with humanity. . . . Yet, over the twelve years of which we are speaking [1518 to 1530], and during the course of what they term the 'conquest,' Europeans . . . butchered, burned alive or otherwise done to death four million souls, young and old alike, men, women and children."[33] If true, that would have meant the Spaniards—a tiny sliver of Mexico's population (in 1525 there were only 150 White households in Mexico City)—somehow managed to capture and kill 913.2 Indians per day (or 38.05 Indians per hour, or 0.6 Indians per minute), a Herculean feat they somehow achieved using early sixteen-century methods and technology such as matchlocks, knives, and garrotes.[34] These Spaniards were apparently superhuman as well as the most tireless, single-minded, maniacal, and determined mass murderers in human history. They must not have eaten, slept, made love, or done anything else for twelve years but kill incessantly—unless they were aided in this monstrosity by a willful army of Native executioners, which is perhaps an even more disturbing thought. Moreover, the Spanish were allegedly killing the very laborers who would have given their encomiendas (grants of labor and tribute) value, meaning that they were not only relentless but also quite stupid, acting directly against their own economic interests with no plausible explanation other than that they were power-mad and intensely cruel.

Las Casas's wild claims notwithstanding, a recent analysis of Mexico's genome reveals a surprisingly stable pre-Conquest and post-Conquest population. In 2014 an international group of forty geneticists and health professionals published a groundbreaking paper in the journal *Science*. Its title was alluring: "The Genetics of Mexico Recapitulates Native American Substructure and Affects Biomedical Traits."[35] One of the members of the team, Carlos Bustamante, recalled, "We were really fascinated by these results because we had expected that 500 years of population movements, immigration and mixing would have swamped the signal of pre-Columbian population structure." Instead this signal, or rather these distinct signals (there are no less than sixty-five different Indigenous groups in Mexico and ten language families, including Nahuatl and Quiché), came in loud and very clear, indicating that in terms of population history there was far more continuity between pre-Hispanic and Hispanic Mexico than had been previously thought based on historical evidence. As Andrés Moreno-Estrada, the lead author of the study, put it: "One would think that all of the [Mestizo] populations would have completely different profiles [from] the native populations because they have been mixed. However, it turns out that these people still reflect the substructures of their specific Native American ancestors."[36]

Thus in Mexico the Indigenous genetic map coincides with the country's geography. A map of Mexico's pre-Columbian populations, which lived in relative isolation from each other, remains clearly discernible in a modern genome map of the country. The team found that divergence increases along a northwest-to-southeast axis, from the northern desert coast on the Gulf of California to Mexico's jungle border with Guatemala. In fact, there is so much genetic variation from one end of the country to the other that the Seris in Sonora in the far northwest are as different from the Lacandon, a small Maya group in Chiapas in the far southeast, as West Europeans are from East Asians.

As expected, the European ancestry of Mexico's Mestizo population matches that of the present-day inhabitants of Iberia. More surprising was the discovery that the Indigenous ancestry of a Mestizo from, say, Sonora, was likely to correspond with that of the local Indigenous people from the same region, as opposed to some other region of the country, illustrating the wide range of genetic variation in Mexico as a whole. The evidence also indicates that Indigenous and cosmopolitan peoples, Mexico's two traditional cultural groups, may be socially and economically distinct but are genetically very similar, "arguing for a strong relationship" between the two. There is also evidence of African admixture in Mexico's population. At 4 percent, it is small but not insignificant.[37]

The historical implications of Mexico's "staggering" genetic diversity have yet to be sorted out. But these findings do raise important questions about the magnitude of Native population decline after the Conquest. If there had been a severe population decline—in effect a near mass extinction event, caused by either wanton violence on a massive scale, as Las Casas would have it, or the unwitting spread of deadly disease—then one would expect to find signs of sharply reduced variation in the gene pool, that is, a genetic bottleneck. But that does not seem to be the case, at least in Mexico. And if the country had been largely emptied out, one would have expected the Spanish to have turned to other sources of labor, perhaps slaves from Africa, on a much more extensive scale. Clearly the different lines of evidence—historical, archaeological, and osseous as well as genomic—have yet to be brought into full alignment.

The North American Paradox

What is also becoming increasingly clear is that pre-Hispanic Mexico was the most advanced region in North America in terms of food production, urban density, and the arts of life, but also a place where, paradoxically, life itself was also harder and shorter than in the upper regions of the continent. In other words, the gains made with the domestication of corn, beans, and squash were more than negated by the lack of domesticated animals, apart from dogs, which Paleo-Indians brought with them across the Bering land bridge, and the native turkey. In the Old World, on the other hand, plant and animal domestication were closely linked, and tame cattle, oxen, horses, pigs, sheep, chickens, and goats provided a reliable source of meat or protein as well as of labor for traction and transportation.

Another crucial and related difference between the Old World and the New World is that in the Old World animal domestication prepared the way for a "secondary products revolution," which allowed for the exploitation of renewables such as milk, eggs, wool, and manure. In North America there were no benefits, of course, to be derived from a secondary products revolution, since there were no animals, apart from dogs and turkeys, to domesticate.[38] Unfortunately the llama, a camelid native to South America and a useful pack animal, was not introduced to North America because the Isthmus of Darién (now the Isthmus of Panama) proved to be an impenetrable barrier; nor did South America's other camelids, the alpaca, guanaco, and vicuña, find their way to North America. The Spanish did report Native rafts off the Pacific Coast of South America, but it is not clear that these balsa craft ever made it as far north as Mexico. If they did, they did not bring South America's domesticated animals to North America. According to the great conquistador Francisco Pizarro, a Native oceangoing raft that he encountered on his way to Peru carried twenty men as well as high-quality manufactured goods, including textiles.[39]

Nevertheless, in North America all of the labor was performed by humans—at great physical and no doubt mental cost. There were no horses, asses, oxen, mules, or other draft animals. According to paleodemographer Robert McCaa,

> Physical and physiological stress seems ubiquitous in Mesoamerica, although somewhat less so than among most peoples in northern North America. Osteoarthritis (degenerative bone disease), likely due to extreme physical exertion, is present in adult skeletal remains from 5,000 years ago in the Tehuacán Valley. High rates of healed fractures, severe dental wear, and advanced osteophytosis are common in the earliest extant skeletal material. Tuberculosis and treponemal infection, forms of syphilis and yaws, date from 3,000 BP [Before Present]. Also common are coral-like lesions on the crania (porotic hyperostosis and cribra orbitalia), severe physiological responses to acute or chronic anemia resulting from nutritional deficiencies, extreme parasitic infestation, debilitating infection, blood loss or some combination of these. The architectural riches of Chichén Itzá contrast starkly with the physiological poverty of its population, which suffered from hard labor, illness, infection, and severe malnutrition. A tally of 752 adult Mesoamerican skeletons . . . reveals women with higher rates of facial fractures (gender abuse?) and more joint disease of the wrists (repetitive stress from arduous labor of grinding corn for tortillas?). Spines of adults of both sexes show severe degenerative wear, averaging 40% or more at Jaina, Tlatilco, Cholula, and Copán (Honduras). The lesson learned from these skeletons is that where the human body was the principal mechanism for growing food, constructing buildings, and moving heavy burdens, the biological price was great. Hard, repetitive work exacted a severe wear on Mesoamerican bodies of both sexes, particularly joints required for mobility, manipulation of objects, or bearing loads.[40]

In the Valley of Mexico (the Aztec Anáhuac, "Land between the Waters"), the practice of cannibalism appears to have been directly related to the depletion of the area's natural resources, leaving the area on the edge of hunger. There were famines in 1501, 1505, 1507, and 1515, and a particularly severe one that lasted from 1451 to 1456. There were no domesticates to speak of, and the area's fish, ducks, and deer were simply insufficient to feed such a large population, driving the Aztec elites to turn to cannibalism as a substitute for animal protein. The Toltecs and the Maya, it should be noted here, also practiced cannibalism, and the hunters, gatherers, and horticulturalists in middle and upper North America ate human victims after they had been made to provide some ritual benefit. The Iroquois competed to eat the heart of a brave prisoner, and the Huron of Canada tormented, tortured, and feasted on their prisoners. But the Aztecs who lived in the protein-poor Valley of Mexico took cannibalism to a level seemingly without parallel in world history.

Water transport (using dugout canoes, or *acalli*) on the shallow lakes—principally the Lago de Texcoco—that lie in the great Valley of Mexico would have mitigated some of the physical demands of daily life there. But everywhere else in central Mexico, including on the Yucatán, somatic energy or human muscle was the only source of power—besides, of course, fire. There was no evidence of any technology—windmills, sails, or waterwheels—which could convert wind and water into power. Moreover, Mesoamericans possessed neither the wheel nor the plow. They planted their seeds using digging sticks, with fire-hardened points. There was one important innovation: the *chinampas*, floating gardens that were tended on the west end of Lake Texcoco. To keep the waters fresh around Tenochtitlán, the Aztecs built a dike, the Albarradón de Nezahualcóyotl. Still, that did not prevent the formation of algae blooms. The *chinampas* were extremely productive—many times more so than the slash-and-burn milpa fields. The Aztecs even found that they could make edible scum cakes from the algae that covered the lake surfaces. But the chinampas were small and, although numerous, incapable of satisfying the dietary needs of the Aztecs. Resorting to the expropriation of their neighbors' resources as well as to the practice of large-scale cannibalism, they created an empire built on fear and resentment and subject peoples eager to throw off the Aztec yoke, even if that only meant trading it for another. In the anthropologist Marvin Harris's compelling words, "We must consider. . . that the availability of domesticated animal species played an important role in the prohibition of cannibalism and the development of religions of love and mercy in the states and empires of the Old World. Christianity, it may yet turn out, was more the gift of the lamb in the manger than the child who was in it."[41]

The temple-palace civilizations of the Old and New Worlds—in Mesopotamia, Egypt, and Mesoamerica—appear superficially similar, despite being separated in time by several millennia. Both sets of societies were certainly hierarchical and can be likened to their top-down signature monuments, Egypt's Great Pyramid of Giza and Mexico's Pyramid of the Sun. But the New World's agricultural revolution was only half a revolution in comparison with what happened in the Old World, where the domestication of plants *and* animals produced a powerful double helix of human culture. It was biogeography that determined this parallel but decidedly unequal fate. And whereas Egyptian and Mesopotamian empires were able to lord it over others because of the mastery they had achieved over their riparian environments—the Nile, the Tigris, and the Euphrates—the Aztecs' drive for power and dominion was fueled by need, not wealth, especially the need for prisoners of war to supply protein through a system of human sacrifice and redistribution. This weakness was only one reason for their society's undoing by the Spanish and their Native auxiliaries. The other was Mesoamerica's lag in development. At the time of contact it can be thought of as in transition from a Neolithic to a Bronze Age society, fatally behind Renaissance Europe.[42]

Using evidence from the Health and Nutrition in the Western Hemisphere database (an osteological collection containing over 12,500 skeletal samples from sixty-five different sites in North and South America), biologists, physical anthropologists, and archaeologists have arrived at a consensus, one that reconfirms the more tentative conclusions reached at the Conference on Paleopathology and Socioeconomic Change at the Origins of Agriculture, held in Plattsburg, New York, in 1982.[43] In the words of anthropologists Richard Steckel and Jerome Rose, "The health index declined throughout the pre-Columbian era, as Western [hemispheric] societies evolved from simple to complex and hierarchical. [Robert] McCaa's analysis also identifies the older pre-Columbian period as healthier in terms of life expectancy. In general, the healthiest populations were hunter-gatherers, and the least healthy lived in large settlements supported by systematic agriculture."[44] In other words, "life *became* 'nasty, brutish, and short' for the typical North American [and South American] with the rise of agriculture, government, and urbanization." So why the shift to a more settled and complex life? Steckel and Rose theorize that it may have been because of "leaders who sought advantages may have encouraged the shift, or it could have been an adaptation to diminishing resources, defense needs, or perhaps a preference for some amenities of urban life."[45]

In the Americas, as elsewhere, demography and disease were closely related. So, too, were demography and social development. Again, according to McCaa, "The bioarchaeological record reveals that Mesoamerican populations (indeed, most ancient peoples) were fragile, weakened by stress, poor nutrition, and ill health. The old romantic notion of strong, robust, healthy populations in Mesoamerica—a pre-Columbian paradise—is poorly supported by settlement patterns and the skeletal evidence." Furthermore, the physical and physiological stress seemed only slightly less ubiquitous among the hunters and gatherers in middle and upper North America.[46]

In fact, life expectancy in ancient America from 5000 BC to AD 500 was thirty-four years, slightly lower than the thirty-five years of ancient Rome and early modern Europe.[47] But as Hobbesian as life once was, the shift from hunting, gathering, and horticulture to sedentary agriculture made life harder still, as well as shorter. More precisely, with the evolution of civilization in lower North America, life expectancy fell to twenty-three to twenty-five years, along with the stature of males, while the pressure to increase fertility rose among females. To put this in another way, over time society in Mesoamerica grew more complex and differentiated—a process focused in a succession of urban and religious centers: Teotihuacán, Tula, and Tenochtitlán. At the same time the overall health of the population deteriorated, as fertility *and* mortality rates sought to find an equilibrium under these new and trying living conditions.[48] It was into this exceedingly brittle world that Europe brought the hammer of conquest, the stress of colonization, and, unwittingly, smallpox, among other epidemiological horrors. The effects, not surprisingly, were shattering.[49]

In 2002 Steckel and Rose summed up the research on the general health of Indigenous peoples in the Americas at the time of contact. Their conclusion is startling and significantly alters our understanding of the European conquest: "While no one doubts the importance of germs, steel weapons, and horses in the ascent of Europeans in the Western Hemisphere, we argue that poor health was also a factor in the speed and ease of conquest. *The populations most easily conquered were also the least healthy, who lived in upland urban areas and relied heavily on domesticated plants* [italics mine]. Nomadic, hunter-gatherer societies, particularly those with horses, posed the greatest military challenges to colonizers."[50]

While Mesoamericans may have lived close to the dangerous Malthusian intersection where population increase met food production, they nevertheless achieved the highest level of social development—that is, societies that were the most complex and socially differentiated—in North America.[51] Indeed, in 1518, on the eve of contact with the kingdom of Castile, the social development of the Postclassic Aztecs and other Mexican polities, such as the Tarascan and Zapotec states, towered above that of every other Indigenous society in North America. And at the end of the century, the social development of the Kingdom of New Spain—an amalgam in part Mesopotamian, in part medieval Europe—even with its shrunken population would still tower above the rest of the continent. As we will see, the explorers Francisco Vázquez de Coronado and Hernando de Soto sought out new Tenochtitláns in the north—the American Southwest and Southeast— but found nothing remotely comparable to the Indigenous civilization that had once existed in highland Mexico.

If poor health put America's Native populations at a disadvantage in their encounter with Europeans, so too did their highly myopic and provincial societies, which were basically social silos isolated from the outside world (a description that could be applied equally to Europe for much of the Middle Ages). Indeed, these Native silos were all but hermetically sealed, raising questions about the extent and frequency of long-distance Native trade. There is no doubt that items were traded at long distances, but this does not necessarily prove the existence of long-distance trade.

The Straits of Yucatán, which separate Mexico from Cuba, are only 120 miles wide. After 1492, the year Christopher Columbus discovered the West Indies, Cuba and the rest of the Caribbean islands were conquered, colonized, and by all accounts meanly depopulated. And yet twenty-seven years later, when in 1519 the Spanish left Cuba for the beaches of Mexico, the Aztec elites were caught totally by surprise. They had no more idea what had befallen the peoples of the Caribbean islands than they did the Guanches and Canarios of the Canary Islands, where Christopher Columbus had established a critical port of call on the way to the Americas. But they were about to be rudely educated. Within two short years they would be forced to call these newcomers "lords." Remarkably, this history would repeat itself almost verbatim in 1530, when Francisco Pizarro arrived in Peru. The Inca elites there knew nothing of what had happened either earlier in the Caribbean or more recently in Mexico, and their ignorance of the outside world proved as fatal to their world as it had to that of their Aztec counterparts. Peru's Atahuallpa would meet the very same fate as Mexico's Montezuma.[52]

Spanish brutality and Native insularity had collided, and the course of North American history was dramatically changed. Looking forward, Hernán Cortés, Mexico's conqueror, envisioned a well-ordered society of Indians and Spaniards, jointly ruled by the nobles or hidalgos ("men of quality") of both races. It was to be a society that avoided, with the help of the Franciscans and other religious orders, the demographic disasters of the Antilles, in particular what had happened to the Taíno on the island of Hispaniola. This new New World was not, however, meant to be. Instead, sixteenth-century Mexico experienced a horrific demographic collapse. Hard numbers vary, but it would appear that the country lost 90 percent of its population over the course of the sixteenth century, although in light of recent genomic evidence the decline might have been much less. Death's sharpest scythe was disease: smallpox, measles, typhus, and influenza from Europe; yellow fever and malaria from Africa; and the indigenous *cocoliztli*.

The worst outbreak of smallpox was evidently the first one, in 1520, one year after the arrival of Cortés. The nineteenth-century historian William H. Prescott described how the plague swept "over the land like fire over the prairies, smiting down prince and peasant, and adding another to the long train of woes that followed the march of the white men. It was imported into the country, it is said, by a negro slave, in the fleet of Narvaez. It first broke out in Cempoalla," north of the modern port of Veracruz. From there, "it spread rapidly over the neighboring country, and, penetrating through Tlascala [Tlaxcala], reached the Aztec capital. . . . Thence it swept down towards the borders of the Pacific, leaving its path strewn with the dead bodies of the natives, who, in the strong language of a contemporary, perished in heaps like cattle stricken with the murrain."[53]

In Europe, smallpox was basically a childhood disease. Those who survived the virulent virus and grew up to adulthood could enjoy a lifetime of immunity from further outbreaks. But in Mexico in 1520, where the disease was unknown, smallpox ferociously struck all ages in "one massive blow," in McCaa's words, leaving few alive to care for the sick. In subsequent outbreaks of the disease, however, survivors from previous outbreaks, now immune, could take care of the next round of victims, mitigating somewhat the pathogen's recurring lethality.[54]

What the survivors of smallpox, whether European or Native, could not do was pass on their hard-won lifetime immunity—which was acquired, not genetic—from parent to child. So both populations, European and Native, were doomed to suffer periodic outbreaks of the disease until the late eighteenth century, when the English physician Edward Jenner's vaccine finally began to bring relief to mankind from this insidious malady.[55] While in London the disease was endemic, killing every year, in Mexico it was epidemic, occurring at seventeen- to eighteen-year intervals. The problem of poor health in pre-Hispanic Mexico, the result of widespread poverty and malnutrition, would persist through the next three and a half centuries, continuing to weaken the population's defenses against disease until late in the nineteenth century. Beginning in 1876, the growth rate accelerated between 0.5 and 1.5 percent, giving Mexico a population of 11.5 million in 1890.[56] This demographic change was due in part to long-overdue improvements in public health and education. Only in the twentieth century, after the Mexican Revolution (1910–1923), would Mexico's population begin to surge. Indeed, if this later growth were plotted on a graph, it would look like the business end of a hockey stick. At 127.6 million, Mexico's population is today seventeen times larger than it was at the time of contact.

There is a consensus that the first post-Columbian epidemic that struck Mexico in 1520 was caused by smallpox, a European disease. If anything, the 1545–48 and 1576–78 epidemics were even more catastrophic. The epidemic of 1545 took the lives of no less than 80 percent of the Native population, making it the worst tragedy in North American history (although, again, these figures might be too high). The epidemic of 1576 may have swept away half of the remaining population. But it appears that the cause of these two epidemics was not a disease introduced by Europeans but the indigenous hemorrhagic fever called *cocoliztli* in the sixteenth century and *matlazáhuatl* in the seventeenth, eighteenth, and nineteenth centuries. The disease targeted the Native peoples in the Central Highlands but not those in the warm low-lying coastal plains. And it notably did not infect Europeans. The relative affluence of the colonizers and the poverty of the colonized may be an important discriminating factor. In any event, the victims of the disease either suffered horribly or perished.[57]

Despite the appalling contraction of the Native population, which declined until the mid-seventeenth century before finally beginning to recover, the survivors nevertheless vastly outnumbered the European population. In 1570 the Europeans numbered 6,644 souls. In comparison, the Indians for that same year numbered 3,366,860. In other words, Europeans made up only 0.2 percent of the total population, while Indians made up virtually all of the rest.[58] That the dominant European population was very low in relation to the rest of the Native population was not unusual. In 1901 the population of British India was close to three hundred million. In comparison, the number who made up the British Raj, the subcontinent's system of governance and security, was minuscule. There were only nine hundred British civil servants and approximately one soldier for every four thousand

Indians. The existence of such a large Native population, and thus of Native laborers and craftsmen—who quickly learned European trades, including the arts of sculpture and painting, especially if they were already skilled in Native crafts—discouraged Europeans workers from emigrating to New Spain and traders from bringing in enslaved Africans. In short, New Spain was by no means viewed as a land of opportunity for Old Spain's "huddled masses" who may have yearned to "breathe free."[59]

During the sixteenth century, however, in the wake of the conquistadors, there was a steady, if small, flow of emigrants from Spain to the Indies, increasing in the 1560s and 1570s. The total number of emigrants has been estimated as between 200,000 and 250,000. That number may be high, but in any event, it breaks down to an average of 2,000 to 2,500 a year, very few by nineteenth-century standards. Men outnumbered women, who made up only a third of the total emigrants. The prime destinations were the viceroyalties of Peru (36 percent) and New Spain (33 percent), followed by New Granada (9 percent), Central America (8 percent), Cuba (5 percent), and Chile (4 percent).[60]

According to Angus Maddison, at the very end of the colonial period (1820) the ethnic composition of Mexico broke down as follows: Indigenous, 3,570,000; Mestizo, 1,777,000; European or White, 1,230,000; African or Black and Mulatto, 10,000 (0.15% of the total population). The ethnic composition of Latin America as a whole was 37 percent Indigenous; 24 percent African or Black and Mulatto; 22 percent European or White; and 16 percent Mestizo.[61] The historian Enrique Semo, who cites Woodrow Borah, a high counter, provides these figures: in 1521, with the fall of Tenochtitlán, the White population of Mexico (that is, Cortés and his men) was little more than 1,500, a merest drop in Mexico's population bucket. By 1570 the population of Europeans and related Mestizos had risen to 63,000; in 1646, to 125,000; in 1742, to 565,000; and in 1772, to 784,000. In the course of two centuries Mexico's non-Indian population—Europeans, Criollos (native-born Europeans), Mestizos, and other *castas* (mixed-blood groups)—went from only 0.7 percent of the total population in 1570 to 27 percent in 1742.[62] Today, however, the majority of Mexicans are Mestizo, although Mexico's Indigenous and its Spanish-speaking cosmopolitan (or Mestizo) peoples are very closely related genetically, indicating the importance of Hispanicization or cultural change in Mexican history.[63]

On *mestizaje* or racial intermingling, Iberians were hardly more enlightened than were other Europeans or other peoples, for that matter. John H.

Elliott has characterized Spanish America as a "pigmentocracy" and described Spanish colonials as obsessed with their genealogy and preoccupied with *limpieza de sangre* ("purity of blood"). "Lineage and honour," Elliott writes, "went hand in hand." The blood of Mestizos, then, was considered tainted by the White ruling elite. Mestizos belonged to neither the Spanish republic (*república de los españoles*) nor the Indian republic (*repúblicas de los indios*), two distinct corporate and officially recognized but not equal identities. (Indians were considered minors, that is, children, in the eyes of the law.) The Mestizos found themselves relegated to what was regarded at the time as an inferior and illegitimate society of darker-skinned *castas* or half-breeds. But as Semo points out, the economy of the *república de los españoles* was not made up of just Whites. It included *peninsulares* (Spanish-born Europeans) and Criollos (American-born Europeans) as well as three groups "removed from their communities," the Mestizos, Indians, and *castas*. And there was more than one type of *casta*. The Mestizos were the result of unions between Europeans or Criollos and Indians; children of unions between Europeans and Blacks were called Mulattos; and children of unions between Blacks and Indians were called *zambos*. In fact, there were numerous distinctions "based on degrees of relationship and gradations of skin colour running the full spectrum from white to black." Spaniards who fell out with their countrymen or who adopted Native customs were known as *zaramullos*.[64]

In short, Europeans were able to imagine a brilliant and enticing New World—but unable to imagine being part of the creation of a new people who had the same opportunities to share in what that new world had to offer. A notable exception to this rule, as we shall see, was Samuel de Champlain, the father of New France. Champlain did envision, and tried hard to realize, a new Métis civilization in North America. This failure of Spanish America—and later of British America, where, if anything, an even more rigid pigmentocracy took form, if not one as taxonomically elaborate—did not prevent the continued social development of the North American continent. It did, however, influence the pace of that development, and ultimately limit its possibilities.

PART I

NORTH AMERICAN CONTOURS

Figure 2. John Webber, *The Inside of a House in Nootka Sound* (detail), 1784. Engraving on paper. John Carter Brown Library, Providence, RI. https://commons.wikimedia.org/wiki/File:The_Inside_of_a_House_in_Nootka_Sound.jpg. Image licensed under CC BY-SA 4.0.

CHAPTER 3

The Renaissance Explores the East Coast

THE SALIENT FACT ABOUT NORTH American geography, according to Ian Morris, is that the continent is only three thousand miles away from Europe, while it is six thousand miles away from Asia. Given the respective widths of the Atlantic and the Pacific Oceans, it was almost inevitable that Europe's mariners would discover the Janus-faced North American continent before Asia's did. And indeed while Renaissance voyagers were exploring the eastern coast of North America in the sixteenth century, the discovery of the continent's western coast would have to wait for three more centuries, was largely conducted by the men of the Enlightenment, and took place within the context of the Pacific world. As we shall see, for most of the period under study here—that is, the European period from 1521 to 1823—the basic outline of North America was unknown. One of the period's great feats was revealing the continent's outline or contours, a process that was not achieved until late in the eighteenth century. And the exploration of North America's vast interior would take yet another century to complete.

The depth of ignorance about North American geography as well as its ethnography during our period was profound. When the United States purchased Louisiana in 1803, it was buying a pig in a poke. It would take explorers from two entirely different ages of discovery, the Renaissance and the Enlightenment, to sort out the many problems. The exploration of North America, in turn, stimulated these very ages of discovery and gave them much of their distinctive character. And there is probably no better example of social power, a key theme of this book, than exploration, except perhaps the colonization that followed.

The First Transatlantic Connection

The European discovery of North America occurred twice: first by Scandinavians—seafaring Vikings—whose reach extended from the shores of the Caspian Sea to Cape Farewell in Greenland, an island discovered by Erik the Red in AD 981, and later, as we will see, by Renaissance Europeans. On a route between 61 and 62 degrees north, the direct distance between Norway and Greenland is 1,500 miles. But this voyage could be broken up by hopping from one group of mountainous islands to another group. As the historian J. H. Parry notes, "From Bergen to Shetland is 180 sea miles; from Shetland to the Faeroes, 120; from the Faeroes to Horn in eastern Iceland, 240; from Snaefelsnes due west to Greenland coast, 350."[1] The Vikings' reach, according to the Vinland sagas and other written evidence, even extended to lands southwest of Greenland—that is, to continental North America.[2]

The credit for the first European to sight the North American mainland goes to Bjarni Herjólfsson, an Icelandic trader who, in 985, became lost on his way to Greenland. Leif Erikson, the son of Erik the Red, acquired Bjarni's ship and in 1000 retraced his errant voyage. In the process he explored three new western lands, which he named, running north to south, Helluland (Flat-Rock Land)—possibly Baffin Island, Labrador, or both; Markland (Forest Land)—possibly Labrador, Newfoundland, or Nova Scotia; and Vinland (Wine Land)—a land described as "so good" or rich that the "livestock would need no fodder during the winter," and where the "temperature never dropped below freezing." Vinland, unlike Greenland, was well inhabited. One may speculate, and many certainly have, that it could have been any one of a number of relatively balmy areas farther down the North American seaboard—Nova Scotia, Massachusetts, Rhode Island, Connecticut, or Long Island.[3] Vinland's location remains an enticing mystery.

The Vikings, or rather their less colorful and more prosaic Christian descendants, probably made only seasonal visits to what is today eastern Canada. Greenland's few ice-free areas are largely treeless, and Markland would have been the closest source of timber. The Davis Strait, which lies between Greenland and the Labrador Peninsula, is only 180 miles wide at the narrowest point, and evidence of ongoing contact between the two lands exists, though sparse. Two and a half centuries after Greenland was colonized, according to a record written on an Icelandic vellum in 1362, "There came a ship from Greenland [in 1347], less in size than small Icelandic trading vessels. It was without anchor. There were seventeen men on board, and they had sailed to Markland, but had afterwards been driven [to Iceland] by storms at sea."[4] The author of another calfskin record concurred but placed the number of the crew of the small, gale-battered North American ship at eighteen. And there is solid archaeological evidence that the Vikings were in eastern Canada. A Norse site was found in Newfoundland at L'Anse aux Meadows (excavated in the early 1960s) in the far north of the island, across from the Labrador Peninsula. The Newfoundland site and Norse base camp were occupied by the Norse in AD 1021, a little over a thousand years ago, when Europeans crossed the Atlantic Ocean for the first time and the Old and New Worlds were thereby joined, however loosely.[5]

If the Vikings possessed superior navigational skills, seaworthy vessels, iron tools and weapons, and livestock (cattle, including one very headstrong bull), these things gave them little advantage, at least in Vinland, vis-à-vis the Native peoples, whom the Vikings called the derogatory *Skræling* ("little barbarians").[6] According to the sagas, the efforts of Thorfinn Karlsefni to colonize Vinland ended in failure due to internal divisions—that is, jealousies over women ("the men who had no wives sought to take those of the married men")—and the outside threat of hostilities from the more numerous and armed Skræling, whom they seem to have antagonized. The sagas relate that the Norse Greenlanders acquitted themselves well in these violent encounters with the Vinland natives, but Karlsefni nevertheless concluded that their situation was in the long term unsustainable. He decided therefore to return to Greenland, from whence his people came. They were not surrounded by enemies there (this situation would change by the fifteenth century, with the southward expansion of the Thule (the ancestors of the Inuit).[7] These medieval encounters left no discernible impact on North America, west of Greenland—but the episode nevertheless made a large mark on North America's modern imagination.[8]

Viking Vinland apparently ended before it got started. But Viking or Norse Greenland prospered—for a time. The population was concentrated in the island's Eastern and Western Settlements, Eystribygd and Vestribydg, both on a habitable stretch of land above Cape Farewell, and each of which was a patchwork of farms and pasturage for cattle and sheep. Centuries before the 1619 establishment of the modern House of Burgesses in Jamestown, Virginia, Greenland's medieval assembly of freemen, the *thing*, met in Gardar (where there was also a Roman Catholic bishopric) in the Eastern Settlement. The *thing* was an ancient Germanic institution (the Roman historian Tacitus referred to it in the first century AD), which had been transplanted in 930 to Iceland, a country the historian Richard F. Tomasson calls Europe's "first new society," and in the process was transformed from a local into a national assembly. According to Tomasson, Iceland's *thing* was a "national legislative and adjudicating assembly, a fair, a marriage mart, a reunion of family and friends, and a national celebration in which a large but unknown proportion of the Icelandic population participated for two weeks each June." Greenland was colonized by Iceland—and connected through trade with Norway—and the Germanic *thing* was transplanted thither.[9]

Tomasson calls Iceland the "most extremely inhospitable environment in which a European people has been able to survive and maintain its culture"—except for Greenland. Greenland was a poor man's Iceland, and its population of 500 remained small, peaking at 3,000 or so. But with the gradual end of the Medieval Warm Period (AD 900–1300), the Norse numbers began to dwindle, and by 1500 had disappeared altogether. In fact, after AD 1300, average temperatures declined and reached their lowest phase—since the end of the last Ice Age—between the years AD 1300 and 1850. Indeed, the demise of Norse Greenland and the subsequent rise of European North America both occurred during this relatively recent and harsh climatic regime known as the Little Ice Age.[10]

The historian Gwyn Jones discusses a number of reasons for the extinction of Greenland's Vikings, including how the changing climate worked against the Norse Greenlanders in at least two ways. Greenland's expanding glaciers and the North Atlantic's growing pack ice increased the range of the Thule people, who originated in northern Alaska around AD 900, gradually expanded across Canada's Arctic islands, and then migrated down into Greenland. At the same time these dangerous and harsh climatic conditions reduced Greenland's trade and communication with Europe. Norwegian trading ships might still have braved Greenland's dangerous waters to bring iron tools and weapons as well as textiles in exchange for wool and wild products, including Greenland's white falcons, which were prized as gifts for princes, and walrus ivory, if there had been profit in it. But as Jones points out, the economic viability of this remote outpost of Western civilization was undermined by the "increased trade in furs and hides out of Russia, the growth of English and Dutch cloth trade as against Greenland's woolens, and the preference of French workshops for elephant ivory over the inferior walrus tusk."[11] Or as J. H. Parry succinctly explains: "The commercial economy of the Greenland settlements broke down, and their subsistence economy was inadequate to sustain them."[12]

These changes probably doomed the settlements. Moreover, in 1349 the Black Death came to the port city of Bergen, Norway, thereby weakening the country as a maritime power and as Greenland's only lifeline. Poor, and getting poorer, as well as all but cut off from Norway, the Norse Greenlanders were left alone to fend off attacks by the Thule. In one encounter recorded in 1379, the Thule killed eighteen of the Norse Greenlanders and enslaved two boys. Still, there is archaeological evidence that the exit of the Norse Greenlanders was orderly, not forced. In 1492 Pope Alexander VI of the infamous Borgias lamented that the last contact between Greenland and the rest of Christendom occurred eighty years before (two years later he would negotiate the division of the world between Spain and Portugal with the Treaty of Tordesillas in 1494). Since 1412, in other words, the colony had been on its own. Evidently news had recently reached the Vatican regarding Greenland's prolonged and malignant neglect, which prompted the papal bull. In this lonely survival of the coldest the Norse Greenlanders, based on a recent study of their diet, made some important adjustments: they shifted from cattle to sheep and goats and substantially increased their reliance on marine foods, especially seal meat. They might have subsisted, like the Inuit Greenlanders, indefinitely, but from the Norse point of view that meant a dreadful, cheerless isolation at the edge of the world. It thus seems more likely that they chose to abandon their homes in Greenland and retreat to Europe.[13]

The end for the Norse Greenlanders does not seem to have come right away, or all at once. What is clear is that sometime during the fifteenth century the long-flickering light of Erik the Red's old, cold colony in the North Atlantic finally blew out.[14] This was not the end of the Norse in Greenland, however. Scandinavia—that is, the unitary personal union of Denmark-Norway from 1524 to 1814—eventually recolonized Greenland in 1721, and today Greenland (or Kalaallit Nunaat, in native Inuit), is an autonomous constitutional monarchy under Denmark's Queen Margrethe II. According to the English historian Thomas Babington Macaulay, a constitutional monarchy is a form of government in which the monarch—in the case of Greenland, the queen—reigns but does not govern.[15] Canada is also a constitutional monarchy, whose royal head—the king or queen of the United Kingdom—reigns but does not rule. It is worth pausing to consider the fact that while monarchy has disappeared from much of Europe, a good swath of North America remains under the sway of European monarchs, if only nominally.

The Second Transatlantic Connection

By the 1300s Venetian bankers had developed capitalism, or the informa-tion technology to bring together the people who start businesses with the people who invest in them. And by the fifteenth century double-entry bookkeeping had been invented, in which accounts were credited, debited, and balanced. This accounting system allowed for the detection of error and thus for much greater financial complexity than was previously possible. In addition, this information technology came to include insurance, currency, stock markets, limited partnerships, and Italy's *contratto di commenda*, as well as other ways of turning savings into investments. Capital formation was slow but cumulative. By the sixteenth century it had grown enough to transform the world. And it did. We often think that Europe conquered the world and got rich doing so. We forget that Europe already had the wealth in the first place to finance its explorations and conquests.[16]

In 1415, at the instigation of its twenty-one-year-old prince, later known as Henry the Navigator, Portugal conquered Ceuta, the Maghrebi port city used by eighth-century Islamic holy warriors to spread Islam to Iberia, after having crossed the Strait of Gibraltar. (At the strait's narrowest point, the Maghreb is only eight miles away from Iberia.) Ceuta was a gateway to the trans-Saharan gold trade. If Islam was losing ground in the lands of the western Mediterranean, just the opposite was the case in the east, a point dramatically driven home when the Christian city and Byzantine capital of Constantinople fell in 1453 to the Ottoman Empire. The Turks came to dominate the trade of southeastern Europe, the Middle East (the old Islamic caliphate), and the land routes to the Orient, thereby challenging the positions of the Mediterranean city-states of Italy and Dalmatia—that is, Venice, Genoa, and Ragusa (today's Dubrovnik in Croatia).[17]

To outflank the Ottoman Turks and their taxes as well as the middle-men, including Venetians, in the ports of the Gulf of Aden, the Red Sea, the Persian Gulf, Egypt, and the Levant, Atlantic Europe sent shipborne human probes (many of these seafarers were Italian, and some of the voyages, while state-supported, were nevertheless financed with Italian capital) to explore Africa. Because they had to figure out how to outsmart the prevailing winds and currents, it took decades for these sail-driven mariners to work their way down Africa's long western coast and examine its great gulf,[18] round its massive cape, and search its large horn—all in order to reach by sea India, the Golden Chersonese (Malaysia), the Spice Islands (the Moluccas, which included Ternate, Tidore, Motir, Makian, and Bachan), Cathay (China), and

Cipangu (Japan). These mariners, the Portuguese Bartolomeu Dias, Pedro Álvares Cabral, and Vasco da Gama among them, sailed past the Gulf of Guinea—where they could obtain Ashanti gold, melegueta peppers, and enslaved Blacks—rounded the optimistically named Cape of Good Hope, and finally crossed the Arabian Sea, from Africa's Malindi Bay to India's Malabar Coast, while others ventured westward across the Atlantic Ocean, eventually adding the Antilles to the Atlantic's Cape Verde, Canary, Madeira, and Azore archipelagos, and in so doing reached lands and seas unknown to the ancients. In the meantime, in 1492 the Catholic monarchs Ferdinand II of Aragon and Isabella I of Castile finally finished the Reconquest, taking back Granada from the Moors, a success that they followed by expelling practicing Jews from the kingdoms of Aragon and Castile with the Alhambra Decree, and they initiated the Conquest of the Americas by supporting the daring and unprecedented voyage of a Genoese mariner, Christopher Columbus.

These explorers learned that the world was much bigger than Ptolemy and other authorities had supposed it to be, although Columbus persisted in the belief that his false Asia—the Americas—*was* Asia, that the West Indies *were* the East Indies, and that the locals he encountered there *were* Indians.[19] As early as 1507 Martin Waldseemüller and Matthias Ringmann, two cartographers from Saint-Dié in the Vosges mountains of France, with great imagination and skill grasped the rough eastern outline of the Americas, lands that were, significantly, depicted as separate from Asia. For now and for some time to follow, the western coasts of the Americas remained *terra ultra incognita*.

The outline of North America appeared very rough indeed—whether portrayed as an island or, alternatively, as a cape, Waldseemüller and Ringmann considered both possibilities in the *Universalis Cosmographia* (see Figures 3 and 4). Nevertheless, they were the first cartographers to inscribe "America," a name which was initially affixed across the landmass of South America, below a drawing of a parrot, and derived from the controversial explorer Amerigo Vespucci, a Florentine who had sailed in the service of Spain. His distant relation Simonetta Cattaneo Vespucci, "La Bella Simonetta," served as the inspiration for Sandro Botticelli's *Birth of Venus* (1485). Later in the sixteenth century the mellifluous name America was applied by the Flemish cartographer Gerardus Mercator to both the southern and northern landmasses of the "New World." The name stuck.[20]

In the push west, the Iberian sea powers and nation-states of Portugal and Spain led the way. In order to settle existing territorial conflicts between

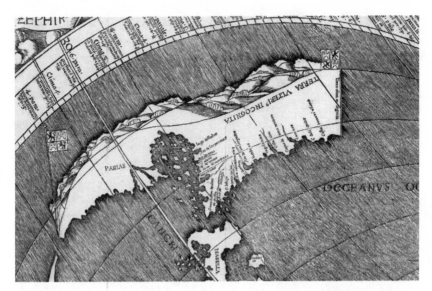

Figure 3. Martin Waldseemüller and Matthias Ringmann hedged their bets. In this detail of their world map of 1507, they show two Americas, each a separate and distinct landmass. The landmass that coincides with what would later be called North America is here named Parias. The strait between the two landmasses is located roughly where Panama is today. Although Vasco Núñez de Balboa did not cross the Isthmus of Darién (Panama) and discover the nearby Mar del Sur (Pacific Ocean) until 1513, Europeans had already clearly grasped or intuited years before that the Americas were shaped like an hourglass—one pinched in the middle. Martin Waldseemüller, *Universalis cosmographia secundum Ptholomaei traditionem et Americi Vespucii aliorumque lustrationes* (detail). [Strasbourg, France (?): n.p., 1507.] Geography and Maps Division, Library of Congress, Washington, DC. https://www.loc.gov/item/2003626426/.

them and avoid future ones, the two countries grandly agreed in 1494 to the Treaty of Tordesillas and later, in 1529, to the Treaty of Saragossa. The former treaty divided up the Atlantic between them; the latter, the world. This initial division was supported by the Spaniard Rodrigo de Borja y Doms, Pope Alexander VI (1492–1503)—the pope who had fretted over the neglect of his flock in Greenland. Portugal's hemisphere ran eastward from Brazil and included the Moluccas. In the latter division, Spain ceded its claims to the Moluccas to Portugal. Diplomats decided that the Moluccas were on Portugal's side of the new demarcation, as were the Philippines, which lay to the north of the Moluccas, a point that the Spanish would choose later to ignore. The Portuguese sphere encompassed much of the known world, from Old Guinea to New Guinea. To Spain went much of

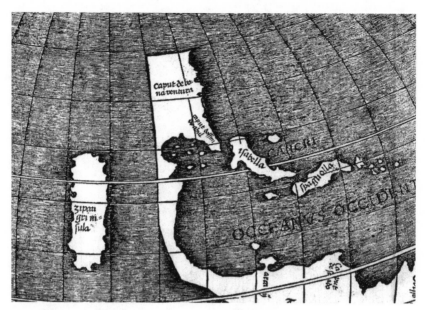

Figure 4. In a separate map of the Western Hemisphere (next to the figure of
Amerigo Vespucci), which was displayed prominently above the world map, the
cartographic duo depicted America as a single landmass. What would later be called
North America was shown not as a separate and distinct island but as a prominent
extension of a single America, specifically as Caput de Bona Ventura ("Cape of Good
Fortune"). Note that the Caribbean islands were roughly the same distance from
North America as was the island of Cipango (Japan; far left). Martin Waldseemüller,
*Universalis cosmographia secundum Ptholomaei traditionem et Americi Vespucii
aliorumque lustrationes* (detail). [Strasbourg, France?: n.p., 1507]. Geography
and Maps Division, Library of Congress, Washington, DC. https://www.loc.gov/
item/2003626426/.

the unknown world—the undiscovered countries—namely the Americas,
except for Brazil, and the Pacific Ocean beyond, including the Philippines
(despite the fact that the archipelago was in Portugal's sphere), which were
named after King Philip II (1556–1598). Spain's hemisphere included the
West Indies, much of South America, Central America, and all of mainland
North America. Thus Portugal was largely excluded from North America
except, technically at least, the eastern portion of Greenland. (Canada's
Labrador Sea and Peninsula, however, were named after the fifteenth-
century Portuguese explorer João Fernandes Lavrador.)[21] The two Iberian
kingdoms more or less adhered to these lines of demarcation, but France
and England studiedly disregarded them. The issue of jurisdiction between

the Iberian rivals was rendered moot, however, with the Iberian Union in
1580, when Portugal came under the rule of the Spanish Hapsburgs (Philip
II, Philip III, and Philip IV). And by the time the House of Bragança, beginning with John IV, the Restorer, finally reestablished Portugal's independence in 1640, the monarchies of France and England as well as the
Dutch Republic had already established colonies in North America, thereby
directly challenging Iberia's global claims.

Verrazzano

The first European we know to have set foot on North American soil after the ill-fated Norse was John Cabot (Giovanni Caboto), a citizen of the
Most Serene Republic of Venice and an explorer who received a commis-
sion from England's Henry VII of the House of Tudor. Cabot and a crew of
eighteen men left the port of Bristol in early May 1497 aboard the *Matthew*
and returned in August, three months later. They made landfall on or near
Newfoundland (Cabot may not have actually stepped foot on the mainland)
and, ignoring, or ignorant of, the Treaty of Tordesillas, claimed the country
for the Albion king. Cabot made a second voyage the following year. But
what happened on this expedition and to Cabot in particular, and whether
he survived it, is far from clear; what has survived is Cabot's name on the
strait between Newfoundland and Cape Breton, connecting the Atlantic
Ocean with the Gulf of Saint Lawrence. Four of five ships, including Cabot's,
were evidently lost at sea. What is clear is that after Cabot's second voyage the English, with a few interesting exceptions, were discouraged from
making any further attempts in the direction of North America. Not until
1587 did Sir Walter Raleigh attempt to settle Roanoke Island, off the coast
of North Carolina. But the approximately 115 colonists he sent, both men
and women, mysteriously disappeared. It is presumed that they were either
killed by, or perhaps were absorbed into, a neighboring Indian tribe, possibly
the Croatoans. Only in 1607 at Jamestown, Virginia, did the English finally
succeed, if with great difficulty, in planting a successful colony. Nevertheless,
the Venetian's late fifteenth-century discovery established England's claim
to Canada. (Newfoundland, incidentally, Britain's oldest colony, did not join
the rest of Canada until 1949.)

Like England's, France's initial exploration of North America failed to
lead to any permanent settlement until the seventeenth century. In 1524
Giovanni da Verrazzano, an Italian navigator and experienced seaman who
may be seen as the representative type of this stage in Europe's cultural

history, sailed under the French flag (he had also Florentine supporters in Rome and Lyons) up North America's Atlantic coast, a long stretch of land between the Florida and Labrador Peninsulas. Earlier, in 1513, Spain's Juan Ponce de León (who had already founded the first European settlement, Caparra, on Puerto Rico) had explored, en route to the island of Bimini, the coasts of Florida ("La Florida"), which he took for another island in the Greater Antilles. Ponce de León later tried to establish a colony on Florida's Gulf Coast, near present-day Charlotte Harbor, in 1521, but was killed by the local Timucua people, who, based on hard experience with other Europeans, distrusted his professions of friendship.

In 1513, while Ponce de León was making landfall in Florida, Vasco Núñez de Balboa would cross the Isthmus of Darién. From the top of a hill he, along with sixty-seven other "caballeros and hidalgos and worthy men," sighted the Pacific Ocean—what he called the South Sea (Mar del Sur). Later, standing in the surf on the Gulf of San Miguel, equipped with buckler and sword and holding a standard of the Virgin and Castile, he claimed in sweeping language this body of water for the royal crown of Castile: "I take and assume royal possession corporal and present of these austral seas and lands and coasts and islands with everything annexed to them or which might pertain to them in whatever manner or by whatever reason or title might or could exist, ancient or modern, in times past, present or to come, without gainsay whatsoever."[22]

In 1519 Alonso de Pineda explored the entire north coast of the Gulf of Mexico but failed to find a northern passage to the Pacific. That same year Ferdinand Magellan set sail with the Armada de Molucca, which initially consisted of a fleet of five ships and a crew of 270 men. The following year he succeeded in finding a southern passage through the Strait of Magellan to Balboa's Mar del Sur, which Magellan called the "pacific sea," and from thence to India. Magellan was killed on Mactan in the Philippines on April 27, 1521. Juan Sebastián del Cano brought the sole surviving ship, the *Victoria*, and eighteen half-dead sailors back from the Philippines to the city of Seville on September 6, 1522. The losses and hardships of the expedition notwithstanding, he had returned with enough spices in the *Victoria*'s hold to pay for the entire expedition. In his extraordinary report to King Charles, Cano declared that at 54 degrees south of the equator, "We found a Strait which passed through Your Majesty's mainland to the Sea of India, which Strait is of 100 leagues and from which we debouched. . . . Your Majesty will know best that what we should esteem and admire most is that we have

discovered and made a course around the entire rotundity of the world—
that going by the occident we have returned by the orient."[23]

During the 1520s the Spaniard Lucas Vázquez de Ayllón sailed up the
coast north of Florida as far as Cape Fear, North Carolina, looking for a passage to the Spice Islands. And Estêvão Gomes, a Portuguese in Spanish service, sailed down the Atlantic Coast from Nova Scotia, also vainly searching
for the same strait.[24] And now, on January 17, 1524, the thirty-nine-year
old Verrazzano set out to replicate Magellan's stunning feat in the much
closer, more convenient, and less tempestuous northern latitudes—to try to
find a fabled northern passage through a "Strait of Verrazzano" to reach the
"blessed shores" of Cathay.[25]

Verrazzano, his brother Gerolamo, and his pilot, Antoine de Conflans,
failed, of course, as did everyone else who would later try to find the fabled
Northwest Passage through North America to Asia. In fairness to all who
tried to do so, knowledge of North American geography would be hard won
and come slowly. And until the continent's land mass and contours were
finally known to their full extent, the Spanish would hopelessly seek the
mythical Strait of Anián through the Pacific coast to Baffin Bay or Hudson
Bay; the French, in their fruitless attempt, would penetrate deep into the
continent via the St. Lawrence River and the Great Lakes; and the English
would sail north, where they dodged icebergs and ice floes in the waters of
the Arctic archipelago in their own futile effort to find a northwest passage
to Asia from either Baffin Bay in the north or Hudson Bay in the west. But
these "voyages of delusion," in the historian Glyn Williams's rueful phrase,
still lay in the future.[26]

Verrazzano was educated in Florence and was an experienced seaman,
one who knew the waters of the Mediterranean and the North Atlantic. In
fact, there is circumstantial evidence that he may have visited North America
as early as 1508, when Thomas Aubert's exploring party left Dieppe, France,
for Newfoundland. Verrazzano's writings reveal him to be an intelligent and
discriminating observer. Indeed, he was the very model of the Renaissance
mariner. In 1524, when he crossed the Atlantic Ocean in search of a route to
Asia, all things seemed possible. This encounter with North America began
at North Carolina's Outer Banks, a string of barrier islands and spits of land
that, unbeknownst to Verrazzano, separate the Atlantic from the mainland.
He believed, however, that this isthmus, which he described as being "one
mile wide and about two hundred miles long," was all that stood between his

ship, the three-masted *La Dauphine*, and the western sea, and from thence to Asia. The explorer mistook any number of sounds—the Pamlico, the Roanoke, the Currituck—for this false sea. In 1529 his brother Gerolamo turned Giovanni's charts into a striking map of the world. In so doing, he divided North America into two large land masses, connected by Verrazzano's thin isthmus. To the south and west of the isthmus lay Terra Florida, which looked a lot like the boot of Italy. Situated to the north and east of the isthmus was what he called "Francesca," after Francis I of France (1515–1547). But Verrazzano's brother named it New France ("Nova Gallia") instead. And wedged in between Francesca and Florida, and opposite the Atlantic Ocean, was Verrazzano's great geographical error: the "Oriental Sea."

Verrazzano's search for an Atlantic entrance to Asia led him up North America's Atlantic coast as far as Cape Breton. Along the way, he used a small boat to make several landfalls in order to survey the country and observe the Native inhabitants. And just as he found that the land varied, so too did he observe differences in, and distinctions among, the peoples of the New World, whom he thought looked like "Orientals." His caution and prudence were evident at every turn, and no doubt go far in explaining what was, on the one hand, a remarkable voyage of discovery, and on the other, one almost free of hazardous missteps and accidents. He missed the Delaware and Chesapeake Bays but not the Lower and Upper New York Bay. He gazed upon New York Harbor but evidently overlooked the mouth of the Hudson River, one of the two great north-south waterways of New Netherland, the other being the Connecticut River. The Hudson River would later serve as the natural border between New York and New England. All that, however, was in the future. As of 1524, New York Bay appeared destined to be French. Verrazzano named the future heart of the American imperium Angoulême, again after Francis I, who was also the count of Angoulême, a city in southwestern France. In 1964 a double-decked suspension bridge that spans 4,260 feet from tower to tower, each of which rises 700 feet from the water, was built in honor of Verrazzano to cross the Narrows and connect the boroughs of Brooklyn and Staten Island, despite the objections of thousands of their citizens. This massive but majestic gateway to the North American continent is sixty feet longer than its Pacific Coast counterpart, San Francisco's Golden Gate.[27]

From New York, the explorer continued past Long Island and Block Island to Narragansett Bay ("Refugio"), north of Rhode Island. Verrazzano gave Rhode Island this name because of its likeness to Rhodes, an island in Greece's Dodecanese chain with which Verrazzano was personally familiar from his earlier maritime career. Of his encounters with Native peoples, he was particularly struck by Rhode Island's Wampanoag and the Narragansett, whom he described as the "most beautiful," with "the most civil customs that we have found on this voyage." He sailed north past Cape Cod and on to the coast of Maine and, possibly, Newfoundland, before finally returning to Dieppe on July 8, 1524.

In these upper northern reaches, Verrazzano found the Native peoples quite different from the others his party had encountered and of whom he had written admiringly. "For while the previous ones had been courteous in manner," Verrazzano observed, "these were full of crudity and vices, and were so barbarous that we could never make any communication with them, however many signs we made to them." The men, he wrote, "made all signs of scorn and shame," including "showing their buttocks and laughing," that "any brute creature would make." Perhaps the rude behavior was born of a suspicion or contempt based on earlier dealings with unscrupulous European sailors or fishermen.

Verrazzano had set sail for Terra Nova on January 17, 1524; less than six months later, by July 8, he had returned to Dieppe and at once reported to the king. Instead of a highway to the Orient, Verrazzano explained, he had found an obstacle, a land that "was unknown to the ancients." And this obstacle, this landmass, was not without great value in its own right. He reported to the king that at different stops "we frequently went five or six leagues into the interior, and found it as pleasant as I can possibly describe, and suitable for every kind of cultivation—grain, wine, or oil. These fields extend for [25] to [30] thirty leagues; they are open and free of any obstacles or trees, and so fertile that any kind of seed would produce excellent crops." In what was one of the grand statements of the Renaissance, Verrazzano told Francis I,

My intention on this voyage was to reach Cathay and the extreme eastern coast of Asia, but I did not expect to find such an obstacle of new land as I have found; and if for some reason I did expect to find it, I estimated there would be some strait to get through to the Eastern Ocean. This was the opinion of all the ancients, who certainly believed that our Western Ocean was joined to the Eastern Ocean of India without any land in between. Aristotle supports this theory by arguments

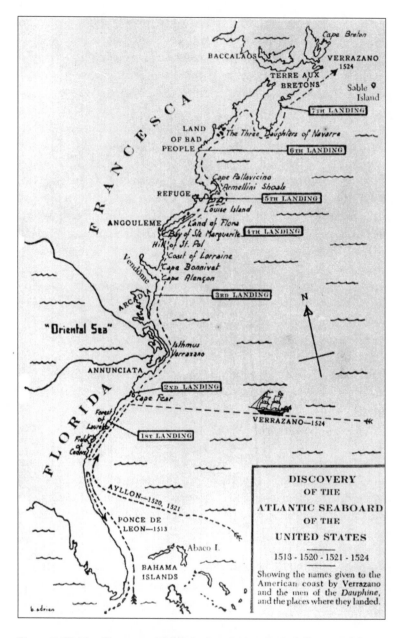

Figure 5. *FR-Map, Verrazano Atlantic Seaboard*, 1950. [08/50] Photograph by Angelo Rizzuto. Anthony Angelo Collection, Library of Congress, Washington, DC. https://www.loc.gov/item/2020635600/.

of various analogies, but this opinion is quite contrary to that of the moderns, and has been proven false by experience. Nevertheless, land has been found by modern man which was unknown to the ancients, another world with respect to the one they knew, which appears to be larger than our Europe, than Africa, and almost larger than Asia, if we estimate its size correctly.[28]

Verrazzano's discovery ranks with Columbus's discovery of the South American mainland, near the mouth of the Orinoco River in Venezuela, in 1498. Unfortunately, Verrazzano did not get to bask in glory in his later years. He made a later voyage, this time to the Lesser Antilles in the Caribbean, where in 1528 he was captured, killed, and cannibalized by Caribs on the butterfly-shaped island of Guadeloupe. It was Verrazzano's brother Gerolamo who named these islands the Insule de Canibali. Today Guadeloupe is an overseas *département* of France.

If Verrazzano had discovered that the way to the Orient was blocked by a continent, the French explorer Jacques Cartier was among the first of many explorers who would nevertheless continue to seek a northwest passage through or around North America to Asia. Under Francis I Cartier would make three voyages (1534–41) and navigate the St. Lawrence River west as far as Montreal. He failed to find a route to Asia or found a colony, but he did put the Huron-Iroquois name Kanata, or Canada, on the map of North America.

Inhumanity and Humanism

In 1521 Lucas Vázquez de Ayllón, a wealthy judge from Hispaniola though born in Toledo, Spain, in 1480, had sent an exploring expedition up the Atlantic Coast. Now, in 1526, he would try to colonize the area, first in Winyah Bay in South Carolina, north of present-day Charleston. Although Winyah Bay, where several rivers, including the Pee Dee, empty, was an estuary rich in fish and wildlife, the Spaniards found the area unsuitable for agriculture and withdrew south to present-day Georgia's Sapelo Sound, where Ayllón with six hundred colonists and one hundred horses founded the first European settlement in what would become the United States: San Miguel de Guadalupe.[29]

The colony, however, was very short-lived. Within two months it was abandoned for a number of reasons: a harsh winter, contaminated water (which killed Ayllón), a revolt of enslaved Blacks (the first in American history), and hostile Natives (with good reason—the local Guale, like the

Timucua, feared enslavement at the hands of the Spanish). The latter reason was tragic, since Ayllón personally opposed the enslavement of Natives. He was a saver, not a slaver. In fact, his expedition included Fray Antonio de Montesinos (in whose arms Ayllón died), whose denouncements of Native slavery in 1511 from the pulpit in the cathedral of Santo Domingo had moved and inspired none other than Bartolomé de las Casas. For his part, to meet the labor needs of the Spanish in the Americas, and spare the Natives from slavery, Las Casas recommended, first, the subsidized immigration of free Spaniards and their families, and second, the expansion of African slavery to the Americas, which he came deeply to regret. Thus San Miguel de Guadalupe—"the Lost Spanish City," according to an historical marker in the city of Beaufort on South Carolina's Port Royal Island—was a failure, but its experience was predictive of Europe's sixteenth-century colonization efforts in middle and upper North America.

A case in point was Santa María de Filipinos, a city founded on Florida's Pensacola Bay by the conquistador and Coronado expedition veteran Tristán de Luna y Arellano. Luna arrived on August 14, 1559, with 500 soldiers, 1,000 colonists and servants, and 240 horses. The expedition rode anchor while an exploring party went inland. He was then to find an overland route from Pensacola Bay to Santa Elena, an area of the Atlantic-coast Sea Islands between present-day South Carolina's Parris Island and Georgia's Tybee Island that Ayllón had explored and named in 1526. Within five days of Luna's arrival, however, a hurricane destroyed seven of his ships, taking the lives of many of the settlers as well as destroying the expedition's provisions. Luna never located Santa Elena, either by land or sea. Two years later he was ordered back to Mexico in 1561, and his ill-fated mission in the North American wilderness was abandoned. It was not until the Spanish were directly threatened by the French—not French corsairs operating from the Caribbean but, at the instigation of French admiral and Huguenot leader Gaspard II de Coligny, French sailors carrying the French flag—that they found the resolve to colonize the Atlantic coast. (Coligny also tried to establish a colony in South America, France Antarctique, on the island of Serigipe—renamed Villegagnon after the colony's leader, Nicolas Durand de Villegagnon—in Brazil's magnificent Guanabara Bay in 1555. The French settlers fell into squabbling factions of Protestants and Catholics, and were expelled by a Portuguese flotilla five years later.) In 1612 the French would try again to colonize South America with the establishment of Equinoctial France, near the equator in what is the present-day Brazilian state of Maranhão. The colony was expelled by the Portuguese in 1615. The

French would finally succeed in South America several decades later with the founding of French Guiana, later home of the infamous penal colony Île du Diable.

In 1562 Captain Jean Ribault, aided by the explorer and gentleman René Goulaine de Laudonnière, built Charlesfort (named after Charles IX) on Parris Island, just south of the present-day US Marine Corps Recruit Depot, to protect French settlers and position the French to easily prey upon Spanish ships passing by on the strong current that runs from the Gulf of Mexico, through the Straits of Florida, and then up the Atlantic Coast. To add insult to injury, many of the French settlers were Huguenots or Calvinist Protestants. To the Catholic Spanish who claimed this territory, this military and religious intrusion was intolerable. Charlesfort was soon abandoned because of internal dissension, and in 1664 a second, largely Protestant colony was established even deeper in Spanish territory, on the Florida coast at or near the mouth of the St. Johns River, where Laudonnière oversaw the construction of a second fort, Fort de la Caroline (Fort Caroline).

As in Charlesfort, the colony soon teetered on the brink of disaster, again because of internal dissension and starvation, as well as poor relations with local Natives. But it was relieved by the timely and very generous intervention of John Hawkins, a fellow Protestant and English sea dog, and one of a number of privateers authorized by Queen Elizabeth to attack Spanish ships and targets. (Unlike Ian Fleming's fictional James Bond, these Elizabethan 007s were real and had real licenses to kill.) Hawkins, a pious privateer (his flagship, a carrack, was named the *Jesus of Lübeck*), also happened to be England's first slaver. Somehow his contradictions resolved themselves in the moral and intellectual world in which he lived, calling to mind the line by the British novelist L. P. Hartley, "The past is [indeed] a foreign country: they do things differently there."

In response to France's provocations the Spanish king, Philip II ("the Prudent"), dispatched Admiral Pedro Menéndez de Avilés to Florida via Puerto Rico. Menéndez was named Florida's first *adelantado*, or governor—which, given Spain's territorial claims and the state of geographical knowledge at the time, made him the governor of all the lands that would one day make up the United States and Canada. Along with five ships carrying five hundred soldiers, two hundred sailors, and one hundred colonists, Menéndez arrived at Cabo Cañaveral (Cape Canaveral, now known as the Space Coast) on August 25, 1665. After learning the whereabouts of the French from the Timucua, Menéndez proceeded up the coast. Three days later he discovered an inlet or harbor where the Tolomato and Matanzas Rivers converged and founded a settlement there. San Agustín, as the new settlement was named, would become St. Augustine, the oldest continuously occupied city of European origin in United States. It was later the site of Spain's imposing stronghold the Castillo de San Marcos, as well as the future terminus of North America's first Underground Railroad; escaped slaves were granted freedom in Florida if they agreed to swear allegiance to the king of Spain and convert to Catholicism, or in exchange for military service.

To provide added protection to Fort Caroline, which looked likely to suffer the same fate as Charlesfort, Coligny sent a naval force of seven ships carrying six hundred colonists, again under the command of Ribault, which arrived in Florida's waters on August 28, 1565. The two European forces soon collided. Menéndez found himself outmaneuvered, but he evaded the French and withdrew to San Agustín. Ribault pursued him but later encountered a storm that wrecked his fleet. The French survivors, including Ribault, washed up onshore near San Agustín.

In the meantime Menéndez subjected five hundred of his men to a forced march north to attack Fort Caroline, which he did on September 30. What followed was a slaughter in which 132 Huguenots were killed or executed. Women and children under the age of fifteen were spared. Laudonnière managed to escape. Others were captured and hanged from nearby trees. To mark the occasion, Menéndez inscribed on a sign: "I do not do this to Frenchmen, but to Heretics." Word of his act raced across the Atlantic world. Two large groups of survivors of Ribault's fleet, Ribault among them, surrendered to Menéndez, only to be put to death by the Matanzas, or Slaughter River, as it was named afterward by the Spanish. Menéndez spared, however, sixteen Breton sailors of the Catholic faith. He went on to rename Fort Caroline "Fort San Mateo," and in 1566 he sailed up the Atlantic Coast to Parris Island (now in South Carolina), where he established Santa Elena, the first capital of Spanish Florida, and built another garrison.

But the French were not through. In 1568 the French captain Dominic de Gourgues—evidently on his own initiative, though one suspects crown involvement at some level)—self-financed an expedition of three ships, carrying 150 soldiers and 80 sailors, to exact revenge on the Spanish at Fort San Mateo for the massacres of Huguenots at Fort Caroline and the Matanzas River. In league with local Natives, notably Chief Satouriana and the chief's nephew Olotocara, Gourgues not only defeated the Spanish and razed the fort but also hung a number of Spanish prisoners from the very same trees from which they had hung Huguenots. Gourgues then mounted his own sign: "I do not do this to Spaniards and sailors, but to traitors, robbers, and murderers."

With his nation's honor restored, Gourgues returned to France with the fallen fort's artillery. Nevertheless the French incursion into the Spanish Main—which, as opposed to the Spanish West Indies, includes New Spain, Florida, Central America, Columbia, and Venezuela—had been terminated with extreme religious prejudice. Henceforth, and until the French explorer René Robert Cavelier, sieur de la Salle, claimed Louisiana for France in 1682, the French would concentrate their ambitions in the Americas on either Canada or the Caribbean, and after the dismal experiences of Charlesfort and Fort Caroline, they would later, as a matter of policy but not always of practice, favor Catholic over Protestant colonists.

As for the Spanish, their presence in upper Florida was problematic. Relations with the local Guale and Orista peoples were strained, and in 1586 the English replaced the French as the major threat to Spain's New World interests. That was the year that the legendary swashbuckling sea dog Sir Francis Drake, John Hawkins's younger cousin, raided and plundered not only the Spanish West Indies but the Spanish Main as well, including San Agustín, which he burned to the ground, reavenging his fellow Protestants the French Huguenots, killed near there by the Spanish nearly twenty years before.

Drake then returned to England via Sir Walter Raleigh's new colony in present-day North Carolina, Roanoke. Founded in 1585, Roanoke, like San Miguel de Guadalupe, Santa María de Filipinos, Charlesfort, and Fort Caroline, would be subsequently abandoned. In reaction to Drake's raid and to England's colonization efforts in North Carolina and Newfoundland— where Sir Humphrey Gilbert (1539–1583), Raleigh's half-brother, claimed St. John's for Queen Elizabeth on August 5, 1583—the Spanish withdrew from Santa Elena for good, moving the capital of Spanish Florida and the colonists of Parris Island to San Agustín. A month after Gilbert left Newfoundland, where he founded Britain's overseas empire, he was drowned in the wreck of the HMS *Squirrel*. He exited the world's stage with a line worthy of his contemporary William Shakespeare: "We are as near heaven by sea as by land."[30]

The European colonization of middle and upper North America took place against a backdrop of intense religious conflict, which ground on at least until 1648, when the peace treaties that were finally concluded in the Westphalian cities of Osnabrück and Münster ended the Thirty Years' and the Eighty Years' Wars, respectively. The English Civil War, the bloodiest conflict in the history of the British Isles, closed three years later in 1651. Out of all of this strife, a new spirit of religious toleration was born on both sides of the English Channel, although it would be tested again and again in the ensuing decades.

While much of the previous history of the English colonization of North America may be seen as a reaction to the religious troubles of the Old World, French Canada started as something different. Sectarian violence bedeviled France, of course, as it did elsewhere. Indeed, Gaspard II de Coligny, who had tried to colonize first Charlesfort and then Fort Caroline, was brutally beaten, defenestrated alive, and then beheaded in 1572 during the St. Bartholomew's Day Massacre. Thousands perished in this wave of assassinations and mob violence carried out by French Catholics against French Huguenots. This event reignited the French Wars of Religion, which went on from 1562 to 1598 and nearly led to France's national disintegration. The long conflict did produce a remarkable king, the pragmatic Henry IV, known as Good King Henry. A Huguenot who had received his military education from Coligny, he nevertheless converted to Catholicism in 1593, four years after he became king, in order to end the stout Catholic resistance to his kingship. It eventually worked; he became accepted and in 1598, in the city of Nantes in Brittany, promulgated an edict granting religious liberty to France's Protestant minority. After decades of sectarian turmoil, Henry supposedly commented, "Paris vaut bien une messe" ("Paris is well worth a mass"); in other words, the peace afforded the nation by a rapprochement between Catholics and Calvinists was worth more than one's private conscience, a stunning admission in an age of religious zealotry.

After years of civil war, Henry embarked on a comprehensive program to revive France's economy. This included an effort to return to North America, beginning in 1599 with the settlement of the Île de Sable (Sable Island, literally "Isle of Sand"), a long, thin, treeless sandbar covered with tufts of marram dune grass, one hundred miles southeast of present-day Nova Scotia. The island would become a notorious shipwrecker, the "Graveyard of the Atlantic." In 1583, in fact, Sir Humphrey Gilbert's ship the HMS *Delight* had sunk in the island's waters after hitting a shoal. It was to this unpropitious place, today known mainly for its stunted feral horses, that the viceroy of New France, Troilus de La Roche de Mesgouez, sent convicts recruited from

France's jails in an effort to combine colonization with rehabilitation. In 1516 the English humanist Sir Thomas More's *Utopia* had conceived of an ideal society set on an imaginary island somewhere in the New World—a thought experiment intended to encourage reform in Europe. The society founded on Sable Island, however, proved to be the very antithesis of More's utopia—or any other utopia, for that matter—degenerating into mutiny, murder, and starvation. In the end, only eleven survivors managed to get back to Europe aboard a passing Spanish ship.

Henry IV would reign for ten more years before he was stabbed to death by a Catholic fanatic in 1610. It was during this period that France recolonized North America. Pierre Dugua de Mons, an aristocrat whom Henry IV had granted a trading monopoly (1604–7) in Acadia, oversaw the establishment of two successful settlements: Port-Royal in Acadia (the use of the name Acadia in North America dates back to Verrazzano), in what is now Nova Scotia, where group camaraderie and good relations with the local Mi'kmaq and Maliseet peoples marked a sharp departure from France's previous efforts; Quebec City, founded on the St. Lawrence River. The success of Port-Royal, it should be noted, followed an initial failure on the Isle de Sainte Croix near the mouth of the St. Croix River between present-day Maine and New Brunswick, where thirty-five colonists out of seventy-nine perished due to scurvy (a cause of death confirmed in 2003 by forensic pathologists). The long Canadian winter of 1604–5 had turned this natural fortress into a prison, cut off as it was from the mainland, and then a graveyard. The Indians would later call this place of misfortune "Bone Island."

In both Acadia and Quebec, Samuel de Champlain, who had seen the worst in his fellow man as he fought in the French Wars of Religion, worked tirelessly to establish and then consolidate a New France. He recorded much of this activity. In the words of the historian Kevin Starr, Champlain was "an able presenter of vivid real-time experience in straightforward prose, and since he was so central to the establishment of New France, the record Champlain created—like the life he lived—remains foundational. Champlain lived history, acted history, made history, was history."[31] In the service of king and country, he made no less than twenty-seven transatlantic voyages between 1599 and 1633. According to Champlain's biographer, David Hackett Fischer, in Champlain's

> thoughts and acts we always find a consuming curiosity about the world. Here was a spirit that was sweeping the western world in the

sixteenth century. Part of it was linked to the Protestant Reformation and the Catholic Counter-Reformation, and to a search for the spirit of God in the natural world. Another part flowed from the Renaissance and its hunger for knowledge. It inspired a fascination with *scientia*, not the modern idea of science but is epistemic ancestor, which was a broader idea of ordered knowledge. With it came a disciplined inquiry, a systematic spirit of observation, a love of study, and a deep belief that knowledge would be immediately useful and beneficial. These values expressed themselves in another quality of Champlain's [writings]: its exhilaration in the act of discovery, not in the sense of being the first to find something, but in the pleasure of revealing it to others.[32]

And just as Champlain wanted a France where Protestants and Catholics lived together in peace, he imagined a New France where old intramural quarrels would be set aside, a society of mutual benefit to the French and the *sauvage*—a term he used to mean nothing more than "forest-dweller." He had a great respect and sympathy for North America's Native peoples, and *sauvage* did not carry for him any negative connotations. It was merely descriptive, not racist; the racial determinism of Arthur de Gobineau was still a good two centuries into the future. Champlain believed in a common humanity, which is not to say he thought that all cultures were of equal value. Far from it. Europeans of the seventeenth century were hardly adherents of cultural relativism, a twentieth-century invention of anthropology. On the other hand, the debates of 1550 in Valladolid between Las Casas and Juan Ginés de Sepúlveda on the intellectual and religious capacity of the American Indians had been settled as far as Champlain and other French humanists were concerned. In fact, Champlain not only admired the intellect of Native peoples but championed their physical condition or general health over that of his fellow Europeans. His vision of a Gallic-Indigenous commonwealth, that is, a new Métis civilization, his *grand dessein* for North America, was, in short, tolerant and humanistic. And admittedly it was also one that perfectly suited an economy based on the fur trade, in which intergroup cooperation was essential, as opposed to mining or agriculture, where the profit in exploiting others often proved irresistible.

In 1605, after the disastrous winter on Saint Croix Island, now an international historic site, Dugua and Champlain moved to Port-Royal (today's Annapolis Royal) on the other side of the Bay of Fundy. The following year

Champlain organized the Ordre de Bon Temps ("Order of Good Cheer"), the first chief steward of which was the young classically trained lawyer Marc Lescarbot, Canada's first poet-historian. Lescarbot's *Histoire de la Nouvelle-France* was first published in 1609 and would go through several editions and translations. He was not only New France's first historian but also New France's first poet. Aspiring to be a Virgil, he wrote the Acadian *Aeneid*, the long poem "Adieu à la France." It is also worth noting that in addition to this history and poem, Lescarbot also wrote *Le Théâtre de Neptune*, a play or masque that was performed, with French as well as Natives in attendance, in the port of Port-Royal in 1606. It was the earliest theatrical production in Canadian history.

The point of the Ordre de Bon Temps was not to provide the colony with a new dining society, although it was that, and a very successful one. It was Champlain's attempt to battle scurvy, the bane of sailors and settlers alike. He had come to believe the disease was related to some kind of nutritional deficiency, having observed that local Natives as well as the colony's own hunters survived the winter without getting the dreadful disease. What these two groups seemed to share in common, besides camaraderie, was the consumption of fresh foods, including fresh-killed meat.

The Ordre de Bon Temps was thus intended not only to promote camaraderie—which it did, as Lescarbot's fulsome account of the society well attests—but also to provide everyone with fresh fish or game and other foods. Members took turns serving as the chief steward, who wore a special medal around his neck and made sure that on his watch the dining tables groaned under the weight of the land's bounty for nobles like Jean de Biencourt, sieur de Poutrincourt, Canada's first composer. The society did not admit the French lower orders; France's class system arrived in North America fully intact. To again quote Champlain's biographer:

> Like most Europeans his age, [Champlain] believed in a hierarchy of orders and estates. But he also believed that, by God's will, people of all nations should be treated with respect. Many of Champlain's French associates shared his way of thinking: Protestants such as Dugua and Catholics such as Lescarbot. Here again, as in many other ways, these men were profoundly influenced by the example of Henry IV. This circle of French humanists were pivotal figures in more ways than one. In the history of Europe they transformed the purpose of the Renaissance into the program of the Enlightenment. In America they also played a vital role. After many failures of French colonization in the sixteenth

century they were the first to succeed. They planted the seed of New France, and bent the sapling to the pattern of its growth. Their history bears witness to the importance of small beginnings in the history of great nations.[33]

But they did invite the sagamore Membertou and other Native chiefs to participate—as equals—in the bonhomie of these culinary events and ceremonies. In fact, good relations with the local Natives were key to the success of Port-Royal and later Quebec. After much misery and death, the French had cracked the code on how to survive—how to live—in the northeast corner of a faraway continent.

The English, in contrast, had many hard lessons yet to learn. Virginia's "Starving Time," the winter of 1609–10, lay dead ahead.

The Ordeal and Odyssey of Cabeza de Vaca

Exploring the continent's eastern coastline was a daunting undertaking. But exploring its vast interior was, if anything, even more so. North America (Canada, Mexico, and the United States) covers 8,408,449 square miles and includes a broad range of biomes, from the frozen tundra of Canada's Northwest Territories to the steamy jungles of the Mexican states of Chiapas, the Yucatán, and Quitana Roo. Or, in terms of fauna instead of flora, from polar bears to iguanas. Canada's total land area is 3,860,000 square miles, making it the second largest country in the world. The third largest is the United States, with its 3,790,000 square miles. Mexico ranks fourteenth, between Saudi Arabia and Indonesia, at 758,449 square miles. Thus to Europeans North America, to the extent that they fully grasped it, appeared as an almost unimaginably immense, largely trackless wilderness, especially the lands north of the Rio Grande and west of the Appalachian Mountains.

Or at least it seemed like a wilderness. It was hardly empty. The wigwams, tepees, longhouses, and igloos of the northern reaches were highly serviceable and ingenious, if few and far between. But in the eyes of Europeans, these structures in middle and upper North America could not but compare invidiously with the great temple-palaces, pyramids, and cities of lower North America or Mexico. Given the sheer size of the North American continent, the alacrity with which the Spanish came, saw, and conquered the continent's most sociopolitically advanced societies was astounding. By August 13, 1521, less than thirty years after Columbus's first landfall in the Bahamas, the expedition of Hernán Cortés had already reached the Valley of Mexico and replaced the Aztec Empire with Spain's own semifeudal, semicapitalist order. In South America the Inca Empire would soon meet the same fate, although fighting there would go on for years. And within two decades of the conquest of the Aztec capital, Tenochtitlán, rumors grew that somewhere to the north lay the famous Seven Cities of Gold.

According to Christian legend, seven bishops and their congregations had fled Spain—as Aeneas and his family had fled Troy—following the invasion of the Moors. These episcopal refugees went to an island somewhere in the Western Ocean, where they went on to found not a new Rome among seven hills but an island where they built seven rich and wonderful cities. When the Spanish failed to find the "Seven Cities of Antilia" or the "Cities of the Seven Bishops," somewhere in the middle Atlantic or the Caribbean Sea, the location of these cities was moved in the Spanish imagination to the mainland of North America, perhaps somewhere north of Mexico. These cities later became known as the Seven Cities of Cíbola, for a Native word that meant "buffalo."[34]

The source of the rumors came from the Odysseus of North America, Álvar Núñez Cabeza de Vaca. His grandfather was Pedro de Vera, the conqueror of Gran Canaria of the Canary Islands. Cabeza de Vaca himself was a distinguished veteran of Spain's wars in Europe. He was appointed treasurer of the disastrous colonizing expedition of Pánfilo de Narváez, making him second-in-command. The expedition left Cuba for Florida's Gulf Coast in 1528, the same year that Verrazzano died for king and country on Guadeloupe Island. Through a series of poor decisions and bad luck, the incompetent Narváez and nearly three hundred men perished after first becoming lost in the Florida interior, near Tampa Bay. Worse, they allowed themselves to become separated from their supply ships. After being reduced to eating their own horses, they then attempted to leave Florida in a flotilla of makeshift barges. Cabeza de Vaca, however, survived the harrowing trip into the Gulf of Mexico and washed up somewhere near Galveston Island and the Matagorda Peninsula on the Texas coast. He was later reunited with three other castaways—Alonso del Castillo Maldonado, Andrés Dorantes, and a Moroccan slave and native of Azamor, a Black man named Estevánico. The quartet then followed Indian trails overland across south and west Texas and northern Mexico, meeting many of the region's Native peoples, such as the Coahuiltecan, to whom they ministered as faith healers.

In 1536, nine long years after Narváez's failed attempt to conquer Florida and having walked over two thousand miles, the four survivors of his expedition finally arrived in San Miguel de Culiacán. New Spain's northwesternmost outpost in the recently created province of New Galicia, Culiacán was founded near the Sea of Cortés in 1531 by the conquistador and human butcher Nuño Beltrán de Guzmán. His biographer called him the very "personification of the Black Legend."[35] Before reaching this remote pueblo and former Native village, the four castaways knew they were getting close to their countrymen when they saw "a buckle from a sword belt around an Indian's neck, with a horseshoe nail sewn to it."[36] This unplanned pedestrian feat proved that North America was wide indeed, contrary to Verrazzano's narrow conception of the land's westward extent. The English, however, would continue to hold otherwise until the seventeenth century, as evidenced by the expansive "sea to sea" land grant of the Virginia charter.[37]

Back in civilization, Cabeza de Vaca reported to the Spanish officials in New Spain's capital, including the viceroy Antonio de Mendoza, who had been appointed as a royal check against Hernán Cortés. Much of Cabeza de Vaca's account was notable for its empathy and anthropological detail. Indeed, if Cortés had changed North America, it seemed that North America had very much changed Cabeza de Vaca. Human- rather than divine-centered, his account was more a product of the Renaissance than of the Middle Ages. And having spent time with Native Americans, he counseled a policy of restraint toward them. But some of his countrymen were not nearly as interested in Cabeza de Vaca's recommendations as they were in his party's reports, based on secondhand Native sources, that large cities lay to the north of Mexico. These reports turned into rumors and spread like wildfire. Many Spaniards immediately jumped to the conclusion that this news confirmed the existence of the fabled Seven Cities of Gold.

Ghosts

In an important sense the Indians were right. There were relatively large settlements to the north in what is now Arizona and New Mexico, two states that, taken together, make up the American Southwest.[38] According to Donald Meinig, place matters. He argues that in prehistoric times the Southwest—Arizona and New Mexico—was physically as well as culturally set apart from other regions in North America, as well as from California and Texas. Bounded by the Mojave Desert, the Colorado River Canyonlands, the Southern Rockies, and the Llano Estacado, the Southwest was home to several Formative cultures. By the time the Spanish arrived, the region's three principal Formative societies had, between AD 200 and 1450, already

waxed and waned. In historic times the Southwest was where the Spanish
and American zones of influence intersected, and home to relatively large
populations of Native Americans.

The Hohokam lived in the Arizona desert along the Gila and Salt
Rivers, the waters of which they had diverted into extensive irrigation networks.[39] In contrast, the Ancestral Puebloans (also known as the Anasazi,
"ancient enemies," in Navajo, though some of their modern descendants
object to the term) occupied the mesas, buttes, and plateaus of the Four
Corners region of Utah, Colorado, Arizona, and New Mexico. And finally the Mogollon resided in the mountain valleys of southeastern Arizona,
southwestern New Mexico, and northern Chihuahua. Their pit houses and
well-preserved cliff dwellings, which like the cliff dwellings of the Ancestral
Puebloan neighbors to the north were defensive in nature, were built near
the headwaters of the Gila River. Abandoned in the mid-fifteenth century,
they were among the first sites to be set aside for protection under the US
Antiquities Act of 1906. The Mogollon produced a distinctive high-quality
black-on-white pottery called Mimbres, which means "willows" in Spanish,
after the Mimbres River.

It is not clear why the Hohokam abandoned their settlements, but the
usual suspected factors are environmental degradation, crop failure from
soil exhaustion (corn quickly depletes the soil of nutrients, especially ni-
trogen), climate change, and civil conflict and/or foreign invasion. When
Anglo-American pioneers arrived in the Salt River Valley after the American
Civil War, they found the old canals and reused them to irrigate their farms;
others, who felt that their land was devalued by what they regarded as nui-
sance canals or ditches, filled these ancient works with dirt. In acknowledgment of their vanished Native predecessors, the pioneers in Arizona named
their new community after the mythological Phoenix, a reborn bird that
rises from the ashes of its burned body. In the Mississippi Valley, Anglo-
American pioneers encountered a similar, if aboveground, problem: the
land was dotted with numerous mounds or barrows, which is why the city of
St. Louis in Missouri was nicknamed the "Mound City." These mounds were
seen as obstacles to progress, however, and almost all of them were removed.

Whatever may have happened to the Hohokam, their likely descendants,
the Tohono O'odham Nation or Desert People (until 1986 known as the
Papago tribe), adapted to the sere and spare life of the Sonoran Desert.
North America's other great deserts are the Great Basin, the Mojave, and
the Chihuahuan. The Sonoran, with its iconic saguaro cactus, runs south of
Arizona's Mogollon Rim to the cactus-studded coast and islands of the Sea

of Cortés. This North American region was bordered by four rivers: the Gila River in the north, the Magdalena River in the south, the San Pedro River in the east, and the Colorado River in the west. The Spanish distinguished the people who lived here, a land they called the Pimería Alta, into the Pima and the Papago tribes. Its pre-Christian spiritual center and home of the creator I'itoli was Baboquivari Peak, located southwest of Tucson and the San Xavier del Bac mission, established in 1692 by the Jesuit Italian explorer Eusebio Francisco Kino. Once united by geography and culture, this region is now bisected by the US-Mexican border.

Like the Hohokam, the Ancestral Puebloans—ancestors of the Hopi, Zuñi, Acoma, and Pueblo peoples—and Mogollon withdrew or abandoned their villages in the late prehistoric period, although it is unclear why. According to dendrochronology, the study of tree rings pioneered by astronomer Andrew Ellicott Douglas of the University of Arizona while he was trying to reconstruct a history of sunspots, there was a severe and prolonged drought in the late thirteenth century (circa 1275–1300)—similar, in fact, to the long "megadrought" that the wider region is experiencing today. But there had been prolonged droughts before. The most likely explanation for the Anasazi and Mogollon outmigration was an intensification of warfare over dwindling resources.[40] Or perhaps the societies of the Hohokam, Mogollon, and Anasazi were all caught in a Malthusian trap, where the population simply outran the food supply, forcing it to adjust downward, chewing off its own leg in order to escape. This cruel fate seems to be what befell Cahokia, the prehistoric mound city near the confluence of the Mississippi and Missouri Rivers. After four centuries (circa 950–1350), the Formative Mississippian culture centered there went into decline in the mid-fourteenth century.

Coronado's Compass

In 1540 Francisco Vázquez de Coronado, at the behest of the viceroy of New Spain, Antonio de Mendoza, assembled a large force in Compostela, the capital of New Galicia, to venture northward. Mendoza wanted to find the cities of gold before New Spain's captain general Hernán Cortés or Hernando de Soto, who was on his way from Spain and at the head of another expedition.[41] Coronado's fully armed force, immortalized in 1905 by the American artist Frederic Remington, was comprised of 230 men on horse, 62 foot soldiers, and a number of friars. The party also included at least 1,000, perhaps as many as 1,300, Mexican Native auxiliaries, armed with atlatls (spear throwers), *macahuitls* (obsidian-edged war clubs), and *tepoztopollis* (halberds), as well as morning stars, mauls, and slings. The use of skilled Native warriors or "Indios Amigos" had been crucial in Cortés's rapid conquest of the Aztecs—a lesson not lost on his successors, rivals, and enemies. In fact, one sometimes wonders who was driving whom to new conquests, the Spaniards or the Indios Amigos. Regardless, it is hard to imagine at the time a more terrifying army than the one led by the Spaniard Coronado, which debouched from Mexico in 1540 to reach as far away as the Wichita villages on the wide expanse of the Kansas plains.

In addition to these human components, Coronado's party also consisted of a thousand horses and six hundred mules, as well as herds of pigs and cattle. The introduction of these animals would change the course of North American history in general, and in particular alter the lifeways of the continent's Native peoples. At the head of this colorful and bawling pageant was Coronado, dressed in a suit of armor that he described as "gilded

Figure 6. Frederic Remington, *Coronado Sets Out to the North*, c. 1890s. Oil on canvas. Wikimedia Commons. https://commons.wikimedia.org/wiki/File:Frederic_Remington_-_Coronado_sets_out_to_the_north.jpg.

and glittering."[42] In 1540 a supply fleet—the ships the *San Pedro,* the *Santa Catalina,* and later the *San Gabriel*—sailed up the west coast of Mexico under the command of Hernando de Alarcón, from Acapulco to the Colorado River, what he called the Buena Guia ("Good Guide"), which he ascended upriver as far as the Yuma Crossing between what is now Arizona and

California. When Alarcón failed to rendezvous with Coronado as planned, he returned, leaving behind a cache of letters at the foot of a tree, which were recovered later by Melchior Díaz, who came instead of Coronado. Díaz called the Colorado River, North America's Nile, the Río del Tizón ("Firebrand River"), a name that stuck for two centuries. Alarcón did record an important discovery: Baja California was not an island but part of the mainland. Coronado, who was nearly five hundred miles away, did not find cities of gold, of course. What he found instead was Hawikuh, one of the six Zuñi cities, or rather villages, of Cíbola, the others being Kyanawa, Pinnawa, Halona, Matsakya, and Kyakima.[43]

We should note that a year before Coronado's departure, Viceroy Mendoza sent an expedition led by Fray Marcos de Niza (Mark of Nice) to the north to reconnoiter the Cities of Cíbola. Estevánico, the Moroccan slave who crossed North America with Cabeza de Vaca, was ordered to accompany the expedition. In fact, Estevánico led an advance party. He later sent word back to Fray Marcos that he had found Cíbola. Why he misrepresented the situation, when there was no city of gold, is not clear. Perhaps it was a case of preemption, and he gambled that there was indeed such a city or cities to make a name for himself. But after Estevánico sent word, Fray Marcos was informed by Native messengers that the Zuñi had killed Estevánico. According to Coronado, they had very good reason: Estevánico had assaulted and killed Native women, "whom the Indians love better than themselves."[44] Hernando de Alarcón, on the other hand, who learned of Estevánico's fate while he was waiting for Coronado on the lower Colorado River, wrote that the "Negro," as he called him, was killed for being a spy.[45] Perhaps afraid that he might meet the same fate as that of Estevánico, Fray Marcos reported to the Viceroy that he espied Cíbola "from a hill where I stood to view it." He reported that the "pueblo has a fine appearance. . . . The houses are as they had been described to me by the Indians, all of stone, with terraces and flat roofs." Fray Marcos then claimed that the "city is larger than the city of Mexico," which was clearly a gross exaggeration.[46]

Why the deception? The debate over Fray Marco's account goes back decades. Historians have tended to accept, with reservations, Fray Marcos's account, while nonhistorians such as cultural geographer Carl Sauer and meteorologist Cleve Hallenbeck believed that Fray Marcos was a bald-faced liar. [47] He certainly told a whopper about the size of Hawikuh. Moreover, Sauer and Hallenbeck do not think Fray Marcos even reached as far north as the present border between the United States and Mexico. They contend— quite plausibly—that the friar's report gave the shrewd viceroy exactly what he wanted: a prior claim to the Seven Cities of Gold, assuming that they were ever found to exist.[48]

Whatever the case, Coronado was angry and disappointed at what he found at Hawikuh, and he sent Pedro de Tovar, one of his captains, north to investigate the pueblos at the Three Mesas of the *Moqui* (Hopi) in the "province of Tusayán." Coronado also dispatched García López de Cárdenas and twelve men to explore a "large river" to the west where there were "people with very large bodies." Cárdenas did not find people with large bodies, but he did find large river gorges. The ensemble of these gorges formed the Grand Canyon of the Colorado River in Arizona, a wonder of the world (and now a national park) that Europeans and European Americans were very slow to appreciate. Without an understanding of geology—of the forces of uplift and erosion—the Grand Canyon is all but incomprehensible.[49] The Spanish did realize that the river at the bottom of the canyon, which they failed to reach because of the incredibly rugged terrain between the vast canyon's rim and the river, was the same as Melchior Díaz's Río del Tizón.

Finding nothing in Arizona, Coronado headed east to the multistory pueblos along the forest- or bosque-dotted Rio Grande Valley, where areas were cleared for fields. Along the way the expedition passed the Acoma and Laguna pueblos. Coronado wintered in 1540–41 at one of the twelve pueblos in the Tiguex (now the Tewa) province (and again on his way back in 1541–1542). This province was located on the banks of the Rio Grande in or near present-day Bernalillo, New Mexico. Close by are the Sandia Mountains, which rise spectacularly to the east of the river. The Tiguex province lies at the very heart of the American Southwest. And at the twelve-hundred-room Kuaua Pueblo, there was a square painted kiva or ceremonial chamber in the community center. Its murals of folk history represent probably the finest examples of pre-Hispanic art in middle and upper North America (the ruins are now preserved as the Coronado State Monument). The Spanish and their Indios Amigos eventually wore out their welcome, however. The Tiguex revolted but were defeated by superior numbers and arms. The Tiguex War was the first Indian war of a great many more between Europeans and Native peoples in what became the United States.[50]

From Tiguex, Coronado left the Rio Grande or Río Bravo del Norte, which the Tewa Pueblo peoples called the the P'osoge ("Big River"). He continued east across the Llano Estacado, a vast featureless tableland shared by New Mexico and Texas, and then on to the *barrancas* (canyons) south of the Canadian River. The most notable of these, which, taken together, actually made up

Figure 7. *Grand Cañon, Arizona, across the Cañon from Point de la Olla*, ca. 1899. Photograph. Prints and Photographs Division, Library of Congress, Washington, DC. https://www.loc.gov/item/2005681078/.

the eroded eastern edge of the Llano Estacado, was Palo Duro Canyon, the second largest canyon in the United States and today a Texas state park. Coronado then followed his compass needle north again, this time with a smaller party, in one last great exertion of energy, past modern-day Wichita, Kansas, in the Arkansas River Valley. But out there on North America's Great Plains, some fifteen hundred miles from Mexico City, he found only seminomadic peoples, buffalo, and an endless ocean of waving grass.[51]

On the totem pole of social development, the people with whom Coronado and his men were most impressed were the Pueblo Indians. The Puebloans lived in compact, terraced or multistoried community dwellings made of stone, adobe, and other local materials, and their communities were autonomous and linguistically diverse. They raised corn, beans, and squash, as well as melons, cotton, and turkeys. In northern New Mexico, along the Rio Grande, the Puebloans practiced agriculture based on irrigation, while those to the west—the Laguna and Acoma, the Zuñi, and the Hopi—used dry-land farming techniques. Everything is relative, and from the perspective of Indian hunters and gatherers in Mexico north of the twenty-first

parallel, the peoples whom Cabeza de Vaca had encountered, these northern food producers must have seemed like they existed in another world
in their well-ordered villages, especially those romantically situated atop
windswept mesas, such as those of the Hopi in Arizona and the Acoma in
New Mexico. It is hardly surprising that in translation, the Spanish confused
Indian descriptions of these faraway villages with their own myths about
gleaming Christian cities.

While Coronado searched for the cities of gold in the American
Southwest, to the east the large expedition of Hernando de Soto, which had
set out from Spain in 1538, was tramping across three thousand miles of
the American Southeast. From South Carolina to Texas and as far north as
Tennessee, he terrorized the Apalachee, the Cofitachequi, the Coosa, and
the Tuscaloosa as he went, in a pursuit of gold, God, and glory that proved
in the end as futile as Coronado's quest. (De Soto had tried to recruit Cabeza
de Vaca as his second-in-command, but Cabeza de Vaca refused and went
to South America instead, having been appointed governor of the province
of Río de la Plata.)[52] De Soto discovered the Mississippi River and the wider Mississippi Valley, but he found also an early death from fever. In 1543
this utterly ruthless and wantonly cruel man was laid to rest in the Río del
Espíritu Santo ("River of the Holy Ghost"), later known as the Mississippi
River. (*Mississippi* is a Chippewa word meaning simply "the great river.") He
was succeeded by Luis de Moscoso Alvarado, who to his credit managed
to evacuate the survivors of De Soto's expedition, some 322 of the original
600 soldiers and servants, from the mouth of the Mississippi to the mouth
of Mexico's Pánuco River, some thousand miles away. He did so by ordering
his men to build a small fleet of pinnaces and using these craft to follow the
present-day coastlines of Louisiana, Texas, and Tamaulipas.[53]

At one point in 1541 the two conquistadors, Coronado and De Soto, were
only several hundred miles apart from each other. Between the two great
overland entradas of Coronado and De Soto, the Spanish had explored
North America from the Carolinas to the Sea of Cortés. These were remarkable and far-flung feats of exploration. The Spanish also launched a number
of voyages up the west coast of Mexico in search of either a strait through
North America to the Atlantic or evidence of gold and other riches. They
found neither. But in 1542 Juan Rodríguez Cabrillo, a Portuguese navigator
in the service of Spain, sailed north along the coast far enough to "discover"
and make landfall in Alta California, what would later become the Golden
State, at points as far north as San Francisco Bay.

The Great Pacific Portage

A notable exception to the Tordesillas and Saragossa demarcations was Spain's colonization of the Philippines, where Ferdinand Magellan (a Portuguese navigator in the service of Spain) perished in 1521 after finding a southern, if harrowing, passage through the tip of South America—the Strait of Magellan—to Asia. The Philippines lay north and west of the valuable Moluccas, which were initially controlled by the Portuguese and later by the Dutch. A Spanish trading post was eventually established on the Philippine island of Cebu in 1565 by Miguel López de Legaspi. Wishing to avoid a repetition of the bloody conquests of the Aztecs and the Inca and the criticisms by Las Casas and others that followed, Legaspi was sent to the islands by the viceroyalty of New Spain, which had been established in Mexico City in 1535, to pacify the Filipinos rather than vanquish them.[54]

From 1565 to 1815 a Spanish Manila galleon carrying goods from China—silk, porcelain, ivory, spices, and other exotic luxuries—crossed the Pacific Ocean once a year on a five-month voyage to Mexico's southwest coast, and thence an overland portage to the port of Veracruz on Mexico's east coast. (In 1527 Cortés had tried but failed to establish a Mexico-to-the-Moluccas trade route with a small fleet built on the Pacific Coast.) For over two centuries this sea-overland route was the preferred one, given the dangers posed by going through the Strait of Magellan or around South American's Cape Horn. The ship put in at the magnificent natural harbor at Acapulco, where the dazed crew could recover from the ravages of scurvy. A feeder line connected Acapulco by sea with the city of Lima in Peru. And every year a galleon from Acapulco—loaded with silver from the mines of Mexico—returned via Guam to Manila Bay in Luzon, where Legaspi, the new Spanish colony's first governor, had moved the seat of government in 1571. Within the Spanish Empire, the Philippines were unique. The archipelago was Spain's only colony in Asia and, in a classic case of "subimperialism," they were subordinate to Mexico or the viceroy of New Spain rather than to Spain. To reach Pacific South America, the Spanish developed two other major portages: one across the Isthmus of Darién and the other up the Río de la Plata and overland to Tucumán, and from thence to the Andean city of Potosí. Thus Spain's American trade was carried on the backs of mules as well as in the hulls of ships.[55]

But before the Manila-Acapulco trade could be established, the transpacific east-to-west and west-to-east routes had to be worked out, which was done by the navigators Alonso de Arellano and Fray Andrés de Urdanet on board the *San Pedro* (1565). It was easy to sail westward from the Americas to Asia by following the northeasterly trade winds and stopping along the way at the conveniently located islands of Guam and the Marianas. The hard part, because of the same prevailing winds, was getting back again. But the two men discovered that after leaving the treacherous waters of the Philippines by way of the Strait of San Bernardino, if they sailed far enough north, past Taiwan and Japan, they could catch the high-latitude westerlies that would propel them across the Pacific to California (the *San Pedro* made landfall on San Miguel, one of California's Channel Islands), and then down the coast to Acapulco. Unlike the east-to-west route, however, there was no port of call on the return voyage.

William Lytle Schurz, the historian of Spain's Pacific expansion, called these two men "as truly pioneers as was Columbus." The two transpacific routes were separated by over twenty degrees of latitude, a distance greater than 1,380 miles (lines of latitude are approximately sixty-nine miles apart). And given that Spanish traders never deviated from these established westward and eastward routes, they never discovered the Hawaiian Islands, which lay in between the two routes and were but a month's sailing voyage from California. This failure seems hard to explain. But according to Schurz, since the Hawaiian Islands "lie outside the zone of the prevailing westerlies in the north Pacific and almost midway between the eastward and westward lanes of the galleons, it was not to be expected that the Spaniards would find them in the ordinary course of the Manila-Acapulco navigation." Moreover, he pointed out, "in the long Spanish epoch in the Pacific the spirit of discovery was early superseded by a cautious business aversion to taking unnecessary risks." This latter statement is very insightful and could be generalized to describe Spain's entire overseas empire after the violent and breathless age of the conquistadors.[56]

Prior to the arrival of the Spanish in the Philippines, the Chinese had reached the islands by junk and bartered silks for gold and pearls. But with the introduction of American silver to the islands, not only were Chinese traders drawn to the islands but Chinese immigrants as well. This silver also subsidized the islands. The Spanish Philippines was primarily a missionary, not a commercial enterprise, and as such the administration ran an annual operating deficit between 85,000 and 338,832 pesos. The treasury in Mexico City made up the difference. There was another aspect of New Spain's transpacific trade that should be noted here: it was strictly regulated by the Spanish crown. The total value of goods could not exceed 250,000 pesos, to limit the flow of cheap silks from China into the markets in Mexico and Peru. This regulation served to protect the vested interests of the merchants in Seville and the textile industry in Andalusia. Thus, early in the European era of North American history, North America was directly connected to Asia, the Golden East, through the limited but influential and long-running trade of Asian silks for American silver.

The Spanish Borderlands

The sixteenth-century explorers Cabeza de Vaca and Coronado laid the predicates for the colonization of New Mexico and Texas. In 1598 New Mexico was colonized by the Mexican-born subimperialist Juan de Oñate—nine years before Christopher Newport, the captain of the *Susan Constant*, sailed into Chesapeake Bay. Oñate led approximately 560 men, women, and children as well as Franciscan priests and brothers into the green valleys and red cliffs of northern New Mexico, where he introduced European culture and technology. Pursuing a policy of viciousness, Oñate was cruel to the Natives in the region, especially the Acoma people.[57] Perhaps the one redeeming act of this conquest was that he brought four thousand head of Churra (later renamed Churro) sheep to the upper Rio Grande Valley, which would subsequently prove essential to the economies of settler and Native alike; the Navajo acquired flocks of the hardy animals through raiding and trading. In addition to European crops, Oñate also brought to the region horses, goats, cattle, donkeys, and poultry. The Spanish also likely introduced chile peppers to New Mexico.

The first Spanish settlement in New Mexico, San Juan Pueblo (today known by its pre-Spanish name of Ohkay Owingeh), was founded near the confluence of the Rio Grande and the Rio Chama. The Spanish capital of the province was later relocated to the outlying pueblo, San Gabriel de Yunque, and then to Santa Fe, located at the foot of the beautiful Sangre de Cristo Mountains, in 1610, only three years after the founding of Jamestown and two years after the founding of Quebec City. The longest road in North America, at 1,850 miles in length, the Camino Real de Tierra Adentro ("royal road of the interior land") linked Santa Fe, a settlement remote beyond compare, and Veracruz on the Gulf of Mexico. In between the mountain village and seaport, and running south to north, were the communities of Mexico City, Guanajuato, Lagos, Zacatecas, Durango, Chihuahua, El Paso, Socorro, and Albuquerque as well as numerous *parajes* (campsites), such as the Paraje de Fra Cristobal, and a ninety-mile waterless and largely level stretch set between New Mexico's Caballo and San Andres Mountains. It was known as the Jornada del Muerto, "Dead Man's Journey," after Bernado Gruber, a German trader who while fleeing the Inquisition in 1670 perished in the desert south of Socorro, New Mexico.

And in the ensuing centuries the Spanish remained in place, except for a short interregnum between 1680 and 1692 when the Pueblo Indians were united and for a time rebelled against their Spanish overlords under the leadership of Popé, a Tewa religious leader from the San Juan Pueblo. After killing four hundred Spaniards, the Natives drove the rest of the colonists into exile at El Paso. After twelve years, Don Diego de Vargas, who had been appointed governor by the viceroy, reconquered New Mexico for the Spanish—with the aid of Pueblo Indian auxiliaries—and reopened the Camino Real, New Mexico's long and dusty lifeline to European civilization. Communication and commerce was carried up and down this road by slow-crawling caravans of mule- or ox-drawn *carros y carretas*, middle North America's first wheeled vehicles.

To the east of the province of New Mexico lay that of Coahuila y Tejas, which the Spanish colonized in the late seventeenth century to counter the perceived threat posed by La Salle to Spanish dominion of the northern *frontera* of New Spain. La Salle was extending the work of the explorers Father Jacques Marquette, a Jesuit-trained fur trader and former philosophy student and musician, and the Canadian-born Louis Joliet, who could play the harpsichord and organ. In 1673 Marquette and Joliet sought a river route to Asia but discovered instead that it was possible to travel by water from the Great Lakes to the Gulf of Mexico, although they took their canoes only as far south as the mouth of the Arkansas River, fearing capture by the Spanish, before turning back to Canada by way of a significant shortcut— the Illinois River. They also found that the Natives of the Mississippi Valley were well disposed to trade, and that this vast region was rich in resources.

In 1682 La Salle pushed into and explored the lower Mississippi Valley, below the mouth of the Arkansas River, two years after the Pueblo Revolt and Spain's (temporary) withdrawal from New Mexico. He claimed the region for France, calling it Louisiane (later Louisiana), and posited that a colony there would link New France (French Canada) with the French Caribbean. And with Spain at war with France, Louis XIV, the Sun King, granted La Salle permission to plan an invasion of coastal New Spain from a base or colony at the mouth of the Mississippi River, which was believed to lie much farther west, and closer to the rich silver mines of Zacatecas, than was actually the case. From the mouth of the Mississippi River, La Salle was to use a small French force as the nucleus of a much larger army made up of Native auxiliaries, thus using the tried and tested practice of the Spanish against them. Instead, in 1685 he mistakenly landed 180 colonists at Matagorda Bay, some five hundred miles away from the mouth of the Mississippi. Three years later the Karankawa Indians massacred the French colonists who had managed to survive on the Texas Gulf Coast into the harsh winter of 1688 and took their children into captivity. La Salle himself was murdered by a fellow Frenchman during a botched effort to bring aid to the beleaguered settlement.[58] To secure Mexico's mines from any further French encroachment, Spain built, beginning in 1690, a network of missions and presidios or forts. Perhaps the most of famous these, San Antonio, Texas, later the home of the Alamo, was founded in 1718.

The old struggle between France and Spain over North America would enter a more peaceful phase, after Spain's Charles II, the country's last Hapsburg ruler, designated the Duke of Anjou, a Bourbon and the grandson of Louis XIV, as his successor. On November 16, 1700, in the Hall of Mirrors at the Palace of Versailles, the Sun King presented the world with Spain's new king, the seventeen-year-old Philip V. Spain's ambassador responded to the news with the incendiary declaration "*Il n'y a plus de Pyrénées*" (There are no more Pyrenees). The balance of power in Europe had been upended, and the the War of the Spanish Succession (known as Queen Anne's War in North America) promptly ensued, dividing Europe into warring camps from 1701 to 1714.

Creating an empire in the North American interior was an intensely hard, immensely huge, and terribly risky undertaking. This heroic effort was something the Romantic historians of the nineteenth century better appreciated and with which they more easily sympathized than we do. Also, their technology was far closer to that of the seventeenth century than is ours, so the world of the conquerors was not so very different from theirs. Indeed, in the nineteenth century, the "Wild West" was still wild. It was a region where Native peoples like the Comanche, the Apache, and Sioux, continued to resist with fierce and even armed determination the coming, as it was once said, of the "white man." Of the French efforts in North America, Francis Parkman, the Boston Brahmin who had personally, as sickly as he was, observed life firsthand on the Oregon Trail, wrote: "Of all their toil and sacrifice, no fruit remained but a great geographical discovery, and a grand type of incarnate energy and will. Where La Salle had plowed, others were to sow the seed." Parkman was eloquent but not quite accurate. In the Willamette Valley, the terminus of the Oregon Trail, Yankee settlers who arrived in the 1840s found it already occupied by French and Native settlers— retired voyageurs who had worked for the Hudson's Bay Company.[59]

Moreover, the French were already back in Louisiana as early as 1699. That was when the Montreal-born Jean-Baptiste Le Moyne de Bienville and his older brother, the soldier Pierre Le Moyne d'Iberville— the first native-born Canadian to receive the Croix de Saint Louis for valor—found and entered the elusive mouth of the Mississippi River. In 1711 Bienville established a French settlement in Alabama at Mobile, and in 1718 he went on to found New Orleans (named after the duc d'Orléans) as a port of deposit or transshipment for the French. In that same year the French Compagnie d'Occident (later renamed the Compagnie de Indes) was granted a monopoly over Louisiana. And the same year that New Orleans was founded, the French Compagnie d'Occident (later renamed the Compagnie de Indes) was granted a monopoly over Louisiana. The Mississippi Valley's economic potential seemed to investors to be all but infinite—as it indeed was. But the value of the company's stocks quickly soared far in excess of the colony's actual earnings (shares rose from 500 to 18,000 livres!). By 1720 the "Missssippi Bubble" had burst. Samuel de Champlain's humanist dream of an ideal and inclusive feudal order in Canada had become in Louisiana— where slavery had been introduced in 1706—a capitalist nightmare in which a colony nearly bankrupted, rather than enriching, its mother country. This was humanism and mercantilism turned upside down.

In the aftermath, New Orleans was made the capital in 1723, and in 1731 Louisiana was turned into a royal colony. Thus, in a variation on the theme of subimperialism, the Canadian Bienville had in fact sowed where La Salle, as well as Marquette and Joliet, had plowed. Moreover, Bienville went on to serve several more terms as Louisiana's governor, retiring to Paris in 1743. Eventually a four-thousand-mile network of trading posts connected the Gulf of Saint Lawrence with the Gulf of Mexico. Clearly the scramble for, and the defense of, European empire drove the early development of North America.

CHAPTER 4

The Enlightenment Explores the West Coast

Where the Sea Breaks Its Back

IN 1718 THE RUSSIAN CZAR Peter the Great ordered two Russian officers, Fedor Luzhin and Ivan Evreinov, to "go to Kamchatka and farther. . . and determine whether Asia and America are united; and go not only north and south but east and west, and put on a chart all that you see."[1] They failed in this endeavor. In 1724 Peter the Great tried again—but this time he put Vitus Jonassen Bering in charge. Bering, who hailed from Horsens, Denmark, was a seasoned but cautious navigator in the Imperial Russian Navy. He reached the Arctic Ocean in 1728 by passing through the strait that now bears his name (Captain James Cook later named the strait in the Dane's honor), proving once and for all that North America was not part of Asia.

This was a major achievement, and 1728 is a date as important in North American history as 1497, the year of John Cabot's landfall. But Bering failed to find a northeast passage, a sea route to China around or through Siberia, or to see or visit the coast of North America. In 1733 Russia launched the Great Northern Expedition, sponsored by the Russian admiralty in St. Petersburg. This time there were two ships; Bering, in his second expedition, commanded the *St. Peter*, and Aleksey Chirikov commanding the *St. Paul*. The expedition contributed to the mapping of Russia's northern coast, from the White Sea to the Kolyma River, and succeeded in crossing the North Pacific in 1741, this time reaching America's northwest coast. Bering thus reconfirmed the existence of a strait between Asia and Alaska and established Russia's imperial claims to North America. The name of this new land, Alaska, comes from the Aleut word *agunalaksh*, which means "the shores where the sea breaks its back."

Bering did not make it home. In 1741 the *St. Peter* wrecked on Bering Island, a seal paradise located in Russia's treeless Commander Islands, geographically the westernmost extension of the Aleutians. Bering perished on December 19, 1741, from scurvy, along with other members of his crew. But some of Bering's men made it back, including the German naturalist Georg Wilhelm Steller, after whom the Steller sea cow and Steller sea lion are named. From the wreckage of the *St. Peter*, the castaways built a boat that took them safely from Bering Island west to the Kamchatka Peninsula in 1742.

The news that the lands and waters of the Commander Islands, the Aleutian Islands, and Alaska—what the Russians called Bolshaya Zemlya, "Great Land"—were rich in fur-bearing mammals, triggered a Russian fur rush. Just as Siberian sable had been traded for profit in China, so too could sea otter pelts, and sea otters abounded in Russia's new Far East. These fur trappers and traders would eventually turn the American northwest, primarily above the fifty-fifth parallel, into a company colony that exploited Native Aleuts and Alaskans. The Russian American Company was chartered and granted an exclusive monopoly by Czar Paul I in 1799, with headquarters in Novoarkhangelsk, "New Archangel," today Sitka, Alaska. It built trading posts from Kodiak Island to the Sonoma Coast in California; one of these, Fort Ross, was located only fifty miles north of Yerba Buena, near what would later become San Francisco. Russian Alaska survived from 1741 until 1867, five years after the Russian American Company's charter expired, when US secretary of state William H. Seward acquired it from the cash-strapped Czar Alexander II. By this time the sea otter, the pursuit of which had drawn the Russians down the coast of North America in the first place, had been driven to near extinction (it has since recovered), so there was little economic incentive to remain and much to gain by selling out, leaving the North American continent altogether. And there were strategic considerations. Despite Alaska's immense resources, the Russian navy at this point was not prepared to defend Alaska should either the imperialist British or the expansionist-minded Americans decide to invade it.[2]

The Rim of Christendom
Alarmed by the threat posed to its imperial interests by Russia from without and by the power and wealth of the Jesuit order from within its American colonies, the Spanish crown expelled the Society of Jesus in 1767 from Spain

and Spanish America. The less powerful and wealthy Franciscan order was allowed to fill the void in New Spain's far northern frontier, which led to an outburst of colonizing activity. Through the leadership of Junípero Serra, the chief of the missions of the Californias, the church started a string of twenty-one missions, running up Alta California from San Diego to San Francisco, to Christianize the California Indians and turn them into good colonial subjects. (During the 1750s Serra had proven himself a capable administrator with the establishment of the five missions of the Sierra Gorda in the Mexican state of Querétaro.) This activity mirrored the string of settlements the Spanish had built along the Atlantic Coast as far north as the Carolinas during the sixteenth and seventeenth centuries.[3]

To protect the Provincias Internas, a large semiautonomous district that included Alta and Baja California, Sonora, Sinaloa, Nueva Vizcaya, New Mexico, Texas, and Coahuila, from Russian, British, or Native attack, Teodoro de Croix, the province's governor and commander in chief from 1777 to 1783, answered directly to Charles III of Spain rather than to Antonio María de Bucareli, viceroy of Mexico at the time. Nevertheless Croix found himself at odds with the viceroy over military policy for this vast territory. The first permanent European settlement north of Mexico on California's Pacific Coast was the presidio at San Diego, established in 1769. The great bay of Alta California, San Francisco, was discovered in 1769—by land, interestingly, not sea—by Gaspar de Portolá, the Spanish founder of San Diego and Monterey and governor of the Californias.

Prodded by threats of European encroachment on the Provincias Internas, Bucareli sent explorers far into the *gran océano boreal* (great northern ocean). In 1774 Juan Peréz, who had made the Manila-Acapulco crossing as a pilot, sailed the *Santiago* from the port of San Blas in Nayarit, Mexico, as far north as latitude 54°40', near the present-day boundary between Alaska and Canada, before an outbreak of scurvy forced him to return to Alta California. Peréz was the first European to see the Pacific Northwest. In 1775 Juan de Ayala, captain of the *San Carlos*, was the probably the first European to enter and navigate San Francisco Bay. Juan Francisco de la Bodega y Quadra and Bruno de Hezeta, however, would take their ships, the *Sonora* and the *Santiago* (Juan Peréz served as the pilot), respectively, as far north as 58°30', near present-day Juneau, Alaska, sighting the mouth of the Columbia River along the way. But scurvy, the bane of seafarers, forced both captains to cut short their voyages. Indeed, scurvy would take Peréz's life. As heroic as were the efforts of these Spanish navigators, their deeds and claims have been largely forgotten, apart from a few place names they left behind. The name of Captain James Cook, on the other hand, who would soon follow in their wake, became immortalized. And his feats still impress.[4]

Captain Cook

In 1779, two hundred and fifty-one years after Verrazzano's demise and 6,088 miles away from Guadeloupe Island, where Verrazzano was killed and eaten by cannibals, Captain James Cook was also killed by islanders on the Big Island of Hawaii. He was not eaten by cannibals, though his body was burned and his bones were prized as trophies. Just as Verrazzano was the very embodiment of the spirit of the Renaissance, so Cook was the exemplar of the Enlightenment. From humble beginnings in Yorkshire in England, Cook rose up from the coal trade to be a captain in the Royal Navy and later proved to be the greatest mariner of the eighteenth century. He knew intimately the waters of the North Sea, the Baltic, the Channel, the Irish Sea, and the gulf and river of St. Lawrence. In 1759, in fact, during the French and Indian War, he played an indirect role in General James Wolfe's successful amphibious landing at the base of the steep side of the Plains of Abraham, behind Quebec. It was on these plains that Wolfe defeated the French general Louis-Joseph de Montcalm, in a battle that took both men's lives. The result, which was decided in a matter of minutes, answered what the nineteenth-century historian Francis Parkman called the "most momentous and far-reaching question ever brought to issue on this continent. . . . Shall France remain here, or shall she not?"[5]

The answer, of course, was that France should not remain, although Canada's largely self-sufficient French-speaking inhabitants continued their lives largely unchanged. There were two small exceptions: the islands of Saint Pierre and Miquelon, both of which lay just south of Newfoundland. According to the Treaty of Paris of 1763, which settled the French and Indian War, the islands, which were valued by French cod fishermen, were to remain in the possession of France. But before the victorious British returned the islands to France, Cook was ordered to survey them first. He continued this survey work aboard the HMS *Grenville* for Newfoundland and Southern Labrador, an endeavor that took several years and several Atlantic crossings to complete. The resulting charts of Newfoundland, the Strait of Belle Isle, and Southern Labrador were outstanding. And in a nation of seamen, Cook's seamanship was regarded as second to none. He also acquired a reputation as a mathematician and astronomer, impressing the

Royal Society for Improving Natural Knowledge with his observations of an eclipse of the sun. From the vantage point of one of the Burgeo Islands— likely the small islet Eclipse Island—Cook used a telescopic quadrant to measure a solar eclipse on August 5, 1766. His calculations matched those taken in Oxford, England, and thus could be used to determine longitude, in this case the coordinates of Newfoundland in relation to Greenwich, providing that "due allowance" was made "for the effect of parallax, and the earths prolate spheroidal figure."[6]

Cook's First Voyage

The exploration of North America was intimately tied to the exploration of the universe, even if the latter preceded the former. One of the great problems of eighteenth-century science was determining the size of the solar system. The English astronomer Edmund Halley's solution to this problem was to measure the transit of the planet Venus across the disc of the Sun from different stations around the world, and then comparing the results. Using the principles of parallax and trigonometry, it would thereby be possible to calculate the size of the solar system, beginning with the distance between Earth and the Sun, defined as the astronomical unit (AU). At the time the solar system consisted of six planets: Mercury, Venus, Earth, Mars, Jupiter, and Saturn. William Hershel discovered Uranus, the seventh planet, in 1781 (the eighth planet, Neptune, was discovered seventy years later). The transits of Venus, however, were very rare events. In fact, none occurred during Halley's entire life span, 1656 to 1742. They took place approximately every 120 years, and when they did, they came in pairs, spaced eight years apart. A transit had occurred in 1761, but because of bad weather, underpreparation, and other problems little data was collected. The next one was due in June 1769. After that, Venus would not pass across the sun again until 1874.[7]

The year 1769, then, offered science a precious opportunity. To take full advantage of it, the Royal Society's Transit Committee worked in conjunction with the British Admiralty (improvements in navigation were seen as dependent on improvements in astronomy), and one of their many plans included sending James Cook, along with Royal Society members such as Joseph Banks and Daniel Solander as well as the artists Sydney Parkinson and Alexander Buchan, to the South Pacific on board the bark HMS *Endeavour*, a refitted collier or coal ship. The transit would be visible in its entirety only over the Pacific, the Arctic, and western North America.

Elsewhere it would be either partially visible (ingress or egress) or not visible at all. Cook's mission was to observe the transit from the remote and tiny island of Tahiti, one of the Society Islands (now part of French Polynesia), and to look for the hypothetical massive southern continent Terra Australis Incognita ("unknown southern land"). Samuel Wallis, captain of the HMS *Dolphin*, had discovered Tahiti in 1767 during his attempt to find the vast southern continent somewhere below Africa, South America, and New Holland (later named Australia). Wallis thought he had glimpsed it.

According to classical theory, as in the writings of Pomponius Mela and Claudius Ptolemy, it stood to reason that a large land mass in the Southern Hemisphere was necessary to balance the lands known to exist in the Northern Hemisphere. The continental hypothesis gained new currency during the Renaissance and was finally tested against hard experience by the Enlightenment.[8]

What explorers, including Cook, found instead, of course, was a group of smaller lands—New Guinea, New Holland, Van Diemen's Land, New Zealand, and numerous coral atolls, islands, and island groups such as the Society Islands, the Friendly Islands, New Caledonia, New Hebrides, and the *mo'ai*-covered Easter Island. Antarctica, the real southern continent, would elude Russian, British, and American explorers until sightings and landings were finally made in the early 1820s. In fact English-born American explorer and sealer Captain John Davis reached Hughes Bay on the Antarctic Peninsula, across the Drake Passage from Cape Horn, on February 7, 1821, in the continent's first recorded landing. Thus, two years before James Monroe proclaimed the Western Hemisphere to lie within the sphere of interest of the United States, Americans were already planting flags outside of this sphere.

Cook observed the transit of Venus (which took five hours and twenty-eight minutes), a task that he and fellow astronomer Charles Green performed at Point Venus, located ten miles west of Tahiti's Matavai Bay, on June 3, 1769. Of the weather on that critical day—actually, that critical hour—Cook recorded that "this day prov'd as favorable to our purpose as we could wish." He then turned his attention to the search for the southern continent, which eluded him. He did, however, chart New Zealand (which, he discovered, was made up of two large separate islands) and the eastern coast of Australia, including Botany Bay, an inlet on the Tasman Sea near modern-day Sydney. He then rounded Cape York and headed home through the Torres Strait (discovered by the Spanish explorer Luis Váez de Torres in 1606). Cook reached England in 1771, but not before he first navigated the treacherous waters of Queensland's Great Barrier Reef, the Labyrinth, where he nearly faced disaster when the *Endeavour* ran aground.[9]

Cook's Second Voyage

Cook's first voyage of discovery was spectacularly successful and inspired two even more ambitious voyages to the Great South Sea. He was promoted to captain, and the employment of scientists and artists was continued. Indeed, the practice became a model for subsequent sea and land explorations. From 1772 to 1775 Cook, on board the *Resolution*, another refitted collier, and in the company of the *Adventure* (under the command of Tobias Furneaux), again vainly searched for the Terra Australis Incognita. On the first voyage he had used lunar distances to fix longitude. But on his second and third voyages he could now check this accurate, if cumbersome, method, which involved the sextant, the *Nautical Almanac*, and complex calculations, against a portable chronometer a mere five inches in diameter—London watchmaker Larcum Kendall's "K1" copy of one of John Harrison's later designs. The K1 allowed Cook to compare local time anywhere on Earth with Greenwich Mean Time (GMT), which was adopted as the universal standard on time and longitude by Europe and North America in 1884.[10]

Cook went on to explore much of the South Pacific between New Zealand and South America, making sweeps far to the south, along the Antarctic Circle and the outer edge of pack ice and icebergs. If there were a southern continent, he concluded, it was near the South Pole and could not be reached by ship. The Antarctic landmass would eventually be sighted in 1820, forty-five years later. Cook's contributions to geography were well known. But his contemporaries were no less impressed by Cook's lifesaving shipboard experiments in the prevention of scurvy, which included the regular consumption of fresh fruit, vegetables, and meats. Indeed, the strict antiscorbutic dietary regime that Cook imposed on his officers and crew, along with his insistence on new standards of ship cleanliness and personal hygiene, is what made his long voyages of discovery to the South Pacific and to North America as successful as they were. In short, that diet and long-distance exploration were closely related was not the least of Cook's many discoveries. For the pathbreaking paper he wrote on diet, which was read at the Royal Society on March 7, 1776, and published in its *Philosophical Transactions*, Cook was awarded the Sir Godfrey Copley Medal, the society's most prestigious prize.[11]

Cook's Final Voyage

Having helped to determine the size of the solar system and added to the sum of geographical knowledge, Captain Cook embarked on his third great Pacific voyage of discovery. Like Verrazzano and many others before him, notably the explorers John Cabot, Sir Martin Frobisher, John Davis, William Baffin, and Henry Hudson, Cook was charged with finding a northwest passage through or over Canada, or, failing that, a northeast passage over Siberia. But this time he was to search for an entrance to either passage from the Pacific rather than the Atlantic Ocean. If the famed circumnavigator succeeded, the British government was prepared to award Cook and his men a prize of £20,000, to be shared equally among them. Cook left England on July 12, 1776, eight days after the representatives of thirteen American colonies declared their independence from Great Britain in Philadelphia on the Delaware River, an event that made 1776 a momentous year in the history of North America and of the British Empire. As if to underscore the latter point, that same year also saw the publication of the first of twelve volumes of Edward Gibbon's inauspicious history *The Decline and Fall of the Roman Empire*. Gibbon, who became a member of Parliament in 1774, enjoyed a front-row seat (although he was actually a "backbencher") on the dramatic fate of North America.[12]

Captain Cook departed Plymouth, England, aboard the refitted HMS *Resolution* for the Dutch-ruled Cape Town, South Africa, where he would be joined by the commander of the HMS *Discovery*, Charles Clerke—once, that is, Clerke was released from debtor's prison, where he was being held for his improvident brother's liabilities. On the first voyage Cook had reached the Pacific via Cape Horn. But on the second and third voyages, he took the west-east route around the Cape of Good Hope, first rounded by the Portuguese navigator Bartolomeu Dias in 1488. Dias's voyage proved that the Indian Ocean was not landlocked, as had been supposed by Ptolemy.

After first stopping at Adventure Bay in Van Diemen's Land (Tasmania) and then at Queen Charlotte Sound in New Zealand, Cook followed a now familiar route to Tahiti and the Society Islands. From there, in late 1777, he headed north to North America, to Sir Francis Drake's "Nova Albion." Two centuries before, Drake had sailed up the west coast of North America, possibly as far north as Vancouver Island ("48. deg."), also in search of a northwest passage. On June 17, 1579, Drake recorded that he put the *Golden Hinde* ashore for repairs at "38 deg. 30 min," at a "convenient and fit harbor." These descriptions suggest he landed at or near what is today Drakes Bay, now part of the Point Reyes National Seashore. Drake's "white banks and cliffs" in this area do indeed look remarkably like the White Cliffs of Dover in Old Albion. Drake claimed the lands north of Mexico for Queen Elizabeth I, noting that the "Spanish never had any dealing, or so much as set a foot in this country" (that is, Albion), "the utmost of their discoveries, reaching only to many degrees Southward of this place." This would make Nova Albion older than either the colonies of Virginia or New England. In fact, Drake and his crew celebrated communion in what is now California, which would make this the first recorded Anglican service in North American history.[13]

In route on January 18, 1778, Cook discovered the convenient and strategically located Hawaiian Islands, making landfall two days later on Kaua'i, on a beach near the mouth of the Waimei River. He named the island group the Sandwich Islands, after John Montagu, the fourth Earl of Sandwich and the First Lord of the Admiralty. In 1775 Cook had named another group of islands, located near South Georgia in the South Atlantic, after the Earl of Sandwich as well. Those islands were later distinguished as the South Sandwich Islands. By the time of Cook's visit, the Spanish had been making annual west-east and east-west crossings of the Pacific, as previously mentioned, from Manila to Acapulco, since 1565—or for nearly two centuries. The west-east route arced north of the Hawaiian Islands; the east-west route, south of them. Cook observed how beneficial a stopover, station, or staging area Hawaii would have been to the "Manila ship."[14] Indeed, the Hawaiian Islands belatedly would come to serve the same strategic role in the history of British and American expansion played earlier by the Atlantic's Cape Verde, Canary, Madeira, and Azores archipelagos—stepping stones for the Portuguese and Spanish navies. On March 6, 1778, and in foul weather, Cook sighted the western coast of North America at "Cape Foulweather," a rugged basalt outcropping. This point lies well above San Francisco Bay, where less than two years earlier the Spanish had established a presidio and a mission to preempt either the British or the Russians from claiming this area.

Cook was under strict orders to steer clear of Spain's Pacific holdings, lest his actions further complicate Europe's already complicated politics. From Cape Foulweather on the Oregon coast, the *Resolution* and *Discovery* sailed north to Nootka Sound on the west coast of the coniferous rainforest-covered Vancouver Island. Cook looked for but failed to find the Strait of Juan de Fuca between Vancouver Island and the Olympic Peninsula, missing it—along with Puget Sound and the Strait of Georgia—just as Verrazzano had missed the Delaware and Chesapeake Bays. He wrongly concluded that the strait had never existed, declaring: "It is in the very latitude we were now where geographers have placed the pretended Strait of Juan de Fuca [which connects the Pacific Ocean with Puget Sound] but we saw nothing like it, nor is there the least probability that iver any such thing exhisted." But he was correct that it was not the Northwest Passage or the Strait of Anián.[15]

At Vancouver Island's Nootka Sound on March 29, 1778, Cook encountered for the first time a Native people of western North America, the Nootka. Unlike so many other first encounters, the expedition's artist, John Webber, captured this New World encounter in a series of evocative drawings and paintings. The Nootka, who lived in long plank houses "one hundred and fifty feet in length, twenty four or thirty broad and seven or eight high from floor to roof," paddled out to and surrounded Cook's ships in their canoes, craft that were "40 feet long, 7 broad and about 3 deep." He was welcomed with ceremony and song, and the two peoples struck up a brisk trade: European nails for Native furs.[16]

In Cook's words:

> A great many Canoes filled with the Natives were about the Ships all day, and a trade commenced betwixt us and them, which was carried on with the Strictest honisty on boath sides. Their articles were the Skins of various animals, such as Bears, Wolfs, Foxes, Dear, Rackoons, Polecats, Martins and in particular the Sea Beaver, the same as found on the coast of Kamtchatka. . . . For these things they took in exchange, Knives, chisels, pieces of iron & Tin, Nails, Buttons, or any kind of metal. Beads they were not fond of and cloth of all kinds they rejected.[17]

In fact the Nootka valued metal to such an extent that Cook reported that "one man offered to barter a child about five or six years of age for a spike-nail; I am satisfied we did not mistake his intention."[18]

On Top of the World

Cook took full advantage of the lumber that could be had from Vancouver's lush temperate rainforest and ordered extensive repairs to be made to the two sloops of his expedition. He wanted to make sure they were ready for the rigors of the long voyage northward, past the Queen Charlotte Islands (renamed the Haida Gwaii in 2010), the Dixon Entrance, and the Alexander Archipelago—a group of eleven hundred islands, including Baranof and Chichagof, that were home to the Tlingit and Haida tribes—and on to, and around, Alaska.[19] On reaching the Gulf of Alaska, Cook thought at one point that he had found the geographer's holy grail: the fabled Northwest Passage. But William Bligh (yes: *that* William Bligh, commander of the *Bounty*) found that the inlet—later named the Cook Inlet by George Vancouver, who like Bligh had also served on Cook's third voyage of discovery, and on the second, for that matter—turned out to be a dead end. The city of Anchorage, Alaska, founded in 1914 as the headquarters of the Alaska Railroad, which runs north to Fairbanks, is located there now. Disappointed, Cook followed the Alaskan coast, which, from the Cook Inlet, ran discouragingly in a southwesterly direction. Cook followed the coast until he reached the Aleutian island of Unalaska, which had been discovered by Bering in 1741 and was now the home of a Russian settlement of the same name.

Cook encountered the subarctic Aleuts and, later, as he explored Bristol Bay and points farther north, the "Esquemaux," whom he distinguished from the Nootka and he associated with the "Greenlander." Their large boats and small canoes, which Cook observed, matched the descriptions of the same craft used by the Greenlanders. (Cook possessed a copy of Moravian missionary David Crantz's book *The History of Greenland, containing a Description of the Country and its Inhabitants and Particularly a Relation of the Mission carried on for Above these Thirty Years by the Unitas Fratrum at New Herrnhuth and Lichtenfels in that Country*, published in London in 1767.) Cook knew that anthropology intersected with geography. If he could find a Greenlander, then Greenland, via hopefully a northwest passage, would not be far behind.[20]

Just as the South West Peninsula of England separates the English and the Bristol Channels, the Alaska Peninsula separates the waters of the Gulf of Alaska from those of Bristol Bay to the north. Cook's two-ship expedition continued north past Norton Sound and on to the Bering Strait. He christened the "Western extremity of all America hitherto known," an incredibly remote place, located at the end of what would come to be called the Seward Peninsula, Cape Prince of Wales. Fifty-five miles to the west was Cape Dezhnyov, formerly East Cape, the easternmost point of the Eurasian landmass. In the middle of Bering Strait lies the Big Diomede Island (Russian) and east of it, a short 2.5 miles away, is the Little Diomede Island (US). Below Cape Dezhnyov lay St. Lawrence or Lavrentiya Bay, which is where

Cook put in and encountered yet another people, the maritime Chukchi—as opposed to the related reindeer Chukchi, who lived farther west in the Siberian interior—who hunted walrus, seals, and whales.

After this stop, Cook continued north past the Seward Peninsula and entered the Arctic or Chukchi Sea, sailed past the Kotzebue Sound and Point Hope, and then headed north and east toward Point Barrow, reaching as far north as latitude 70°44 ′ before skirting a compact wall of ice that "seemed to be ten or twelve feet high at least." The existence of this barrier thwarted any hope of finding a route to Baffin Bay on the Atlantic side of North America. Cook thus proved that there was not only no Terra Australis Incognita but no Northwest Passage, either, although that certainly did not end the search for an ice-free short cut to Asia.[21] He then tried to find a northeast passage over Siberia, sailing as far as Cape North (now Cape Schmidt) before being forced back by bad weather and the threat of more ice there as well. But even this failure confirmed that Asia and America were separate and not joined somewhere farther north. Intending to try again the following year, Cook retreated south to winter in Hawaii. Unfortunately, after having at first evidently mistaken Cook for the returning god Lono, the Hawaiian islanders tragically killed him on February 14, 1779, at Kealakekua Bay on the Big Island's Kona Coast, in a stupid dispute over a stolen cutter or small vessel.

Cook's men nevertheless attempted again to find a Pacific entrance to the Atlantic, but met with no more success than had their intrepid late commander. His discovery of the Hawaiian archipelago set in motion a

Figure 8. John Webber, *Kealakekua Bay and the Village of Kowroaa*, 1779. Ink, ink wash, and watercolor. Wikimedia Commons. https://commons.wikimedia.org/wiki/File:John_Webber_-_%27Kealakekua_Bay_and_the_village_Kowroaa%27,_1779,_ink,_ink_wash_and_watercolor.jpg.

series of events that fatefully pulled the Pacific islands—Hawai′i, Maui, Kaho′olawe, Lāna′i, Moloka′i, O′ahu, Kaua′i, and Ni′ihau—into the Atlantic-centered rather than the Asian world, resulting ultimately in the Hawaiian Islands becoming politically a part of North America. The Kingdom of New Spain administered the Philippine Islands, it should be noted, until Mexico's independence in 1821—making them, as it were, a colony of a colony. In 1898, with the Spanish American War, these islands were brought back into North America's orbit by the United States and colonized all over again. They remained under US control until they were temporarily seized by the Japanese during World War II. In 1946, after nearly four centuries of Spanish, American, and Japanese rule, they finally achieved their independence.

In the twilight glow of the eighteenth century, a very rough outline of North America could be found on the world's maps, as if a mist had slowly cleared to reveal the existence of a great mountain. In the decades that followed, every indentation and crenulation of North America's coastline along the Atlantic Ocean, the Gulf of Mexico, the Gulf of California, the Pacific Ocean, and the Arctic Ocean would be surveyed. According to the *World Atlas*, the length of this coastline comes to an estimated 143,744 miles—3.5 times longer than the coastline of the European Union, at an estimated length of 41,000 miles, inclusive of Great Britain. Of Mexico, the United States, and Canada, Mexico's 5,797 miles of coastline is the shortest of the three. The United States has 12,380 miles of coastline, more than twice as much as Mexico. Canada has an astounding 125,567 miles of coastline, dwarfing its two neighbors to the south. In fact Canada's coastline, as already noted, is the longest of any nation in the world.

Ares and Aphrodite
In the spring of 1768, between Samuel Wallis's discovery of Tahiti and James Cook's arrival on the island to observe the transit of Venus, the French explorer Louis-Antoine de Bougainville made landfall there. The expedition consisted of two ships, the *Boudeuse* and the *Étoile*, and its mission was to circumnavigate the earth. Bougainville claimed Tahiti for France, naming it Nouvelle Cythère after Cythera, the mythical birthplace of Aphrodite. A veteran of the Battle of the Plains of Abraham in 1759, Bougainville was probably best known for a colorful plant from Brazil, the bougainvillea, which his botanist, Philibert Commerçon, named after him. But Bougainville's descriptions of Tahiti as an island paradise and erotic playground, unspoiled as

yet by civilization, sounded a theme that supported the social evolutionary arguments of Jean-Jacques Rousseau, a critic of private property, notably in his 1754 *Discourse upon the Origin and the Foundation of the Inequality among Mankind*, and one that would go on to have a profound impact on the Romantic imagination of western Europe and North America.[22]

Here is Bougainville's own fulsome praise of Tahiti:

> Nature has placed it in the finest climate in the world, embellished it with the most attractive scenery, enriched it with all her gifts, filled it with handsome, tall and well-built inhabitants. She herself has dictated its laws, and they follow them in peace and make up what may be the happiest society on this globe. Lawmakers and philosophers, come and see here all that your imagination has not been able even to dream up. . . . Having an elementary knowledge of those crafts that are adequate for men who still live in a state close to nature, [they work] but little, [and they enjoy much of] the pleasures of society, of dance, music, conversation, [and] indeed of love. . . . Men have several wives and girls all the men they want. . . . As long as I live, I shall celebrate the happy island of Cythera. It is the true Utopia.[23]

This was mythmaking par excellence. It was no accident that in 1891, over a century after the *Boudeuse* and the *Étoile* had departed Tahiti's turquoise waters and white coral-sand beaches, the Postimpressionist artist Paul Gauguin would choose this idyll to paint. Indeed, even today tourism is Tahiti's major economic activity, which speaks to the enduring strength of the island's charms, the news of which the voyages of Wallis, Bougainville, and Cook brought to the world's attention.

By Bougainville's account, Tahiti was unique. Few other societies, even those among the Pacific islanders, enjoyed the felicity of that particular place. Cook, however, had the advantage of seeing Tahiti on multiple occasions, and learned that war and misfortune were as much a part of Tahitians' life as was love—Ares no less than Aphrodite. In fact, Cook's return visits to the Pacific allowed him to register the changes that were occurring in Tahiti and elsewhere, sometimes very rapidly, as a result of contact between Europeans and Native peoples.

On Cook's second visit to the Maori of Queen Charlotte Sound, New Zealand in June 1773, the captain of the *Resolution*—who referred to Pacific Islanders and Native Americans as Indians—paused to reflect:

During our short stay in this Sound I have observed that this Second
Visit of ours hath not mended the morals of the Natives of either Sex,
the Women of this Country I always looked upon to be more chaste
than the generality of Indian Women, whatever favours a few of them
might have granted to the crew of the Endeavour it was generally done
in a private manner and without the men seeming to intrest themselves in it, but now we find the men are the chief promoters of this
Vice, and for a spike nail or any other thing they value will oblige their
Wives and Daughters to prostitute themselves whether they will or no
and that not with the privacy decency seems to require, such are the
consequences of a commerce with Europeans and what is still more
to our Shame civilized Christians, we debauch their Morals already
too prone to vice and we interduce among them wants and perhaps

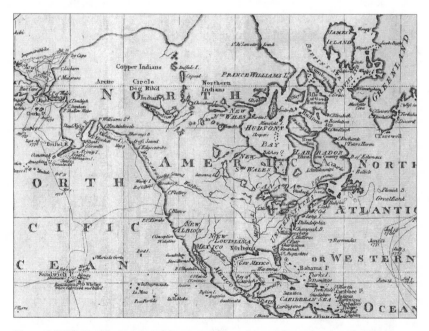

Figure 9. With Cook's voyages of discovery, the outline of the continent of North
America comes finally into focus. Thomas Bowen, *A New and Complete Chart of the
World; Displaying the Tracks of Captain Cook and Other Modern Navigators* (detail),
1790. Engraving, scale ca. 1:75m, sheet: 19 ½ x 15 in. (49.5 x 38 cm). Wikimedia
Commons, https://commons.wikimedia.org/wiki/File:A_new_and_complete_chart_
of_the_world;_displaying_the_tracks_of_Captain_Cook_and_other_modern_naviga-
tors._Drawn_and_engraved_by_T._Bowen._RMG_L7509.tiff.

diseases which they never before knew and which serves only to dis-
turb that happy tranquillity they and their fore Fathers had injoy'd.
If any one denies the truth of this assertion let him tell me what the
Natives of the whole extent of America have gained by the commerce
they have had with Europeans.[24]

Cook's sympathy, however, distorted the nature of both civilization and
simpler lifeways. Unlike traditional civilization, the European civilization
of Cook's day, of which his own voyages of discovery were a prime example,
was no longer merely self-reproducing. Western civilization, which included North America, had become dynamic, progressive, and increasingly expansive, leading to the very sort of moral reflections and sense of difference
found in Cook's journals. After all, European exploration was undertaken
to find alternate routes to the advanced civilizations of the East. But in the
process Europeans encountered new lands as well as peoples at different
levels of social development. And given the asymmetries in wealth, power,
and technology—which included "spike nails"—between the West and the
Rest, it is very hard to imagine how tragedy could have been avoided in
these new cross-cultural and unmediated interactions, the adverse impact
of which was felt as deeply in the South Pacific as it was in North America.

Interlude

I must study Politicks and War that my sons may have liberty to study Mathematicks and Philosophy. My sons ought to study Mathematicks and Philosophy, Geography, natural History, Naval Architecture, navigation, Commerce and Agriculture, in order to give their Children a right to study Painting, Poetry, Musick, Architecture, Statuary, Tapestry and Porcelaine.

John Adams to Abigail Adams, 1780

CHAPTER 5

A Short History of Cultural Evolution

DURING THE EIGHTEENTH CENTURY NORTH America in varying degrees, embraced the Enlightenment of western Europe. Before resuming our narrative of the exploration of North America, we should pause to consider for a few pages what this change, or rather this set of changes, meant for the continent. Because Enlightenment thought not only informed the exploration of western North America, it also helped transform North America's self-reproducing societies into powerful dynamos of social development and cultural evolution.

Cultural Versus Organic Evolution

The French naturalist Jean-Baptiste Lamarck was wrong about biology. Organisms do not, as he supposed, pass on characteristics acquired in their own lifetimes to their offspring. A giraffe, for example, that learns to stretch its neck to reach leaves higher up a tree cannot then pass on a longer neck to the next generation. Biological evolution does not work that way. But Lamarck was right about human history. Humans individually or collectively learn new things all the time. And they may pass on this newly acquired knowledge to the next generation through formal or informal means. This is precisely how cultural evolution, or what one might call Lamarckian evolution, works. And the idea was discovered and given full expression by the Enlightenment.[1]

The modern idea that cultures have evolved, which is the central theme of this book, and that they have the capability to progress, however, did not originate with the advent of critical history during the Enlightenment, marked by the eighteenth-century histories of David Hume, William Robertson, and Edward Gibbon.[2] Rather, the genesis of the idea formed earlier in the sixteenth and seventeenth centuries, when English philosopher Francis Bacon looked back to antiquity and opined that modern inventions have set the modern world apart from the ancient world. "We should notice the force, effect, and consequences of inventions," Bacon observed, "which are nowhere more conspicuous than in those three which were unknown to the ancients; namely, printing, gunpowder, and the compass. For these three have changed the appearance and state of the whole world: first in literature, then in warfare, and lastly in navigation; and innumerable changes have been thence derived, so that no empire, sect, or star, appears to have exercised a greater power and influence on human affairs than these mechanical discoveries."[3] Bacon was making the case for the moderns in the ancients-versus-moderns debate that grew out of the Renaissance, with the rediscovery of classical learning, and intensified during the scientific revolution. Modern Europeans, Bacon argued, could see farther and better than their ancestors because they had powerful new optical instruments, such as the telescope and the microscope. And, crucially, because of the scientific method (the testing of hypotheses), the moderns had the tools and means to think better than the ancients.

Not to be outdone by the scientists, scholars also developed the "humanistic method" to think better, which perhaps no one expressed as well as did the Victorian educator Matthew Arnold. In his 1869 essay "Culture and Anarchy," he wrote that culture ought to be the "pursuit of our total perfection by means of getting to know, on all the matters which most concern us, the best which has been thought and said in the world; and through this knowledge, turning a stream of fresh and free thought upon our stock notions and habits."[4] Implicit in Bacon's argument for the superiority of the present over the past was the notion of progress: that knowledge could be increased and society, therefore, improved upon over what it had been before. This ethos was probably the most important export from western Europe to North America. It was also a major source of social power. It enhanced the abilities of a society not only "to get things done" but to get things done in ever better ways.

Dynamic versus Static Societies

The New World of Bacon was not just geographical; it was also psychological, a new state of mind. In short, as reflected in the methods of Bacon and René Descartes—and later in the work and achievements of Isaac Newton and John Locke—Western society had become "dynamic," to use the term of

David Deutsch, a British physicist and philosopher of science. To Deutsch, a "static society involves," in contrast to a dynamic one, a "relentless struggle to prevent knowledge from growing."[5] This conservatism was not irrational, since without science there was no way to test whether a new idea was true or useful. Thus in static societies authorities sensibly viewed all ideas or innovations with caution, if not outright suspicion or alarm. Cultures that reproduce themselves by avoiding innovation and adhering to tradition— where sons and daughters learn to copy their fathers and mothers' ways of doing things—may be static but are also stable, which was a crucial achievement in what was otherwise a dangerous and unpredictable world. During the Middle Ages, that long period between the fall of Rome and the rebirth of classical learning, Europe was a prime example of a static society, one that strove to reproduce rather to re-create itself, as its countless and nearly identical churches and cathedrals indicate.

Dynamic, as opposed to static, societies, on the other hand, were exceedingly rare. To quote Deutsch again, modern Western civilization is "the only known instance of a long-lived dynamic (rapidly changing) society."[6] Unlike the participants in static or traditional societies, participants in Western civilization were aware, sometimes keenly so, that change had occurred or was occurring during their own lifetimes, and they believed that change would go on to remake their children's world as well. In 1776 and 1789 Americans and the French, respectively, both embraced revolutionary change. As these two revolutions demonstrated, change was not a random occurrence but could be intentional and directed. But change also brought unintended consequences.

With the rise of freer markets, freer and regular elections, amendable constitutions, scholarly criticism, peer review, due process, freedom of the press, patents, double-entry bookkeeping, and many other processes and mechanisms of self-correction and transparency, including the very study of history itself, change became self-perpetuating and its pursuit was institutionalized within new, fiercely competitive and increasingly powerful nation-states as well as within other forms of intrastate organizations, such as the joint stock company and later the business corporation. Even the simplest associations came to keep minutes and to divide business into old and new.

These new freedoms certainly did not emerge all at once or everywhere. The development of a liberal or free culture, after all, was complex and multifarious. But the liberal ideal was grasped early, and by the end of the eighteenth century progress toward its full realization had been made on a number of fronts, from Paris to Philadelphia. At the same time, the belief took hold that the future would or should be better than the past; that the next generation could expect to live better than the last. And in fact from the early nineteenth century to the present the West, lagged by the Rest, with the disparities between the two steadily narrowing, did become, in Benjamin Franklin's terms, healthier, wealthier, and wiser.[7]

Thus the great significance of the scientific revolution had far less to do with the science that the Bacons, Newtons, and Lockes produced during the seventeenth century than it did with the new and improved way of thinking that marked this change in intellectual history and which made possible the Enlightenment that followed in the next century. Reason, to say nothing of faith, was no longer enough. To quote Deutsch again, Europe's thinkers began to seek "good"— that is, testable—explanations. On the significance of this important break with the past, Deutsch declared that

> the sea change in the values and patterns of the whole community of thinkers, which brought about a sustained and accelerating creation of knowledge, happened only once in history, with the Enlightenment and its scientific revolution. An entire political, moral, economic and intellectual culture—roughly what is now called the "West"—grew around the values entailed by the quest for good explanations, such as tolerance of dissent, openness to change, distrust of dogmatism and authority, and the aspiration to progress by individuals and for the culture as a whole. And the progress made by that rich and varied culture, in turn, promoted those values.[8]

In short, the West hit upon a variety of methods to test and, crucially, self-correct for error. The United States in particular embraced these new methods of thinking. Its amendable constitution was Exhibit A, a fact that goes far in explaining its remarkable dynamism.

Europe and America

Modern Europeans began not only to compare themselves with, and distance themselves from, their ancient but civilized ancestors from Greece and Rome but also to compare their cultures (or their common European civilization) with, and distance it from, the Native cultures of the New World—peoples and lands unknown to the cosmographer Claudius Ptolemy and the other ancients. To Europeans, the American aborigines seemed primitive because they lived closer to nature, if not actually, as they thought, in a state of nature. This idea served as the philosophical jumping-off point for seventeenth-century social contract theorists like Bacon's contemporary Thomas Hobbes and John Locke. By the eighteenth century an entire line of thought had emerged from the evolutionary notion that as primitive America now is, civilized Europe once was. Going to America, or the Pacific Islands, meant one traveled horizontally through space and went vertically backward through time. Thus, with the Renaissance, Europeans discovered the ancients, their learned forebears, in their newly stocked libraries of translated texts; in the Age of Discovery and well after, they encountered in real time and throughout the Americas representatives of what they took as their more primitive or savage progenitors. America was regarded, in short, as Europe's distant mirror.

The West's Clenched Fist and Invisible Hand

The ancients-versus-moderns debate, sometimes framed as the fight between authority and progress, or what Jonathan Swift satirized in 1697 as the "battle of the books," exhausted itself by the end of the seventeenth century.[9] The idea of progress, however, not only survived into the next century but expanded and thrived, and later, in the writings of the Scottish Enlightenment philosophers, became richly adorned in theory but firmly based in common sense and in Scotland's own sense of recent history—the divide between the Highlands and the clannish old ways, on the one hand, and the Lowlands and the newer law-based, market-driven society on the other. As scholar Duncan Forbes points out, the Scottish philosopher Adam Ferguson was born "practically on the line" between the Highlands and the Lowlands and took a "cool look at both sides of the medal of modern civilization," and what Ferguson and his fellow countrymen, including Adam Smith, "saw as the paradox of the progress of commerce and manufactures giving rise on the one hand to personal liberty and security, the blessings of the rule of law, but at the same time and equally inevitably producing a second-rate sort of society full of second-rate citizens pursuing comparatively worthless objects."[10]

In short, the theory of progress had replaced the old declension narrative of sacred history, which traced the fall of man from Adam and Eve to Noah and Moses, then to Christ the Redeemer, and finally to the expectation and eschatology of the Second Coming.[11] In contrast, the new secular version of history, as traced by Ferguson in 1767 in his "An Essay on the

History of Civil Society," was one of ascension, as "rude" states evolved into "polished" ones. Rather than salvation, humankind was pointed toward ever greater refinement. In the Enlightenment's shift from a God-centered to a human-centered history—and from a Jerusalem-centered map to a Eurocentric world geography—man arose out of nature rather than the Garden of Eden. Humans then started their long career hunting and gathering. Hobbes had imagined that this primitive and savage state of affairs was a time when

> every man is Enemy to every man; the same is consequent to the time, wherein men live without other security, than what their own strength, and their own invention shall furnish them withall. In such condition, there is no place for Industry; because the fruit thereof is uncertain; and consequently no Culture of the Earth; no Navigation, nor use of the commodities that may be imported by Sea; no commodious Building; no Instruments of moving, and removing such things as require much force; no Knowledge of the face of the Earth; no account of Time; no Arts; no Letters; no Society; and which is worst of all, continuall feare, and danger of violent death; And the life of man, solitary, poore, nasty, brutish, and short.[12]

Eventually, however, animals were domesticated, easing the struggle for existence. In this pastoral or Arcadian stage, barbarians—a social grade higher than savages—came into being. They also invented and cultivated the simpler arts. As more time passed, plants were domesticated, giving rise to a higher level of culture—to an agriculture. In this stage, civilization replaced barbarism, and the rude arts became ever more polished and refined. One of the key mechanisms, if not the most important one, that propelled humanity forward from a "solitary, poore, nasty, brutish, and short" life was war. War made the state, Hobbes's "Leviathan," and the state, in turn, made peace.[13] Ferguson agreed, adding,

> The strength of nations consists in the wealth, the numbers, and the character, of their people. The history of their progress from a state of rudeness, [was], for the most part, a detail of the struggles they have maintained, and of the arts they have practiced, to strengthen, or to secure themselves. Their conquests, their population, and their commerce, their civil and military arrangements, their skill in the

construction of weapons, and in the methods of attack and defence; the very distribution of tasks, whether in private business or in public affairs, either tend to bestow, or promise to employ with advantage, the constituents of a national force, and the resources of war.[14]

Since this was the eighteenth century, when the Industrial Revolution (what the British mathematician and historian Jacob Bronowski called the English Revolution) was still inchoate, the highest stage of development seemed to contemporary observers to be a society based on commerce, trade, and some manufacturing, including incredibly productive pin factories.[15] Indeed economist and philosopher Adam Smith, one of Ferguson's contemporaries and fellow countrymen, boldly argued in his 1776 *The Wealth of Nations* that these market activities alone, if allowed to proceed unhindered by undue government regulation, would eventually make the whole world rich. Thus, between Ferguson's clenched fist of the battlefield and Smith's "invisible hand" of the marketplace, Enlightenment thinkers had not only described mankind's ascent but were prescribing new ways for mankind to ascend. In other words, they discovered by means of wars and markets that humans could break the "cake of custom," as the Victorians would later call it, and take charge of their own future.[16]

The Rise and Fall of Empires

The Enlightenment worked out schemes for how societies evolved or, as the case may be, devolved. In the first book of his six-volume history of Rome, which appeared in 1776, Edward Gibbon famously advanced a two-part explanation for the decline and fall of the Roman Empire. The Latin West succumbed, he contended, to the spread from within of an increasingly intolerant monotheism, namely Christianity, and in the end it failed to repulse the barbarian invasions of the Goths, Vandals, and Huns. The Greco-Roman East, on the other hand, was assailed from without by barbarian Arabs and, later, from without by the barbarian Turks who had converted to another monotheism, Islam. Thus, both halves of the Roman Empire were destroyed by barbarism and monotheism. Barbarians were, by definition, less civilized than Romans. And monotheists were, by definition, intolerant of other faiths. In this respect, differences in culture and cultural or social development were crucial to Gibbon's narrative.

But these differences were in no way baked into anyone's DNA or racially determined. Enlightenment evolutionism was universal and self-evident—it

applied to all peoples, in the past and in the present. Indeed, Gibbon pointed out that the very barbarian territories that had been carved out of the
Roman Empire would one day evolve into the civilized states of Europe,
such as Gibbon's own England. And in time these new states not only
caught up with Rome but improved upon and eventually surpassed Roman
civilization in terms of social development. As Gibbon saw it, the period of
the Renaissance, a term coined by the nineteenth-century historian Jules
Michelet, marked the rebirth of Rome, which had been destroyed centuries
before by barbarism and superstition. And with the scientific revolution
and the transatlantic Enlightenment—Benjamin Franklin was as much a
product of this era as was Voltaire—these moderns were convinced that
they would soar past the Ancients.

The situation across the Atlantic was different, however. In the New
World, members of Europe's transplanted civilization believed they were
surrounded on every side by "savages" or "barbarians." Later, nineteenth-
century historians like Francis Parkman and William H. Prescott, who
continued to look at history through a Gibbonian lens, saw the rise of an independent Latin South and Anglo North as triumphs of Western civilization
over American savagery and barbarism.[17] A fear that these victories would
be reversed haunted the Romantic imagination of the nineteenth century.
A case in point was the American Thomas Cole's painting *The Course of
Empire* (1833–36), which is located at the New-York Historical Society. It
consisted of five separate paintings, each representing a different stage in
the rise and fall cycle of empire: *The Savage State*; *The Arcadian or Pastoral
State*; *The Consummation of Empire*; *Destruction*; and, finally, *Desolation*.[18]

The End of American History

There were many agricultural revolutions. But there was only one Industrial
Revolution, which started in the English Midlands and spread from there
to the rest of the world. One of the intellectual consequences of this transformation was that the evolutionism or stage-theory of culture of the
Enlightenment was all but eclipsed by the evolutionism of the nineteenth
century, which gave rise to two important variations on the older theme:
Marxism, which explained social development in terms of class struggle,
and social Darwinism, which emphasized the survival of the fittest within
different races as well as between them. Other writers, especially from the
Americas, were drawn less to how cultures evolved or progressed and more
to the conflicts that were produced when two cultures at different stages of

development came into conflict, such as when the peoples of Europe collided with the peoples of the Americas.

One of the most influential books in Latin American literature and history was Domingo Faustino Sarmiento's 1845 *Civilization and Barbarism: The Life of Juan Facundo Quiroga, and the Physical Aspect, Customs, and Practices of the Argentine Republic*. The 1840s was a decade when the future of Sarmiento's Argentina, and much of the rest of Latin America, including Mexico, appeared very much in doubt. According to Sarmiento, Latin America was locked in a struggle between the opposing forces of European civilization, that is, "intelligence," which was focused in the port city of Bueno Aires, and "indigenous barbarism," which he equated with "matter" and the wild Pampas. Sarmiento believed that in the Argentine Republic the "nineteenth and the twelfth centuries live[d] together: one inside the cities, the other in the country." And for Sarmiento, the New World was where European civilization was engaged in an ongoing clash with American barbarism, represented by its caudillos, military strongmen, and dictators, from Argentina's Juan Manuel de Rosas to Mexico's Antonio López de Santa Anna—the villain, from the Texas perspective, of the Battle of the Alamo in 1836.[19]

In 1893, not quite fifty years after the appearance of Sarmiento's *Facundo: Civilization and Barbarism*, and a little over four hundred years after Christopher Columbus discovered San Salvador, an island in the Bahamas, thereby changing the course of world history, Frederick Jackson Turner delivered a paper, "The Significance of the Frontier in American History." He did so at the meeting of the American Historical Association, which met in Chicago, where the World's Columbian Exposition was being held to celebrate Columbus's four-hundred-year-old achievement. Turner's paper would prove as influential in Anglophone America as Sarmiento's book did in Latin America. In fact, Turner *invented* American history.[20]

Like Sarmiento, Turner saw American history as a struggle between Indigenous barbarism, or what he called savagery, on the one hand, and civilization on the other. The dividing line between these two stages of cultural or social development was the American frontier, a line that moved west continuously from the founding of Virginia in 1607 up to 1890, when the nation, having supposedly exhausted its free land, subjected its indigenous peoples, like it or not, to assimilation, to be turned into God-fearing, property-loving farmers. At the same time, America's farmers of European and African descent were abandoning their farms in droves to work and live in the country's booming cities. For Turner, the struggle between civilization and savagery was central to American history. The frontier was significant, he argued, because it was the act of settling it that had turned Europeans into Americans, producing a new, rapidly evolving democratic civilization, one thoroughly independent, politically and culturally, of Europe's. But now that the frontier—according to Robert P. Porter, the superintendent of the 1890 Census—was closed, that chapter of American history was at an end, Turner believed; subsequent American development would follow in Europe's footsteps.[21]

Andrew Jackson, after whom Turner's father had given his son his middle name, bore a strong resemblance to Sarmiento's caudillos, especially his contemporary Juan Manuel de Rosas. Both men were noted Indian fighters, and both cleared lands for European settlement. But whereas Rosas established a dictatorship in Argentina, Jackson, following the presidencies of Monroe and Adams, turned the American republic into a popular democracy with the spread of the franchise to all men of European descent, a signal event in the political evolution of the United States and the point where the narrative of this book draws to a close.[22]

In *Facundo* Sarmiento expressed his opposition to Rosas's tyranny, while Turner wrote "The Significance of the Frontier" to analyze and celebrate the sources of American liberty and individualism. And while Sarmiento called for the influence of more European culture on the manners of his country, Turner celebrated the America's distinctive way of doing things. In prose bordering on poetry, these two men offered powerful explanations for the history and culture of their respective countries, and more generally for Latin America and Anglophone America—the former typified by gauchos or vaqueros, the latter by the not-so-different cowboys. In return, Sarmiento and Turner were each offered power themselves. Sarmiento would go on to serve as the president of Argentina, and Turner, who had befriended Woodrow Wilson as a graduate student at Johns Hopkins University in Baltimore, Maryland, would later serve as one of President Wilson's postwar planners.[23]

Darwin and Marx

At the end of the nineteenth century the president of the American Historical Association, James Ford Rhodes, observed that the 1859 publication of Darwin's *On the Origin of Species* marked the dividing line between two intellectual worlds: "Evolution, heredity, environment, have become household words, and their application to history has influenced everyone who has had to trace the development of a people, the growth of an institution, or the establishment of a cause. Other scientific theories and methods have affected physical science as potently, but no one has entered so vitally into the study of man."[24] To be more accurate, Darwin put biology into evolution (a word he initially did not use). Jean-Baptiste Lamarck and others, including Darwin's own grandfather, Erasmus Darwin, had tried to do the same, but not convincingly. The theory of natural selection, the discovery of which Charles Darwin shared with Alfred Wallace, made organic evolution finally acceptable to science. Darwin and Wallace were both inspired by Thomas R. Malthus's 1798 *Essay on Population as It Affects the Future Improvement of Society*. Malthus postulated that human populations would in time always outstrip their environment, forcing the survivors into a grim competition for resources. Malthus's fatalism stood in sharp contrast to the optimism of Robertson and other Enlightenment thinkers.

In the wake of Darwin, the nonorganic theory of evolution of the Enlightenment had all but been forgotten. But obviously there was a great deal of continuity between eighteenth-century and nineteenth-century nonorganic evolutionism, as indicated by the evolutionary stages of Ferguson, on the one hand, and Sarmiento and Turner on the other. The anthropology of Sir Edward B. Tylor and the New York railroad lawyer Lewis Henry Morgan were other cases in point.

In *Primitive Culture*, published in 1871, two years after the publication of Matthew Arnold's *Culture and Anarchy*, Tylor produced the classic, nonorganic definition of culture: that "complex whole which includes knowledge, beliefs, arts, morals, law, customs, and any other capabilities and habits acquired by a man as member of society."[25] And in 1877 in *Ancient Society*, Morgan, who had conducted extensive field work among the Iroquois (he was adopted by the Seneca), fleshed out the now very familiar, nonorganic, tripartite scheme of cultural evolution: first savagery; then barbarism; and finally civilization. While for Ferguson the drive for security was one of main drivers of cultural evolution, for Morgan it was the development of better food production technologies. As Morgan put it: "The great epochs of human progress have been identified, more or less directly, with the enlargement of the sources of subsistence."[26]

Morgan's thinking was, however, somewhat ambivalent on this point, probably because he was not an armchair theorist but had extensive experience in the field, meeting in person, for example, with members of the

Iroquois nation. On the one hand, he believed that a "common principle of intelligence meets us in the savage, in the barbarian, and in civilized man." This was quite literally an enlightened point of view. Ferguson similarly observed in 1767, "We are generally at a loss to conceive how mankind can subsist under custom and manners extremely different from our own; and we are apt to exaggerate the misery of barbarous times, by an imagination of what we ourselves should suffer in a situation to which we are not accustomed. But every age hath its consolations, as well as its sufferings. In the interval of occasional outrages, the friendly intercourse of men, even in their rudest condition, is affectionate and friendly." In other words, ages and stages may come and go, but there is a durability to mankind's intelligence and humanity.[27]

On the other hand, Morgan acknowledged what would have seemed obvious to his European and European American contemporaries, which was that the "Aryan family" had become "the central stream of human progress, because it produced the highest type of mankind, and because it has proved its intrinsic superiority by gradually assuming the control of the earth." Here we see the unfortunate blurring of the Aryan family, of race, with evolution's highest type, and with it notions of racial superiority, as proposed by the French writer Arthur de Gobineau, who once served as secretary to Alexis de Tocqueville; that all men are *not* created equal.[28] This view marked an abandonment of one of the Enlightenment's most important self-evident truths. In the second half of the nineteenth century we see the comingling of biology and culture, of the organic and the nonorganic. Even so, the Aryan Morgan nevertheless believed that the actual timing of the West's attainment of modern civilization was largely a matter of luck; that it "must be regarded as an accident of circumstances."[29] This was more the language of a cultural evolutionist, one with an appreciation of the role of contingency in history, than a racial determinist like Gobineau.

The bearded duo Karl Marx and Friedrich Engels considered Morgan's cultural evolution to be essential to understanding their own parallel theory of developmental stages, namely: first slavery, then feudalism, and finally capitalism. Indeed, according to Engels, "in America, Morgan had, in a manner, discovered anew the materialistic conception of history, originated by Marx forty years ago."[30] Despite Morgan's emphasis on technology rather than race, the anthropologist Marvin Harris notes that a "generation of anthropologists" was "brought up to believe" that Morgan was a racial determinist, which discredited him and other nineteenth-century evolutionists, and, ignorant of Morgan's eighteenth-century antecedents, this generation believed "that the division of cultural history into the universal stages of savagery, barbarism, and civilization" was Morgan's "ill-advised late-nineteenth-century accomplishment." With Morgan, cultural evolution was conflated with organic evolution, actually with social Darwinism, after Herbert Spencer.[31]

The high point of nineteenth-century evolutionism came in 1896, with the completion of Herbert Spencer's multivolume work *The Synthetic Philosophy*. The first of ten volumes, *First Principles*, appeared in 1862, followed by *Principles of Biology* (two volumes), *Principles of Psychology* (two volumes), *Principles of Sociology* (three volumes), and *Principles of Ethics* (two volumes). A schoolteacher and a railway civil engineer, Spencer sought to apply the principles of evolution, including Darwin's theory of natural selection, to biology and to culture alike. Spencer was not content to describe. He prescribed that governments restrain themselves in order to allow for maximum competition in the marketplace and elsewhere, for that was, he argued, the key to progress in every sphere of human activity. Spencer, it should be noted here, was influenced by Auguste Comte, the French philosopher and founder of sociology. Comte, who believed there was an order and logic to the development of knowledge, divided the course of human history into three clear stages of development: the theological, the metaphysical, and the positive or scientific. (There are almost as many developmental schemes as there are evolutionists!)

While Spencer adopted a laissez-faire philosophy in regard to government's role in the economy and in society, which was influential primarily in the English-speaking world, the followers of Comte, especially in Latin America, including Mexico, arrived at the opposite conclusion. In the second half of the nineteenth century the positivists in Mexico—the *científicos*, as they were called—urged the government of Porfirio Díaz to engage in social engineering to fast-forward, leapfrog, or accelerate the country's evolution and thereby catch up with the more advanced societies in western Europe and North America.[32]

The rejection of social Darwinism, which started at the end of the nineteenth century, was complicated. In the new historical discipline (for which the American Historical Association was founded in 1884), Turner's frontier theory was free of the class reductionism of the Marxists and of the racial determinism of the social Darwinists or scientific racists. In many respects it was a refreshing throwback to eighteenth-century evolutionism, directionality, and progress. Indeed, it was an explicit and forceful rejection of the Anglo-Saxon and Eurocentric race-based germ theory that prevailed in American historiography during the 1880s and 1890s. At Johns Hopkins, Turner's mentor had been the historian and germ theorist Herbert Baxter Adams, author of *The Germanic Origin of New England Towns* (1882).[33]

Like Marx, Turner was interested in social change. Whereas Marx emphasized class conflict within a society, Turner was more interested in the conflict between societies at different stages of development, namely in the violent collision between civilization and savagery on the American frontier. Also, whereas Marx wrote of individuals in terms of their class interests, Turner was interested in individuals principally as representatives of different stages of social development. For instance, Turner's writing is peppered with references to individuals as hunters, herders, farmers, town builders, and, later, regional or sectional types.[34] Turner was certainly guilty of harboring a narrow nationalism, and his ideas lost much of their relevance in the broader campaigns to save Western civilization during the world wars and the ideological struggles of the twentieth century. After an extended stay in Europe and the crisis of World War I, Turner adopted a more civilizational approach in which he saw Europe more as a close sister to America than an estranged relative. Still, his earlier evolutionary, exceptionalist, and narrative ideas, which were notably free of the racism of his times, nevertheless had a lasting impact on American historiography.[35]

The Two Cultures

In 1959 the English novelist and chemist C. P. Snow warned that Western civilization was splitting into two cultures, not one European and the other American, or one Anglo-Saxon and the other Spanish, but a culture of math, science, technology, and engineering, on the one hand, and of the arts and humanities on the other. Snow believed that for the developed West to render effective aid to the underdeveloped world, it was crucial to repair the growing breach between these two cultures in order to create a united front. The year 1959 was, after all, the height of the Cold War's struggle between capitalism and Communism, or West and East, and he was very clear that he wanted the West to win. Snow was critical of both cultures for their basic ignorance of each other, but his real target was, in his view, the backward-looking and condescending humanities—the "intellectuals as natural Luddites," a reference to bands of English cotton and woolen mill workers who in the 1810s destroyed machinery that threatened their jobs rather than embracing changes in the workplace that came with innovation.[36]

The Bad Renaissance

The divide or breach that Snow described, while real enough, was hardly new. The Victorian art critic John Ruskin believed that Western civilization had gone off the rails (although he would not have appreciated the metaphor) with the rebirth of classical learning and the influence of Greek and Roman models on European literature, art, and politics. This change was represented by the replacement of medieval Gothic art, which was communal and organic, with the "rigid, cold, and inhuman" geometry of the Renaissance and its emphasis on individual genius and ego rather than on the anonymity of the medieval craftsmen whose creative independence and vitality was showcased in the magnificent Gothic edifice the Palazzo Ducale, or Doge's Palace, in Venice.

In *The Stones of Venice* (1851–53), John Ruskin charted the rise and fall of La Serenissima through its architecture, marking its height with the triumph of the Gothic and, in the third of three volumes, its "fall" with the advent of the "Roman Renaissance," a style that for Ruskin was exemplified in the Biblioteca Marciana, or Library of St. Mark. The Renaissance was characterized by the "pride of science," the "pride of state," and the "pride of system," in which knowledge was arrogantly reduced, or "caged," and "manacled" to philosophy. In other words, an earlier Christian calmness was replaced by the discordant individualism of the pagan world. To Ruskin, the Renaissance "preferred science to emotion, and experience to perception." His cultural history is a perfect inversion of the Enlightenment historiography that the Renaissance—after a thousand-year hiatus of backwardness, fear, and superstition—restored high civilization to Europe. For Gibbon, as we have seen, the Renaissance marked the rebirth of Rome, while for Ruskin it was the cultural movement that murdered the Middle Ages. To Ruskin, the Renaissance was "cold, rigid, inhuman; incapable of glowing, of stooping, of conceding for an instant. Whatever excellence it has is refined, high-trained, and deeply erudite," unlike the Gothic's "quaint fancy, rich ornament, bright colour, something that shows a sympathy with men of ordinary minds and hearts." Ruskin was not only a historian but also a social critic—one who warned his fellow Victorians that without moral regeneration, England was at risk of becoming history's third failed thalassocracy, after first Tyre and then Venice. Indeed, Ruskin's utopian views—he believed there was "no wealth but life" and that "the country that is richest" is the one that "nourishes the greatest numbers of noble and happy human beings"—anticipated the welfare state as well as the philosophy of the United Nation's Human Development Index.[37]

In reaction to Victorian England's putative money-grubbing and materialist culture, Ruskin championed the Pre-Raphaelite Brotherhood and helped inspire the Arts and Crafts movement. The Pre-Raphaelites tried to recapture in their representational paintings the magic and romance of an imagined Arthurian or Christian pastoral past. Ruskin's Romantic counterparts in America were the Transcendentalists Henry David Thoreau and Ralph Waldo Emerson and the artists Thomas Cole, Frederic Edwin Church, and Albert Bierstadt of the Hudson River and Rocky Mountain schools. In North America—whether in the eastern woodlands and river valleys or later in the western plains, mountains, and deserts—artists learned early on to substitute the continent's natural landscapes and geology for Europe's legends and antiquity. Nevertheless, this European and North American art had at least one thing in common: it was a form of redemption, either from the weary Ozymandias cycle of the rise and demise of civilizations or, as an escape to nature, from the dispiriting realities of the Industrial Age.

This fundamental criticism, which formed the original basis of the cultural divide between the arts and the sciences that would later so worry Snow, had the more immediate effect of dividing the Anglosphere into two types of architecture—one classical, the other medieval. The US Capitol (designed by the Scottish-trained physician Dr. William Thornton), the White House (constructed by the Irish-born architect James Hoban), and Thomas Jefferson's Monticello were all built in the neoclassical style, characterized by proportion, symmetry, simplicity, and grandeur. These qualities appealed to the revolutionaries of the Enlightenment as well as to the Enlightenment's despots, such as Russia's Catherine II.

To compete with republicanism and to stress the virtues of monarchy and tradition, the British Houses of Parliament, including St. Stephen's Tower (later the Elizabeth Tower, best known as Big Ben) in Westminster and the government edifices on Canada's Parliament Hill, which overlooks the Ottawa River, were all built in Gothic Revival. This elaborate and decorative style with its pointed arches, pitched roofs, crenulated parapets, high spires, and finials was intended to evoke a bygone era of old castles and abbeys and, significantly, a stable, if stratified and hierarchical, Christian social order. Ruskin would champion Gothic Revival on aesthetic as well as moral grounds.[38]

Good-Bye to All of That

World War I was a catastrophe for Western civilization. Unsurprisingly, the generation, wounded or otherwise, that followed in the wake of that terrible conflict rejected outright much of the world that had preceded it: the Victorian era, with its certitudes and hierarchies, including racial hierarchies and social developmental schemes and stage theories. As we have seen, in anthropology the cultural relativists led by Franz Boas and later by his students, among them Margaret Mead, rejected the theory of cultural evolution that had dominated eighteenth- and nineteenth-century thinking, along with "any grading of cultures in hierarchical systems."

And it was understandable that the work of Victorians—from the poet Rudyard Kipling, author of "The White Man's Burden" (1899), to art critic John Ruskin—was also left, with little or no ceremony, on the ash heap of history. *Good-Bye to All That*, the title of the brilliant 1929 autobiography or memoir of the British Great War veteran and writer Robert Graves, well captured the tenor of those times. And in the century after World War I, especially since the 1960s and 1970s, the idealistic efforts by cultural anthropologists and social historians to de-center and democratize the study of culture and history have only gathered pace. But in a classic instance of the dragon swallowing its own tail, scholars from the arts and humanities did rediscover Ruskin and embrace him as a true intellectual forebear, which in turn only further widened the divide between Snow's two cultures.[39]

But as admirable as is so much of this scholarship, it does leave some of history's biggest questions or problems unanswered or unsolved, not the least of which was: Why the Rise of the West? This question dates back at least to the Age of Enlightenment, when, in the words of the historian Ian Morris, "European intellectuals realized that they had a problem. As problems went, it was not a bad one: they appeared to be taking over the world, but did not know why. Europe's revolutionaries, reactionaries, romantics, and realists went into a frenzy of speculation on why the West was taking over, producing a bewildering mass of hunches and theories."[40] It is little wonder that one of these ideas, cultural evolution, originated during the rise of Europe and North America. The idea also remains useful in explaining that time period, as I endeavor to show in this study.

PART II

THE HISPANOSPHERE

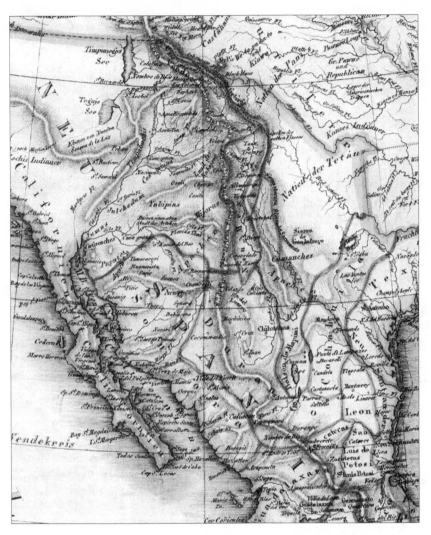

Figure 10. Carl Ferdinand Weiland, *Nord America*, detail of New Spain, 1820. Hand-colored engraved map, 21 5/8 x 20 ½ in. (55 x 52 cm). Lionel Pincus and Princess Firyal Map Division, New York Public Library, https://digitalcollections.nypl.org/items/510d47da-f0b5-a3d9-e040-e00a18064a99.

CHAPTER 6

The Two Mexicos

Eschatology and Empire

LONG BEFORE ENLIGHTENMENT SCHOLARS SUCCEEDED in replacing God as history's motive force with secular theories of ever-increasing social complexity and differentiation, medieval Christian theologians and mystics—who saw the hand of God in history, and everywhere else, for that matter—had devised different histories of ever-increasing spiritual development. From the perspective of sixteenth-century New Spain, as historian John Phelan has pointed out, the most important of these histories was the one put forward by Joachim of Fiore, a twelfth-century Italian mystic and Cistercian abbot. Joachim used the hallucinogenic Book of the Apocalypse to interpret the past and, significantly, predict the future. He divided history into two ages, the age of the Father, from Adam to Christ, and the age of the Son, from Christ to the year 1260. These ages corresponded with the Old and New Testaments, each lasting forty-two generations. Drawing on the idea of the Trinity, Joachim believed in a third act for humankind and thus predicted the coming of a final and deeply spiritual age, that of the Holy Ghost. Joachim believed that this millennial kingdom of the Apocalypse, a golden age of love and contemplation, would follow a time of troubles. According to this Joachimite eschatology, the church of the popes would be replaced by the church of the mendicants.[1] To the Spiritual Franciscans—an extreme group within the Franciscan order that was zealously dedicated to the vow of poverty—Joachim's prophesized Messiah was none other than the founder of their own order, Saint Francis of Assisi, who was born in 1181 or 1182. Francis founded the Order of Friars Minor in 1209, during the twilight of Joachim's age of the Son.

For Renaissance navigators like Christopher Columbus, who saw himself as a Joachimite figure, and for Franciscan missionaries to the New World like Gerónimo de Mendieta, "geographical exploration and colonization" were viewed as "the fulfillment of the prophecies of the apocalypse." Before Columbus and the discovery of the West Indies, the Roman Catholic or Universal Church was universal in name only. Since the Great Schism of 1054 between the Eastern Orthodox Church and the Western Roman Church, Catholicism had been confined to the far western peninsula of the Eurasian landmass—that is, Europe. And with the steady advance of Turkish Muslims into the Balkans after 1453, and the Protestant Reformation, which began in 1517 when Martin Luther of Wittenberg, a German monk and theologian, questioned the church's dubious practice of selling indulgences, much of western Europe was lost to either the infidels or to the heretics. However, as the Age of Discovery dawned, Europe found that the world could be circumnavigated by a single ship, as Magellan's Armada de Molucca had proved. It was now possible—for the first time in the fifteen hundred years since it was issued—to act on the calling of Mark 16:15, "Go ye into all the world, and preach the gospel to every creature."[2]

In 1492 Queen Isabella and King Ferdinand had overseen the end of the long Reconquest, reclaiming all of Spain from the Moorish invaders (Islam was later banned). They had expelled all Jews—except for the *conversos*, those who chose conversion over exile—from the country and backed the exploration of the Genoan mariner Columbus, who would go on to discover a sea route not, as hoped, to the East Indies but rather to the West Indies, new lands teeming with pagans or "heathens"—peoples who were not Christian, Jewish, or Muslim. Over the course of the next century kings Charles I and V, rulers of the Spanish and the Holy Roman Empires, and King Philip II, who ruled both Spain and Portugal, would fight to reunify all of Christendom on one front, and on a second front defend Europe in a religious war against the Turks. At home the Spanish Inquisition, established in Spain in 1478 and extended—and recharged with the zeal of the Counter-Reformation—to New Spain in 1571, was used to persecute Jews, Muslims, heretics, and Native backsliders.[3] And on yet a third and crucial front in the religious wars of the sixteenth century, King Charles and King Philip—both of the House of Hapsburg, which ruled Spain from 1516 to 1700—would also contend by bringing cross and crown to New Spain as well as to the rest of the Americas.

The War of Native Independence

It was Hernán Cortés—a thirty-five-year-old Spanish conquistador from the poor and thinly populated region of Extremadura, perhaps best known today for its acorn-fed hams—who brought the civilization of medieval Europe to the North American mainland.[4] His fierce determination and political genius are well known[5]—his strategy, tactics, and allies less so. After Francisco Hernández de Cordóba and Juan de Grijalva had established the existence of the North American mainland, in 1517 and 1518, Diego Velázquez de Cuéllar, the governor of Cuba, dispatched Cortés to this new land in search of gold and slaves. Cortés arrived at San Juan de Ulúa, the site of the future fortress of the same name, just off the Mexican mainland, in April 1519, a 1 Reed year in the Aztec fifty-two-year calendar. He commanded a force of 508 soldiers (including some 200 veterans of Grijalva's expedition), 100 sailors, and 16 horses. Cortés claimed that he was no longer under Velázquez's authority, prompting the jealous governor to try to reign him in by sending a second force. But Cortés was able to recruit these new soldiers to his side, adding to the size of his army. He burned his ships to concentrate the minds of his men,[6] and took the shrewd expedient of founding Veracruz, the first European settlement in North America, where he had his soldiers-cum-citizens elect him to the positions of captain general and chief justice in the first European elections held in North American history. They also befriended the local Totonac people, who happened to despise the Aztecs, or Mexica. (*Aztec* is a political term, while *Mexica* refers to ethnicity.)

Through his Indian interpreter Malintzin or La Malinche—known as Doña Marina after her conversion to Christianity in 1519—who spoke Nahuatl, the language of the Aztecs, Cortés learned that while there was indeed an Aztec or Mexica empire centered on the great island city of Tenochtitlán, an almost unassailable fortress, there was no sort of Pax Azteca in place. Instead, he found a widely detested Aztec tyranny and a country riven with conflict. Indeed, one of the chief characteristics of the Postclassic stage of development was militarism and large-scale warfare. To exploit the situation, Cortés adopted a divide-and-conquer strategy. Mexican poet and diplomat Octavio Paz described what happened next. The "various city-states allied themselves with the conquistadores or watched with indifference—if not with pleasure—the fall of each of their rivals, especially the most powerful, Tenochtitlán."[7]

If Cortés's strategy was classic, his military tactics were state-of-the-art, having been recently honed by the battles of the Reconquest and Spain's Italian campaigns against the French. By the late Middle Ages, mounted knights had been replaced by tercios, units of foot soldiers who were disciplined, drilled, and organized into companies of pikesmen, swordsmen, archers, and arquebusiers.[8] The key to this evolving system, as the historian Douglas A. Daniel explains, "was mutual support among the different companies. If one unit/weapon type failed, all might be lost. To ensure against this . . . individual units were relentlessly trained to work together. This discipline enabled a commander to move and use his units efficiently, as well as keep them together in the face of an enemy attack."[9] Just as there are three things that matter in real estate—"location, location, location"— military success is the result of three factors: "coordination, coordination, coordination."

If in Europe cavalry units had declined in importance relative to infantry, in clashes with Native forces in North America, where the horse had been unknown until the Spanish introduced the animal, the military value of mounted horsemen enjoyed, as Daniel put it, a "renaissance." He concludes: "The Aztecs . . . although disciplined and ordered in their own units, had neither the effective close-order formations of the Spanish nor any consistent method of preventing the Spanish cavalry from operating at will, at least on the open battlefield." The Aztecs were armed with axes, atlatls, slings, clubs, bows and arrows, and the *macquauitl*, a wooden paddle embedded with razor-sharp blades of volcanic glass, that is, obsidian. This weapon was fierce looking, to be sure, but not very durable. To wield it was to swing it—it was four feet long—and to do so a warrior needed a lot of room. The Aztec formations were therefore loose and open, putting the Native warriors at a distinct tactical disadvantage relative to the Spain's closed formations and cavalry units, the latter of which could and did break and outflank Native lines. To defend themselves, the Aztecs carried shields and wore helmets. They also wore thick, quilted cotton armor.

Military organizations typically reflect the structure of their societies, and the Aztec army was no exception. It was divided into two basic ranks: elite fighters and veteran commoners, just as Aztec or Mexica society was divided into the *pipiltin* (nobles) and the *macehualtin* (commoners). And it was centered on the *calpulli*, "great house," whose members were related by blood and kinship, an important social as well as economic unit. The *calpulli* provided the state with tribute or taxes in kind, corvée labor, and military regiments.[10] It is notable that the Aztec troops were conscripted, whereas the Spanish forces were made up of volunteers, gentlemen adventurers motivated by the expectation that they would share in the spoils. And while the Aztecs traditionally fought to capture captives for sacrifice or to eat later, the Spanish sought to kill the enemy in the here and now—a very different thing.[11]

To oppose the Aztecs' hierarchical political-religious-territorial structure, the Spanish conquerors had thus found an effective strategy and enjoyed superior tactics. They also found that they had numerous Native allies eager to rally to their side. En route to Tenochtitlán in highland Mexico, the Spanish, aided by Totonac guides, encountered and defeated the Tlaxcalans in a series of battles. Perhaps inspired by the Totonac-Spanish alliance, the ruler of the Tlaxcalan city of Tizatlan, Xicotencatl (baptized as Lorenzo Xicotencatl) convinced his countrymen that the Spanish could help them defeat their traditional enemy, the triple alliance of the three *altepetl* (ethnic city-states) Mexico-Tenochtitlán, Texcoco, and Tlacopan. The king of Mexico-Tenochtitlán dominated in the south, the king of Texcoco in the northeast, and the king of Tlacopan in the northwest. While in theory the allied kingdoms were equal, the Tenochca king was nevertheless preeminent. He directed the imperial armies, and significantly, the tribute or loot was taken to Tenochtitlán *before* being distributed among the three kingdoms.[12]

As recently as 1515 Montezuma II, the Aztec king, had tried but failed to conquer Tlaxcala. The agreement reached between the Tlaxcalan leaders and the Spanish gave Cortés thousands of Native troops and a base of operations close to the Aztec capital, which lay only seventy miles to the west. Other groups of Indians, many of them subjects of the Aztec Empire, rushed to join the Spanish coalition as well. Each group was motivated by its own intense local patriotism or loyalty and was eager to escape or avoid Aztec rule, Aztec cannibalism, and Aztec demands for tribute as well as human lives to be sacrificed by Aztec priests on Aztec altars to Aztec gods. We should note that the existence of almost continuous warfare in pre-Hispanic Mexico created internal cohesion. As Enrique Semo put it, individual "communities lived in constant distrust of one another, ready at all times to defend themselves or to attack. These social units revealed a remarkable cohesion and capacity for survival. They resisted the onslaught of conquest, depopulation, and the expansion of large private properties, rising time and time again from their own ruins."[13]

The Mesoamerican sun god Tonatiuh, whom the Aztecs associated with Huitzilopochtli, the god of war—said to be a hummingbird who comes from the south—had an insatiable thirst for human hearts and blood, which fueled the god's daily arc across the sky. The Aztec priests had convinced themselves that the only way for the sun to continue its daily peregrination across the sky was constantly to offer it human blood, usually drawn from the knifed-opened chests of hapless prisoners of war as well as slaves. In a temple on top of a pyramid, the victims were forced by four priests to back spread-eagled over a stone altar. A fifth priest used an obsidian knife to cut out the victim's heart while he or she was still alive. The heart was burned as a sacrifice and the corpses of the sacrificed hurled down the pyramid steps to fall in a heap at the base, where they were taken up to be cut up and consumed. In 1487, during the reign of Ahuitzotl, Montezuma's predecessor, twenty thousand victims were sacrificed at the dedication of the Templo Mayor (Main Temple) in Tenochtitlán, a pyramid on the top of which were two temples, one dedicated to Huitzilopochtli and the other to Tlaloc, the god of rain. To accomplish such a sanguinary feat, the Aztecs formed four lines of prisoners, each line extending for two miles. A team of executioners then worked day and night for four days to kill them all. By the beginning of the sixteenth century, the Aztecs were consuming between fifteen and twenty thousand people every year. Mesoamericans may not have domesticated animals, but the Aztecs learned how to herd and slaughter humans like cattle.[14]

As the Spanish conquistador Andrés de Tapia reported (and as has been corroborated by recent archaeological evidence), the Aztecs also used the decapitated skulls of men, women, and children—the Aztecs did not discriminate—to build the Huey Tzompantli (Great Skull Rack), flanked by two trophy towers, sixteen feet in diameter and over five feet tall, of horizontal rows of skulls arranged cheek by jowl, as it were, one row stacked atop another.[15] The skulls on the outer ring of each tower faced outward, while those on the inner ring faced in. Built between 1486 and 1502, this grim edifice of skulls, lime, stone, and wood was located in front of the Templo Mayor complex. Roughly the size of a basketball court, the *tzompantli* itself was between thirteen and sixteen feet tall and contained, the Spanish estimated, as many as 136,000 skulls. It would have been an awesome and terrible sight.

Human sacrifice certainly had religious significance, and perhaps an evolutionary role.[16] And it was no doubt driven by dietary imperatives, namely the lack of sufficient animal protein. But the Huey Tzompantli was also manifestly a demonstration of social power, an unambiguous political message that Aztec rulers intended for friends and enemies alike: "We are your overlords."

Cortés banned human sacrifice and other horrific practices as early as 1520—even before the fall of Tenochtitlán—and offered the enemies of the Aztecs a way out of their thralldom. Naturally, many took the offer only too willingly. Even the city of Texcoco, a member of the triple alliance, broke with the Aztecs, whose power it resented, and joined the Spanish. Mesoamerica's diplomatic revolution of 1519–21, which pitted the ever-shrinking Aztec alliance against Cortés's ever-ballooning coalition, was a crucial factor in Spain's dramatic and swift conquest of Mexico. Simply put, for many Indians the Spanish conquest of the Aztecs meant their own liberation from tyranny and death.

In 1521 the Spanish laid siege to Tenochtitlán for ninety-five days. To seal off the island-city, the Spanish built thirteen brigantines armed with cannon to patrol Lake Texcoco—west of the Albarradón of Nezahualcóyotl, which ran north and south, dividing the lake into two parts. The Spanish naval force was reinforced by a thousand Native canoes in what must have been a remarkable nautical sight.[17] This combination of land and naval power was decisive. The geographical advantage of the Aztecs had been turned wholly against them.

The isolated and soon starving inhabitants of the besieged city were then struck by an epidemic of smallpox, which hit the entire population all at once, since no one had been previously exposed to the disease, further weakening their ability to resist what was as much a European conquest as it was a massive Native insurrection or war of independence. Nevertheless, the fall of the marooned city was a calamity of epic proportions. The Aztecs lost everything and, to quote Octavio Paz again, "died alone, abandoned by their friends, their allies, their vassals and their gods."[18] On August 13, 1521, a pivotal date in North American history, Cuauhtémoc, the last Aztec *tlatoani* (great chief), surrendered to Cortés the city as well as the rest of the empire, consisting of 371 different tribes and peoples, with a combined population numbering in the millions. The prize covered an area of eighty thousand square miles and spread from the Gulf Coast to the Pacific Slope, although outside the Valley of Mexico, Aztec power was largely tributary.[19] The date August 13, 1521, was also independence day for millions of Native Americans who were at last free of the Aztec yoke.

Telescoping Social Development

To secure this new Spanish empire or confederation, Cortés continued the diplomacy he had started during the Conquest: reward his friends, punish his enemies, and at every opportunity extend his reach. The principal source of wealth in Mexico was its labor—there was precommercial mining of gold and silver, but on a very limited basis—and the Aztecs had already created a large tributary state that, with a little effort, could be reintegrated into a new Spanish empire. The Spanish became aware of this fact through Native interpreters and codices, especially the Codex Mendoza (1541).

In the Aztec Empire, which was based on a nonmonetary economy, tribute was paid with labor (those massive stone temples and pyramids did not build themselves) and commodities, such as cotton, chia seeds, pumpkins, corn, amaranth, tomatillo, cacao, hot peppers, beans, maize, lamb's quarters, turquoise, jade, obsidian, precious feathers, and certain flowers—marigolds, dahlias. Tribute was paid by the *macehualtin* to the *pipiltin*, and it was considerable. According to the Codex Mendoza (1541), the tribute in grain collected from 371 villages was sufficient to feed a population of 361,641 for a year. In addition to grain, the state also collected 2,896,261 textile goods (blankets, wraps) and 220,000 pounds of cotton.[20]

Cortés divided up the conquered lands of the Mexica into encomiendas (jurisdictions or spheres) of temporary grants of land and labor, naturally setting aside the biggest and richest portions for himself. There were twenty-three thousand Indians in his encomienda. These grants were also the principal way for Cortés to reward the men who had served him well, since the shares of the Aztec booty did not go very far. The encomiendas were not, however, property, as Enrique Semo has pointed out. They were usufruct. As Semo explains, the "Crown retained ownership of the land and natural resources. The Indians were free—the king's, not the encomendero's, subjects. The encomienda was inalienable, it could not be sold or transferred; when the encomendero passed away, possession reverted to the Crown. Nor could it be bequeathed." Given the highly provisional nature of the encomienda, grantees lost little time exploiting the situation. They did so by trying to convert their grant of Indian tribute into profit-making enterprises that produced items valued by Europeans—precious metals, hides, wool, wheat, dyes, sugar, silk, and cotton—and could thus be exchanged for money. These various enterprises, taken together, gave the encomenderos a degree of self-sufficiency, as well as supporting a style of life befitting a lord in Spain: in short, the dream of every conquistador. By turning their usufruct into paying propositions, these new lords, along with the members of a rapidly growing private sector (who in turn competed for Native labor), built the economy of New Spain.

To get there, the encomendero quickly, and brutally, dragged Mexico out of the Stone Age and into the sixteenth century, as Enrique Semo dramatically put it. To be sure, the distance in social development between Postclassic Mexico and sixteenth-century Spain was large, though not nearly as large as the cultural chasm that later in the nineteenth century yawned wide between the Native peoples in middle and upper North America and the Europeans of the United States and the Dominion of Canada. For the Native peoples of these two countries, the pace of social change was perhaps even more shocking, traumatic, and disorienting.[21]

New Spain's Checks and Balances

It fell to the local Native rulers, or caciques—whose collaboration with the Spanish was essential to the success of the empire—to see to it that the customary obligation to pay tribute continued to be met. Yet in fact this tribute was rechanneled to the new overlords, the encomenderos, who initially numbered around three hundred, or about 40 percent of the total survivors of Cortés's entrada. Altogether, 506 individuals would hold encomiendas in New Spain. This was a system of indirect rule in which the Spanish controlled the country by controlling hundreds of local caciques. The Spanish could not have conquered Mexico without Native help. And since they made up only a tiny sliver of the total population, neither could they have ruled it without Native cooperation.[22]

Mesoamerica's Native political institutions, at least initially, survived the Conquest, and the day-to-day life of average Indians changed little, except that they no longer had to worry about being captured and eaten or otherwise put to death by the Aztecs. And since the Spanish suppressed intertribal warfare in the areas under their control, the threat of becoming a military casualty dwindled to zero. On the downside, epidemic diseases were omnipresent, deadly old ones and terrible news one alike. The slow-motion demographic collapse that followed the Conquest, if not as severe as was once believed, put enormous strains on the old despotic tributary system.[23]

After the Conquest, Spain's captains not only rewarded their friends but also their Native allies, such as the Tlaxcala, bestowing on them privileges and mercies (*fueros*) and sparing them the encomienda. They did subject the Tlaxcala to evangelization—for the Spanish, Native acceptance of Christianity was nonnegotiable, just as it had been back in Spain for the Moors, Jews, or for that matter ordinary Spaniards. But the Tlaxcala had otherwise survived the Conquest intact. In fact, Tlaxcala continues to exist today as one of federal Mexico's thirty-one states. In North America's long and turbulent history of Native-White relations, this is a truly an astonishing fact. On the other hand, the Spanish turned their full wrath and fury upon their enemies, the Aztecs or Mexica. They used coerced Native labor to pull down the Aztec temples, holy places, and idols, and to remake Tenochtitlán—just as the Aztecs, once a conquering people from the north, had taken part in the destruction of the capital of the Toltecs. Upon the ruins of this Postclassic city the Spanish built the capital of New Spain, christening it La Ciudad de México, and erected a new government. Some fifty miles to the south of Mexico City, Cortés, who was granted the title of Marquess of the Valley of Oaxaca in 1529, built a heavily fortified palace on a fine perch in Cuernavaca in the Mexican state of Morelos, where he ruled as the great lord of the south. The poor boy from Extremadura had made good. He was North America's first self-made millionaire.[24]

As wealthy as they were for their day, the encomenderos, including Cortés, did not operate unchecked. To oversee the king's possessions in the New World, the Spanish monarchy evolved into a highly centralized structure as the chaos of the Conquest gave way to a new stable order in New Spain. The king administered his American possessions through the Consejo de Indias (Council of the Indies; the Spanish insisted on stubbornly calling the Americas the Indies long after Columbus's grand error of geography had been realized. Indeed, the Philippines, located in Southeast Asia, were administered as part of the Americas). Based in Seville, the Consejo de Indias oversaw the viceroyalties, captaincies general, and other subdivisions. Until 1535 New Spain had a string of governors, beginning with Cortés in 1522. But given New Spain's growing importance, in 1535 it was turned into a viceroyalty. The viceroy, the first of whom was Antonio de Mendoza, resided in Mexico City and acted in the sovereign's name. Thus, in the Kingdom of New Spain (and it was a kingdom, not a colony), the encomenderos and their descendants answered to the viceroy. To place a check on the chief executive official, there was the Real Audiencia (Royal Court) of Mexico City, founded in 1527, and, after 1548, that of Guadalajara, the jurisdiction of which included northern Mexico and what would become the southwestern United States. (The province of New Mexico was founded in 1598 by the Criollo conquistador Juan de Oñate.) The viceroy and the audiencia both possessed executive as well as judicial powers. And each reported to the crown, not to each other.[25]

The Two Republics of Mexico

The Kingdom of New Spain was divided into two republics: the *república de los españoles* (republic of the Spaniards) and the *república de los indios* (republic of the Indians), the immensely more populous of the two. The economy of the former was based on wheat, sugarcane, cattle, and silver, produced primarily in the north, while that of the latter drew on the production of corn, agave, beans, and chilies, primarily in the south, for largely internal or domestic consumption. Indians could find themselves in both republics. As members of the *república de los indios*, they paid tribute; they could also be coerced by the encomenderos or officials of the crown, or both, into working for the *república de los españoles*. The natural economy and isolation of much of the Indian world survived the colonial era; it would not finally break down until the Porfiriato in the late nineteenth century (in fact, only 10 percent of the entire transactions of New Spain—whether in the *república de los españoles* or the *república de los indios*—were carried out in official currencies like the gold peso or the silver real. The rest of the transactions— that is, the vast majority of them—were conducted by barter or in local currencies. (For units of exchange the Aztecs had used small copper axes or hoes, *tajaderos*, one of which was worth eight thousand cacao beans, Mesoamerica's other main unit of exchange). Outside Mexico, however, the Mexican silver peso was so important that it served as the world's first international currency. In 1535 Viceroy Antonio de Mendoza established La Casa de Moneda de México, Mexico's, and for that matter North America's, first mint. It was here that the famous silver eight-real coins (eight being the equivalent of one gold unit) were minted. Alexander von Humboldt, who visited Mexico toward the end of the colonial era, estimated that the total value of gold and silver minted at La Casa de Moneda de México since the Conquest exceeded five billion pesos.[26]

The *república de los españoles* was also predominately urban. By 1640, 57 percent of Mexico's European population lived in ten cities; by 1774, 61 percent lived in twelve cities. These two worlds were separated by centuries of social development. The republic included numerous representative corporate entities such as universities, cathedral chapters, and confraternities, as well as merchant and craft guilds, which in turn elected officials. While representative assemblies were established in the English colonies early—Virginia's General Assembly or House of Burgesses, made up of freemen, was founded in 1619—there were no equivalent bodies in Spanish America. On the other hand, the Spanish had since Roman times set great store in the city and its subordinate countryside. And perhaps no unit of government in New Spain was more important or fundamental than the *ayuntamiento* or *cabildo*, the self-governing town council that represented all the heads of households who owned land.[27]

The *república de los indios* was also largely self-governing and enjoyed the protection of the crown, which tried to check the cupidity of colonists by means of a powerful bureaucracy. This republic, in effect, segregated Indians from Spaniards and the Mestizos. Indians continued to pay a feudal tribute, as they had before the Conquest, but they were exempt from the *alcabala*, or sales tax.[28] In each main town there was an administrative center, the *cabecera*, and subordinate villages, the *pueblos sujetos*, regional governments that protected Native rights and culture. In 1542 the crown incorporated Indians by declaring them its subjects and vassals, and in this important sense the population of New Spain was made whole. Finally, to facilitate the crown's control over the Indians, the Native population was reorganized into congregations, or *reducciones* (settlements of converted Indians), first by the mendicant orders and later by civil authorities, while at the same time it was dramatically contracting in size throughout the sixteenth century due to disease. This process was so thorough and socially transformative that Mexico's present-day Indian communities owe their origins, as Semo argues compellingly, more to the colonial than to the precolonial period. It should be added that members of both republics, Spanish or Indian, could seek redress for a wrong from the viceroy or the audiencia, or appeal directly to the Consejo de Indias and thereby to the king himself.[29]

Rapine

Following Cortés but rarely possessing his intelligence, imagination, or skill were other conquistadors, like the infamous Nuño Beltrán de Guzmán, whom the crown supported as a counterweight to Cortés. Guzmán was noteworthy primarily for his ruthlessness and brutality, sharing the same wanton violence employed by Spain's Hernando de Soto in the Americas and Portugal's Vasco da Gama, Francisco de Almeida, and Afonso de Albuquerque in Africa, on the Malabar Coast, in Malacca, and elsewhere. The goal was to create dread, to attract and to keep allies, and to enlist local guides or navigators. There was a method to these men's murder, and it was often extremely effective.[30] But for all of the Guzmáns who practiced rapine—ignoring Pope Paul III's bull of June 2, 1537, Sublimis Deus, which declared that Indians were rational human beings or true men with rights of freedom and property, and thus not to be physically abused, much less enslaved—there were also those, like the explorer Álvar Núñez Cabeza de Vacas and the friar Antonio de Montesinos, who urged restraint. Europe produced savers as well as slavers.

In western Mexico, in what is now Michoacán, Guzmán was received peacefully by the Tarascans, after the Aztecs or Mexica the most powerful people in Mexico (the Tarascan capital was Tzintzuntzan). Yet even though the Tarascan *cazonci* or leader Tzimtzincha-Tangaxuan II had earlier made a treaty of understanding with Cortés, the utterly vicious Guzmán had him tortured, dragged from a horse, and burned alive in 1530. Guzmán succeeded in subjecting northwestern Mexico and enslaving numerous Indians (who were conveniently said to have been in "rebellion") in what came to be called New Galicia (now the modern states of Aguascalientes, Colima, Jalisco, Nayarit, and Sinaloa, as well as parts of Durango, Querétaro, San Luis Potosí, and Zacatecas.[31] Guzmán also founded the city of Guadalajara (today Mexico's second largest, with a population nearing 1.5 million), home of New Spain's second audiencia. But his violent methods terrorized the Indians and eventually provoked the Mixtón War of 1540–42, which pitted the Spaniards and their Native allies, the Tlaxcalans and now the Mexica (the descendants of the Aztec Empire had switched over to the winning side), against the Chichimeca. The term *chichimeca* ("barbarian" or "savage") was used by the settled, civilized Nahua peoples (and adopted by the Spanish) to describe nomadic and seminomadic tribes like the Caxcanes and the Zacatecos, who lived north of the Valley of Mexico. Social development was both universal and relative. At the same time, in the faraway Rio Grande Valley of New Mexico, as we have seen, a similar intercultural army under the leadership of Coronado waged war with the Tiguex.

In the process of these conquests, Guzmán put the *black* in the black legend of Spanish cruelty, a blanket condemnation started by Bartolomé de las Casas and which has since been uncritically extended to all European colonialism. The full limit of Spain's empire in North America, it should be noted, would not be realized until the late eighteenth century. While central Mexico fell in a matter of a few years, the conquest of southern Mexico took decades, while that of the Yucatán and northern Mexico,

above the twentieth parallel, took centuries. In the late eighteenth century a great burst of missionary activity in Alta California also extended
the effective border of the Hispanic monarchy northward as far as San
Francisco Bay.[32]

Restraint

Military conquests come at a price. For the crown, the encomienda was an
indirect and cheap way to pay for military campaigns and extend, at the
same time, its power and reach. But the crown—through its Real Audiencia
in Mexico City—naturally regarded the encomenderos, a new nobility who
controlled thousands of tributaries, with suspicion, fearing that one or all of
them might one day turn rogue, perhaps even declaring their own autonomous fiefdoms. Thus it repeatedly tried to curb their power, though it did
so in the name of protecting the Indians from overwork and abuse. To this
end, the New Laws of the Indies were passed in 1542, the same year that
Las Casas's excoriation *A Brief Account of the Destruction of the Indies* was
published. They replaced the encomienda (at least on paper) with the repartimiento, a public "labor apportionment" under the control of the crown
instead of the encomenderos. The repartimiento drew on two traditions:
the medieval Spanish system of forced public labor, and the pre-Hispanic
Indian *cuatequil*, or summons, in which Native villages, as commanded by
their lords, drafted a percentage of their able-bodied male adults to labor on
public works like temples or irrigation projects on a rotational basis.[33] The
essential difference between the two forms of appropriation was that the
labor provided under the encomienda benefited the encomendero directly;
repartimiento labor, in contrast, was intended for the common good. It was
also defined as having to be compensated. And while the work involved
may have enriched an individual European or Criollo owner of a mine,
plantation, or ranch, it was justified because the work served the greater
interests of the Hispanic economy.

The New Laws also banned Native slavery, in theory, though it continued
in some fashion throughout the colonial era, in particular in the sugar mills
and in the *obrajes* (workshops). But the real turning point in European-
Native labor relations was 1576, when almost half of the Native population
may have been carried away by the indigenous plague *cocoliztli*. Prior to
that year, according to historian Charles Gibson, "the Indian population was
sufficiently large and the number of Spanish employers sufficiently limited
to permit low quotas and rounded numbers in agricultural drafts. But with

the depopulation of the late 1570's and after, *jueces repartidores* [Native labor regulators], on their own authority, resorted to quotas in excess of two percent." Gibson concludes that the "repartimiento system of the late sixteenth century" had become "everywhere one of compulsion and abuse," like the encomienda it was intended to replace, and that "it received ongoing criticism from the clergy," the colony's conscience. However, in the competition for labor, the clergy was hardly a disinterested party. The system of repartimiento or state coercion of Native labor continued throughout the colonial era.[34]

The Desagüe de Huehuetoca:
Social Power versus Social Development

By the middle of the seventeenth century, Mexico's Native population had begun to recover. But long before that demographic tipping point was reached, the Spanish and Criollo elites in Mexico City had become committed to diverting the lake water surrounding Mexico City, which nature had captured in an endorheic basin, to protect their urban properties in the capital from periodic flooding. The Aztecs had built dikes, elevated mounds, and *calzadas* (radial causeways) to control and contain the water. The Albarradón de Nezahualcóyotl, a dike built in the mid-fifteenth century by the poet-ruler Nezahualcóyotl, divided Lake Texcoco to form the artificial lake Lago de México, the shallow waters of which surrounded the Aztec capital Tenochtitlán. Twenty-three feet wide and ten miles long, the dike ran from Atzacoalco in the north—near Tepeyac Hill, where Juan Diego, according to Catholic tradition, met the Virgin of Guadalupe—to Iztapalapa in the south, and served to separate the brackish water of Lakes Texcoco, San Christobal, Xaltocan, and Zumpango in the east and north of the valley from the fresh water of Lakes Mexico, Xochimilco, and Chalco in the west and south. (These lakes were very shallow, averaging less than three feet in depth, and during the dry season the surface area would shrink significantly due to evaporation.)

In 1553, 1580, 1604, and 1607, Mexico City was inundated by devastating floods. The Spanish therefore opted for a radically different approach: drain the valley itself by building a complex water diversion system, which they called the Desagüe de Huehuetoca. This massive hydraulic project was started in 1607, when Mexico's Native population was near its nadir, and conducted under the direction of the German-born royal cosmographer, Enrico Martínez.[35] The project required the skills of technicians and the labor of thousands of Natives workers and cost millions of pesos to build and maintain. According to the scholar Louisa Schell Hoberman,

> Starting from the northernmost of the valley lakes, Lake Zumpango, the desagüe stretched a total of 8.02 miles over terrain rising 110 feet. It extended 3.89 miles from Lake Zumpango to the town of Huehuetoca at the northwest corner of the valley. From there it became a tunnel, continuing 3.84 miles to a spot called the Boca de San Gregorio. An exit canal of 0.39 miles conducted the water from that point to the gulch of Nochistongo, then to the Tula River, and, finally, out to the Gulf of Mexico. The tunnel was between 5.5 and 8.25 feet wide and about 11 feet high throughout. At its deepest point it lay 149 feet below the surface of the earth.[36]

The tunnel failed in the catastrophic flood of 1629, leaving the streets of Mexico City submerged for five years. As a result it was converted into an open canal or trench, the Tajo de Nochistongo. The conversion was enormously labor-intensive, and the canal required near-constant maintenance and improvisation to keep it clear. While the Spanish undertook this massive project, one of their spies noted that the encroaching English on the eastern shore of the continent, far to the north and east, had managed to erect a small three-sided fort of hewn wood on a poorly drained, malaria-prone site on the northeast bank of the James or Powhatan River.[37] The two projects—Fort James and the Desagüe—capture perfectly the different magnitudes of England and Spain's respective colonial efforts in the early seventeenth century.

The Spanish plan to drain and remake the entire Valley of Mexico eventually succeeded, with Lakes Zumpango, Xaltocan, San Cristóbal, Texcoco, and Chalco reduced and largely emptied. Lake Xochilmilco, to the south of Mexico City, remains a vestigial reminder, like an aquatic appendix, of the valley's once-extensive lacustrine environment. After visiting the Desagüe, Alexander von Humboldt pronounced it "one of the most gigantic hydraulic operations ever executed by man." Humboldt found that the Native Mexicans entertained "the most bitter hatred against the desague of Huehuetoca." In 1616, for example, no less than ten thousand repartimiento laborers worked on Mexico City's elaborate drainage system. The work was coerced and dangerous, and the wages were low.

In Middle and Upper North America, social power and social development complemented and reinforced each other, as we shall see. But this virtuous circle is never guaranteed. In fact, in Mexico the two worked against each other. On the one hand, the Desagüe was a good example of social power, if by that one means a society's ability to control its environment. On the other hand, this control, which was wielded by the few, came at the expense of the many—a situation not unlike that on the plantations of the American South. Indeed, according to Humboldt, "Many thousands of Indian labourers have been almost constantly occupied in the desague for two centuries; and it may be considered as a principal cause of the poverty of the Indians in the valley of Mexico."[38] He further opined, "The prosperity of the whites is intimately connected with that of the copper-colored race, and there can be no durable prosperity for the two Americas until this unfortunate race, humiliated but not degraded by long oppression, shall participate in all the advantages resulting from the progress of civilization and the improvement of social order!"[39]

Over two hundred years after Humboldt's visit, another student of the Desagüe, Vera Candiani, a Marxist and environmental historian, has fleshed out and elaborated upon the Prussian aristocrat's original insight into one of the root causes of Mexico's persistent poverty and inequality. And her conclusion, like that of Humboldt's, is hard to gainsay. To quote her on this important point:

> By transforming the physical, hydrological, and biological environment of the basin, the Desagüe irreversibly changed the conditions of life for everyone in it, rendering it more amenable to Spanish patterns of production. By keeping alive into the late colonial era the method of coerced Indigenous labor, it brought into play the protections conferred by the crown upon Indigenous villages and thereby had a hand in sustaining the peasantry as a class. By allowing elites in the city to remain focused on rentier priorities rather than productive ones while other sectors of this class were expanding capitalist social relations and modes of production into a variety of locales and activities, it militated against "founding capitalism," to borrow John Tutino's phrase, in all of New Spain. . . . Though "merely" a collection of excavations and built structures, the Desagüe mediated the superimposition in space of two distinct forms of society—the one transplanted by Europeans

vested in primarily private relations of property and production and
the one surviving from the pre-Hispanic period vested in primarily
communal ones. Each form of social organization had its own way
of valuing land and water and their respective biota. Outwardly divided by ethnicity, Hispanics and indigenes were more fundamentally
distinguished along the axis of social class. Each class and class sector had very different interests, and their conflicts played out in the
Desagüe-modified terrain of the basin, regulated by a dynastic state
apparatus with its own priorities. The complex and contingent process
of colonization that occurred in the basin was shaped largely by this
class-based conflict.[40]

Thus, the Desagüe de Huehuetoca—a unique adaptation and feat of
European engineering with Native elements and Native labor, organized
according to a pre-Hispanic labor regime, which primarily benefited
the Spanish and Criollo urban elites and their properties and modes of
production—goes far in explaining Mexico's economic and social underdevelopment, at least in the Valley of Mexico, relative to its North American
neighbors.[41] In short, the public benefit of the Desagüe was very narrow,
while its social cost ran very deep.[42] As we shall see, the impact of the mining industry on Mexico's development, in contrast to that of the Desagüe,
would be far more positive.

Mexico's Silver Lining

What brought the golden age of the encomenderos to its last act, the period from 1521 to 1550, was the rise of silver as a valuable commodity and
the catastrophic decline in the Native population, especially in the *cocoliztli* epidemics of 1545 and 1576. As the European or Criollo population
in Mexico steadily increased, the economy began to diversify and become
more self-sufficient. Its exports came to include wheat, textiles, dyes (cochineal and indigo), pottery, sugar, furniture, and other manufactures. This was
especially true after mid-century, with the discovery and development of
vast silver deposits in Mexico's Sierra Madre.[43] (In 1546, at roughly the same
time, the Spanish discovered the Cerro Rico in the viceroyalty of Peru). The
conquistadors in North and South America had failed to find the mythical
El Dorado, or the Seven Cities of Cíbola, although not for want of trying.
But what they did find was no less fabulous: the mother lode in Mexico and
a mountain of silver in Upper Peru (present-day Bolivia). These ores were,

however, of lower grade and resisted smelting, the traditional technique in Europe and the Americas for treating silver ore.[44]

In the 1550s, however, miners in Mexico learned how to refine low-grade silver ore by using an amalgamation or "patio" process involving mercury or quicksilver to separate the silver from the ore. The mercury was imported from Spain, where deposits were found at Almadén in the Sierra Morena. Once this technique began to be employed, Mexican silver truly became a transatlantic product.[45]

With the discovery of Mexico's mother lode, the invention of the patio process, the availability of Spanish-mined mercury, and the capital raised by joint-stock companies, Mexico's days as an inward-looking agrarian feudal and tributary state—the vision of the encomenderos—were numbered. Indeed, by 1600 the mining industry was contributing more than 80 percent of Mexico's total exports, with cochineal and cattle hides coming in a very distant second and third place, respectively. The silver-producing regions of Mexico included Zacatecas (the largest), Guadalajara, Guanajuato, Pachuca, Mexico City, San Luis Potosí, Sombrerete, and Durango. To find sufficient labor to work the mines, the Spanish initially relied on Indian draft labor within the old Aztec Empire. But by 1598 volunteer wage earners in the mines began to outnumber the disappearing repartimiento laborers, and eventually there were more European and Mestizo than Indian miners. The mines in the north had always relied on free labor, although such was not the case in the refining mills, which were worked largely by enslaved Africans.[46]

Natives from Michoacán and elsewhere migrated to the north to work in the mines on a permanent and professional basis. Moreover, the labor supply was never an issue for the Mexican mining industry, which at the time was the largest extractive industry in the world, since at most it needed only fifteen thousand workers. This was so because only so many men could fit into a horizontal adit, go down a vertical shaft, or go in a circle around a whim. It should be noted that while Mexico's mines were dominated by free wage labor, Peru and Bolivia relied at the same time on a forced labor system called the mita. Labor was the mining industry's main cost, reaching as much as 75 percent. However, with supportive crown policies—the *quinto real* (royal fifth) was reduced to a tithe, or *diezmo*—the industry thrived. The amount of Spanish silver export from the mines of Mexico and Peru was so large as to cause global inflation. In fact, no less than 90 percent of Mexico's silver was removed from the country.[47]

The Great Recovery

The turnaround of Mexico's population that occurred in the seventeenth century was probably due, at least in part, to better nutrition resulting from the introduction of new crops and new technology—wheeled transport, iron tools, and the plow (instead of digging sticks), to say nothing of draft animals. Seventeenth-century Mexico literally had the best of both worlds. Not everyone could own livestock like cattle, pigs, sheep, and goats, but even the poorest of the poor could afford chickens, which became ubiquitous in rural and urban Mexico. The Spanish thus introduced a very important source of protein—*huevos*—to the Native diet in what was a sort of democratization of the Columbian exchange. And to the Native staple of corn tortillas was added another staff of life: *blanco pan*, wheat bread. Now Mexico could not only feed itself without resorting to eating the flesh of its neighbors; it could clothe itself, too. *Obrajes* (workshops) and *tejedores* (weavers) produced wool fabric in towns such as Puebla, Coyoacán, and Querétaro.[48] The population recovery of the seventeenth century, however gradual, suggests that living standards must have improved over the course of the century, although the rates of infant mortality (nearly 300 per 1,000 live births) and death (life expectancy at birth was thirty to thirty-five years) would nevertheless remain stubbornly high and low, respectively, until the start of a major demographic transition in the twentieth century.

In the meantime Mexico City, the center of New Spain, became an important global crossroads. Linked to Asia by Acapulco and the Manilla galleons, and to Europe by Veracruz and the Spanish galleons and treasure fleets, via the Cuban port and safe haven of Havana, the city lorded it over the rest of Mexico. Moreover, during the seventeenth century, the officials and merchants of Mexico City more than their counterparts in Seville came to manage the affairs of the colony, as Spain's House of Hapsburg slipped into a century-long decline in what was for Europe a turbulent century of wars, depressions, and epidemics. France gradually replaced Spain as the dominant power in Europe, culminating in the France of the Sun King, Louis XIV, and the brilliant court of Versailles. Politics and culture, however, are not always entirely in sync. While American treasure did help finance Hapsburg Spain's Golden Age, that florescence lasted well into the seventeenth century and gave the world two of its greatest lights: the writer Miguel de Cervantes and the artist Diego Rodríguez de Silva y Velázquez.

The Bourbon Miracle

During the sixteenth and seventeenth centuries, Mexico's economy was neither feudalistic nor capitalistic. It was, as Enrique Semo has argued, a "heterogeneous system," one part feudalism, one part tributary despotism, and one part simple mercantilism. In developmental terms, it was precapitalist, or in a state of embryonic capitalism. Semo provides an unabashed and sparkling-clear Marxist analysis of Mexico's colonial economy:

> The system was made up of two basic structures: the *república de los indios* (despotic tributary) and the *república de [los] españoles* (feudal capitalist). The former consisted, on the one hand, of all the Indian communities and, on the other, of the *encomenderos*, the royal bureaucracy, and ecclesiastical hierarchy. The surplus product from the [Indian] communities took the form mainly of tribute in labor, kind, or money. The forces of production underwent some change, but they were not developed much more than in pre-Hispanic times. The latter emerged from the process of colonization and *mestizaje*. Its basic units were the *estancia*, the *hacienda*, the mill, the mine, the workshop, and the *obraje*. The income of the dominant classes derived from the surplus labor of Indian and African workers, granted in *encomienda* or distributed in *repartimiento* to Spanish properties as slaves, free wage laborers, or *peones*, and from the commercial exploitation of communities and independent petty commodity producers. . . . In the North, mining and extensive cattle raising prevailed and peasant communities were weak. In the center, developed communities [that] coexisted with sizable Spanish enterprises. In the South, the [Indian] community remained strong and Spanish colonization advanced slowly. The apex of the system was one and the same: the Crown, the Church, and the metropolitan and dominant classes.[49]

There is a good deal of merit to this basic sketch, although it fails to emphasize the importance of the dynamic role played by the silver industry in Mexico's eighteenth-century economy. Colonial Mexico was not a static society locked in class conflict. One can only speculate on what Mexico might have been had the mining industry survived, but it was wrecked: indirectly by France's Revolution and Napoleonic Wars, and directly by Mexico's own wars of insurgency and independence, which pitted New Spain's Criollo hacendados (owners of large estates) against the *peninsulares*, Spanish-born officials of the crown.

One of the crown's priorities in the aftermath of the War of the Spanish Succession was to increase the production of silver in Mexico's mines. Since the crown owned the mercury mines of Almadén in Spain, it enjoyed a monopoly over an item that was indispensable to the patio process. The crown used this monopoly very wisely, increasing the supply of mercury and at the same time lowering its unit price. These actions reduced the crown's per-unit income from its mercury sales. However, as the Spanish scholars Rafael Dobado and Gustavo A. Marrero demonstrate, this policy, an early instance of supply-side economics, was "more than counterbalanced by an increase in the revenue from taxation on silver extraction, since more silver was thus produced and fiscally controlled. Moreover, the positive backward linkages that mining had with other sectors . . . also had a positive impact on aggregate demand, on the level of general economic activity and consequently on non-mining tax receipts." The consequent rise in Mexico's silver production under the Bourbons was impressive (though just as impressive was the subsequent collapse of the mining industry, after Mexico gained its independence from Spain). And the rise would have not occurred on the scale that it did without the security of property under the rule of law.[50]

As Dobado and Marrero succinctly put it: "The imperial state did not confiscate income or assets that belonged to individuals who were exploiting mineral deposits." The mining laws passed to this effect under the Hapsburgs, such as the Ordenanzas del Nuevo Cuaderno of 1584, were later reinforced by the Bourbons' Reales Ordenanzas of 1783. The economic progress made under the Bourbons would be undone, however, by events in Europe, which provided the international context in New Spain for first the insurgency of 1810–15 and then the fight for independence in 1820–21.[51]

From 1700 to 1809 Mexico's silver industry averaged an annual growth rate of 1.8 percent, thus inviting comparison, as Dobado and Marrero further point out, to British coal production in the second half of the eighteenth century. Mexico also surpassed Peru as Spain's major silver producer. By 1800 silver represented 75 percent of Mexico's total exports, followed by cochineal and sugar. And Mexico's mines—by 1800 there were at least three thousand of them, all in private, mostly middle-class hands—produced two-thirds of the world's output of silver. In the economic shorthand of Dobado and Marrero: from 1720 to 1800 "mercury consumption in New Spain" was up; "silver production in New Spain" was up; "economic activity in New Spain" was up; "tax collection in New Spain" was up; and "fiscal surplus remittances to the metropolis and other colonies" were up. New mining centers—a "dense network" of five hundred of them and North America's first mining boomtowns (after Zacatecas) and industrial operations—also popped up all over northern Mexico, including the Bajío, a Goldilocks geographical and cultural region in central and northern Mexico, which comprises the nonmountainous areas of the states of Guanajuato, Querétaro, Aguascalientes, and San Luis Potosí as well as eastern Jalisco and northern Michoacán. This was the core or heart of New Spain, outside of Mexico City, and later the center of Mexico's independence movement. (The Dolores of Miguel Hidalgo y Costilla's Cry of Dolores, or Grito de Dolores, is a town situated between San Miguel and San Luis Potosí). Unlike the south, the north was also where *españoles* (White Europeans) and Mestizos outnumbered Natives, which worked against forced labor. In the north, "mining was based on the existence of a free labour market with a high mobility of well-paid miners."[52] On this point, the modern views of Dobado and Marrero essentially agree with those of Alexander von Humboldt, the Prussian savant and mining expert. As the historian Jaime E. Rodríguez O. sums up the situation, at "the end of the eighteenth century, New Spain—with a population of nearly six million—was the richest, most populous, most developed part of the Spanish Monarchy in America."[53]

The rich art and architectural legacy of Fresnillo, Guanajuato, San Miguel el Grande (renamed San Miguel de Allende after independence), Sombrerete, Querétaro, Silao, Zacatecas, and other mining or mining-derived cities can still leave the mouth of the visitor agape in wonder. Indeed, the colonial city of Zacatecas, founded in 1546, represented perhaps in its time the zenith of European urbanism in North America. It was as though Florence, Italy, had been copied and replicated at the foot of Mexico's Cerro de la Bufa. True, Zacatecas, San Miguel, and other cities may not have been home to a Michelangelo or a Leonardo da Vinci, but they were nevertheless home to architects, builders, and painters of a very high order.

A roll call of distinguished names would include those of Miguel Cabrera, Nicolás and Juan Rodríguez Juárez, Juan Correra, Cristóbal de Villalpando, José de Ibarra, Miguel Antonio Martínez de Pocasangre (who painted the Sanctuary of Atotonilco, Mexico's Sistine Chapel, which lies to the northwest of San Miguel toward Dolores), and Juan Patricio Morlete Ruiz. And just as crucially, all of these artisans and artists had patrons—in San Miguel el Grande, for example, the Criollo families of Malo, Lámbarri, Moncada y Berrio, Allende, Landeta, Aldama, Sautto, Verver y Vargas, Lanzagorta, Humanrán, and de la Canal—who possessed the wealth to pay for their services. Manuel Tomás de la Canal alone spent more than 200,000 pesos on San Miguel el Grande's beautification.

By 1777 Juan Benito Díaz de Gamarra, an Italian-educated professor at San Miguel's College of San Francisco de Sales, was able to declare the town of San Miguel el Grande "one of the most beautiful and celebrated in this northern America."[54] He was most assuredly right. Gamarra introduced Enlightenment thought to New Spain and authored *Elements of Modern Philosophy* (1774) and *Errors of Human Understanding* (1781). He literally taught his students how to think on their own—a precondition, certainly, of independence.

The mines and their wealth also stimulated suppliers centered in towns such as San Miguel, where wool, leather, animal fat, meat, soap, candles, ironwork, saddles, hats, and serapes (derived from Otomí blankets) were made and grains, fruits, and vegetables traded. And the mines, the richest in the world, favored the careful cultivation of the surrounding country-side, which reminded Humboldt of the beautiful fields in France. Bourbon Mexico, like the capitalist United States a century later, had become a land of "increasing returns" and "positive feedbacks."[55]

Still, we have to qualify this pretty picture. Spain had indeed relaxed its iron grip on Mexico's economy beginning in 1778, allowing more free-dom to trade—but only with Spain and other points within the Spanish Empire. In other words, there was more trade within what remained very much a closed system. One of Spain's great statesmen and figures of the Enlightenment, Gaspar Melchor de Jovellanos, was indeed a disciple of Adam Smith. But Jovellanos's country remained mercantilist, thinking in terms of the wealth of a *nation*, rather than the wealth of *nations*. And so while increased trade did lead to more growth within the Spanish Empire, which benefited Mexico, it was not nearly enough to compete with the British Empire, the very embodiment of the Enlightenment's clenched fist and invisible hand.

To illustrate the difference: in 1762 Spain permitted fifteen ships to en-ter the Cuban port of Havana. The following year, after eleven months of British occupation (this was the time of the Seven Years' War), the British, in contrast, allowed *seven hundred* ships to drop anchor and conduct business. Havana was transformed by this sudden and intense economic activity. By the late eighteenth century there was simply no comparison between the trade of the Spanish and that of the British Empire, a point easily lost in the noisy rhetoric of the American revolutionaries. The Spanish monopoly was crippling, serving only the interests of small groups. Moreover, the Spanish feared not only trade in foreign goods but also the exchange of foreign ideas, especially after 1789, with the start of the French Revolution. (To be fair, the threat of these radical new ideas had a chilling effect in Quebec as well.) In any event, by this point the days of Spanish mercantilism, reformed or otherwise, were numbered. The turmoil caused by the French Revolution and France's subsequent Napoleonic Wars, with their attendant naval blockades, would violently shake the American fruit off Spain's colonial tree, except for the islands of Cuba and Puerto Rico (the latter was not far from Hispaniola, where Spain's great imperial adventure in the Americas began). As Spain's fortunes in its North American enterprise started to falter, British and Yankee traders were only too eager to take advantage of the nation's European distractions and calamities.[56] And unfortunately the turmoil in Europe, as reflected in the troubled reigns of Spain's Charles IV (Carlos IV, 1788–1808), Napoleon's older brother Joseph Bonaparte (1808–13), and Ferdinand VII (Fernando VII, 1813–33), would all but destroy Bourbon Mexico's social and economic gains, leaving the country weak and dangerously isolated.

CHAPTER 7

Mexico's Axial Age

Our Lady of Guadalupe

WHEN THE GERMAN PHILOSOPHER KARL Jaspers called the middle centuries of the first millennium BC the Axial Age, he used *axial* in the sense of "pivotal." With this term, he referred to the remarkable advances in ethical and religious thinking that occurred in the four classical civilizations of Eurasia at this time—civilizations we consider classical because their legacy continues to influence our own times. In China, there appeared the Hundred Schools of Thought, including Confucianism, Daoism, and Legalism; to the south, in India, a modified ancient Hinduism gave rise to Buddhism and Jainism; the Middle East produced Zoroastrianism and Judaism (and later the Abrahamic religions of Christianity and Islam); and rational philosophy originated in the eastern Mediterranean. This revolution in thought, specifically the Western variant of it, was brought to Mexico beginning in the sixteenth century and was later extended throughout the continent of North America.[1]

All of these Old World traditions shared a social background of growing affluence, which changed behavior as well as thinking, from a "narrative and analogical style," to quote the scholar Nicolas Baumard, to a more analytical and reflective style, probably due to the increasing use of external memory tools," (that is, writing).[2]

This evolving technology allowed peoples, or at least the elites among them, to record and thereby externalize or objectify their beliefs. Writing opened up a critical distance—quite literally—between man and text, believer and belief, mythos and logos, and the local and the universal. It is possible, of course, to have good thinking without writing; but it is impossible to have good writing without good thinking. And it was this linkage that accelerated the evolution of culture, giving humanity the tragedies of Aeschylus, the *Analects* of Confucius, the Book of Psalms, and much else.

Among the peoples of the Americas, the Maya alone invented a written language that corresponded to their spoken word. They wrote their language in codices, folding books made of fig-bark paper, or carved it into stone—both costly and tedious processes. Most of the codices were destroyed by Christian priests in fits of religious zealotry. In fact, there are only four extant: the Madrid, Paris, Dresden, and Grolier codices. Based on the available evidence, the Maya recorded information of almanac interest (for example, when to go to war) or dynastic interest (that such and such a king was born in such and such a place and in such and such a year). If Maya writers expressed thoughts of a higher order, they have been sadly lost to posterity. In any event, writing in pre-Hispanic North America was probably limited to a very small elite, as had long been true in Eurasia and elsewhere.

On the significance of literacy to social development, Walter J. Ong, a professor of English literature and a Jesuit priest, has expressed the idea as well anyone:

> Oral cultures indeed produce powerful and beautiful verbal performances of high artistic and human worth, which are no longer even possible once writing has taken possession of the psyche. *Nevertheless, without writing, human consciousness cannot achieve its fuller potentials, cannot produce other beautiful and powerful creations* [italics mine]. In this sense, orality needs to produce and is destined to produce writing. Literacy . . . is absolutely necessary for the development not only of science but also of history, philosophy, explicative understanding of literature and of any art, and indeed for the explanation of language (including oral speech) itself.[3]

In Europe, literacy spread with the Christian conversion of the continent, a very slow and halting process that vied at times with the spread of Islam (as in Spain and Sicily) and created productive tensions between church and state, with lasting political consequences. Christianity was not tolerated in the Roman Empire until the early fourth century. And it would take centuries more for monks and missionaries under the institutional leadership of the papacy to spread the gospel of Roman Catholicism from the old cities of the Mediterranean basin to the rural backwaters of northern and western

Europe. This involved countless conversions at different times and in different places, which sometimes required creative adaptations and repurposing of local customs, beliefs, and sacred places with the exotic Roman import. The replacement of pagan tree worship with Christmas trees, wreaths, and garlands was but one example of this process of appropriation and assimilation. Not until the late fourteenth century, over a thousand years after the conversion of the emperor Constantine in AD 337, were the pagans of the Grand Duchy of Lithuania, the last pagans in Europe, finally baptized prior to joining a dynastic union with Poland. To put it another way, one of the great achievements or cultural transformations of the Middle Ages was the conversion of the entire continent of Europe to Christianity.[4] We should note that both Iceland and Greenland were converted in 1000, so European paganism did have a very brief life in North America (Greenland was settled fifteen years earlier by Eric the Red). In the eleventh century a bishopric was established in 1126 at Gardar, where the Cathedral of Saint Nicholas was built. This faith was extinguished with the retreat or destruction of the Norse settlements in the fifteenth century, but was reintroduced by Danish Lutherans in the eighteenth century.[5]

It is in the light of this European history that the Christianization of Mexico is perhaps best understood. On the heels of their military conquest, the Spanish delivered the Requerimiento (Requirement) of 1513 to the defeated Natives, demanding that they convert or face enslavement or, worse, death. The Franciscans, led by Fray Toribio de Benavente (or Motolinía, "the poor one"), arrived in New Spain in 1524, followed by the other mendicant orders—the Dominicans in 1527 and the Augustinians in 1533. In Europe, the mendicants had taken care of the urban poor. In Mexico they wished to evangelize as well as to take care of the needs of the Native population, who resided largely in the countryside.

The mendicant orders sorted themselves out by region. The Franciscans established themselves in the north, the Dominicans in the south, and the Augustinians in the unclaimed spaces between the other two.[6] The Jesuits followed much later, in 1572, and focused on the needs of the urban elites, the *peninsulares* (Spanish-born Europeans) and the Criollos (Mexican-born Europeans). The Jesuits, notably the Italian Eusebio Francisco Kino, also established missions in the far northern frontier of the country, "the Rim of Christendom," comprising the Pimería Alta (Sonora and Arizona) and Baja California as well as New Mexico and Texas.[7] Among the many accomplishments of Kino, the "padre on horseback," was his proof that—contrary to the commonly held belief at the time, as depicted on existing maps—California was not an island. (Hernando de Alarcón and others had long before pointed this fact out, but that knowledge was promptly forgotten because it was useless at the time.) Kino's map of 1705, which showed the clear outline of the Gulf of California and the land passage from Pimería Alta to Alta California, was a major contribution to the understanding of the geography of North America.[8]

The orders set themselves a monumental task: the conversion of pagan Mexico. In the words of the French authority Robert Ricard, "Before the arrival of the Spaniards, paganism had permeated the whole life of the Indians, from birth to death, from the temple to the hearth, in war and in peace. Such was the life that had to be imbued with Christianity."[9] The Spanish prohibition against human sacrifice (the whole point of Christ's crucifixion, from the missionary's point of view, was that it obviated any further need for such acts) and cannibalism, ritual or otherwise, struck at the heart of this belief system, which took as many as twenty thousand victims a year—to say nothing of the fearsome tyranny it required and the terror it induced. But the friars went well beyond that. In seven years, the Franciscans claimed to have destroyed twenty thousand idols. If we take the church men at their word, that came to 2,857 per year, or nearly 8 idols per day. That was a lot of grabbing and smashing.

And they developed a strategy that was sharply attuned to the basic cleavage of Native society. First, they would bring about the deep conversion of the Indian nobles or *caciques*, above all their sons, who were set aside and instructed in special schools; and second, they would employ a much lighter standard of conversion for the *macehualtin*, whose guarded ignorance would protect them from error. To this end, the friars introduced the ethics of the Axial Age to pagan Mexico, which was no small thing. They did it by reducing the Ten Commandments to one simple golden rule: "Do unto others as you would have them do to you, and do not do unto them as you would not have them do unto you."[10]

Many colonists (or rather "subjects"), to say nothing of the Indians themselves, helped create a new civilization in North America. The church's contribution began with Motolinía's friars, known as the Twelve Apostles. In 1524 they walked on bare feet from Veracruz to Mexico City (a distance of 227 miles), where they were welcomed by none other than Hernán Cortés. The great conquistador knelt in the dust and kissed the hand of their leader, Martín de Valencia, in a gesture of humility and deference performed in front of a gathering of Spanish and "astonished" Indian nobles and *caciques*.[11] Cortés intended that the past of the Antilles—one stained black by exploitation and depopulation—would not be the future of Mexico. And his efforts did bear fruit.

According to tradition, in 1531, seven years after the prodigious pedestrian feat of the Franciscans, the Virgin Mary first appeared as a light-brown-skinned woman (Our Lady of Guadalupe) to an Aztec convert, Juan Diego, who had been born in 1474 as Cuauhtlatoatzin.[12] In several subsequent apparitions, Mary asked Diego—significantly in the native language of Nahuatl rather than in the tongue of the conqueror—that a shrine be built to her on Tepeyac Hill, north of, but now encircled by, Mexico City. Juan Diego—now known as Saint Diego—obliged. This event, which started at the center of Mexico and eventually spread to the periphery, marked the beginnings of Mexico's mass conversions and baptisms, a complex cross-cultural phenomenon that involved far more than the European coercion of Native peoples. It was an enculturation that took decades, if not centuries, to complete.[13] As in Europe, it involved appropriation—in pre-Hispanic times, for instance, there had been a shrine at Tepeyac Hill, where the Aztec earth goddess Tonantzin was worshipped.[14]

And as in Europe, it also involved assimilation, a cross-cultural process and as such a two-edged sword. Located at Tepeyac Hill today is a new, modern Basilica de Guadalupe (the old colonial-era structure had become destabilized and dangerous), complete with moving walkways to whisk millions of visitors each year past the physical evidence of Mary's encounter with Juan, namely her image imprinted on his *tilma*, or cloak (the artifact is encased in bullet-proof glass). Tepeyac is perhaps the most widely regarded sacred space in North America and one of the most important pilgrimage destinations in the entire Christian world.[15] Moreover, the image of Our Lady of Guadalupe has become a potent symbol of Mexican nationalism. In 1810, at the start of Mexico's war of independence against Spain—essentially an inverted crusade rather than a belated chapter in the age of Democratic revolution—Miguel Hidalgo y Costilla, a Mexican priest-turned-revolutionary, marched under the banner of the Virgin to the battle cry "Long live the Virgin of Guadalupe and Death to the Spaniards."[16]

One may reasonably question the level of sincerity or depth of comprehension of the numerous individual and group conversions that occurred in post-Conquest Mexico; according to one report by Motolinía, fifteen thousand baptisms were performed in Xochimilco by two priests

Figure 11. N. Currier, *Nuestra senora de Guadalupe: our lady of Guadalupe*, ca. 1848. New York: N. Currier. Hand-colored lithograph. Prints and Photographs Division, Library of Congress, Washington, DC. https://www.loc.gov/item/2002710685/.

on a single day. Over time, however, Christianity would take deep root. In 2014, according to the Pew Research Center, 81 percent of Mexican adults identified as Catholic, the highest percentage in Latin America. This near denominational monopoly would set Mexico far apart from its more religiously diverse North American neighbors. Indeed, if British North America, with its Mayflower Pilgrims and Massachusetts Puritans, was a product of the Protestant Reformation, then Catholic Mexico and Catholic Quebec were continuations of medieval Europe, and both were influenced by the Counter-Reformation.[17] Historian Kevin Starr is right to assert that there can be "no understanding of American culture and history without an understanding of the role played by Catholic peoples in the unfolding drama of the American experience," from colonial times to the present. This statement is also true of the experiences of both Mexico and Canada.[18]

Literacy and the Inquisition

Unfortunately, the program of salvation light for the Indian masses, once implemented, was never substantially modified. Toward the end of the colonial era Mexico had a population of six million, but only a negligible number of primary schools. Education had been, and very much continued to be, confined to the country's urban elites. In 1925, over a century after it achieved its independence from Spain, Mexico's literacy rate was still barely 36 percent, and female literacy was even lower. The church bears much of the blame for this sad state of affairs. While it certainly possessed the resources to teach the masses to read and write, it persisted in the belief that ignorance was bliss. In sharp contrast to the role the Catholic Church played in Mexico, the Church of Sweden, which was Protestant, launched a literacy campaign based not on school but on family instruction or homeschooling. From 1660 to 1720, the literacy rate went from 35 to 90 percent—and this in a country which was overwhelmingly agrarian at the time. This was because Martin Luther's catechism was required reading. The notion as well as the reality, then, of near universal literacy existed in the Western world during the colonial era and was nearly achieved in Scandinavia.[19]

Indeed, the church owned more than half of the land in use in Mexico, and as New Spain's most important moneylender (merchants were another) it possessed two-thirds of the capital in circulation. Moreover, the church directed its loans principally to hacienda owners in return for *censos* (liens) on their real estate. The hacendados typically used these loans for the purchase of luxury items or to build sumptuous homes and estates—that is, on conspicuous consumption rather than on investments that could have made Mexico's economy more productive and diversified. Thus the church not only kept the people of Mexico ignorant but also hindered the country's economic development. In Europe the Protestant Reformation had challenged the church's authority over education, and there were numerous translations of the Bible into different vernaculars. But there was no such movement in New Spain. The colonial Holy Office of the Inquisition, established in New Spain in 1571, had done its job all too well.[20]

In his *Historia eclesiástica indiana*, the sixteenth-century Franciscan millenarian and historian Gerónimo de Mendieta described the limits of literacy in Mexico:

In all the towns there has been built a school. In the same school, in a room by itself, or in the same one if it is large, reading and writing are taught the children of the important people, after they have learned Christian doctrine, which is the only thing taught to the common people out there on the patio, and having learned this they are dismissed so that they can help their parents in their farming or jobs, although in some places there was some carelessness in making this difference (especially in the small villages, where there are few people) so that all the children were taught without distinction, the sons of the principal persons and of the common people, to read and write in the schools, and from this there follows that in these towns the common people rule and command over the plebeians, having been elected to these offices by being the most capable and sufficient.[21]

Mendieta's history was completed in 1596, toward the end of his life (it was not published until 1870, however, after it was unearthed by the Mexican scholar Joaquín García Icazbalceta).

For using literacy as a measure of social development, New Mexico serves as a case in point. Although founded as a colony in 1598, the province did not receive its first printing press until 1836, two hundred and thirty-eight years later and well after Mexico's independence from Spain! This far northern country, which was roughly bisected by the Rio Grande, may have been (and still is) a land of enchantment, but it was decidedly not a land of enlightenment—a description that applies equally well to Old Mexico.[22] In short, education was limited almost entirely to New Spain's elite, whether of Native or European descent, a group that did include women such as the remarkable and self-taught nun and thinker Sor Juana Inés de la Cruz. Still, in 1811 Mexico City's newspaper, the *Diarío de México*, had a single day's print run of only seven thousand copies.[23] It is hard to gainsay the historian Henry Bamford Parkes's conclusion, however dated, that the church's contribution to colonial Mexico was a "despotic government, a privileged priesthood, and an ignorant laity."[24] And it is not hard to understand the subsequent deep anticlericalism and reformism that infected Mexico's politics in the nineteenth and twentieth centuries. The colonial church was in the business of saving souls, not minds.

To put Mexican literacy into an Atlantic context, with the advent of printing, the ability to read and write rose in Europe between 35 and 40 percent during the sixteenth century. It fell again during the wars and depressions of the seventeenth century, but by the mid-nineteenth century about half of the population of Europe was literate. Literacy was generally higher among the upper classes, among males, and in urban areas. And it was generally higher in northern than in southern Europe, the latter being largely Catholic, relatively poorer, and more rural. White literacy in British North America was higher than in Europe, and universal White literacy was achieved earlier in North America—where the gap in the literacy rate between men and women was also narrower—than in Europe. But there were significant discrepancies between regions and races. In New England, literacy was higher than elsewhere; native-born White literacy was higher than for immigrant Whites, and White literacy was higher than it was for non-White groups. On the other hand, the rate of literacy in Spain remained quite low. As late as 1860, three out of four people aged ten or older in the land of Cervantes could not read or write; by 1940, it was still as high as one out of four. As it was in Spain, so it was in Mexico.[25]

Feeding Souls and Stomachs

If the early missionaries or evangelists in Mexico believed that as far as the masses were concerned, ignorance of anything beyond the catechism was bliss, this does not mean that they did not care about social development. On the contrary, this is why there was, to quote Robert Ricard again, the "teaching and development of agriculture, the introduction of new crops and industries. . . the opening of roads to facilitate the transport of food, the building of aqueducts. . . the founding of hospitals. . .[and] the organization of primary schools, technical schools, and schools of music."[26] These schools, however, were intended for the children of the Native elite, not for Mexico's masses, and they replaced the *calmecatl*, the old Aztec schools in which students learned about the prephonetics and hieroglyphic writing of the pictograph codes.[27] By 1532 more than five thousand students were enrolled in monastery schools throughout central Mexico—in Acapistla, Cholula, Coyoacán, Cuahutitlan, Cuernavaca, Huejotzingo, Tepeaca, Texcoco, Tlalmanalco, Tlaxcala, and Tula. The largest of these schools, with a student body of six hundred, was San José de Belen de los Naturales (Saint Joseph of the Natives), located in Mexico City and founded by Fray Pedro de Gante. It was at this school that Arnald of Bassac, a French Franciscan, offered instruction in Latin for the first time in Latin America.[28]

In 1536, to facilitate further the evangelization of the Native population, the Franciscans founded the college of Santa Cruz de Santiago de Tlatelolco. A boarding school, it offered a curriculum based on the seven liberal arts of the *trivium* (grammar, logic, and rhetoric) and the *quadrivium* (arithmetic, geometry, music, and astronomy).[29] The student body was exclusively Indian (and male). To be accepted to North America's first institution of higher learning, a student had to be "an Indian born of a legitimate marriage, from caciques or noble birth and not of 'macegual,' despicable or blemished origin, or marked because of their own vulgar behavior or that of their parents."[30] By 1699 the college had been turned into an elementary school, but not before it had produced several generations of alumni who helped the friars to write vocabularies, doctrines, and histories as well as to serve as teachers and administrators.

The Augustinians founded another college in Mexico City in 1537, this one open to Natives and Europeans alike. Unlike the Franciscans and the Augustinians, the Dominicans opposed educating Native peoples on the grounds that it would invite heresy—a view widely shared among the European population, including the former conquistador Don Jerónimo López. On October 20, 1541, Lopez wrote Emperor Charles V, beseeching him to close the college of Santa Cruz de Santiago de Tlatelolco on the grounds that Natives would draw the wrong lessons from their education, confusing, for instance, the teachings and moralities of the Old and New Testaments.[31] Spanish artisans, with their guild mentality, had a less elevated motive for keeping Natives ignorant: they wanted to keep from them the secrets of their skills to prevent competition. Nevertheless there emerged a class of technically trained Native artisans in various crafts and trades—blacksmiths, carpenters, tailors, shoemakers, painters, and stonecutters.[32]

In addition to new crafts and trades, Europeans also introduced new crops, notably wheat, which was raised on estancias located near urban areas, and livestock—sheep, cattle, pigs, and especially chickens, namely, the Mediterranean hen.[33] Still, beef consumption was also important—as were hides for export. In Mexico, cattle herds grew dramatically during the 1500s, as did the number of slaughterhouses among the Native as well as the European and Mestizo populations. By the seventeenth century as many as twenty thousand head of cattle were driven from New Galicia to New Spain.[34] Mexico's emergent vaquero culture and hacienda system had roots in Iberia; the same cultural complex would later greatly influence the storied cowboy and ranch traditions of the American West.

But if the missionaries tried to Europeanize or Westernize the Natives, they nevertheless sought at the same time to protect them from the corrupting influences of Europeans, Spanish and otherwise. To do so, they worked to keep the majority of the Indians isolated or congregated—physically in their own villages or pueblos, and linguistically in their own languages. Throughout the colonial era the Spanish used Nahuatl, the lingua franca of pre-Hispanic Mesoamerica, as an official language for documentation and communication.[35] This policy of isolation and/or segregation had a profoundly negative long-term effect. As Ricard put it, the isolation opened "a gulf between the two elements" and kept "the Indian mass outside the general evolution of their country." The result of this policy was that "one of the essential problems of Mexico [was how] to incorporate the Indian into civil and civilized life," and thereby address the country's ancient problems of poverty and inequality.[36] This was written in 1934 in the midst of the Great Depression. In fact, as of August 10, 2021, eighty-seven years later, according to Mexico's National Council for the Evaluation of Social Development Policy, as reported by BBVA Research, 56 million Mexicans, nearly 44 percent of the nation's population, live below the poverty line, many of them in southern states like Chiapas and Oaxaca, which have large Native populations. Of these 56 million Mexicans, nearly 10.8 million, or 8.5 percent, live in extreme poverty. Since Ricard, there has been a great deal of scholarship on Mexican inequality. But he was right: there are still two Mexicos.

Hispanic civilization or urbanism, which segregated Mexico into the *república de los indios* and the *república de los españoles*, drew on both Native and European elements. It also included notable innovations. The growth of cities is usually associated with nineteenth-century industrialization, but in New Spain it was the sixteenth century that witnessed a golden age of urbanization. New cities and towns were founded for military and commercial reasons, as well as to keep Indians apart and thereby protect them from Europeans. In contrast, the old Native community or *altepetl* lacked boundaries or centers.

These new European cities replaced pre-Columbian irregularity with Spanish geometry and were based on gridiron or checkerboard plans, already known in the Old World and not unknown in the New, as in Teotihuacán and Tenochtitlán. What was different was the plaza, or public square, where the town's two main axes met, the four sides of which were lined with religious and civil buildings. The plaza was the gathering point and heart of the community, a fact as true today as it was then. Mexico City's Zócalo is only the most famous and monumental example. According to historian George Kubler, "Mexican plazas . . . are unprecedented in general European practice, but for a very few exceptions. Their form is suggested, not in coeval European towns, but in Italian theory of the fifteenth and sixteenth centuries, where the relation between open spaces and house blocks was an object of constant study."[37] Also notable were Mexico's churches, which were surrounded by a courtyard and walls. Interestingly, the churches were fortified while the rest of the town was left open to attack. This was a defensive decision meant to protect the defenders from a rebellion from within as well as secure them from an attack from without. On Mexico's urbanism, Kubler concludes that this "program constitutes one of the most important chapters of civic art in occidental history. It enjoyed dimensions not often encountered in Europe: the dimensions of free experiment, surging expansion, and unlimited resources. There is nothing to compare with it either after the Roman Empire or before the industrial creations of the nineteenth century."[38]

And if the *república de los indios* and the *república de los españoles* were initially divided by race, they were united by the Hispanic town plan, which would later serve, as the population recovered and expanded in the seventeenth and eighteenth centuries, as the basis of a common civilization. For example, Santiago de Querétaro, a city distinguished by a stunning Romanesque aqueduct—five and a half miles long, seventy-five feet high, and with no less than seventy-five arches—is a good example of a Hispanic space, and center of social power, where Indians, Europeans, and Mestizos learned to live and work together. Situated between Mexico City and the mines of Zacatecas, Querétaro was founded as a pueblo de los indios in the sixteenth century, but as Mexico's mining sector expanded and the economy grew, it became a cosmopolitan pueblo de los españoles in 1655.

It should be noted that given Mexico's size, its population density was low. But by 1800 there were nineteen or more towns with a population greater than ten thousand, according to Humboldt—which meant that 9.1 percent of Mexico's population was urban (in comparison, 6 percent of the US population was urban in that year). In terms of population, Mexico City was the largest city in North America—and still is. Humboldt estimated that the population was somewhere between 135,000 and 200,000, 67,500 of whom were European Mexicans or Whites. But urban development in middle and upper North America was catching up with Mexico's; both Philadelphia and New York City had reached a population of 60,000 by 1800. Still, Mexico's rate of urbanization compared favorably at the time with the average for Europe, outside of the Netherlands and Great Britain.[39] In conclusion, for much of the colonial period it was an oxymoronic fact that Mexico was both more urban and less literate than the rest of European and largely Protestant North America.[40]

Counting Dollars and Souls

By turning to macroeconomic history, we can try to answer the question of what all of this means for the social development of lower North America or Mexico. For 1500, the late Angus Maddison has estimated Mexico's population at 7.5 million souls (Spain's at the time stood at 6.8 million) and calculated Mexico's per capita GDP at $425 in 1990 international dollars.[41] By 1600, despite a drastic drop in population and a decline in GDP to $1.1 billion, from $3.2 billion in 1500, Maddison's estimated per capita gross domestic product for Mexico in 1600 had actually increased to $454. And how does the seventeenth century look in terms of the numbers? According to Maddison, Mexico's per capita GDP increased from $454 in 1600 to $568 in 1700. Mexico's total GDP in 1700 was $2.6 billion, up from $1.1 billion in 1600 but, remarkably, down from $3.2 billion from the start of the sixteenth century.[42]

To put these figures into a continental perspective, in 1700 Mexico's GDP was nearly thirty times as large as Canada's and nearly five times as large as that of the prefederal and federal United States (this term refers to a national account, that is, to the territory that becomes or is the United States; depending on the context, this is true of the terms *Canada* and *Mexico* as well). For the first two centuries after Cortés, then, Spanish North America's social development, as defined by per capita GDP, was ahead of that of both middle and upper North America. Looking ahead, however, these two regions—the Hispanosphere and the Anglosphere—would trade places by 1820. In this respect, the eighteenth is the most crucial century in North American history.

We should note that Maddison based his calculations, in part, on the work of John H. Coatsworth, a leading scholar of Latin American history whose own per capita GDP numbers for Mexico were significantly higher: $550 for 1500, and $755 for 1600. Not only were Coatsworth's numbers higher for both years, but the increase in GDP he showed during the sixteenth century was much greater. These differences notwithstanding, Coatsworth concluded:

> It is now generally accepted that the areas of Latin America under effective Spanish or Portuguese control probably enjoyed per capita incomes on a par with Western Europe and at least equal to the British colonies that became the United States well into the eighteenth century. Maddison . . . estimates that in 1700 the thirteen British Colonies in North America had a per capita GDP well below the Caribbean and Mexico and barely equal to the average for Latin America. Others have put Cuba's GDP per capita higher than that of the United States until the 1830s, though Mexico had already fallen well behind by 1800.[43]

The Great Land Redistribution

During the seventeenth century, despite its ups and downs, the Mexican economy turned from the earlier exaction of tribute—labor and goods— by the encomenderos, as well as crown and church, to the production of livestock, clothes, foodstuffs, and mineral wealth, above all silver. This production occurred on the largely Criollo-owned haciendas, estancias, *minas*, and *obrajes* and was intended for both in-country consumption and international export. This development marked a fundamental shift of economic activity away from the *república de los indios* to the *república de los españoles* and occurred only in Spanish North America, where the Native population was conquered and incorporated, rather than in British

North America, where the Native population was pushed back, removed, assimilated, or simply overwhelmed. In the continent's upper regions, the populations of Natives and Europeans, as they faced each other across a slowly advancing western frontier, were often either roughly equivalent in size or the Europeans enjoyed, or would soon enjoy, a decisive numerical advantage. In colonial Mexico, on the other hand, Europeans remained a small and distinct minority of the total population.[44]

These differences set Mexico apart from the rest of North America, where the factor endowments of land, labor, and capital would arrange themselves into very different permutations, with very different socio-economic consequences. Indeed, during the seventeenth and eighteenth centuries, Mexico had produced a semipeasantry, while at the same time a yeomanry took form in the continent's land-abundant Anglosphere. In 1500 the hunting, gathering, and horticultural economy of what became the United States could support only 2 million people, whereas the modern US economy can support 331.5 million. The only question was: On what basis or bases would this revolution in land redistribution proceed—by purchase, diplomacy, or war? Moreover, Canada possessed an even larger land mass and, in 1500, at 250,000, it had an even smaller Native population. The redistribution of land there followed along the same lines as it did in the prefederal and federal United States. In both territories today, Native peoples make up a distinct minority—between 2 and 4.5 percent of the overall population.[45]

These profound differences cannot be overstated. They ensured that during the nineteenth century Mexico's economy would be dominated by the hacienda, and its politics by the hacendados, while in the United States and Canada the economic and political interests of the homesteader as well as the entrepreneur, both of whom were united by the political ideology of "free soil, free labor, and free men," were paramount. (In the United States, the cherished ideal of the homestead was enshrined in national law with the passage of the Homestead Act of 1862, this after the plantation South had seceded from the Union and was still in rebellion, and in Canada, ten years later, as the Dominion Lands Act.) The differences between life on the hacienda and life on the homestead captured in microcosm the differences between Latin and British North America. However, there were also similarities, as between the large plantations and the institution of slavery in the American South and the haciendas and peonage in Mexico, especially in the center and south.[46]

Alice and the Red Queen

*"Well, in our country," said Alice, still panting a little, "you'd generally get to
somewhere else—if you run very fast for a long time, as we've been doing."*

*"A slow sort of country!" said the Queen. "Now, here, you see, it takes all
the running you can do, to keep in the same place. If you want to get somewhere else, you must run at least twice as fast as that!"*

— Lewis Carroll, *Through the Looking Glass*

During the colonial period Mexicans as a whole enjoyed peace and security, a working economy that satisfied basic needs, a meaningful and ethical
religion that organized life from cradle to grave, and a system of justice for
all, but they were also, as a whole, poorly educated and illiterate. To requote
Walter J. Ong: "Without writing, human consciousness cannot achieve its
fuller potentials, cannot produce other beautiful and powerful creations."
Yet under an older standard, Mexican society grades very high under
Spanish rule, for it enjoyed stability, order, and peace. Hobbes would have
bowed his head in respect, even admiration, at this New World Leviathan.
But how does Mexico fare if judged by a modern standard, one in which
the happiness or well-being of the individual is taken into account? In other words, was the average Mexican—an imaginary composite of Whites,
Mestizos, and Natives—happy? This is a tough but very important question,
and it is hardly an ahistorical or an anachronistic one. Indeed, the question,
while modern, is also as ancient as it was central to Western philosophy.

In the fourth century BC, Aristotle gave much thought to the subject of
happiness and concluded that it was a state at once subjective and moral, as
well as objective and dependent on the existence of certain material conditions. However virtuous and wise people may be, in other words, if they
are cold, sick, or hungry, it is difficult for them to be happy—a point clearly
illustrated in the psychology of Abraham Maslow's hierarchy of needs.
And in 1776 Thomas Jefferson declared to a candid world that the pursuit
of happiness was an inalienable right for all men; that there could be no
real happiness without liberty—or without security, we should promptly
add. Measuring this pursuit in both its subjective and objective senses is,
however, a challenge, especially in times remote from our own.

To create a measurement for the present, in 1990, more than two hundred years after the writing of the American colonies' Declaration of

Figure 12. John Tenniel, "The Red Queen's Race," from *Through the Looking Glass* by Lewis Carroll, 1871, Wikimedia Commons, https://commons.wikimedia.org/wiki /File:Alice_%26_Red_Queen.jpg.

Independence, Pakistani international development theorist Mahbub ul Haq created for the United Nations a way to quantify happiness or well-being, the Human Development Index (HDI). This annual measurement and national report card looks at three basic factors: longevity, per capita income, and education. As it turns out, we do know enough about life in colonial Mexico, a country that had been Christianized and Hispanicized, to hazard an educated guess on all three of Haq's accounts. In 1820, by this measure, Mexico's general state of well-being lagged well behind that of its two North American neighbors, Canada and the United States. Moreover, it would fall even further behind, and dramatically so, in the decades from 1820 to 1870—the deeply troubled period after Independence and the start of the Porfiriato.

Before we turn to longevity, which is a strong indicator of health in general, let us look at Mexico's population history over the course of the colonial era. As we have seen, the Columbian exchange of plants, animals, and technologies benefited both the Old and New Worlds. However, the exchange of diseases—New World syphilis for Old World smallpox, for one—was primarily a one-way disaster.[47] As a result of the introduction of new pathogens, Mexico's population crashed in the sixteenth century. The country's immunological vulnerability was no doubt exacerbated by the "physiological poverty" that existed at the time, as indicated by extant skeletal evidence.[48] On the other hand, recent genetic research in Mexico and in Hispaniola calls into question the veracity of the historical record. The population may have been much smaller and the Conquest not nearly as violent or disruptive as scholars had previously supposed.[49] Alas, as much as has been learned about sixteenth-century North America, it remains an opaque time and place. In any event, by the mid-seventeenth century Mexico's population had made a U-turn. And it headed back toward fifteenth-century levels in the course of the eighteenth century. It did not, however, fully recover in absolute terms until the middle of the nineteenth century (the population of middle and upper North America recovered—in purely raw numbers—a century earlier). To put muscle and tissue on these bones, Mexico's population stood at 7.5 million in 1500, 2.5 million in 1600, 4.5 million in 1700, 6.6 million in 1820, and 7.6 million in 1850.[50]

Mexico was not an immigration destination for Europeans as were its two North American neighbors. Still, its population growth, due largely to natural increase, was impressive. This was especially so after November 30, 1798, when King Charles IV ordered a massive program, to be carried out by his physician, Francisco Javier de Balmis, to vaccinate New Spain, including the Philippines, and the rest of Spanish America, against smallpox. Dr. Balmis convinced New Spain's viceroy, José de Iturrigaray, to have his own son vaccinated, thereby setting a royal example for all of Mexico. In respect to Spain's relationship with its colonial possessions, the Balmis expedition of 1803, the first of its kind and a superb example of social power, was probably imperial Spain's finest hour.[51] Since the vaccine survived in vitro for only twelve days, Balmis used twenty-two children—orphans from Spain—as human "refrigerators" to keep the vaccine fresh (every ten days he infected two new children with serum taken from the pustules of two sick children, a relay that was repeated until the expedition arrived in New Spain). The infected children became sick but did not die. On the voyage from Acapulco to the Philippines, Balmis recruited another twenty-six children, Mexican boys aged from four to fourteen, by paying the parents to part with them. The campaign vaccinated approximately three hundred thousand people all over the world.[52]

During Mexico's subsequent national period, intermittent vaccination campaigns followed. Indeed, taming smallpox and other killer diseases was a major triumph of man over nature and pointed forward to a brave new world of falling death rates and, for a time, persistently high birth rates, which produced a major population explosion. In 1900, at 13.6 million, Mexico's population had nearly doubled since 1850. By 1950, at 28.5 million, it had more than doubled again since 1900. And by the year 2000 it stood at over 100 million, having nearly *quadrupled* since 1950.[53]

The rise or fall of a population is one gross measure of social well-being. From 1521 to 1850 Mexico experienced one of the most violent and emotional roller-coaster rides in world history, one that stands on par with the horror Europe experienced in the fourteenth century with the Black Death. But based on rough estimates over the duration of the colonial era, Mexico also enjoyed a slow but steady recovery, beginning in the middle of the seventeenth century, although not everywhere or all at once. It is hard to interpret this development—a feat of survival and endurance in the face of large-scale suffering—in any other way except to say that Mexico's population recovery from the introduction of Old World diseases was a major national triumph, one made possible by the solicitous care of millions of single individuals for millions of other sick individuals. As for the general health of Native Mexicans, who made up the majority of the population, it may not have been much better during the colonial era than it was before the arrival of Cortés, but at least it was no worse.[54]

Still, life expectancy from birth, as the historical demographer Robert McCaa has pointed out, was very low—fewer than thirty years for men and women—just as had been the case in the agrarian societies of prehistoric Mesoamerica. Between puberty and menopause, there were birth intervals of thirty-six months to produce a total fertility rate of 8.5 children per woman. McCaa hypothesizes a model of vital rates of "high but slowly easing pressure" in which birth rates drifted downward from perhaps 60–70 per 1,000 population per annum in the fifteenth century, to 55–65 in the eighteenth, and 50–55 in the nineteenth (and 20–25 by the end of the twentieth).[55] This high-pressure demographic system of high mortality but even higher fertility—characterized by marriage at a very young age among a large percentage of the female population—accounts for Mexico's growth, which improved during the colonial era and the nineteenth century, but only very slowly.

By measuring longevity over the period from 1521 to 1823, we see that life under the Spanish may not have been as "poor, nasty, and brutish," to quote Hobbes, as it had been under the Aztecs. Still, it remained "short." And in respect to education or literacy, there was almost no improvement over this period—a stain on the church, since it was primarily responsible for the country's education. To be fair, the salvation of the soul was regarded as more important than the full development of the mind. On the other hand, this was not an either/or proposition. More than that, the church actively and paternalistically strove to keep the Mexican mind closed, through the Inquisition and the lack of any meaningful education beyond teaching of the catechism and the rudiments of the Castilian language. Class distinctions existed, as we have seen, but in general free inquiry and expression were stifled to suppress any possible challenge to the church's authority. In Europe, the church could not control the spread of the Reformation, a movement that divided Christendom and was seen by Rome as a spiritual catastrophe. But it could control or suppress thought in Mexico, where Catholicism reigned uncontested, simply by using the powerful Mexican Inquisition to starve the country of outside intellectual nourishment.[56]

At the same time, church-directed and controlled expression thrived, as demonstrated by the elaborate and fulsome styles of the Baroque and Rococo—or the Spanish Baroque or Churrigueresque, which flourished in Mexico. Indeed, there is architecture in Mexico equal to or surpassing that of its counterparts in Spain and Italy. The magnificent Churrigueresque facade of the Cathedral of Our Lady of the Assumption in the mining center of Zacatecas is only one brilliant and stunning case in point. This and numerous other architectural and artistic pearls notwithstanding, in longevity and literacy we have little choice but to rank Mexico well behind its North American neighbors, of which more later.

It is in Haq's third factor, per capita income, which is based on per capita gross domestic product, that we see a notable improvement over the course of the colonial period. In 1500, despite Mexico's productive milpas and chinampas (floating gardens, which were grounded as the Desagüe de Huehuetoca drained the shallow lake waters), the country's per capita GDP stood at $425,[57] only $25 higher than the $400 per capita GDP of the hunting, gathering, and horticultural economies in middle and upper North America. This minimal difference explains why many foragers were reluctant to adopt farming. At the individual level, the material benefits of agriculture were negligible, whereas a life of soil and toil was absolutely detrimental to one's health. This was true in the Americas as well as elsewhere in the world.

But the advantages of shifting from foraging to farming, at least from the standpoint of the elites or of society as a whole, become clear at once if we consider the matter in the social aggregate. That is, if we multiply that extra $25 of individual income by 7.5 million, which was the size of Mexico's population in 1500, we get $187.5 million. A society can do things with that kind of money: build massive stone pyramids, field large armies, and maintain vast empires. This is why we find these very things in Mexico, with its sedentary agriculture, and not in middle and upper North America at that time. In fact, in 1500 Mexico's GDP was $3.2 billion in 1990 international dollars—thirty-two times bigger than that of Canada, which stood at only $100 million, and four times bigger than the $800 million of the prefederal United States. Simply put, Mexico's economy produced a surplus.[58]

Put another way, in 1500 Mexico was, relatively speaking, North America's economic powerhouse—and it possessed social power. But the country was also plagued by a profound social inequality, as the division of Mexican society into *pipiltin* and *macehualtin* attests. What is more, this sharp class divide was perpetuated and even reinforced by the Spanish, who were quick to realize and seize the sources of Mexico's social power for themselves. Three centuries after the Conquest, Humboldt was forced to conclude that Mexico had become, or rather continued to be, the "country of inequality." As he put it: "Nowhere does there exist such a fearful difference in the distribution of fortune, civilization, cultivation of the soil, and population." In fact, Humboldt thought that the closest analogy to Mexico's "political and moral state" was Russia, with its deeply divided society of nobles and serfs.[59]

By 1820 Mexico's population had climbed to 6.6 million and its GDP had increased to $5 billion, having doubled since 1700, while its per capita GDP had risen also to $759 (again in 1990 dollars). These numbers are impressive by Latin American standards. But in the context of North America, Mexico was, in the geography of Lewis Carroll, a "fast" country: it took all the running the Red Queen could do just to stay in place, so she would fall behind her more dynamic neighbors in the "slow" northern region of the continent. And with the destruction during the struggle for independence of Mexico's once-dynamic mining sector, which did not recover for half a century, the Red Queen lost even more ground.

But we are getting ahead of ourselves. In 1820 Mexico's GDP was 6.7 times larger than Canada's—but it had been nearly 30 times larger in 1700. Moreover, and this fact is telling, Canada's per capita GDP of $904 that year was greater than Mexico's. Its population was also much smaller, at 816,000. And while in 1700 Mexico's economy was five times larger than that of the prefederal United States, 120 years later it had shrunk in size relative to its North American neighbor's. In fact, in 1820 US GDP, at $12.4 billion, was more than double that of Mexico. The US population, at 9,981,000, was also larger now than Mexico's at 6,587,00, as was the per capita GDP of the United States at $1,257—not quite twice that of Mexico's at $759. What is especially striking is that the US GDP and per capita GDP were also greater than Spain's GDP of $12.3 billion and per capita GDP of $1,008, even though Spain's population, at 12.2 million, was larger.[60] By 1820, then, the remarkable growth of the US economy had transformed not only North American relations but those of the North Atlantic as well, pointing to a new era in world history.[61]

CHAPTER 8

The Two Spains

The Great Reversal of Fortune

IN 1500 THE SOCIAL DEVELOPMENT of lower North America or what would become Mexico was more advanced than that of middle North America, or what would become the United States, and upper North America, or what would become Canada. The reverse would be true three centuries later, a change that would alter the course of North American history. Nowhere on the continent north of the twenty-first parallel had social development exceeded the Formative stage, which had peaked in the thirteenth and fourteenth centuries with the Cahokian, Ancestral Puebloan, Hohokam, and Mogollon cultures. To the south of that line on the globe, however, Central Mexican civilizations had peaked during the Postclassic stage (AD 1000–1521). The gap as of 1500, then, between the Postclassic stage of lower North America, with its much greater social differentiation, and the Archaic stage of middle and upper North America was very wide.

From this perspective Mexico stood in sharp relief from the rest of the continent, where Archaic peoples harvested the seasons' offerings using sophisticated hunting and gathering techniques as well as practicing horticulture. And in the case of many Eastern Woodland, Californian, and Pacific Northwest Native peoples, the Archaic stage represented a cultural climax—a way of life that might have survived indefinitely—had, at the risk of sounding romantic, the rest of the world not punctured this ancient equilibrium between man and nature. And in comparison with Archaic middle and upper North America, Postclassic Mexico was rich, especially in labor. So much so that Mexico's wealth would draw Iberian conquistadors to it like bears to honey.

Over the course of the next three centuries, as we have seen, the population of Spanish North America fell during the sixteenth century and then

179

wound back up, like a yo-yo, during the seventeenth. As the population re-covered from 1600 to 1700, the per capital GDP likewise shot up from $454 to $568, as did the total GDP, which went from $1.1 to $2.5 billion in 1990 international dollars. From a low of 2.5 million in 1600, Mexico's population had reached nearly 6.6 million by 1820, according to Maddison's estimates, which was still below its pre-Hispanic high of 7.5 million, while Mexico's per capita GDP and GDP exceeded the pre-Hispanic ceilings to reach $759 and $5 billion, respectively.[1] These were substantial gains for a pre-industrial economy and were due, in no small part, to the wealth produced by the country's rich silver mines. By the end of the colonial era not only had Mexico's population largely rebounded, even if it was now made up of a different mixture of peoples, but its per capita GDP had also increased, from $425 to $759. Still, for all of Mexico's gains in social development, which, tragically, would be lost in the half century after Independence, the country was soon to be surpassed by the rest of Anglophone North America and Francophone Quebec.

A Tale of Two Cities: Madrid and Mexico City

The wars and rumors of wars and the diplomatic arrangements and rear-rangements of eighteenth-century Europe read much like the endless ge-nealogies of the Old Testament. But while the latter have little relevance to the history of North America, the former could not be more germane. They were the European causes of many American effects.

In 1700 Charles II died heirless, bringing the Spanish Hapsburg dynasty to a close. The War of the Spanish Succession, which involved much of Europe, broke out the following year and lasted up to the signing of the Treaty of Utrecht in 1713. As a result, Felipe V (Philip V)—the grandson of France's Louis XIV and the first of the Spanish Bourbons—was recognized as the king of Spain and Spanish America; he would rule until 1746, save for nine months in 1724. As a result of its defeat in the conflict, Spain was also shorn of many of its European possessions, while in North America, Bourbon France lost Acadia, Newfoundland, and Hudson Bay, leaving to New France the colonies of Canada and Louisiana. This was still a vast country that was united by the St. Lawrence River, the Great Lakes, and the Mississippi, all of which connected the Gulf of Saint Lawrence with the Gulf of Mexico. In 1718 *le pays des Illinois* or "Illinois country," which would eventually make up the modern American states of Illinois and Missouri, was detached from Canada and joined to Louisiana.[2] Closer to home, Spain lost Gibraltar and

Minorca to Great Britain (England and Scotland had been united by acts of their respective parliaments in 1707). On the other hand, Spain emerged from this war more united than it had ever been, and for the first time it had a more centralized and efficient administration.

During the second half of the eighteenth century, both the Hanoverians in Britain and the Bourbons in Spain sought greater control over their American colonies, this with an eye to generating more revenue to maintain their expensive empires.[3] But in retrospect Europe's attempt to subordinate North America's Kingdom of New Spain and the thirteen intensely proud Little Englands along the Atlantic Coast as well as Nova Scotia, Newfoundland, St. John's Island (renamed Prince Edward Island in 1798), and, after 1763, the province of Quebec was a mistake of epic and tragic proportions. The exception to this rule was Britain's policy toward Catholic Quebec, as evidenced by the Quebec Act of 1774. It was remarkably generous and accommodating, so much so that the Protestant English colonists elsewhere on the continent became suspicious of the crown's motives, which proves that no good deed in this world goes unpunished.

Although the French Bourbons had as a result of the French and Indian War lost Louisiana to Spain in 1762 and Canada to Britain in 1763, France did retain colonies in the West Indies, including Saint-Domingue (Haiti). France would go on to squeeze or exploit Saint-Domingue to the point that Black Haitians, the vast majority of the colony's population, rose up in revolt in 1791, inspired by the French Revolution. Napoleon would later try to reclaim the once rich colony but failed in the endeavor. Also in 1763, Spain exchanged Florida for Havana, which Britain had captured. Britain subsequently divided Florida into East Florida (with St. Augustine as capital) and West Florida (with Pensacola as capital), the latter of which extended from the Apalachicola River, the border between the two Floridas, to the Mississippi. Britain would return the Floridas to Spain twenty years later, as part of the price of losing the War of American Independence.

Royal absolutism, domestic control, and fiscal efficiency constituted a reform program of enlightened despotism, which crossed the Pyrenees from France to Spain. José de Gálvez, inspector general to New Spain from 1765 to 1771—dispatched by King Charles III—is usually credited with introducing to Mexico major administrative, judicial, and especially fiscal reforms, with the primary aim of increasing revenues to the government. This program of so-called Bourbon Reforms included, significantly, the expulsion of the Jesuits in 1767 from all of Charles III's lands, calling to mind the purges of 1492; the occupation of Alta California, beginning in 1769 with the founding of the presidio at San Diego; the establishment in 1776 of the Provincias Internas, to better regulate and protect the northern frontier, from Texas to the Californias; and the creation of the intendancy system. As a result, Mexico was reorganized into twelve intendancies by the Royal Order of December 4, 1786. Sowing future discord, the new intendents were to be chosen from Spanish subjects, not those born in Mexico. All of these changes were made to create a centralized government and a modernized empire, with Spain at the center of what was a confederation of disparate kingdoms and lands.

For enlightened despotism—one way to characterize Bourbon Spain and Mexico—to succeed, one needs enlightened despots. Unfortunately for Spain, in 1788 Charles III was succeeded by his son Charles IV, an incapable dimwit and cuckold who relied for advice entirely on a sole minister, the less than competent and inexperienced Manuel de Godoy, the lover of Queen Maria Louisa. To be fair, the foreign crises that faced Spain in the 1790s were unprecedented. The French Revolution in 1789 violently shook Europe's *ancien régime*, of which the Spanish monarchy was Exhibit A. And before the revolution in France was over, the upheaval had taken the life of Charles IV's Bourbon relation Louis XVI ("Citizen Capet"), in early 1793, despite Spain's efforts to save his head from the national razor. These events ruptured the old *pacte de famille* between the Bourbon rulers of France and Spain. Spain had tended to side with France in the latter's many European and colonial wars, the French and Indian War (1754–63) and the American Revolutionary War (1775–83) among them, but the decapitation of the French king upended this tradition, and Spain ended up going to war with its old trans-Pyrenean ally.

In 1794 France invaded and occupied parts of Spain in the War of the Pyrenees (1793–95). Spain's own territorial integrity had thus been seriously threatened. A panicked Godoy and much-relieved Charles IV were able to end the war, which cost Spain nearly twenty-six thousand casualties, with the Peace of Basel in 1795. At the same time Godoy addressed American grievances over issues relating to the Floridas and the Mississippi Valley, thus settling matters, at least for the time being, on New Spain's northern borders as well. The following year, in a dramatic volte-face, Godoy decided to return to Spain's old policy of siding with the French against the British, even though the *pacte de famille* that was the rationale for it had been violently dissolved by France's National Convention. Thus, with the resulting Treaty of San Ildefonso of 1796 between Spain and France, Godoy had turned Great Britain, a powerful ally of monarchical Spain against republican France in the War of the First Coalition, in which the War of the Pyrenees was but one self-contained theater, into an enemy. There were no less than seven coalition wars between 1792 and 1815 against either revolutionary or, after 1799, Napoleonic France.

Portugal, significantly, continued to fight with their British ally against the French. With this diplomatic reversal, Godoy had given his sovereign and countrymen the worst of all possible worlds, to turn upside down the famous phrase of Voltaire's Candide. Spain was now caught between an unpredictable and ideologically hostile land power, France, on the one hand, and a resolute and hostile sea power, Britain, on the other.

The essences of these two militaries were soon personified in the master commanders of France's Napoleon Bonaparte, who became first consul of France in a bloodless coup in 1798, and Britain's Admiral Horatio Nelson. Moreover, Spain's Iberian neighbor, Portugal, was now Spain's enemy. Except for a short respite following the 1802 Treaty of Amiens, the "Definitive Treaty of Peace," which was signed by Napoleon's older brother, Joseph, and the Marquess Cornwallis, better remembered by Americans for his surrender at Yorktown, the Anglo-Spanish War raged for eleven years, from 1797 to 1808. Now that Spain had switched sides, Britain extended its naval blockade of France to include Spain. This act had enormous consequences for North America, since it cut off Spain from Mexico and, for that matter, the rest of its American empire, as well as starving the country of customs, a vital source of government revenue.

Under these intolerable conditions, Spain's nobles finally revolted in March 1808 in Aranjuez, a royal estate located south of Madrid, against Godoy's ministerial despotism. Godoy was dismissed, and Charles abdicated in favor of the treacherous crown prince Ferdinand VII. Napoleon, understandably disgusted with and distrustful of these Bourbon intrigues, fatefully decided to turn on his former ally and invade and occupy Spain itself, posing as the savior of national Spain. He lured Charles, Ferdinand, and Godoy to the Basque city of Bayonne, France, where he treated Ferdinand like a misbehaving child and forced him to return the Spanish crown to his father. Charles was then given no choice but to abdicate in favor of Napoleon, who then had his brother Joseph relinquish the crown of Naples and made him king of Spain instead. Charles and Godoy went to Rome, while Ferdinand was imprisoned in the Château de Valençay, the estate of the diplomat Charles-Maurice de Talleyrand—a gilded cage to outclass all other gilded cages. Napoleon then ordered Marshal Joachim Murat south to occupy Madrid. These actions united the British and the Portuguese, along with the Spanish people, against France.

None of this occurred in a vacuum. The crisis in Old Spain sent alarums throughout the Americas, where Spain's army of 125,700 men, many of them native-born Americans whose loyalties to Spain or to their own patria would soon be tested, was left on its own to hold together an empire of millions that stretched from the Rio Grande to the Río de la Plata. The sad face of the reconquest of America was that of the Spanish general Pablo Morillo, known as El Pacificador ("Peace Maker"), who led an expedition to New Granada in 1815. Unlike Hernán Cortés, who promised his men riches beyond reckoning, all Morillo could offer his force was poor pay and other privations as well as the grim prospect of a lonely grave in a foreign land. Times had changed.[4]

The Incredible Cortes of Cádiz

Charles IV's feeble rule and disastrous foreign policies had undermined, in some quarters, support for Spain's old regime. The majority, however, in this profoundly Catholic, conservative, and loyal country feared the secular French and their revolutionary notions more than their own incompetent Christian leaders. A popular revolt took hold, starting first in Madrid on Dos de Mayo, May 2, 1808, and then spreading across the country. Thus began the Peninsular War (1808–1814), which pitted the Spanish, British, and Portuguese against the invading French in a war of national liberation—for God, king, and patria—fiercely and passionately fought with regular as well as guerilla tactics.

In July 1808 at the Battle of Bailén in Andalusia, where Pablo Morillo first distinguished himself on the field of battle, the Spanish dealt the Napoleonic army its first defeat, inviting intervention by Napoleon himself to regain control of the country—something he never accomplished. And on August 21 British general Arthur Wellesley (later the Duke of Wellington) defeated Jean-Andoche Junot at the Battle of Vimeiro, a village near Lisbon, cutting the French general off from his home country and ending France's first invasion of Portugal (but not before the Portuguese royal family had fled to Brazil). Napoleon was not fighting soldiers alone but ideas, and he had stirred up a hornet's nest. He preferred a different metaphor, however, calling the war his "Spanish ulcer." The family compact between the French and the Spanish had become the family conflict.

In January 1810 the French marshal Nicolas Jean-de-Dieu Soult, who had reinvaded Portugal the previous year but met the same fate as Junot, took Seville, the capital of rebel-controlled Andalusia. In so doing he forced the Supreme Central Junta, Spain's ruling body in the absence of the monarch, to flee to the island fortress of Cádiz, home and destination port of the American treasure fleets and last holdout of the Spanish rebellion. The British blockade had strangled the port's economy back when Britain and Spain were enemies, but now the junta invited the British troops into Cádiz, to defend it against a French attack and what later occurred instead, a long siege. Thus it was that British general Thomas Graham, a Scottish aristocrat, faced off against the forces of France's Marshal Claude Victor-Perrin, while the Spanish junta appointed a Council of Regency, charged with calling for the election of deputies to a "General and Extraordinary Cortes," a parliamentary body similar to France's Estates General, except that this body was both transatlantic and transpacific. The Cortes of Cádiz faced three daunting challenges: to reform the monarchy; to defend Spain from France; and to preserve the empire.

The Cortes of Cádiz was a national assembly, and its legal basis was as simple as it was remarkable: in the absence of the king, sovereignty reverted back to the people. It met for three years between September 24, 1810, and September 20, 1813. The assembly was not made up of deputies or representatives from Spain only but rather, as Jaime E. Rodríguez O. has pointed out, from the entire Spanish Empire, including New Spain and the Philippines, where elections were held for it. Spain's American colonies enjoyed real representation, not the merely virtual representation afforded Great Britain's American colonies, which was a major point of contention between the two sides of the Atlantic. In other words, the Cortes of Cádiz was the first truly transatlantic representative governing body and one of the great, if belated and underappreciated, achievements of the Enlightenment. To quote Elliott, the Constitution of 1812 "transformed Spain and its American possessions into a single nation-state, based on a much wider franchise than that of the Anglo-American world, since it included no literacy or property requirements." Of the approximately 220 deputies who served in the Cortes of Cádiz, 67 were from the Americas. A third of them were clergymen, one-sixth were nobles, and the rest were professionals or middle-class men. Two of the *cortes*'s notable deputies and Criollos were the New Spaniards Miguel Ramos Arizpe of Coahuila and the Tlaxcalan José Miguel Guridi y Alcocer.[5]

The result of this extraordinary and Hispanic, rather than solely Spanish, meeting was the radical Constitution of 1812, or Political Constitution of the Spanish Monarchy. Unlike the US Constitution, the document created three *unequal* branches of government, with the executive and the judiciary branches both subordinate to the legislature, the *cortes*. The power of the king was therefore greatly reduced. The church was to come under the control of the state. And the constitution abolished seignorial institutions, the Inquisition, Indian tribute, and forced labor—in Spain *and* in the Americas. The Constitution of 1812 was in theory as revolutionary as the great charters of freedom produced by the American and French revolutions, actually far more so, yet historians rarely speak of a "Spanish Revolution" because the idea failed to be realized. Still, it merits our attention because history's dead ends often shed light on the roads that were actually taken.

The Constitution of 1812 also expanded the franchise to all men, including Mestizos and Native Americans. However, as the historian Elliott notes, "concession of full citizenship rights" to Indigenous people did nothing to improve their situation; if anything, it worsened it, because "equality meant an end to the system of legal protection they had hitherto enjoyed, leaving them still more exposed to [Criollo] exploitation."[6] Excluded from the franchise were men of African descent, convicted criminals, members of religious orders, domestic servants, and public debtors. Since the number of those disqualified was very small, the size of the qualified electorate was very great.[7] In 1813, no less than 93 percent of Mexico City's adult male population was on the electoral register.[8]

For Americans—namely the Criollos, and above all the hacendados, wealthy merchants, and mine owners—who wanted more autonomy and home rule, all cities and towns with more than a thousand inhabitants were given their own *ayuntamientos* or town halls, and twenty provincial deputations were created, six of them for New Spain. These new bodies were to be popularly elected. The Constitution of 1812 was, in short, liberal, and with its large expansion of the electorate, it was as potentially as far-reaching in its effects as was Jacksonian democracy, a popular movement that spread across the United States beginning in the 1820s. And in certain respects this new Hispanic order anticipated the British Commonwealth of Nations by over a century. The Constitution of 1812, however, was suspended, at least temporarily, and then suspended again permanently.

Napoleon finally allowed Ferdinand VII to leave the Château de Valençay and return to Spain. There was perhaps no one more out of touch with his country, literally and figuratively, than was Ferdinand. In May 1814 he abolished the Cortes of Cádiz and repudiated its liberal constitution.

And after six years of fighting to rid Spain of a foreign power, a war that took 215,000 to 240,000 military and civilian lives, he tried with the support of reactionaries in Spain and in the Americas to restore the absolute monarchy, in effect reconquering the Americas. Spain's army of liberation was now to do an improbable about-turn and become a foreign army of subjugation.

The war in the Americas dragged on without conclusion until 1820, when a score of Spanish battalions in Cádiz, which were waiting to be shipped out to the Americas, mutinied. General Rafael del Riego of Asturias and other liberals forced Ferdinand to concede to the restoration of the Constitution of 1812, thereby ushering in three more years of liberal rule, the "Liberal Triennium." In 1823, however, France intervened yet again in its southern neighbor's internal affairs; Louis XVIII (whose reign lasted from 1814 to 1824, except for a hundred days in 1815) sent an army to liberate Ferdinand from his liberal ministers.

Liberty without Security

Jaime E. Rodríguez O. probably said it best: "The emancipation of most of America—that is, the Western Hemisphere—may be best understood as a series of reactions by the settlers to the actions and events that occurred in their mother countries."[9] To wit: Ferdinand VII's abdication in 1808 and subsequent French captivity created an intolerable situation for Spanish officials in New Spain, who arrested its viceroy, José de Iturrigaray, and reluctantly supported the new king, or at least did not actively oppose him. However, loyalty to Ferdinand, not Joseph, Napoleon's brother, ran deep and wide in Mexican society, even among the Native population. And as in Spain, juntas or conspiracies formed to oppose French authority as well as to support Ferdinand. And everyone in Mexico seemed to want to defend the Lady of Guadalupe.

Others sought complete independence, or autonomy under Ferdinand, including one conspiracy, based in Querétaro, involving Miguel Hidalgo y Costilla, a priest from Dolores. As a student Hidalgo had been known as El Zorro, "The Fox"—the crafty one. The uprising also involved Ignacio Allende, a Criollo officer from San Miguel.[10]

Allende had attended the College of San Francisco de Sales and served as a second lieutenant in San Miguel's Regiment of the Queen's Dragoons, the emblem of which was Saint Michael the Archangel. He later answered the call of Viceroy Iturrigaray to defend New Spain from Great Britain—France and Spain's enemy at the time but later Spain's ally against France. Iturrigaray had the support of the *ayuntamiento* of Mexico City, but the city's audiencia distrusted him, fearing that he would break from Spain. Despite everything that had happened in the three-century interim, New Spain's creaking imperial machinery still worked; this ancient colonial institution worked as exactly as it was designed, back when the threat to the monarchy was sixteenth-century conquistadors going rogue. The subsequent coup against Iturrigaray, led by the Spaniard Gabriel J. de Yermo on September 15, 1808, left Allende disaffected. The Criollo officer now began to yearn for independence from a French-controlled Spain, but hoped for a separation achieved with a minimum of social conflict and with honor, as had been largely the case with the American Revolution of 1776.

In September 1810 Allende and Hidalgo, who were otherwise polar opposites, initiated the war for Mexico's independence. From his church in Dolores, Hidalgo issued the morally contradictory Cry of Dolores, "Long live the Virgin of Guadalupe and death to the *gachupines* [Spaniards]!" Unlike Allende, Hidalgo hoped to incite the maximum amount of social and racial conflict—and he succeeded. Thousands of local Indigenous people and Mestizos heeded the call to arms, and nearby Guanajuato was pillaged. Some five to six hundred Spaniards, who had barricaded themselves inside the Alhóndiga de Granaditas, a massive and imposing public granary, were slaughtered to a person.

The next year Allende and Hidalgo were captured and executed. Their severed heads were placed in separate iron cages, along with the heads of two other rebel leaders, and hung from a hook on each of the four corners of the granary for all the world to see. As grisly as was this warning against further insurrection, the fighting nevertheless continued. Hidalgo was immediately replaced by other leaders, among them José María Morelos and Vicente Guerrero, who in 1829 would become the president of Mexico and thereby the first Black president in North American history. (Guerrero's father, Pedro Guerrero, was of African descent; his mother, Guadalupe Saldana, was Native.) Before it was over, the war—which pitted rebel against royalist—would consume somewhere between 250,000 and 500,000 souls, a staggering number. In contrast, the casualties in America's earlier Revolutionary War were approximately 25,000, out of a population about one-third the size of Mexico's (approximately 2 million versus 6 million). Mexico had paid very dearly for its freedom.[11]

In a strange twist of history, Mexico's independence from Spain was secured not by revolutionaries but rather by conservatives, led by Augustín de Iturbide, an upper-class Criollo who had fought on the side of the royalists. In 1820 the liberal revolt in Spain convinced Mexico's elites that the time had come to establish an autonomous monarchy under the Constitution of 1812, which was the essential idea behind Iturbide's Plan of Iguala. Iturbide then made common cause with Guerrero and the other insurrectionist leaders against Spain. This left Juan O'Donojú, the Spanish viceroy, with little choice but to agree to Iturbide's terms. On August 24, 1821, he signed the Treaty of Córdoba, thereby granting Mexico its independence. The Spanish government, however, refused to recognize the treaty. And by maintaining troops until 1825 at San Juan de Ulúa, a fortress on the island of the same name, within shelling distance of the port of Veracruz, the Spanish in effect and out of malice and spite kept a gun pressed up against the temple of the new nation. The United States, on the other hand, was quick to recognize its new North American neighbor, along with Columbia, Peru, Chile, and Argentina, on December 12, 1822.

Under these conditions, it is hardly surprising that no European prince would agree to accept Mexico's offer of an American throne. Therefore Iturbide took the predictable and fateful step of declaring himself an emperor and Mexico an empire, which the Central American provinces of Guatemala, El Salvador, Honduras, Nicaragua, and Costa Rica subsequently joined. His rule proved largely arbitrary, and his open borders policy was a national disaster. William Becknell, a Missouri trader, immediately took advantage of the situation to trade American goods for Mexican silver and pelts. His initial success set off a commercial contagion that led to the establishment of the Santa Fe Trail, a New World Silk Road that linked St. Louis with Santa Fe via Bent's Fort on the Arkansas River. (The Cimarron River Cutoff, to the south, was an alternative route.) And in the ensuing years the Old Spanish Trail from Santa Fe to Southern California became increasingly important as New Mexicans used it to trade wool for Californian horses, which in turn enlarged Santa Fe's growing commercial importance.

On January 4, 1823, moreover, Iturbide permitted Anglo-Americans to establish a colony in Texas on the Brazos River. Three months later, on March 19, 1823, with his coalition in tatters and facing armed opposition from Antonio López de Santa Anna and Guadalupe Victoria, Augustín I abdicated and fled to Europe aboard a British vessel (he later returned, was captured, and was executed by a firing squad). Guatemala then seceded, except for Chiapas, along with the other Central American provinces, and on November 1, 1823, the Mexican empire was proclaimed an independent republic: the Federal Republic of the United Mexican States—a highly problematic proposition, as it turned out.

Republics were very rare things in those days, and one of the most famous that had existed, the First French Republic (1792–1804), had raised serious questions about the viability and sustainability of this particular form of government.[12] Nevertheless Mexico, which had been a stable kingdom for three centuries, now embarked on a radical experiment for which it had little preparation. For decades to come the Mexican people would find their country pulled violently toward one pole, that of tradition and monarchy, and then back again toward the opposite pole of republicanism, anticlericalism, and individual liberalism. Needless to say, this political extremism or instability, punctuated by numerous *pronunciamientos* (calls to arms), retarded Mexico's economic and social development during a good part of the nineteenth century and then again in the early twentieth century with the outbreak of the Mexican Revolution in 1910.

The Spanish monarchy was far greater than its individual parts, a point that became increasingly clear as this once major weight and social power in world politics atomized into many smaller, poorer, struggling, and disparate parts. In the Americas the empire had been reduced to the islands of Cuba, Puerto Rico, and—until 1825, when Spain finally withdrew its forces from San Juan de Ulúa. The Philippines had been under the jurisdiction of New Spain for 250 years, from 1565 to 1815, but Spain took direct control of the islands after Mexico's independence and ended the trade between Mexico and the Philippines. This severed North America's direct connection to Asia until the Spanish-American War of 1898, when Spain ceded control of the Philippines (and Guam) to the United States. This reestablished an important old tie between North America and the East. The archipelago became independent of the United States in 1946, but it has been a strategic ally ever since. In 2021 the Philippines renewed the Visiting Forces Agreement with the United States as a check against China's growing ambitions in the waters of Southeast Asia.

In contrast to its northern neighbor, which had won its independence from a rising power, one sympathetic with the United States, Mexico, its economy in ruins after a decade of war, separated from a humiliated and hostile mother country in sharp decline. In fact, for years Spain had used

Cuba as a base to threaten Mexico's territorial waters and Mexico itself. And in 1829 Spain attempted again to reconquer Mexico. To do so, it sent a fleet under the command of Admiral Ángel Laborde to land troops at the port of Tampico on the north bank of the Pánuco River. But Mexico's army (it possessed no navy to speak of) defeated Spain's army under General Isidro Barradas in the Battle of Pueblo Viejo on September 11, 1829, a date that marked a key turning point in North American history. Not until the end of 1836, however, would Spain finally recognize Mexico's independence under the Treaty of Santa María-Calatrava.

But by that time, Mexico had already lost the Central American provinces in the south, and in the north, Anglo-American settlers and Tejanos in Texas had lost all confidence in Mexico's federal government, if not its prospects at remaining a viable independent nation. After a short but successful rebellion that ended with the decisive Battle of San Jacinto on April 21, 1836, Texas went on to form—at Mexico's territorial expense—another North American republic. Like Texas, in 1841 the Yucatán also declared its independence from Mexico. But in exchange for Mexico's military help in putting down an internal revolt—the interminable 1847–1901 Caste War between the Native Maya and the Hispanic Yucatecos—the Republic of the Yucatán agreed to rejoin the United Mexican States in 1848. By this time, Mexico had lost additional territory—the modern states of New Mexico, Arizona, and California—to the United States.[13]

Unlike the United States and the United Kingdom, which early on formed a special and enduring relationship that well served the interests of both nations, Spain's early position toward an independent Mexico was adversarial. Indeed, in 1823 US and British interests in the Americas were so congruent that George Canning, the British foreign minister, suggested to US president James Monroe that the two countries issue a joint statement of policy. The former US presidents Thomas Jefferson and James Madison both urged Monroe to accept this remarkable offer to share the Western Hemisphere, but Monroe's secretary of state, John Quincy Adams, demurred. He thought the United States should issue its own separate and apt statement rather than appear to "come in as a cockboat in the wake of the British man-of-war." Adams prevailed, and the US statement, which the British fully and tacitly supported, became known as the Monroe Doctrine, although "the Canning-Adams Doctrine" would have been more accurate. Mexico, on the other hand, had no Great Power guardian. Even if Spain had been inclined to play such a role, it was too weak to do so. The long Spanish peace was over. In fact, none of the newly independent American nations, including Mexico, could afford to build a navy worthy of the name, and thus found themselves at the mercy of those nations that could, namely the United States, Britain, France, and Russia. This lack of security early in Mexico's history, coupled with its ongoing political turmoil, profoundly shaped and hindered the country's development and made general prosperity all but an impossibility.

Mexico's Social Power

The wealth of the Kingdom of New Spain, principally its silver, helped to make Old Spain a great power for nearly three centuries, deeply complicating European politics and fueling Europe's rivalries in North America, as well as stimulating Europe's economy. After the line of Spanish Hapsburgs had exhausted itself in the withered and misshapen body of Charles (Carlos) II, also known as "Carlos the Mad" or "the Bewitched," the wealth of the American empire continued to allow Spain's Bourbons, the dynastic successors to the Hapsburgs, to play great-power politics until the Peninsular War. In fact, with the Treaty of San Ildefonso, which along with the Treaty of Paris of 1763 concluded the Seven Years' War (also known as the French and Indian War), Spain acquired all of the French colony of Louisiana, including the future site of St. Louis, a river town founded the following year by the French fur traders Pierre Lacléde and Auguste Chouteau. This marked the high point of Spain's territorial claims as a North American power.[14]

Historians of North America have charted the fortunes of dynastic houses, empires, colonies, plantations, and companies such as the Virginia Company, the New Netherland Company, the Hudson's Bay Company, and the Russian-American Company, as well as its many churches and religious orders. They have studied the continent's myriad peoples and focused on the pageant of intrepid, tragic, and remarkable figures—Cortés, Father Kino, Samuel de Champlain, Abigail Adams. But in the pursuit of these numerous historical and biographical stories, one thing has become obscured, or even lost from view entirely: the continent of North America—a place united by many things but not the least of all the three-century expansion of Western civilization into almost its every nook and cranny. In fact, given the complex interplay and inseparability of North America and Europe, it is perhaps more useful to think in terms of a transatlantic or simply an Atlantic civilization, with strong Pacific interests. For that is what it was. And the dramatic rise and dynamic development of this civilization is our real story, one with global consequences. Moreover, it is a story, as Angus Maddison, Ian Morris, and other scholars have shown, that has clearly measurable traits, even if the results are as rough as a frontier cabin made of ax-hewn logs.

Mahbub ul Haq and Morris are both students of social development. The difference between them is that Haq measured longevity, income, and education in order to define happiness or general well-being, while Morris measured social power by examining four traits, those of "energy capture," "social organization" (city size is used as a proxy), "information technology," and "war-making capacity."[15] The work of both men is very useful, but Morris's, which focuses on a society's ability "to get things done," adds a crucial dimension to our understanding of North America's cultural evolution, a process that produced the world's sole remaining superpower—for now.

Let us take each of Morris's traits in turn, beginning with the energy capture of foods (for humans and animals), fuels (for cooking or manufacture), and raw materials (for construction, clothing, metallurgy, and so on). To put these numbers in context, the total food and nonfood energy capture of the simplest hunter-gatherer societies is around 4,500–5,000 kilocalories per person per day (KPPPD). In contrast, the figure for the contemporary United States is an astonishing 230,000 KPPPD! The contemporary global average is 50,000 KPPPD.[16]

With these figures in mind, the West's energy capture in 1500—at the beginning of the great global convergence and the start of North America's colonial era—was 27,000 KPPPD. A century later this consumption had climbed by 2,000 to reach 29,000 KPPPD. In 1700 the consumption level had increased by 3,000 to reach 32,000 KPPPD. For the first time since AD 100—the height of the Roman Empire, when the Mediterranean-centered West had topped out at 31,000 KPPPD—the North Atlantic–centered West had finally surpassed the old Roman high water mark by 1000 KPPPD. At one point between AD 700 and 900—the "Dark Ages"—it had dipped as low as 25,000 KPPPD.[17]

However, it is not until the eighteenth century that things began to improve noticeably, as we see a striking increase of 6,000 KPPPD, which puts Western energy capture in 1800 at 38,000 KPPPD, or an increase of 11,000 KPPPD, since Columbus first sailed the ocean blue. By 1800, to quote the Beatles, life in the West was "getting better all the time." And, not surprisingly, Enlightenment thinkers on both sides of the North Atlantic came to adopt a faith in progress, which they saw unfolding all around them and which is still very much with us, as the West and the Rest continue to getter richer and healthier.[18]

The real breakout, of course, occurred during the nineteenth century, when the industrial or fossil fuels revolution fully kicked in, a revolution that had started in the previous century in Britain's Midlands. During the nineteenth century, KPPPD in the West increased by a whopping 54,000 to reach 92,000. To look at this huge surge in another way, in the West from 1 AD to the year 1800 KPPPD grew from 31,000 to 38,000, a gain of only 7,000 KPPPD. By the end of our period, then, which is 1823, life in the West had improved significantly. But the real gains that followed the intellectual, political, industrial, and social revolutions that swept away the old regimes of the North Atlantic world were not widely felt until well after 1823—and much later in the case of Mexico, which did not find stability and security until the 1870s, with the establishment of the Porfiriato and the recovery of the mining industry.

Morris uses the size of urban populations as a proxy for social organization, since a "long tradition of research in the social sciences, and particularly in archaeology, anthropology, economics, and urban studies, has demonstrated the strong relationships between the size of the largest settlements within a society and the complexity of its social organization."[19] With this academic tradition in mind, we may see that from 1521 to 1823 North America became the home of what would become two of the world's largest cities, New York and Mexico City. In 1820, according to the fourth US Census, New York's population stood at 123,706, making it the largest city north of the Rio Grande (the second largest city, Philadelphia, with a population of 63,802, was a little less than half the size of New York). Five years later, in 1825, New York's dominance would be assured with the opening of the Erie Canal, a project that fundamentally altered North America's economic and urban geography and in the process blunted the ambition of Montréal's merchants to funnel trade with the West and the commerce of North America's inland waterways through the St. Lawrence River. It is hard to think of a better example of social power than the construction of the Erie Canal, which stands in contrast to Mexico City's ambiguous Desagüe de Huehuetoca. To put these facts into a transatlantic and continental context, by 1800 London, with a population of 900,000, had already become the largest city in the world after Beijing. And in 1827 Joseph Bouchette, a veteran of the War of 1812 and the surveyor general of Lower Canada, stated that the population of Canada's leading urban and commercial center, Montreal, numbered 32,000 souls.[20]

For the population of Mexico's leading city, one may turn to the authority of Humboldt. He derived his estimations from Mexico's first census, the Revillagigedo census of 1793 (named after the viceroy and count who ordered it).[21] According to this census, the population of Mexico City was 112,926 in 1790. Humboldt thought this figure was much too low, and after considering the tables of consumption and the number of births and burials as well as making comparisons with the cities of Europe, he estimated it as somewhere north of 135,000, suggesting that it could be as high as 200,000, making Mexico City the largest city not only in Mexico but in all of North America.[22] And he was certain that the population of Mexico City, as well as the rest of the country, had "made the most extraordinary progress" since 1793, enthusing that

> the augmentation of tithes and of the Indian capitation, and of all the duties on consumption, the progress of agriculture and civilization, the aspect of a country covered with newly constructed homes, announce a rapid increase in every part of the kingdom. How are we to conceive then that social institutions can be so defective, and a government so iniquitous, as to pervert the order of nature, and prevent the progressive multiplication of our species in a fertile soil and temperate climate? Happy the portion of the globe where a peace of three centuries has almost effaced the very recollection of the crimes produced by the fanaticism and insatiable avarice of the first conquerors![23]

US historians often begin their histories with those first conquerors and the fall of the great Mexican city of Tenochtitlán in 1521. But after that, Mexico basically disappears from the narrative until well into the national era, with the start of the Mexican War in 1846, three hundred and twenty-five years later. But a lot happened in lower North America in between those two epic events, not the least of which was the remarkable transformation of Tenochtitlán into Mexico City. The size of Tenochtitlán deserves our attention because it speaks to the complexity of Postclassic Mesoamerican society and to the tragedy of its destruction. By the same token, the fact that after three centuries Mexico City was still the largest city on the continent should have—at the very least—an equal claim on our historical imagination, for it speaks to Mexico's enduring social complexity.

Morris's trait of "information technology" is more complicated than that of literacy. For one thing, he includes numeracy and notes the differences over time between male literacy, which was very low, and female literacy, which was even lower. He also distinguishes gradations between three levels of literacy: full, medium, and basic. For the period covered in this study, 1521 to 1823, the technology involved was printing (Johannes Gutenberg developed printing with movable type in the fifteenth century), although among the educated, letter writing remained very important. To Morris the chief significance of printing was "to generate more and cheaper materials, rather than to transform information storage and retrieval the way that the telegraph and the Internet would do in the nineteenth and twentieth centuries." Printing did that, to be sure. But it did much more. It was, above all, a technology of reproduction. A printer could reproduce maps and other forms of information not just "more and cheaper," but *identically*—and it could do so quickly. And that was printing's real power. In the preprinting era, maps, for example, were individually and painstakingly hand drawn and thus subject to human error. Printing did not eliminate mistakes, of course. The typo was cursed by the first printers. But in the long view, printing's real historical significance is that it made mass literacy a possibility.[24]

In the meantime, the role that literacy played in Europe's conquest and colonization of North America, and its influence on the rest of the world, cannot be overstated. The skills of reading and writing were crucial to Europe's military, commercial, and religious designs and activities. For literacy was social power, a truth fully grasped by the Jesuit Chinese missionary Matteo Ricci (he died in 1610): "The whole point of writing something down is that your voice carries for thousands of miles, whereas in direct conversation it fades at a hundred paces."[25] In directing the affairs of New Spain from Seville and, after the Guadalquivir River silted up, the port of Cádiz, this is certainly how the officials of the church and crown regarded the power of writing.[26]

There is wide agreement among scholars, including Morris, that literacy is a positive trait and that it correlates with social development and modernization. This is certainly the view shared in these pages. The ability to read and write are skills that may open new horizons. Those who possess these skills simply have more options in life than those who do not. There are scholars, however, who view literacy as a "constraining" or "conforming" force, rather than as a force for liberation and creativity. If true, these are very fine distinctions that may apply to very particular circumstances in certain parts of Europe and British North America. But not to Mexico. In a country of mostly have-nots, literacy was the almost exclusive enjoyment of a small minority who possessed the country's wealth and power.[27]

The trait perhaps most obviously associated with social power is a society's capacity to make war. According to Morris, comparisons of war-making capacity must "come down to measuring the destructive power available to society," by which he meant "the number of fighters they can field, modified by the range and force of their weapons, the mass and speed with which they can deploy them, their defensive power, and their logistical capabilities."[28] In New Spain, for much of the colonial period, the military problems were relatively minor. The viceroy, like the pope today, was protected by a simple guard of halberdiers. There were three basic threats, but all were successfully met by the deployment of understrength companies.

The first of these threats was the protection of the Gulf Coast, in particular the port of Veracruz, from invaders and raiders. Veracruz is where Hernán Cortés landed in 1519, and where US general Winfield Scott would later invade in 1847. Defending Veracruz posed a special challenge, given its location in the disease-ridden lowlands. Highlanders were naturally terrified of going somewhere that they might very well contract malaria or *el vomito negro*, or yellow fever. Veracruz's shippers and merchants wanted a military presence at the port, while soldiers and their officers preferred to protect the port at a distance, in cantonments located in the more salubrious temperate highlands.

The second problem involved protecting the northern frontier from raiding Natives, especially the Comanches—the Lords of the Plains.[29] In time, the Spanish learned, as did the French and English, that it was easier to purchase peace with gifts—medals, colorful clothes, uniforms, swords and other weapons, and even bugles—than to impose peace by force from afar. And the third problem pertained to the need to police against rural banditry and urban uprisings. The latter point was driven home in 1692, when riots broke out in Mexico City over food shortages and the viceregal palace was set on fire.

During the eighteenth century the rise of Great Britain threatened Cuba, New Spain, and the Isthmus of Darién (as early as 1671, the daring British buccaneer Henry Morgan had landed on Panama's Caribbean coast, traversed overland through the jungle to the Pacific Ocean, and attacked Old Panama City from the rear). The turning point in Madrid's strategic thinking, however, came near the end of the Seven Years' War, with the British siege and occupation of Havana in 1762. It was clear that the ad hoc and provisional approach of the past to Mexico's security was no longer sufficient; New Spain now required a permanent military force, one that should consist of infantry, dragoon, cavalry, artillery, and engineering units.

There was also a need to change Mexico's old lax, complacent military attitude and replace it with a new sense of martial urgency. One of the biggest problems the Spanish authorities faced was deciding what role the Mexicans themselves should play in this new military response, given Spain's old reluctance to arm and train locals. After various experiments, the Spanish crown in 1788 finally approved a system of defense involving regulars and militias, Spanish as well as Mexican officers, which at least on paper pooled up to 40,000 men for service. For a peacetime army, this was impressive. To put this size in perspective, during the American Revolutionary War, the US Continental Army never had more than 20,000 men in service at any one time, versus Great Britain's opposing force of 50,000 men, plus 30,000 Hessian auxiliaries.[30]

As the European situation deteriorated during the 1790s, and Spain found itself increasingly distracted, the Mexican army was steadily "Mexicanized," adding more Mexican officers and soldiers. Spanish doubts about the army's reliability and effectiveness proved unfounded; according to the military historian Christian I. Archer, Mexico's Bourbon Army, designed to repel foreign invasion, remained loyal after the Hidalgo revolt in 1810 and fought well until independence in 1821, when the royalists and the insurgents joined forces to form the "Army of the Three Guarantees"—that is, of religion, independence, and union—after the Plan of Iguala. The insurgents had been successful against the royalists only when they "adopted new tactics and unconventional guerilla warfare."[31]

North America and the Military Revolution

During the centuries between the fall of Granada and Napoleon's invasion of Spain and Russia, Europe underwent a military revolution. The Chinese may have invented gunpowder—a mixture of potassium nitrate, charcoal, and sulfur—but it was the Europeans who realized its military potential. The development of artillery, and the constant search for ways to improve the accuracy and range of these guns, changed everything; with this new technology, the once mighty fortresses of medieval Europe could be pulverized, perhaps beginning with the fall of Constantinople in 1453. A turning point in military history, which was recognized as such by contemporaries, was the French invasion of Italy in 1494, two years after the reconquest of Andalusia and the discovery of the Americas by Christopher Columbus. France's Charles VIII sent eighteen thousand men and a siege train of forty guns. Florentine observer and historian Francesco Guicciardini summed up the significance of what had happened next:

> Before the year 1494, wars were protracted, battles bloodless, the methods followed in besieging towns slow and uncertain; and although artillery was already in use, it was managed with such lack of skill that it caused little hurt. Hence it came about that the ruler of a state could hardly be dispossessed. But the French, in their invasion of Italy, infused such liveliness into our wars that, up to the year 1521 [the present, for Guicciardini], whenever the open country was lost, the state was lost to it.[32]

The answer to this new firepower was the bastion, a type of fortification that could resist artillery bombardment because it was lower, thicker, and ended in an outward-pointing angle. It was also designed to contain mutually supporting and interlocking fields of fire. The dialectic between offensive and defensive military capabilities—between mortar and masonry—was expensive, and only princes who could afford to do so could play this dangerous game of escalating point and counterpoint. But spend as they might, neither Philip II of Spain, nor Louis XIV, nor Napoleon Bonaparte of France could achieve military dominance over Europe, even with such important innovations as the *levée en masse* (mass national conscription). Instead, the continent was the scene of constant warfare and shifting alliances—a military and economic competition that was extended to and shaped North America.

Indeed, the real end of masonry fortification systems occurred in 1862 during the American Civil War, with the fall of the massive and supposedly unbreachable Fort Pulaski, with its high moated walls of solid brick, seven and a half feet thick. (After the War of 1812 exposed the vulnerability of the United States to foreign invasion, Fort Pulaski had been built, along with Fort Sumter and forty other citadels, as part of the country's new system of coastal fortifications.)[33] The fort, on tiny Cockspur Island at the mouth of the Savannah River, was occupied by a Confederate garrison. But after only thirty hours of bombardment, during which new rifled cannons spun a numbing 5,275 projectiles (which works out to close to 176 pulverizing shells an hour) from federal batteries on Tybee Island, over a mile away, the fort's massive walls, embrasures, and casements began to crumble, forcing Confederate commander Charles H. Olmstead to surrender to Union engineer captain Quincy A. Gillmore. The fall of Fort Pulaski signaled the end not only of old fixed, stand-alone masonry defensive structures (reinforced concrete structures were another story) but also marked the transition from the old smoothbore cannon and its thick round shots or balls to the revolutionary rifled cannons, which could fire heavy, cylindrical exploding shells.

Not only were Europe and North America's fortifications and fields of battle transformed, but so was the character of naval power. Once upon a time, military ships were built to ram and board. But with the advent of artillery, ships could be turned into sail-driven dirigible platforms, bristling with cannon. It was this change, and the growing economic wealth that lay behind it, that eventually allowed Europe to bring and hold not only North America but, for a time, much of the world under its influence.

After the West Indies, Mexico was one of the earliest prizes in this conquest. Middle and upper America would follow a century later. But whereas the Atlantic seaboard, the St. Lawrence Gulf and Valley, and the Trans-Appalachian West would face almost two hundred years of constant warfare between Europeans and Native Americans and between rival European empires and Indigenous alliances, from 1521 to 1810 group conflict in the Kingdom of New Spain was—except for ongoing warfare on the northern frontier—largely suppressed, giving much of the country something it had never enjoyed before: peace. And this Pax Hispanica lasted, as Humboldt exclaimed, for "three centuries!" This was an impressive feat, by any measure. The nineteenth century, however, would be a very different story. Relatively weak and alienated from the now-declining power of Spain, Mexico would find itself embroiled in almost constant internal conflicts and *pronunciamientos* as well as the target of foreign invasions. And in sharp contrast to contemporary Mexico and to their own earlier sanguinary colonial era, the United States and Canada would enjoy the blessings of "free security," courtesy of the Pax Britannica.[34]

PART III

THE ANGLOSPHERE

Figure 13. Unknown artist, *Log Cabin*, n.d. Print. Prints and Photographs Division, Library of Congress, Washington, DC. https://www.loc.gov/item/2003663901/.

CHAPTER 9

Neo-Europes and Middle Grounds

The First Wild West

THE NEW EUROPEAN SOCIETIES THAT took root in lower, middle, and upper North America were determined, at least initially, by the Treaty of Vervins of 1598 between Henry IV of France and Philip II of Spain, mediated by the papal legates of Clement VIII. The treaty ended France's ghastly wars of religion. It also set the terms by which the Spanish and the French, and by implication the English and the Dutch, would struggle for control of the West Indies and the Florida coast. The lines were clear. In the area west of the Azores archipelago and south of the Tropic of Cancer, there were to be no rules; in this, Europe's first Wild West, the different powers were free to pursue their interests without restraint. And soon this far-away zone of conflict, where there was "no Peace beyond the Line," was extended west and north to encompass all of North America.[1] European civilization would eventually find its way to the northern reaches of this faraway continent and largely undiscovered country. But the devil-take-the-hindmost imprecation at Vervins (a small French village in Picardy, near the Hapsburg Netherlands) goes far to explain much of Europe's bloody expansion into what would become, and in good part long remain, English America—or, after the 1707 union between England and Scotland, British North America. Unlike Spanish or lower North America, which was dominated by one European power, Spain, the vast region north of the Rio Grande was the scene of intense European rivalry and Native-European conflict for control of the rest of the continent.

New France

We have traced the history of New Spain. We will now look at the other Neo-Europes of North America. After several abortive efforts in the sixteenth century—by Jacques Cartier in Montreal, Sir Humphrey Gilbert in Newfoundland, and Sir Walter Raleigh in Roanoke—Europeans in the seventeenth century finally succeeded in founding colonies along the Atlantic Seaboard, north of Florida, and down the St. Lawrence Valley. They did so largely by means of joint-stock companies, a brilliant financial innovation in the history of capitalism. These organizations could raise pools of capital while limiting the liability of individual investors.

In 1606 King James I granted a charter to the Virginia Company of London. The following year the company established Jamestown and the first Anglican parish on the broad James River. Under the firm hand of Captain John Smith, a military veteran with a storied career, this colony encompassed the Chesapeake Bay region as far west as the Blue Ridge Mountains. It was one divided by nature into three regions or provinces: the tidewater, the piedmont, and the valley and ridge. Spanish tobacco—the mild-tasting *Nicotiana tabacum*, introduced by John Rolfe in 1612 from the Spanish Main's Orinoco Valley (the local variety, *Nicotiana rustica,* was bitter)—flourished in the low country or bottomland and proved to be a reliable cash crop. Indeed, tobacco supported the colony's economy for nearly two centuries. If the Church of England took root in Virginia, the Pilgrims and the Puritans found refuge in Massachusetts from Europe's religious storms. The city of Boston was founded in 1630. With its fine harbor, this "City on a Hill" became the spiritual as well as the commercial heart of New England.

Not surprisingly, the French followed closely on the heels of their English rivals with a North American colony of their own. Samuel de Champlain had fought in France's wars of religion for King Henry IV and had traveled to New Spain, Cuba, and Venezuela, observing at first hand the intricate workings of the Spanish Empire. He was an ideal choice to lead France's colonial efforts in North America. In 1604, as the king's envoy, he helped to establish a beachhead in Acadia, the maritime area that is now Nova Scotia, New Brunswick, and Prince Edward Island.

The original settlement was founded on an island in Passamaquoddy Bay, an inlet of the Bay of Fundy and home of the world's highest tides—between what is today New Brunswick and Maine, near the mouth of the St. Croix River. But it was soon abandoned for Port-Royal, a site on the opposite or eastern side of the Bay of Fundy. The colony held promise, but

Figure 14. William Hole, *Virginia / discovered and described [sic] by Captan [sic] John Smith, 1606; graven by William Hole*, 1612. Map. Prints and Photographs Division, Library of Congress, Washington, DC. https://www.loc.gov/item/2003670836/.

it was also extremely vulnerable to naval attack from the Gulf of Maine and was abandoned in 1607, the year that Jamestown was founded. In 1608 Champlain, a true visionary and deservedly considered the Father of New France, founded the city of Quebec on the north side of the St. Lawrence River, opposite the Norumbega peninsula.

It was a strategic point. The promontory above Quebec City, called Cape Diamond, overlooked the narrows of the St. Lawrence River below, marking the dividing line between the Atlantic Ocean and the continent's vast interior. Champlain had found his Dardanelles, which separated Europe from Asia, or his Strait of Gibraltar, which divided the Atlantic from the Mediterranean Sea. Later, in 1620, Champlain built a fort on top of the promontory. The economy of this defensible, if lonely, and strikingly impressive outpost of Western civilization was based on the trade of European goods for Native furs and pelts, especially that of the beaver (the noble *Castor canadensis*). New France would eventually comprise the five colonies of Canada, Acadia, Newfoundland (Plaisance), Hudson Bay, and Louisiana.[2]

To encourage this activity—in 1624, there were fewer than sixty people in the city of Quebec—Cardinal Richelieu, Louis XIII's brilliant and capable minister, arranged a charter for the Company of New France, or Hundred Associates, in 1627, modeled on the joint-stock companies of England and the Netherlands. The Edict of Nantes notwithstanding, Cardinal Richelieu saw to it that henceforth only Catholics were permitted to immigrate to New France. Moreover, as in Mexico, the Catholic Church came to dominate the life of the colony of New France. The Jesuits or "Black Robes," including Father Jean de Brébeuf, a missionary, arrived in New France in 1625 to spread the gospel. Brébeuf was later tortured and martyred by the Iroquois in 1649, when they attacked and destroyed their regional rival, the Huron nation, France's ally and partner in the fur trade, becoming one of the eight *saints martyrs canadiens*, or "Canada's Martyrs." In the meantime, the Scots founded short-lived settlements at Port Royal in Nova Scotia ("New Scotland") and New Galloway on Cape Breton Island in 1629, before the French reasserted their claims to Acadia.

With the disappearance of the Huron from the shores of the lake from which they took their name, the French—whose population in Quebec numbered fewer than one thousand in 1650—had no choice but to turn to French laborers, a class that came to be known as the *coureurs de bois*, or "runners of the forest," to take up the slack. To feed and supply the *coureurs de bois* and barter with the Indigenous tribes, the French brought in more laborers to clear the land and farm the St. Lawrence Valley. Thus the Iroquois attack on the Huron fundamentally altered the character of the French presence in North America; it turned Quebec into a settler, as opposed to a trading, colony. After 1681 licensed traders were known as voyageurs, while unlicensed or renegade traders were called *coureurs des bois*. But these independent men were of no less importance to the French fur trade. In the west they explored the *pays d'en haut*, or "upper country," and built economic and familial relationships with Native peoples.[3]

Due to the six-to-one ratio of men to women, the European population along the St. Lawrence Valley remained very small. One scholar estimates that during the French period as many as 27,000 immigrated to Canada, but only 31.6 percent actually remained.[4] French Canada's European population would depend not on immigration but on natural increase, the turning point of which occurred in the 1660s, with the arrival of 800 *filles du roi*, "daughters of the king," between 1663 and 1673. These women were part of the imperial agenda of Jean-Baptiste Colbert, Louis XIV's controller-general of finances, to increase the size of the population of New France. (Colbert's man on the ground was the capable Jean Talon, the intendant and ardent mercantilist who arrived in Canada in 1665.) At least a third of these single or widowed women came from the home for the destitute, the Hôpital Général de Paris. Each endowed by the court with a dowry of fifty livres, these women soon found husbands and a rustic respectability. Moreover, in what almost sounds like a fairy-tale ending, these unions and the families they produced would form Quebec's founder population.[5]

The native-born European population reached 15,000 in 1700, when the male-female ratio had normalized.[6] In 1755, before the British conquest (the decisive Battle of Quebec on the Plains of Abraham occurred in 1759), the European population had increased to 62,000, and by 1771, after the conquest, to 80,000. In contrast to the Spanish conquest of Mexico, the British conquest of Canada (Quebec and Ontario) left no discernible mark on nativity, marriage, and mortality rates, which remained constant.[7] On the contrary, in the postconquest years the British Province of Quebec thrived. And in contrast to the English colonies, this steady, and indeed remarkable, growth rate was due almost entirely to natural increase, the excess of births over deaths (the annual rate was a vigorous 2.5 percent, which meant a doubling of the population every thirty years), not to immigration from the old country. Important reasons for this growth had to do with the high fertility of Canadian women as well as low adult mortality, both of which, in turn, can be partly attributed to the highly salubrious Canadian environment. During their childbearing years, women in the St. Lawrence Valley had, on average, two more children than did women in France. And a French Canadian family, on average, had between seven and eight children—and 40 percent of these families had at least ten children.[8] In short, the *filles du roi* program was arguably one of the most successful government initiatives in North American history. From these humble acorns grew a mighty oak forest: a viable, healthy, self-sustaining, and largely homogenous population—a veritable *société française*.[9]

Eventually the arable lands on both sides of the St. Lawrence River, from the Gulf, past Quebec City and Trois-Riviéres, and upriver to the Lachine Rapids (near the riparian island and site of Montreal), were granted to seigneurs, or landed gentry—the nobility, the clergy, military officers, and civil administrators. These seigneuries were cleverly divided into long, narrow *rangs* or lots, typically about 500 feet wide and 5,000 feet long, each of which was laid out perpendicular to the river. Thus each strip of field or pasture had on one end a narrow frontage on the river, and on the other a narrow access to a forest or to a road that ran parallel to the river. Over the course of the French period, beginning in 1627, approximately 220 seigneuries were granted. These lands were worked by tenants called habitants, who made up 80 percent of Canada's European population. In theory, this was Old World manorialism. But New World conditions—namely, New France's or Quebec's factor endowments of abundant lands, small population, few markets, and isolation—worked against the system. The seigneurs found that they could not live by rent alone, as could the nobility in France, and were obliged to find other sources of income. They also mixed much more with the rest of society, unlike their aloof counterparts across the water.

In fact, France's sugar islands—Guadeloupe (where Verrazzano had met his demise), Martinique, and Saint-Domingue—were forced to turn to the British colonies for needed supplies rather than to Canada, with its small surpluses of wheat and other produce. In 1700 the European population of Canada stood at only 15,000 souls (towered over by the Native population, at 185,000, though it was spread out over a much larger territory).[10] Thus while the seigneur tried to augment his rental income, the habitant was concerned with his or her own subsistence—the production of roughly 2,500 calories per day—to the exclusion of almost everything else. By 1700 the per capita GDP of European Canada was $800 (in 1990 dollars), or exactly double that of the per capita GDP of Native Canada, with its hunting, gathering, and horticultural economy. The average per capita GDP (European and Native) or multicultural estimate of Canada was $430.[11] The seigneurial system survived the British Conquest and was not officially abolished until 1854.

New Netherland and New Sweden

In 1609 Henry Hudson, in the employ of the Dutch East India Company (officially the Vereenigde Oostindische Compagnie, or United East India Company), explored his riparian namesake. He sailed the *Halve Maen* (Half Moon) up the Hudson River as far north as Albany and Troy (the Hudson River is tidal as far north as Troy) at roughly the same time that New France's Samuel de Champlain was heading down his lacustrine namesake from Quebec. Unbeknownst to them, the two explorers—in the vicinity of Lake Champlain, Lake George, and the Hudson River—came within a few miles and several months of meeting each other, paralleling Coronado and De Soto's near miss in the wilderness in 1541.[12]

Figure 15. S. Hollyer, *Henry Hudson's Half Moon, 1609*, c. 1909. Engraving. Prints and Photographs Division, Library of Congress, Washington, DC. https://www.loc.gov/item/2005689539/.

Hudson's voyage inaugurated the Dutch colonization of North America, followed by Adrian Block's four voyages between 1611 and 1614. In 1624 the colony of Nieuw Nederlandt or New Netherland was founded by the West India Company, and a lucrative trade in furs was established with the Native Americans. Dutch settlers (many were French-speaking Walloons) were also drawn to the region, which was bounded by the Delaware and Connecticut Rivers. Four decades later, however, the Dutch director general or governor, "Peg Leg" Peter Stuyvesant, surrendered political control of the colony to an English fleet (since his fellow citizens refused to fight for him, he had no choice). On September 8, 1664, New Amsterdam became New York City.

The West India Company was founded in 1621 as a joint-stock company, inspired by the famous and pioneering Dutch East India Company, which was chartered in 1602. One of the company's first orders of business was to establish the colony of New Netherland (also called Novi Belgica, "New Belgium"). In Indonesia the Dutch were lured by the promise of the spice trade. In North America they were drawn by the potential of the market in furs, a commodity they planned to funnel down the Hudson Valley, away from the English and the French. And in this endeavor they were very successful. By mid-century an astonishing eighty thousand beaver pelts a year were passing through Manhattan and on to Europe (the fur pelts were turned into fine felt, which in turn was made into fashionable hats for the well-to-do). The Dutch had aligned themselves with the Iroquois, principally with the Mohawk tribe, against the French and their Indigenous allies, the Algonquin and the Huron. The stakes were high. To secure the coveted role of middlemen in the fur trade, the Iroquois proved willing to destroy the Huron in Ontario in what amounted to a genocidal assault in 1649.

But the primary objective of the Dutch during the Eighty Years' War with Spain (1568–1648) was not the profitable fur trade but the use of North America as a staging area to harass Spanish shipping. The Dutch colony was comprised of the incredibly rich and bountiful lands that lay to the south of the St. Lawrence River, stretching from the Connecticut River or "Fresh River" in the northeast to Virginia in the southwest. Apart from numerous safe havens and its dry sandy beaches, New Netherland encompassed a harbor at the mouth of the Hudson River, where it emptied into New York Bay—possibly the finest harbor in the world, and the key to North America's future economic development. When it came to buying good real estate, the Dutch were second to none.[13]

In 1626 colonial governor Peter Minuit (a Walloon from Wesel) had acquired Manhattan, the site of the future financial capital of the world, from the chiefs or sachems of the Manhattans for sixty guilders worth of goods or trinkets. Minuit would later run afoul of his bosses (*boss* being a loanword from the Dutch *baas*) in Amsterdam and be recalled from the colony, but Manhattan, the capital of New Netherland but nevertheless a company town, at least as far as the West India Company was concerned, would prove its utility as a military base and eventually achieve a degree of self-government. Captain Willem Blauvelt, for example, a privateer who commanded the Dutch frigate *La Garce*, was well known for sailing into Floridian and West Indian waters and bringing back to Manhattan one Spanish prize after another. And in 1653 the city received, despite the grudging reluctance of its governor-general, a municipal charter—and the name New Amsterdam—providing for a government rooted in Roman-Dutch law.

Under the aggressive reign of Gustavus Adolphus, Sweden became a great power in Europe and entered a golden age. But in 1632 Gustavus, a Protestant, disappeared from history in the violent confusion of the Battle of Lützen in Saxony-Anhalt in what is today Germany. The battle was part of the Thirty Years' War, a conflict between Protestants and Catholics that overlapped with the last thirty years of the Eighty Years' War between the Dutch and the Spanish (military conflict in Europe was basically incessant).[14]

One of the important results of the Thirty Years' War was the delay in the unification of Germany until the nineteenth century. After Gustavus's death and during the ensuing regency of Christina, Axel Oxenstierna, the Swedish chancellor, continued the expansionist policies of Gustavus and engaged the services of the cashiered West India Company employee Minuit.[15] In 1638 the Dutchman went back to North America to found Nya Sverige or New Sweden, locating the colony on the lower Delaware River, which happened to be territory claimed but weakly defended, as Minuit well knew, by the Dutch. Needless to say, the New Netherlanders regarded the Swedes (and the "forest Finns" who came with them) as interlopers.[16] During its short life, the colony had four governors, the third and most important of whom, Johan Björnsson Printz, was a former military officer and a giant of a man—weighing in at four hundred pounds—who had fought for Sweden in the Thirty Years War. Printz's girth did not slow him down; he served as an energetic and capable, if autocratic, governor for eleven years, beginning in 1642.[17]

In 1655 the Dutch, under Peter Stuyvesant, the director general of New Netherland and the Dutch Antilles, that is, Curaçao, Bonaire, and Aruba, reclaimed the territory of New Sweden for the Dutch with a flotilla of seven vessels and three hundred soldiers. Like Printz, Stuyvesant resented any challenge to his authority. And like Champlain, Printz, Smith, and Myles Standish, Plymouth Colony's military leader, Stuyvesant was no stranger to combat. In 1644 he had lost a leg on Saint Martin to a cannonball in a failed effort to recapture the Caribbean island from the Spanish.[18] Without opposition, Stuyvesant took over the thinly populated colony of New Sweden (with less than four hundred souls), including Fort Christina—later Wilmington, Delaware—from the recently installed governor Johan Risingh, and thus restored Dutch control. While Stuyvesant was away dealing with the Swedes, however, Native American warriors killed or captured 250 Dutch settlers in a raid on Manhattan in the so-called Peach Tree War. This war was reportedly set off when Henry van Dyke, a Dutch farmer, killed a Native American girl for eating peaches from a tree in his orchard, but it may have had less to do with the theft of a single farmer's peaches than with the shift in power represented by the events in the lower Delaware Valley.

The replacement of New Sweden with New Amstel (later known as New Castle), a Dutch settlement founded by Stuyvesant to control the Delaware River, was more a change in management, if it even could be called that, than any kind of real subjugation, especially in the region north of where the Cristina and Brandywine Rivers reach the Delaware. The Dutch,

Swedish, and Finnish—Protestants all—lived in peace with each other and with the Lenapes, Susquehannocks, and other local Natives on a sort of middle ground, where no one power or interest predominated. The spirit of these equitable relations lasted after the old colony was granted to the Englishman and Quaker William Penn in 1681. Another legacy of New Sweden was the "American" log cabin, an ancient vernacular architecture imported from Scandinavia by the Finns.[19]

New Netherland had survived conflicts with the Natives such as Kieft's War (1643–45), the Peach Tree War (1655), and the Esopus Wars (1659–63). But less than ten years after the fall of New Sweden, in 1664, New Netherland was forced in turn to surrender to the English in Europe's seemingly endless game of musical chairs, although the Dutch colony had already lost significant territory in Connecticut and Long Island to the more numerous and land-encroaching New Englanders.[20]

This change in fortunes was executed by Captain Richard Nicolls, the agent of the Duke of York (later James II), brother of England's Charles II. The Stuart monarch had been restored to the English throne in 1660, ending England's Interregnum, which had begun in 1649 with the tyrannicide or regicide, depending on your politics, of Charles I. Along with three hundred soldiers, Nicolls seized the city of New Amsterdam and Fort Amsterdam, both located on the southern tip of Manhattan, without firing a single shot, and served ably as the English governor of the colony until 1668 (he was killed in action in 1672). It was Nicolls who renamed New Amsterdam as New York, after the Duke of York. English warships also seized the village of New Amstel. Thus the Dutch, who numbered by then around 9,000 (1,500 in New Amsterdam), were conquered, but like the Swedes in the Delaware Valley, they found the English yoke light. Their lives went on pretty much as before. This was true in Manhattan, up the Hudson Valley; in Fort Orange, later Albany, near the confluence of the Hudson and Mohawk Rivers in the Mohawk River Valley, the original gateway to the West and later the corridor of the Erie Canal; and in Beverwyck, which, with a population of one thousand, was in 1660 the largest community after New Amsterdam, 150 miles away. It was even true on the Manor of Rensselaerswyck surrounding Fort Orange, the most famous of North America's patroonships or semifeudal estates—counterparts to the seignories of New France, the haciendas of New Spain, and the plantations of the American South.[21]

Conquered but undefeated, the Dutch thrived and passed on to New York City a tradition of relative tolerance and egalitarianism. This remarkably open state of mind, which set New York apart from the rest of British America, was born out of the long Dutch struggle for independence from Spain and its policies of mind control in the Eighty Years' War (1568 to 1648), which left the Low Countries divided and the Dutch Protestants in the north committed to representative government and religious freedom, whether they called Amsterdam or New Amsterdam home. (The southern provinces, which would include Belgium and Luxembourg, on the other hand, remained under the control of Hapsburg Spain until the War of the Spanish Succession.) The English recognized these Dutch liberties. In fact, in 1664 Nicolls guaranteed them in the Articles of Capitulation, a document drawn up on Stuyvesant's *bouwerij*, or farm (an area later known to New Yorkers as the Bowery).[22]

Thus the struggles and conflicts of seventeenth-century Europe—but not necessarily Europe's violence—were projected, if faintly at this point, onto North America, an ocean away. It is noteworthy that New Netherland, New Sweden, New England, and Virginia were all, like their mother countries, Protestant (New France, like New Spain, was of course Roman Catholic). How one prayed mattered to seventeenth-century Europeans. In 1655 Stuyvesant was able to take over New Sweden without any loss of life. Three years later, in 1658, the Dutch fleet defeated the Swedish fleet in the Battle of the Sound (the Sound of Øresund, the body of water that narrowly separates Sweden from Denmark), thereby freeing up the vital Baltic trade to the Dutch Republic that the Kingdom of Sweden had sought to control. In this single engagement, there were 2,600 casualties. Similarly, the English fleet fought the Dutch for commercial advantage in several full-scale naval wars, beginning in 1652 with the First Anglo-Dutch War (there would be two others in the seventeenth century) between England and the Netherlands. There were no less than 5,500 casualties in this first conflict alone. And, yet for all of this violence in Europe, in North America Nicolls, like Stuyvesant, was able to effect a peaceful transfer of power.

The English takeover of New Netherland had profound implications for the North American fur trade. With control of the Hudson River Valley now in English hands, the English eventually replaced the Dutch as allies of the Iroquois and became an even greater threat to New France and France's American Indian allies. Moreover, in 1670, the first cousin of Charles II, Prince Rupert of the Rhine, a true Renaissance man, received a royal charter granting him trading privileges in the lands making up the vast watershed of Hudson Bay, which served as the legal basis for North America's oldest surviving corporation, the Hudson's Bay Company. And just as New York was named after Charles II's brother, Rupert's Land, as this vast land in the north came to be known, took its name from the king's cousin.

Thus the English now controlled two key sources of the fur trade—the Hudson River and Hudson Bay. This meant that the French settlements along the St. Lawrence River Valley were caught in a great commercial pincer movement. To parry England's deft moves, the French pushed west into the Great Lakes and south to the Gulf of Mexico. After Jean Talon returned to France in 1672, the governor-general of New France, Louis de Buade, comte de Palluau et de Frontenac and veteran of the Thirty Years' War, established Fort Frontenac on Lake Ontario near the source of the St. Lawrence River, one of a growing string of French forts. Thus the St. Lawrence River was now fortified on both ends, from Quebec City to Fort Frontenac. And in 1682 La Salle, a seigneur in New France, explored the Mississippi Valley, calling it Louisiana after the Sun King, Louis XIV. This region was subsequently secured by the native-born Canadian Pierre Le Moyne d'Iberville in 1702 (his brother Jean-Baptiste Le Moyne de Bienville, as we have seen, founded New Orleans and was long involved in the administration of Louisiana). The region was divided into Basse-Louisiane (lower Louisiana) and Haute-Louisiane (upper Louisiana), also known as the Pays des Illinois (Illinois country). The dividing line between the two was the Arkansas River. The economy of this new colony functioned very simply: the farmers of the Mississippi bottomlands of Illinois basically fed the Gulf Coast settlers of New Orleans, Mobile, Biloxi, and Natchez with wheat and flour, ham, salt pork, dried beef, and venison. Furs and lead were also exported downriver from French Illinois. As of 1752, the population of French Illinois was approximately three thousand, one-third of it either enslaved Blacks or Natives.[23]

It is worth remembering here that the Dutch briefly regained control of New York City in 1673 but returned it to the English the following year. Fifteen years later the Dutch invaded England itself, at the instigation of Parliament, to rid the country of its monarch, James II, a Catholic convert—a pious decision, perhaps, but a politically foolish one—in what was called the Glorious Revolution. James chose to flee to France rather than to stay in England to fight. William of Orange, a stadtholder and Protestant, and his wife Anne, the daughter of James II but also a Protestant, went on to reign as joint sovereigns. Queen Anne, who survived William, was the last of the Stuarts. More significantly, these events produced the English Bill of Rights, another landmark document in the evolution of Anglo-Dutch liberty and tolerance, which contrasted sharply at the time with the royal absolutism of the Spanish and French monarchies and, by extension, with the governance of their respective colonies in North America.

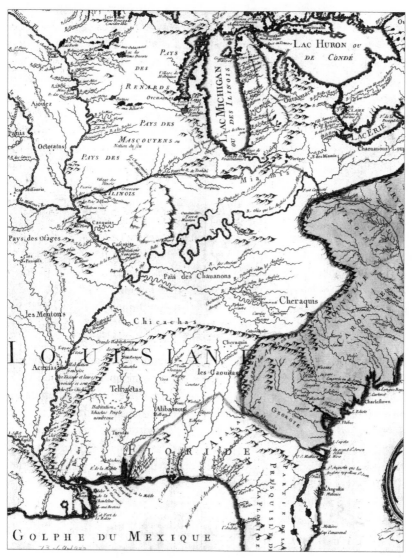

Figure 16. Jean Baptiste Nolin and Jean-Francois Daumont, Detail of *Carte du Canada et de la Louisiane qui forment la Nouvelle France et des colonies angloises ou sont representez les pays contestez* (detail). Map. Paris: Chez Daumont, 1756. Prints and Photographs Division, Library of Congress, Washington, DC. https://www.loc.gov/item/73694932/.

North America's Dark and Bloody Ground

The two peaceful changes in North American colonial governance—the takeover of New Sweden and of New Netherland—were the exceptions to the rule. In contrast, as we shall see, the fraught colonial relations of the Protestant English and Catholic French resulted in two centuries of on-again, off-again warfare in North America, with profound implications for the continent's social development. The French and English wars with the Native Americans were particularly vicious. They began almost immediately with the first settlements and were continued by these European parties or their respective successors, the US and British or Canadian governments, intermittently, for nearly three centuries.[24] Samuel de Champlain and his Algonquin and Montagnais allies went to war with the Iroquois Confederacy or the Haudenosaunee tribes, which included the Mohawk, the Oneida, the Onondaga, the Cayuga, and the Seneca (and, after 1722, the Tuscaroa) as early as 1609 near Lake Champlain. This was the first skirmish of the Fur Wars, which during the seventeenth and eighteenth centuries were fought out in the St. Lawrence River Valley, the Ohio Country, and the lower Great Lakes region. Champlain killed two Iroquois warriors with a single shot from an arquebus, thereby introducing European firepower to upper North America and commencing a long-standing blood feud between the Iroquois and the French and their Indigenous allies.

At the same time in Virginia, only two years after the founding of Jamestown, war broke out between the English and the Pamunkey tribe, and it dragged on until 1614, when the colonists returned Pocahontas, the abducted daughter of Chief Wahunsenacawh, or Powhatan. Pocahontas married the Englishman and tobacco farmer John Rolfe, but tensions between the two groups continued as the English seeded more and more lands with tobacco, the colony's economic and profitable mainstay. The peace was shattered on Good Friday, March 22, 1622, when the second of the three Tidewater Wars broke out. Opechancanough, Powhatan's brother and now head of a confederation of some thirty tribal groups, numbering around eight thousand, launched a brilliant coordinated attack that wiped out 347 colonists, reducing the population to 1,240 (although disease, not violence, remained the colony's greatest killer).

The military disaster forced James I, king of England (and of Scotland, as James VI), to revoke the company's charter. In 1623 his court assumed direct responsibility for, and control of, what was now no longer a corporate but a crown colony. Fighting continued until peace was finally reached with

peonage—although this was based more on credit than actual bondage—to the country's new Criollo landlords, the hacendados. The social transformation that occurred in English-speaking North America did so through a cycle: first, immigration, driven in part by England's enclosure movement; second, European-Native warfare—with the advantage on the European side; and third, land clearing, accomplished by hand and ax.

The enclosure movement, which largely began in England and later spread to the continent, transformed western Europe's communally held arable lands into individually owned and managed farms. Land enclosure was the precondition for modern farming. And in a sense Europe's enclosure movement was extended to North America as individual freeholders acquired Native American lands, which were also held in common, although land tenure in New France, New Spain, and New Netherland passed first through a distinct manorial phase. In the English colonies, the practice of indentured servitude could be regarded as a form of serfdom, if a very temporary one (four to seven years). The process of turning the continent of North America into real estate overwhelmingly benefited European Americans, although in the nineteenth century liberal reformers in Mexico, the United States, and Canada such as Miguel Lerdo de Tejada, Henry Dawes, and John A. Macdonald tried to make "allotment in severalty" and other assimilationist programs work for Native peoples as well, usually with mixed, if not tragic, results. On the other hand, the enclosure of North America, which took nearly four centuries to complete, released the continent's enormous productive capacity, thereby transforming the North American as well as the world economy. To sum up this dramatic change, in 1500 North America supported a population of a mere 9,750,000; by 1820, toward the close of our period, this number had almost doubled to 17,384,000. Today (2020), North America supports a population of no less than approximately 493 million—or nearly a half a billion people![26]

But we are getting ahead of ourselves. The opening of free land on the western edge of settlement was a process that acted to keep down the price of real estate. Indeed, by the end of the seventeenth century landownership in America—in the northern as well as in the southern colonies—was widespread.[27] According to historian Allan Kulikoff,

All but 4 of the first 238 inhabitants of Salem, Massachusetts got land, and later arrivals fared nearly as well, eleven-twelfths (134 of 146) getting land. . . . In three towns in Essex County, Massachusetts, in the late seventeenth century, half the men owned land before they were thirty, as did 95 percent of men over thirty-six. Before 1660 two-fifths of Connecticut settlers, most of them young men, had no land, but by the 1690s six-sevenths of all farmers owned land. . . . In 1660 four-fifths of the white men in Charles County, Maryland, were landowners; as the opportunity for former servants to get land plummeted, the proportion of owners among taxable men declined to seven-tenths in 1675 and six-tenths in 1690. . . . In both 1687 and 1704 nearly two-thirds of the household heads in Surry County, Virginia, held land, as did three-quarters of householders in Talbot County, on Maryland's Eastern Shore, in 1704. Landownership, moreover, might have been nearly universal in early Pennsylvania; during the 1690s eight-ninths of the householders in one Chester County township owned land.

And as Benjamin Franklin put it:

Land being thus plenty in America, and so cheap as that a labouring Man, that understands Husbandry, can in a short Time save Money enough to purchase a Piece of new Land sufficient for a Plantation, whereon he may subsist a Family; such are not afraid to marry; for if they even look far enough forward to consider how their Children when grown up are to be provided for, they see that more Land is to be had at Rates equally easy, all Circumstances considered.[28]

This development, the ubiquitous freehold farm, along with a light tax burden to support a bare minimum of public services—forts, roads, schools, jails, courts, ports, and poor relief—were the key underlying conditions for the general prosperity of colonial British America.[29] Or to use the old formulation: with land there was liberty. In contrast, the fiscal system of the crown in Spanish North America remained feudalistic in nature in that "all known production or income had to be taxed." And unlike the English system, it was all but indifferent to the needs of commerce and manufacturing.[30] On these matters, the political scientist Alvin Rabushka concludes:

When the dust settled on the seventeenth century, 250,000 colonists had secured for themselves the power to tax and spend that was largely free from governors and their officials sent from England, appointed by the proprietors, or selected from among themselves in the charter colonies. Even when rates, poll taxes, duties, and other levies were authorized by elected representatives to colonial legislatures, taxpayers sought to minimize their taxes in every imaginable way, from hiding real assets to undervaluing farmland to making payment in substandard commodities to outright refusal to pay. The first century of the American colonies set a firm low-tax foundation that underpinned the economic freedom of generations of Americans to come.[31]

The upshot was this: in 1700 the per capita GDP of Europeans and Africans in prefederal America was $909 (in 1990 dollars), while that of Native Americans was $400 (the maximum value, according to Maddison's estimates, of a hunting, gathering, and horticultural economy).[32] GDP for that year was $527 million. In contrast, Canada's multicultural estimate (Europeans and Natives) of per capita GDP was much lower, at $430 ($800 for the European population), while Mexico's per capita GDP was significantly higher, at $568. Thus, in 1700 Mexico's GDP was $2.5 billion, or five times larger than the prefederal US GDP at $527 million and nearly twenty-nine times larger than Canada's GDP at $86 million (GDP for Canada's European population was $12 million; for its Native population, $74 million).[33]

Eventually the freehold farm of British North America and the relatively easy access to land in New France would go far in explaining the growing gulf in social development between British and Spanish North America, which would accelerate rapidly after 1800, with the spread of the latter's large haciendas, estancias, and minas. In Mexico the ownership of the means of production and exchange belonged, as an old-fashioned Marxist would have it, to the few—specifically to those who belonged to the *república de los españoles*. As for the more populous *república de los indios*, the private plot—separate from the community—did not exist. In the words of Enrique Semo, an old-fashioned Marxist, "Peasants in Mexico had not cut the umbilical cord that bound them to the community. . . . In Western Europe, small property owners constituted the basis of most struggles against feudal lords. Their emancipation from the yoke of serfdom laid the foundation for the proliferation of petty commodity production, the threshold of capitalism." However, if Native communities in Mexico did not possess private property, American Indians were, as Humboldt had observed, not serfs. They were a free people, but they did not possess the private property rights to secure that freedom, a crucial difference that would distinguish Mexico from the rest of North America and one that goes far to explain, along with the country's belated industrialization, Mexican underdevelopment. In the nineteenth century, liberals would try to privatize the American Indian commons—as well as church lands—with the Ley Lerdo (Lerdo law) of 1856 in order to create a genuine Native yeomanry. But this well-intentioned reform ended up instead benefiting the large landowners.[34]

But again, we are getting ahead of ourselves. In 1676 Bacon's Rebellion soon turned into a civil war between the colony's loyalists—some of whom were Royalists from England who had fled in the 1650s from Oliver Cromwell's Commonwealth and Protectorate (1649–60)—and the rebels. Bacon, the rebel leader, would succumb to typhus and dysentery, the "bloody flux," in October 1676, but not before his men burned down Jamestown, the capital of Virginia. The uprising confirmed to the colony's planter elite that enslaved Blacks or bondspeople were preferable to White indentured servants, a class that eventually, as they fulfilled their covenants or contracts, became free and therefore a potential menace to society—providing they did not die of disease first. The opening of lands in the backcountry to free Whites, however, greatly mitigated this threat, while the involuntary servitude of Blacks ensured that planters would have a tractable workforce and a profitable business. Dutch traders introduced African slaves to Jamestown, Virginia, as early as 1619.

In Canada (Quebec), the colonial economy did not favor the growth of slavery because the economy's two principal industries required little manual labor: the fur trade was controlled by a small group of professionals and essentially relied on the labor of Native fur trappers, and the manual labor of French families was sufficient for the colony's small family-farm operations. The American South and French Louisiana, on the other hand, did.[35] The gradual turn to forced, racialized lifetime labor—that is, the perpetual slavery of peoples of African descent—was momentous, a change that had become clear by 1705, when the House of Burgesses passed Virginia's infamous Slave Codes. And France's *code noir* (slave code) was later extended from the West Indies to Louisana in 1724. The "peculiar institution" set Virginia and the South on a social trajectory different from that of New England and the rest of the North, as well as in large rural patches throughout the South, where the ideal as well as the reality was the freehold farm. But slavery was similar to the labor situation that existed in central and southern Mexico, even if slavery itself was abolished in Mexico in 1829.

Next to the French seignory, the Dutch patroonship, and the Spanish or Criollo hacienda, the stark and binary master-slave relationship that existed on the southern plantation was the most extreme form of social and labor organization anywhere on the continent. Large-scale, single-crop plantation agriculture of tobacco, indigo, cotton, or sugar was profitable to a few—the planters or owners. Indeed, slavery allowed for the amassment of huge fortunes, sustained an opulent and even an aristocratic way of life, and concentrated political power in the hands of a small elite. And to protect the economic as well as social institution of Black slavery, this White elite (and political oligarchy) found it useful to make common cause with middling and poor Whites—a political, social, and racial possibility that did not exist in the West Indies or Mexico. In this way and in this region, race transcended class and a powerful new European American identity was forged, which largely distinguished the American from the Canadian and Mexican experience. Slavery also helped to stimulate multilateral trade flows, which in turn hastened the full transition to capitalism. But to the many—the hapless Blacks whose unrequited toil supported the American South's network of sugar, tobacco, and cotton plantations—work and living conditions were in the main physically brutal, mentally stultifying, and spiritually enervating. Whatever slavery contributed to America's social power, it took away from the country's social development. In these terms, the institution of slavery was to the American South what the Desagüe de Huehuetoca was to central Mexico.[36]

America: A Better Europe

Slavery was eventually abolished in North America, but not before a profound revolution in moral perception across the Western world, albeit one that did not occur everywhere or all at once. Indeed, according to the distinguished scholar David Brion Davis, the abolitionist movement marked the dawn of a new age of reform, a second Axial Age, in which slavery as well as serfdom, along with many other ancient practices such as torture, suttee, dueling, footbinding, public execution, flogging, bear baiting, and impressment, came under the scrutiny of an increasingly candid world. For millennia slavery was regarded everywhere in the world as a normal, even necessary, practice. And then suddenly, in the late eighteenth century, the West produced critics, from religious as well as secular quarters, whose attacks on the execrable institution ultimately resulted in its demise—*despite* slavery's growing economic importance and profitability in the next century. The chorus of abolitionists producing music that could be heard on both sides of the Atlantic included John Wesley, Thomas Clarkson, William Wilberforce, William Roscoe, Angelina Grimké, William Lloyd Garrison, the freedman Frederick Douglas, John Brown, and Harriet Beecher Stowe.

There was, we should note, an important precedent. The colony of Georgia (named after King George II) was founded in 1733 by the soldier, philanthropist, reformer, and colonial trustee, James Edward Oglethorpe.[37] Georgia, an original program of the Enlightenment, was to serve as a refuge for the poor and oppressed. America was always at its best when it tried to be a better Europe. The plan was for these deserving souls to receive a second chance in the New World by learning to produce wine, olive oil, and silk—in a place where slavery, rum, lawyers, and Catholics were prohibited—for export to England.[38] Parliament explicitly banned slavery in 1735.[39]

The colony was a refuge, perhaps, but it was hardly a safe haven, located as it was in the "debatable" or contested land of cabbage palms and salt marshes that lay between the English in South Carolina, the Spanish in Florida, and the French in Louisiana, along with the various Native allies of these European powers. Of immediate concern, Oglethorpe worked swiftly to establish friendly relations with Chief Tomochichi of the Yamacraw tribe, a small local band of Lower Creek people. This diplomacy proved successful, based as it was on mutual interest. It gave the fragile English colony a security that probably could not have been achieved through the show or force of arms alone.

However, with the breakout of the War of Jenkins' Ear or Guerra del Asiento, as the Spanish called it, in 1739, between Britain and Spain, Georgia found itself in the middle of an ongoing imperial rivalry that had suddenly turned violent. The following year Oglethorpe tried but failed to capture St. Augustine. However, in 1742, two years later, on the Georgian sea island of St. Simons, where six years before Oglethorpe had prudently established Fort Frederica, the colony's military headquarters, Oglethorpe and the Georgia militia repulsed a Spanish invasion.

St. Simons had once been the site of two Spanish missions: Santo Domingo de Asajo and San Buenaventura de Guadalquini, two of a string of Spanish towns, missions, and presidios or garrisons that had stretched up the eastern seaboard. These were built during the sixteenth and seventeenth centuries to protect the Spanish transatlantic convoys or treasure fleets from English and French privateers as well as to Christianize local Natives, such as the Yamasee. These hoary claims notwithstanding, with Oglethorpe's victory over the Spanish in the Battle of Bloody Marsh, Georgia's future was secured and Britain, not Spain, would become master of the American Southeast, the coastal region above the mouth of Florida's St. Johns River.

Despite this military success, after two decades Oglethorpe's admirable utopian experiment failed, and in 1752 the trustee-governed colony was turned over to royal control. The ill-advised efforts to produce wine, olive oil, and silk had come to naught. Interestingly, unlike silk, peaches, which also originated in China, thrived in Georgia. The fruit had been successfully introduced earlier by Franciscan missionaries to St. Augustine, Florida, and later planted on St. Simons and Cumberland Islands. But they were not grown in Georgia as an important orchard crop until King Cotton was finally dethroned by the Civil War.

Of even greater significance than the agricultural failures of Trustee Georgia was the abandonment of the ban on slavery. To Oglethorpe's chagrin, his victory over the Spanish had removed the security argument for the ban on slavery, since African slaves who could expect freedom from the Spanish in exchange for military service were no longer seen as potential collaborators or fifth columnists. In 1751 Parliament repealed its 1735 ban on slavery in Georgia, and within three years Georgia adopted a slave code virtually identical to the slave code of South Carolina. In fact, South Carolina's planters soon brought their slave-based rice economy to Georgia's Lowcountry, while Savannah (which means a flat tropical grassland), Georgia's capital, evolved into a major cotton exporter. The colonial capital had been founded in 1733 by Oglethorpe on Yamacraw Bluff, located some sixteen miles up the Savannah River from the Atlantic.

All that seemed to remain of the original humanitarian ideals of Oglethorpe and the other like-minded trustees was Savannah's innovative urban design. The city was planned around a geometrical system of squares, or small parks. The six squares that Oglethorpe originally laid out were later expanded in number to twenty-four. Today twenty-two carefully manicured squares remain, each shaded by live oaks festooned with Spanish moss, and many adorned with monuments or fountains and semitropical flora, making Savannah one of the most graceful and charming cities in North America.[40]

One Step Forward, Two Steps Back

While it is true that Parliament reversed its ban on slavery in Georgia in 1751, in the longer view what is significant is that Parliament banned the institution in the first place, back in 1735, establishing the possibility that it could do so again. And if Parliament could ban slavery in one colony, it could in theory ban the institution everywhere it had jurisdiction—that is, throughout the entire empire. Over time, this idea gained more supporters than opponents.

In 1787 the Society for the Abolition of the Slave Trade was founded in London, and in 1793 the House of Assembly in Upper Canada, at the behest of lieutenant governor John Graves Simcoe, passed an act preventing the further introduction of slaves into the province. After Parliament's 1735 prohibition of the institution in Georgia, this was the first piece of legislation in the British Empire to limit slavery, which explains why the Underground Railroad (a network of Good Samaritans and sanctuaries created to help escaped American slaves find freedom) would terminate in Windsor, Ontario, just across the river from Detroit, Michigan, and thus outside the jurisdiction of US law enforcement (the US Fugitive Slave Acts obliged northern officials to return runaway slaves to their southern owners). The Underground Railroad also ran south to freedom in Mexico, as it had once done in Florida, but was not nearly as well organized, according to historian Sean M. Kelly, as was the much better known northern operation.[41] The British later used their navy, at considerable cost, to suppress the slave trade, which was abolished in 1807, although the trade continued illicitly long after that date. The institution of slavery itself was finally eliminated throughout the British Empire in 1833, which included Canada, exactly one century after Oglethorpe founded his utopian colony.

The scholars Chaim Kaufmann and Robert Pape have called Britain's efforts to stop the Atlantic slave trade, which went on from 1807 until 1867, the most expensive example of "international moral action in modern history," adding that

> Britain carried out this effort despite its domination of both the slave trade and world sugar production, which was based on slave labor. In 1805–1806 the value of British West Indian sugar production equaled about 4 percent of the national income of Great Britain. Its efforts to suppress the slave trade sacrificed these interests, brought the country into conflict with the other Atlantic maritime powers, and cost Britain more than five thousand lives as well as an average nearly 2 percent of national income annually for sixty years [from 1807 until 1867, when, as a result of British coercion, Cuba finally banned the importation of slaves].[42]

The abolition of slavery in the United States took a more circuitous, longer, and ultimately much more violent route than did that in Britain.

In 1784 Thomas Jefferson, an extraordinarily complex and contradictory man, tried to outlaw slavery in all the new states to be carved out of the western territories, north as well as south of the Ohio River, in a bold proviso to the Territorial Governance Act of 1784. The legislation was ratified by Congress, but Jefferson's anti-slavery plank was defeated by one vote. In 1786 he lamented, "The voice of a single individual . . . would have prevented this abominable crime from spreading itself over the new country. Thus we see the fate of millions unborn hanging on the tongue of one man, and heaven was silent in that awful moment! But it is to be hoped it will not always be silent and that the friends to the rights of human nature will in the end prevail."[43]

The good news was that they did. Three years after 1784's two steps back, the friends of human rights took one very big step forward with the Northwest Ordinance of 1787, outlawing slavery north of the Ohio River in the new Northwest Territories, though they failed to prevent it from expanding in the Southwest Territories—across the Deep South and onto the plains of Texas. The fate of slavery in the Great West had not been sealed one way or the other, however. The struggle between the forces of freedom and slavery over the region's future would produce a series of sectional crises—firebells ringing in the night—and compromises. Like the United Kingdom, the United States had ended the slave trade in 1807, as delegates had agreed to do twenty years earlier at the Constitutional Convention of 1787. But the abolition of chattel slavery would not occur in the United States until 1865.

During the Civil War (1861–65), the Union Army, which included separate Black units (by the end of the war Blacks made up 10 percent of the Union Army's manpower), succeeded in preserving the United States from dissolution as well as liberating nearly four million Americans from bondage. It did so, in part, with General Sherman's famous (or infamous) 1864 march through Georgia from Atlanta to Savannah, a sweeping scorched-earth campaign that broke the back of the Confederacy. Preserving the Union and thereby nobly saving Abraham Lincoln's "last best hope" as well as ending slavery in the Anglosphere's last holdout were civilization-altering victories. But soldiers, alas, can march much faster than the pace of social change, as was sadly proved by the truculent South's postwar resistance, yet another two steps back, to the one step forward of Reconstruction.[44] In respect to emancipation and in a respectful nod to whiggish history, a school of thought that posits that history has a progressive directionality, it is worth remembering that the very wording of Jefferson's failed antislavery proviso of 1784, the so-called Lost Clause, reappears or is found again in the text of the Thirteenth Amendment. This latter measure, passed in 1865, eliminated slavery in the United States once and for all.[45]

CHAPTER 10

Transatlantic Wars and Transcontinental Treks

The Repetition of History

The authorities in New Spain did have to contend with Native hostilities, especially in the underpopulated northern provinces, where missions and presidios were built in tandem for a good reason. But throughout the colonial period, New Spain was largely free of European rivalry and warfare. This was true until the Dos de Mayo uprising against Napoleon Bonaparte's occupation of Madrid on May 2, 1808, and the ensuing Peninsular War. The Spanish called this war the Guerra de la Independencia (War of Independence), and its memory has been preserved in the haunting paintings and prints of the artist Francisco Goya.

This European war begat numerous other wars and uprisings, including Mexico's own long war of independence from Spain from 1810 to 1821, which left the country independent but chronically unstable and insecure. The unity Mexico briefly achieved in its struggle to evict the peninsulares or *gachupines* ("those without spurs") was important but ephemeral. The winners of Mexico's revolution, after all, were the Criollo hacendados, who had rid their country of the Spanish and, from their standpoint, Spain's stifling viceregal bureaucracy and mercantile controls. From the Spanish point of view, this bureaucracy had served as a check on first the encomenderos and, later on, the hacendados. With this check removed, the hacendados—some conservative, some liberal—were free to pursue their own interests in an endless series of struggles for power. Given its weak democratic character, perhaps what Mexico needed was a monarchy, or some type of a strongly unifying institution. In the first flush of independence, the conservative Augustín de Iturbide, who was a better general than a politician, tried to establish a constitutional monarchy and an empire. Tragically, this North

American political experiment ended almost as soon as it began. Decades of civil strife, punctuated by foreign invasion, ensued.[1]

These constitutional and military struggles left the Native and Mestizo masses, who had little or no stake in the outcome, largely undisturbed and almost completely indifferent to those who made claims of leadership. This indifference would prove fatal; history rarely repeats itself, but in Mexico it surely did. And while the outcome was the same, the role that Natives peoples played could not have been more different. As we saw, in 1519 the Spanish landed near Veracruz and marched to Tenochititlán, where they defeated the Aztecs. Along the way, they enjoyed the enthusiastic support of numerous Native allies eager to help destroy the hated Aztecs. This support was crucial to the success of Hernán Cortés.

Fast forward three hundred and twenty-six years, to March 9, 1847, when General Winfield Scott, at the head of a US force of ten thousand troops, landed south of Veracruz, in what was the largest amphibious landing in North American history. This was a prime example of social power—a society's ability to get things done. From the coast, Scott and company marched inland to Mexico City, after defeating a superior Mexican force led by Antonio López de Santa Anna in the Battle of Cerro Gordo. Scott entered Mexico City in triumph on September 14, 1847. This time Native peoples neither aided nor hindered the advance of the invading army. And given that they numbered in the millions by this time, their population having recovered to pre-Cortesian levels, their involvement, either way, would have been greatly impactful, if not decisive. The American invaders could have found themselves in the same predicament in which the British found themselves in 1775 at Lexington and Concord, where they were surrounded and harassed by the local militia. And if American troops in Mexico had encountered strong popular resistance and been forced to turn the invasion into a retreat back to Veracruz, they could very well have shared the same fate as did British forces in their humiliating march back to Boston, or their more recent and disastrous withdrawal from Kabul to a British garrison in Jalalabad in 1842, when they had no choice but to run a ninety-mile gauntlet of Afghan tribesmen. That ordeal ended with the last stand and massacre (near the village of Gandamak) of Sir William Elphinstone's expeditionary army—sixteen thousand soldiers, sepoys, civilians, and camp followers—in the rugged foothills of the Hindu Kush. Only one European survivor got through to Jalalabad.

In Mexico, as it turned out, there were no Native equivalents of a Paul Revere or of Minutemen (although the Americans were slowed down by yellow fever, as well as other maladies that they encountered in Mexico's coastal lowlands). And there were no gauntlets to run, only Native inaction, which proved key to the US victory over its southern neighbor. Once again in Mexican history, a small force of foreign invaders had conquered a land of millions. What the Americans found in Mexico was a deeply divided society, or congeries of societies—a nation without a common nationality, little social power, and no general will.[2]

Out of the Smithy of War

In sharp contrast, middle and upper North America during the colonial era were the scenes of almost endless European conflict, much of it between agents and forces of the French and British Empires and their respective Native allies or proxies. In this respect, the history of middle and upper North America reads more like the history of Europe than does that of New Spain. And throughout, of course, Native tribes negotiated or fought for their own reasons. From 1689 to 1783 the region north of the Rio Grande and east of the Mississippi was but one of several theaters in a seemingly endless succession of European wars: what was known as the War of the Grand Alliance or the War of the League of Augsburg in Europe (1689–97) was called King William's War in North America; Europe's War of the Spanish Succession (1702–13) was North America's Queen Anne's War; Europe's War of the Austrian Succession (1744–48) was North America's King George's War; and Europe's Seven Years' War (1754–63) was called the French and Indian War in North America.[3]

The last conflict, however, differed from the others in two very important respects: first, the war actually started in North America, involving none other than George Washington, a twenty-two-year-old Virginian and future founding father of the United States. This was due to British colonial opposition to France's expansion into the Ohio River Valley, below the confluence of the Allegheny and Monongahela Rivers. The war then spread from North America to Europe, instead of the other way around, as had been the case in all of the previous colonial conflicts mentioned. This difference demonstrated North America's growing importance vis-à-vis western Europe. Second, and again unlike previous colonial conflicts, the French and Indian War produced a decisive result. The American colonists, with the help of the British, were able to drive the French—though not the habitants, voyageurs, or *coureurs des bois*—out of North America. Voltaire famously dismissed the loss of Canada in the novel *Candide* (1759), sneering that the country was little more than *quelques arpents de neige*, "a few acres of snow." The great philosophe apparently made no note of the many acres of wheat and vegetables up and down the St. Lawrence Valley or of New France's vast wealth in natural resources, chiefly furs, hardwood timber, and fish. In fact trade with French Canada—which was largely economically self-sufficient, although it did buy wine and brandy from the home country—did not amount to much, and was paltry in comparison with the sugar profits of the West Indies. This point was well understood by the French mercantilist Étienne François, comte de Stanville and duc de Choiseul, one of the architects of France's global strategy.

Having fought the French for decades, the triumphant Americans to their great dismay and chagrin found themselves banned by the Royal Proclamation of 1763 from the much-coveted lands west of the Appalachian divide. The proclamation was issued on October 7, six months after the signing of the Treaty of 1763, which had spelled out the terms of the peace with France. This so-called Proclamation Line was imposed by royal action to placate Native peoples such as the Ottawa leader Pontiac, who was then leading a pan-Indigenous rebellion (1763–66) against the British by attacking their forts, starting with Fort Detroit, to be followed by attacks on defenseless settlements. The Royal Proclamation was a perfectly rational response to a deadly serious situation. And if the line was a barrier to American westward settlement—although its declaration hardly stopped Daniel Boone and his fellow emigrants from crossing the Appalachians and moving into the hollers of Kentucky in 1773, it was, and remains, an important legal precedent for the First Nations of Canada. For while the British crown claimed territory in North America, existing aboriginal rights and title were nevertheless recognized, and aboriginal lands could only be ceded by treaty with the crown. The same principles would later inform the US Indian Non-Intercourse Act, last modified in 1834.

In 1763 the British also created the province of Quebec, which the crown's officials would rule with an unusually light, if not sympathetic, hand. The conciliatory Quebec Act of 1774 that Quebec governor Guy Carleton, First Baron Dorchester, urged Parliament to pass was a model of restraint. It not only retained French law—the *coutume de Paris*—and preserved the seigneurial system but also supported the Roman Catholic Church, which was as deeply entrenched in Quebec as it was in New Spain. The Quebec Act's tolerance of things French and Catholic raised suspicions among the largely Protestant English Americans, who saw their interests subordinated first to the Native and second to the French peoples of what not so long ago had been New France (Canada) and was now the British province of Quebec. Moreover, ever since the ascendancy to power of Oliver Cromwell, the Lord Protector, and the passage of the Navigation Acts in the seventeenth century, England had sought to exert greater control over the economic affairs of its North American colonies. But it was not really until France's eviction from the continent in 1759 (the habitants remained behind) as a result of the decisive Battle of the Plains of Abraham that aspects of the theory of mercantilism became the actual practice of His Majesty's government. The following year the young King George III (he was only twenty years old) ascended the British throne. His reign, the third longest in English history, lasted an impressive fifty-nine years and ninety-six days, from 1760 to 1820, although beginning in 1811 his son, later George IV, became regent when George III was declared unfit to rule.

The new province of Quebec was situated in between Rupert's Land to the north, the English Thirteen Colonies to the south, and what was (as of 1762) now Spanish Louisiana to the west. One result of the French and Indian War was that Louisiana, the western half of the Mississippi basin, including the city of New Orleans, was transferred from New France, which now ceased to exist, to New Spain and its administration (which lasted from 1762 to 1801). Finally, during the French and Indian War the British enacted a new policy, the Rule of 1756, a measure of the Seven Years' War by which Britain would not trade with neutrals who traded with her enemies. This policy had no bearing on the Thirteen Colonies, but it would later have momentous consequences for the independent United States during the French Revolution and the Napoleonic Wars and was a cause of the War of 1812. In this respect, the Seven Years' War and the War of 1812 are related events.

Taken all together, these postwar territorial arrangements fully addressed the long-standing issues of the military history of colonial North America. This was no small feat. But by hemming in, and cutting off, English-speaking colonists from the rest of the continent, the British now found themselves working against, or at cross-purposes with, the success and future of their rapidly growing and increasingly prosperous colonies. The population of the prefederal United States was nearly 1.6 million in 1760. By 1780, one year before the surrender of General Cornwallis to General Washington and the French commander Jean-Baptiste Donatien de Vimeur, the comte de Rochambeau, on the Yorktown peninsula (Cornwallis had been cut off from the sea by French admiral François-Joseph-Paul de Grasse's French fleet of thirty-seven ships, including twenty-eight ships of the line, in the

Battle of the Capes), the American population had swelled to nearly 2.8 million, a whopping 74.4 percent increase in twenty years. And over the next decade, from 1780 to 1790—as the United States shifted from being a weak confederation of states to becoming a much stronger federation— the growth of the American population accelerated even further, reaching approximately 3.9 million souls by 1790, the year of the first US census. This was the demographical context for America's democratic revolution of 1765–83, and the war that it produced, events that exposed and corrected the illogic of British imperial policy and restored America's population-fueled westward expansion into the North American continent.[4]

The American Revolutionary War saw the French return to the North American theater to assist the American colonists or rebels, once the latter had proven their martial mettle in the decisive Battles of Saratoga of 1777. The following year, in a plucky demonstration of America's emerging social power or, perhaps more accurately, social spirit, the audacious Scots-born American captain John Paul (alias John Paul Jones) took the Continental Navy sloop-of-war the *Ranger*, and with it the revolution, into England's own home waters, having boldly entered the Irish Sea through St. George's Channel. Later, in 1779, aboard the USS *Bonhomme Richard*, named in honor of Benjamin Franklin, along with a small squadron of ships—the *Pallas*, *Vengeance*, and *Alliance*—Jones sailed from France into the North Sea. Near the chalk cliffs of Flamborough Head on the coast of Yorkshire, he engaged a British convoy coming from the Baltic. In the midst of grueling four-hour gunnery duel, in which Jones ultimately prevailed over the HMS *Serapis*, he was asked to surrender by Captain Richard Pearson. In reply, Jones spat out the words "I have not yet begun to fight." These feats, which were more propaganda victories than anything else but no less important for being symbolic, served as the heroic antecedents for America's spectacularly daring, power-projecting, and morale-raising air raid, led by James Doolittle, on the Japanese archipelago in 1942, early in World War II. For his dash and derring-do, John Paul Jones, the toast of Paris, was presented with a sword and made a *chevalier*, or knight, by France's Louis XVI.

To weaken its old rival Britain, France sought a strong United States. The French habitants or Quebecois, however, parted company with their Old World cousins, returning Voltaire's indifference, if not disdain, with compound interest. The secularism and radicalism of the French Revolution, with its contradictory ideals of *liberté, égalité, and fraternité or death*, would sunder even further the French of Quebec from their radical sansculotte cousins across the water. Throughout the American Revolution, the Quebecois chose to remain loyal to the British Crown, a sentiment only strengthened by America's failed invasion of Canada in 1775.

In fact, the first major campaign of the American Revolutionary War, after the Battle of Lexington and Concord, was to take Montreal, Quebec City, and the riparian country between the two and thereby liberate the Canadians from British tyranny. (At the start of the war, there were twenty-three British colonies and territories in North America.) The Americans failed. And in this very important regard, the American effort to drive the British out of the continent was only partly realized. The French Canadians were later joined by the American Loyalists, or United Empire Loyalists, as they were called in Canada. Perhaps the most notable of these was William Smith, a former New York chief justice. Between 80,000 and 100,000 thousand Loyalists fled the Thirteen Colonies—half of whom, including 3,500 free Black Loyalists, went to British Canada for land and the promise of security. In addition to these refugees, Britain granted land along the Grand River in Ontario to its Native allies, the Six Nations of the Iroquois or Haudenosaunee Confederacy, who had been forced to cede most of their lands in New York's Mohawk Valley. Thus one of the underappreciated results of the American Revolution was demographic: the size of Canada's European population was diversified and dramatically increased in size, and its Native population was augmented as well.[5]

In the Peace of Paris of 1783, which concluded the American Revolutionary War—at the expense of the province of Quebec—Britain relinquished to the Americans all of the lands south of the Great Lakes as far as the thirty-first parallel, the border between the United States and the British colonies of East Florida and West Florida, which were ceded back to Spain, and from the Atlantic Ocean to the Mississippi River. Navigation on the Mississippi River, North America's longest river, was to remain open to the citizens of both Britain and the United States, although the port of New Orleans remained under Spanish control until 1801. On paper, then, the United States came out of the war exceedingly well indeed. The British negotiators had shrewdly directed America's energies westward, away from Canada. However, the actual alienation of all of these lands in the Trans-Appalachian West from their Native occupants would be another matter for another day.[6] Moreover, US independence from Great Britain had the unintended consequence of seeding the origins of a second North American nation: a bicultural Canada, which encompassed what are now the provinces of Ontario, Quebec, Newfoundland, New Brunswick, Nova Scotia, and Prince Edward Island, and ultimately a transcontinental nation. And this bicultural as well as bilingual entity would prove that a house divided against itself, contrary to the US experience, could not only stand but actually endure and even thrive.[7]

It should be noted that while the Revolutionary War fighting in North America stopped with the Battle of Yorktown, the war between Britain, Spain, and France nevertheless continued in Europe. Moreover, the costs of having supported the Americans against the British produced a fiscal and constitutional crisis in France. The French nobility refused to pay higher taxes, forcing the French monarchy in 1789 to summon the Estates General, which had not been convened since the troubled regency of Marie d' Medici. (Louis XIII was only eight when his father Henry IV, "Good King Henry," was assassinated in 1610.) This institution, which dated back to 1302, was made up of three estates, or classes: the clergy, the nobility, and the commoners. After members of the Third Estate took the Tennis Court Oath on June 20, 1789, swearing not "to separate, and to reassemble wherever circumstances require, until the constitution of the kingdom is established and consolidated upon firm foundations," the Estates General was transformed into the National Assembly. This act started the French Revolution and marked the beginning of the end for France's *ancien régime* but not for its monarchy, which would be restored in 1814, when Louis XVIII became king. As interrelated as were North America and western Europe, their transatlantic histories would become even more entangled and confused over the course of the next quarter century.

The Birth of a Nation

The Loyalists who relocated in Canada were largely of a middling sort. They were Protestant and spoke American English. A few had gone south to the havens of East and West Florida. Many more went north and settled either to the east of Quebec in the Maritimes—Nova Scotia, Cape Breton, St. John's Island, the Gaspé Peninsula, and the Saint John River Valley. In 1784, to accommodate the influx of Loyalists, New Brunswick was carved out of Nova Scotia at the point west of the Isthmus of Chignecto. Few Loyalists went to either Newfoundland or St. John's Island, where the land had been divided up among a small number of absentee owners from Britain and was already occupied by French Acadian refugees from the French and Indian War. (Other French Acadians went elsewhere, including Louisiana, where their descendants became known as the Cajuns, while many returned to western Nova Scotia in the 1780s and 1790s to take up new homes.) The Loyalists also settled to the west of the seigneuries of Quebec on the lands north of the St. Lawrence River, where Natives were few in number, as far as the Z-shaped Bay of Quinte on Lake Ontario. By 1791 the English-speaking population of this area had grown to 14,000, large enough that a separate colony was created for them by the British Parliament with the passage of the Constitutional Act of that same year. The new colony (now Ontario) was named Upper Canada, but businessmen and bankers in Montreal nevertheless controlled its economic development. To the east, with its larger French-speaking population of 150,000, the old colony of Quebec was renamed Lower Canada. The boundary between the two Canadas was the Ottawa River.

The Constitutional Act had been promoted by the capable Sir Guy Carleton (Lord Dorchester), the governor in chief of British North America from 1786 to 1796. It provided Canada with a constitution based on the general principles of the British constitution. However, there was a critical and unfortunate difference. In the Thirteen Colonies, the elected assemblies had been strong and the appointed governors weak, while in the Canadas, after 1791, the situation was the exact opposite. In Great Britain after the 1688 revolution there was a cooperation of powers between crown and Parliament, or between the executive and the legislative spheres. During the eighteenth century this constitutional development gave Great Britain a strong and stable national government—too strong, from the American perspective. In the United States, after the 1776 revolution, the American distrust of the executive led to the separation or division of powers, enshrined in a written constitution, as opposed to Great Britain's reliance on custom as well as an unwritten acknowledgment of a body of precedents. The result was a relatively weak central government—at least, that is, until the Civil War, an event that altered, for better and worse, the relationship between the federal government and the states.

In the aftermath of the American Revolution and with the French Revolution in full progress, Carleton as well as William Smith and British foreign secretary Lord William Grenville sought a third way for Canada. According to the Constitutional Act, there was to be a governor in each colony representing the crown. There was also to be an elected legislative assembly, to represent local people of property. Under the British system, the crown was willing to choose many of its chief ministers from the House of Commons. Despite this fact, in Canada the governors were to appoint their own executive and legislative advisers, which meant that they were not of the assembly, or unaccountable to it. This disjunction between the British and the Canadian systems initially worked. But in time dissatisfaction with it grew in Canada, leading to rebellions in 1837 and 1838 in Lower and Upper Canada and calls for responsible government, that is, the Westminster system. The act also provided for lands (the clergy reserves) to support an Anglican establishment (in the English-speaking colonies) and a peerage for a hereditary upper house, neither of which succeeded in the end. The egalitarian conditions of the frontier and the existence of free land worked against the rise of a landed aristocracy in Canada, just as they had done in America.

Scylla and Charybdis

The new United States produced a remarkable number of leaders and thinkers who were every bit the equal of their flinty-eyed European counterparts, whether the subject was statecraft or improvements in agriculture. Nevertheless these Founders, perhaps none more astutely than General George Washington, recognized the importance of sea power. Several weeks after the surrender of Cornwallis at Yorktown on October 19, 1781, Washington observed in a letter to the Marquis de Lafayette that "no land force can [act] decisively unless it is accompanied by a Maritime superiority; nor can more than negative advantages be expected without it, for proof of this, we have only to recur to the instances of the ease & facility with which the British shifted their ground as advantages were to be obtained at either extremity of the Continent & so their late heavy loss the moment they failed in their Naval superiority."[8] With a navy consisting of no more than six frigates, the Early Republic was hopelessly outmatched by the British and French navies. And yet it was between these monsters of Scylla and Charybdis that the American merchant marine had to try to navigate the Atlantic if it were to trade in Europe. The sea trade of Canada's colonies, on the other hand, enjoyed the British Empire's full protection, even as the gaze of that empire turned from North America to the other side of the world. Cornwallis may have left North America a defeated general, a failure he survived with his military reputation intact. But he went on to become the governor-general and commander in chief of India.

In addition to these harsh maritime realities, the dawn of the Early Republic was darkened by the violent political storms that swept over Europe during of the 1790s. The French Revolution of 1789 had turned by

1793, with the execution of King Louis XVI, into a declaration of war on monarchy and royalism everywhere, including Great Britain, Spain, and the Netherlands, with its hereditary stadholderate, which disappeared in 1795 along with the old republic (William V and his family fled to England).[9] And to fight a counterrevolution at home and spread its radical ideas across Europe, France introduced universal conscription to fill the ranks—the *levée en masse*. This new and much enlarged army would become Napoleon's Grande Armée.

These events polarized American politics (to say nothing of Europe's) into on one side pro-French Jeffersonians and Madisonians, partisans known as the Democratic-Republicans, and on the other the New England–based, British-leaning Hamiltonians, or the Federalists, as they were called. George Washington and John Adams led the latter faction. It is impossible to separate the emergence of America's two-party system from the general US reaction to European politics, in particular to France's revolutionary upheaval. The two were inextricably related.

If at the end of the eighteenth century North America and western Europe were comparable in terms of social development—longevity, per capita income, and literacy— a yawning chasm nevertheless existed in social power between the two regions. Indeed, there was very little the newly minted United States, with its minuscule navy, could do in the face of Europe's massive sea power, especially Britain's. In this maritime world, the young republic was at a great disadvantage. President Washington, whose term as the nation's first chief executive spanned the crucial years from 1789 to 1797, responded by proclaiming his country's neutrality in the continuing hostilities, a foreign policy borne out of necessity but one that perfectly matched means with ends. On the other hand, if the Early Republic was weak at sea, it had strength on land—in North America—whereupon it could more easily apply pressure on Europe and its Native allies. These realities were reflected in the two key treaties of this period: Jay's Treaty of 1794, between the United States and Great Britain, and a 1795 agreement between the United States and Spain, Pinckney's Treaty.

President Washington sent John Jay, the US chief justice and envoy extraordinaire who had been involved in the negotiations in the earlier Peace of Paris of 1783, to negotiate a treaty with the highly capable Lord William Grenville, the British foreign secretary. The result of these talks was the Treaty of Amity, Commerce, and Navigation of 1794 between His Britannic Majesty and the United States of America, commonly called Jay's Treaty. The treaty normalized trading relations between the two nations, although Britain restricted American shipping from its lucrative ports in the West Indies. Before the Revolution, Americans had exported flour, beef, pork, salted fish, naval stores, and bar iron to these islands and their hungry enslaved populations. But with these new restrictions, this vital trade fell by as much as half. A good part of one side of the trade triangle had been removed. The Canadians could only try to make up the difference. In 1807, after Napoleon in the Berlin Decree of November 21, 1806, imposed his Continental System, forbidding the import of British goods into Europe, Britain retaliated with a counterblockade, the Orders in Council. These blockades rerouted Atlantic trade flows. For example, Britain turned from the Baltic region to New Brunswick's forests of spruce and pine to supply its Royal Navy with timber. This was a boon to Canada, but Britain's counterblockade would serve as one of the main causes of the War of 1812 between Britain and her deeply affected former colonies, the United States.[10]

If these policies squeezed America's transatlantic trade, the agreement Jay and his counterpart had reached on North America's intracontinental commercial intercourse, specifically in regard to the crossing of the shared border between Britain and the United States, was remarkably enlightened and very generous. If not an open border, it certainly came very close to being one. According to article 3 of the treaty,

> It is agreed that it shall at all times be free to his Majesty's subjects, and to the citizens of the United States, and also to the Indians dwelling on either side of the said boundary line, freely to pass and repass by land or inland navigation, into the respective territories and countries of the two parties, on the continent of America (the country within the limits of the Hudson's Bay Company only excepted) and to navigate all the lakes, rivers and waters thereof, and freely to carry on trade and commerce with each other.[11]

These terms were also practical, given the poor state of geographical knowledge at the time and the amount of manpower that would have been required to regulate the traffic on such a long border. In fact, surveys were to be created and commissions appointed to settle the existing boundary disputes; in the northeast, the issue was which river was the St. Croix River, the dividing line between New Brunswick and Maine, and in the northwest, whether the Mississippi River extended as far north as the Lake of the Woods (it does not; the river's source was found to be Lake Itasca).

The treaty ignored the impressment of American sailors by the British, who claimed that they were British deserters, but not the contentious issue of Britain's continued occupation of forts in New York, Vermont, Michigan, and Ohio and its arming of Native peoples. The latter point was critical; since the Peace of Paris, American pioneers had been streaming west into the Ohio River Valley, where they fought over land with area tribes such as the Lenapi (Delaware), Shawnee, Illinois, Wabash, Miami, Ottawa, Ojibwe (Chippewa), and Potawatomi.[12]

As governor of the Northwest Territory, Arthur St. Clair was charged with trying to persuade or compel the Native peoples in the Ohio River Valley to cede their lands to the United States, which they understandably refused to do. Indeed, St. Clair's defeat at the Battle of the Wabash River in 1791 against a force of confederated Native groups led by the Miami chief Michikinikwa—Little Turtle, as he was known in the Anglosphere—was the single worst rout of a US army (mostly poorly trained militia) by Native warriors in American history. Little Turtle's followers included Tecumseh, the future Shawnee chief. Nearly a thousand of St. Clair's people were slain, including women and children accompanying the army as well as officers and militiamen. In reaction, George Washington appointed "Mad Anthony" Wayne, a bold and capable officer who had distinguished himself in the Revolutionary War, to serve as commander in chief of the US Army. Wayne took two years to train his men properly before taking the fight back to the Ohio Country. On August 20, 1794, at the Battle of Fallen Timbers near Fort Miami, a British supply post on the Maumee River, Mad Anthony's "Legion," which included regular army, Kentucky militia, and Indigenous scouts, succeeded in routing a much larger Native force. Serving as Anthony's aide-de-camp was a young William Henry Harrison, who would be elected in 1840 as the ninth US president. Throughout US history, past wars have made future presidents.

The casualties on both sides at Fallen Timbers were light, but the battle's consequences were profound. Several months later, on November 17, 1794, King George III's government acceded to Jay's demands that the British quit their forts in the Northwest Territory to honor, finally, the original terms of the Peace of Paris of 1783. Jay's Treaty cost Britain almost nothing, but it reflected the reality that the republic across the English Channel, not the fledging republic on the other side of the Atlantic, was Britain's real and indeed mortal enemy. The following year, on August 3, 1795, Little Turtle's confederation agreed under the Treaty of Fort Greenville to cede to the

United States much of the Old Northwest. This included territory that would be reorganized into the future states of Ohio, Indiana, Michigan, and Illinois. Little Turtle, who would go on to become a national celebrity and meet personally with George Washington, also forsook any further violence against the Americans. Tecumseh, however, and his brother Tenskwatawa, "the Prophet," vowed to fight another day. To do so, the two would organize another pan-Indigenous confederation to try vainly to stop America's westward expansion.[13]

From the Native perspective, Jay's Treaty pointed toward the end of an era, which would finally close with the War of 1812. Whether one views this fierce early nineteenth-century Native resistance to European American encroachment as heroic, tragic, or both, it would have been impossible without British collaboration and arms, the latter supplied to Native allies through a conduit of frontier forts via Canada. Similarly, via Spanish Florida the Spanish supplied their Native allies in the Old Southwest, the region that stretches from South Carolina to Louisiana, or what would later be called the Deep South. Hunters, gatherers, and horticulturalists simply did not possess the social capability to make guns, gunpowder, and bullets of their own. They were therefore hopelessly and dangerously dependent on others, to wit Europeans—the British in the North, the Spanish in the South—for the modern instruments of war.

Jay's Treaty was followed in 1795 by the "Treaty of Friendship, Limits, and Navigation between Spain and the United States," which came to be known as Pinckney's Treaty, after the US envoy Thomas Pinckney of South Carolina. Like Jay's Treaty, this agreement, which was reached by Pinckney and Manuel de Godoy (Charles IV's prime minister of everything, including the amorous attentions of the queen, Maria Luisa of Parma), basically restated, as had Jay' Treaty, the original terms of the Peace of Paris of 1783, confirming the Mississippi River as the western border and the thirty-first parallel as the southern border, respectively, of the United States. And Pinckney's Treaty was negotiated for the same reason: it was in Spain's interest to have friendly relations with the United States, with whom it shared long borders in North America. In addition, this agreement allowed American ships duty-free passage through, and the right of deposit in, the port of New Orleans. Finally, to please the Americans, Spain abandoned its efforts to use Native peoples to create a buffer zone in the Old Southwest, much as Britain had done in regard to the Old Northwest, although it would not abandon the idea entirely until 1814, with the conclusion of the War of

1812. Moreover, the two treaties were similar, but the public perception of them in the United States was not. Pinckney's Treaty was widely acclaimed, especially in the South and West. Jay's Treaty, on the other hand, was very unpopular, above all with Democratic-Republicans who saw in it an alignment of the United States with America's former enemy, and a repudiation of the nation's revolutionary ideals to boot.

By treating with Great Britain and Spain, Washington effectively rendered hollow the Treaty of Alliance and the Treaty of Amity and Commerce that the United States had signed with France back in 1778, all of its professions of neutrality notwithstanding. In the great contest of the time for European supremacy between Britain and France, the United States had taken sides, although it tried hard to do so on its own terms. Alexander Hamilton, the US secretary of the treasury, was even against repaying the country's war debt to France, insisting the money had been loaned by, and thus owed to, the French monarchy, which had been abolished in the French Revolution, not to France's radical First Republic (1792–1804), to which the revolution had given birth. Franco-American relations continued to deteriorate under France's high-handed foreign minister Charles-Maurice de Talleyrand, who was behind the brazenly extortionist XYZ Affair. In fact by 1798, the same year the US Congress created the Department of the Navy, the two republics were in a state of undeclared war at sea, primarily in the Caribbean. This conflict, which the US Navy waged with just fifteen vessels, with more under construction, was called the Quasi-War (1798–1800), since it was never officially declared a war as such.

The Louisiana Parity

In the meantime France changed the world—again. On November 9, 1799 (18 Brumaire, year VIII of the republican calendar), Napoleon Bonaparte overthrew the Directorate and made himself first consul. Napoleon's political ambitions were boundless, and they included the restoration of the French Empire in the West Indies (the slaves in the French colony of Saint-Domingue on the island of Hispaniola had been in revolt since 1791) and Louisiana, but not in Canada—at least not yet. To this end, Napoleon and Talleyrand negotiated with the John Adams administration (1798–1801) an end to the Quasi-War with the Convention of 1800 or Treaty of Mortefontaine, which terminated America's military alliance with France. There would not be another such entangling alliance until 1949, when the United States signed the North Atlantic Treaty. And in the Treaty of San

Ildefonso on October 1, 1800, the Court of Madrid secretly agreed to ret-
rocede Louisiana and New Orleans (the Floridas remained under Spanish
rule, as they had been since 1783) to the French in exchange for the kingdom of Etruria in Tuscany for Charles IV's son-in-law, the Duke of Parma.
Even more ominous, the Spanish then closed the port of New Orleans to
American trade. Just like that, the United States woke up to rumors that
the somnolent Spanish empire that had been its neighbor was being replaced by another empire, one that was revolutionary, bellicose, and led by
an enormously ambitious thirty-one-year-old military genius who was determined that France would once again become a North American power.
Furthermore, with the Peace of Amiens in 1802, which marked a cessation or
brief pause in the endless war between France and Great Britain, Napoleon
was able to free up men and resources to devote to his transatlantic project.

John Adams's successor as president, Thomas Jefferson, and Jefferson's
secretary of state, James Madison, would learn from Rufus King, a Federalist
and the US minister to the Court of St. James, that a Napoleonic Louisiana
was no mere rumor. Jefferson, both a Francophile and an Anglophobe, faced
with deep chagrin the prospect of war with France, given Napoleon's ambitions, and the probable need for an alliance with Britain, given America's
military weakness. But Napoleon's dreams of a second North American
empire would be dashed on the hard rock of Hispaniola.

Napoleon ordered the general Charles Leclerc, his brother-in-law, and
twenty-three thousand soldiers to regain control of Saint-Domingue, the
French colony on the western end of Hispaniola and the nearby island of
Tortuga. The colony had once been rich. On its plains nearly two-thirds
of the world's sugar had been grown; and in the mountains above, more
than half the world's coffee.[14] Leclerc and company landed in 1802 and
were initially successful. They captured the former slave and military leader
Toussaint Louverture—who had declared himself dictator for life—in an
act of French bad faith, and sent him to Fort-de-Joux in France, where he
died in 1803. But instead of regaining control of the colony, Leclerc's army
contracted yellow fever from the island's mosquitoes, an epidemic that dec-
imated his men and took Leclerc's life. Moreover, the well-grounded fears
that the French would reimpose slavery on a largely Black population, as
Napoleon had done in Guadeloupe and in other possessions—even though
revolutionary France had abolished slavery in 1794—led to yet another
revolt. This time, under the leadership of Jean-Jacques Dessalines, the rebels offered effective military resistance.[15] The French surrendered in 1803,
and Dessalines, an African-born former slave, declared the entire destitute

and war-ravaged island of Hispaniola, now called Haiti, independent from France.[16] Dessalines would go on to name himself Emperor Jacques I and, for good measure, launch in the spring of 1804 a genocidal campaign to kill most of Hispaniola's remaining European population. The slave-based society of middle North America's southern mainland watched these events unfold in dismay.[17]

In April 1803, with his North American plans in disarray, Napoleon decided to sell Louisiana to the United States. This gave him funds to wage war against Britain, and the battle between the two European powers resumed in May 1803. The agreement also greatly accelerated the demise of the Spanish Empire in North America by creating a long border that was difficult, if not impossible, for New Spain to defend against an increasingly aggressive United States. President Jefferson had already instructed Robert Livingston, the US minister to France, and minister extraordinaire James Monroe to negotiate the purchase of New Orleans, a port of key strategic and economic importance. Talleyrand's offer to sell New Orleans as well as the rest of Louisiana—a vast territory, much larger than the current American state of Louisiana, that in the event of war with Britain would be exposed and vulnerable to attack by land from Canada and by sea from the Gulf of Mexico—was thus met with great relief by the Americans. Jefferson easily put aside his constitutional scruples (a strict constructionist, he in theory did not believe that a president had the authority to acquire new territory) and, with the British bank Barings financed the asking price of $15 million. It was thus that with the Louisiana Purchase in 1803, Jefferson, the apostle of limited government, doubled the size of the United States. In so doing, he dramatically altered the course of North American history.

But it was Robert Livingston and Napoleon who expressed in writing the real significance of the Louisiana Purchase. "We have lived long," Livingston wrote, "but this is the noblest work of our whole lives. The treaty which we have just signed . . .will change vast solitudes into flourishing districts. From this day the United States take their place among the powers of the first rank; the English lose all exclusive influence in the affairs of [North] America." As for Napoleon, he thought the Louisiana Purchase "strengthens forever the power of the United States" and that he had "given England a maritime rival, that will sooner or later humble her pride."[18] He was right about the former, but wrong about the latter.

In short, the United States had adroitly used its advantages to purchase social power as well as parity with Europe—thus leaving the rest of the Americas, Asia, Africa, and Oceania far behind. Or rather, at this point in

Figure 17. Unknown artist, *Napoleon Bonaparte*, mid-nineteenth century. Oil on wood, 18 1/4 x 15 in. (46.4 x 38.1 cm). Metropolitan Museum of Art. Image licensed under CC0 1.0.

time, she had purchased the potential of social power and of parity with Europe; the United States had yet to turn the Louisiana Purchase's enormous economic potential into social capability. But it was only a matter of time. In 1776 Jefferson had declared that all men were created equal. True enough. But the societies or cultures that men were born into were anything but equal. Social power was made, and some societies made or purchased more of it than others.

In 1803, a mere two decades after the Peace of Paris of 1783, Jefferson's Louisiana Purchase paved the way for the United States to turn the valleys of the Mississippi and the Missouri into money—endless raftloads of it. In doing so, it would become one of the major players in the newly emerging international system, a system that would by the 1870s be anchored by the United States, the United Kingdom, Canada, France, Italy, Germany, and Japan. These very nations, two of them North American, would vie with each other during the twentieth century's two world wars but later make up the Group of Seven (G7), an international organization comprising the world's largest national economies, once they had finally learned to cooperate with each other in the decades after World War II.[19]

The Two Treks of Mackenzie

A century after the treks of La Salle and Father Kino, Europeans and European Americans remained ignorant of much of North America's vast interior geography, including the lands that made up the Louisiana Purchase. This would change dramatically in the late eighteenth and early nineteenth centuries. In British Canada the fur trader Alexander Mackenzie, born in Stornoway, Scotland, in 1764 and described by a contemporary as "blond, strong and well built,"[20] led two important overland expeditions for the North West Company, whose Canadian agents were based in Montreal but whose "wintering partners" were located deep in Indian country.

Britain's Hudson's Bay Company, chartered in 1670, had a monopoly on the fur trade in the Hudson Bay drainage basin, a huge territory known as Rupert's Land. The basin's surface waters flow east from the Continental Divide to the Atlantic Ocean. With the Peace of Paris of 1783, which concluded the American Revolutionary War, the fur trade country south of the Great Lakes (Ohio, Indiana, Michigan, Illinois, Wisconsin, and Minnesota)—centered on the trading posts of Detroit, between Lake Huron and Lake Erie, and Michilimackinac, between Lakes Huron and Michigan— was ceded to the new United States.[21] The North West Company, which was formally organized in the winter of 1783–84, sought to gain control of the lands outside the Hudson's Bay Company monopoly, as well as those claimed by the new United States. That left all of western Canada, a vast region extending from Grand Portage on western Lake Superior all the way across the continent to the Georgia Strait, where fur-bearing animals filled the forests and plains.

Much of this country was unknown to Europeans. To explore it Mackenzie, then twenty-five years old, left Montreal in 1789 for Fort Chipewyan on the far western shore of Lake Athabasca ("Lake of the Hills"), with the primary objective of finding a "Passage by Water through the N.W. Continent of America from Athabasca to the Pacific Ocean."[22] From Fort Chipewyan he canoed 290 miles down the Slave River to Great Slave Lake, deep in the interior of Canada, between Great Bear Lake to the northwest and Lake Athabasca to the southeast.[23] Named after the Slavey people and, at 2,015 feet, North America's deepest lake, Great Slave Lake is the source of what would later be called the Mackenzie River. The Mackenzie's main stem issues from the western arm of the Great Slave Lake and stretches north through eleven hundred miles of forest and tundra, draining the largest river basin in Canada. In some places up to four miles wide, this liquid immensity flows northwest through the Great Bear Lake or Sahtú Lands and on past the Arctic Circle. There it separates into three main channels to form the Mackenzie Delta, bordered in the west by the Richardson Mountains and in the east by the Caribou Hills, before debouching into the Beaufort Sea, which is part of the Arctic Ocean.

Mackenzie's expedition downriver took forty days; the journey back up-river, fifty-nine.[24] He made the journey in the company of a Chipewyan guide named English Chief (with his two wives), four French Canadian *voyageurs*—Joseph Landry, Charles Ducette, Francois Barrieau, and Pierre de Lorme (two of whom were joined by their wives)—and a clerk, the German John Steinbruck. Everyone returned safe and sound. After Cook, safe returns were now de rigueur. Mackenzie believed that his later name-sake, the Mackenzie River, was "Cook's River," which Peter Pond, a Yankee fur trader, thought ran west from Lake Athabasca to empty into Cook's Inlet on the Gulf of Alaska.[25] Mackenzie tested Pond's theory but found that the Northern Rockies formed a rampart, forcing the river away from the Mer d'Ouest ("Western Sea") to what he called the Northern Ocean (our Arctic Ocean). The negative result of Mackenzie's overland expedition complemented the negative result of Cook's third voyage in that they both eliminated the possibilities of the existence of a northwest passage.

In 1792 Mackenzie tried again to reach his Western Sea. This time, his par-ty of ten men (two of whom had accompanied Mackenzie to the Arctic and two of whom were Native guides), left Fort Chipewyan to travel west into the Northern Rockies by canoeing up the Peace River. The party crossed the 120th meridian west of Greenwich, which ran along the Continental Divide and would form the upper border between the provinces of Alberta and British Columbia, avoiding grizzly bears and other dangers along the way. Mackenzie negotiated rivers and streams—though he decided to eschew the Fraser River—and followed Native trails, some of them "very good and well traced," over the rugged terrain of the Pacific Slope, gathering intelligence from local Natives—some friendly, some not—along the way, until he finally reached the Bella Coola River, teeming with salmon, on the Pacific coast of British Columbia. His descriptions of the large plank houses of the Pacific Northwest tribes matched those made earlier by Captain Cook. To mark the occasion, Mackenzie used some "vermillion in melted grease" to inscribe "in large characters" the memorial: "Alexander Mackenzie, from Canada, by land, the 22nd July, 1793."[26] They then returned to Fort Chipewyan, again with everyone alive and well.

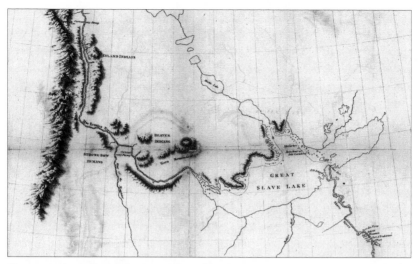

Figure 18. Alexander Mackenzie, *A Map of Mackenzie's Track from Fort Chipewyan to the North Sea in 1789* (detail), 1801. Map, 23 ¼ x 21.65 in. (59 x 55 cm) Courtesy Library of Congress. https://www.loc.gov/item/2002625187/.

Cabeza de Vaca was the first European to cross North America. Mackenzie was the first to cross North America above Mexico. By reaching the Pacific Ocean, he realized the dream of many an explorer, dating back almost three centuries to John Cabot's landfall on Newfoundland in 1497. Unfortunately, he missed George Vancouver by only forty-three days. Captain Vancouver, who had sailed on Cook's second and third voyages, was surveying the Pacific Coast, from San Francisco to Cook's Inlet, at the time. On June 10, 1793, he weighed anchor and left Bella Coola in British Columbia. This marked yet another tantalizingly close encounter of two explorers in the wilderness, calling to mind the near misses of Coronado and De Soto in 1541 and of Champlain and Hudson in 1609. Taken together, Mackenzie's difficult overland trek through the eastern and western watersheds of the Northern Rockies and Vancouver's meticulous survey of North America's coast, including the Strait of Juan de Fuca, in the grand tradition established by Cook, seemed to have finally settled the question of whether there was a sea passage through North America.

It was nearly a decade before Mackenzie published his *Voyages from Montréal through the Continent of North America to the Frozen and Pacific Oceans in 1789 and 1793.*[27] Less than two months later, on February 10, 1802, he was knighted. He later followed up his transcontinental feat by joining with the Scottish peer Thomas Douglas, Earl of Selkirk (also known as the Lord Lieutenant of Kirkcudbright) to pressure the Hudson's Bay Company into ceding part of Rupert's Land, namely the Red River Valley and the home of the Métis. In 1811 Lord Selkirk (who was nearly kidnapped when he was seven by the American patriot or pirate John Paul Jones), founded a colony in the valley for poor Scots—victims of the Highland Clearances.

In the time between Mackenzie's Arctic and Pacific expeditions, Spain and Great Britain had nearly gone to war over an incident at Nootka Sound on the west coast of Vancouver Island. In 1789 Spain's Esteban José Martínez seized four British trading vessels of the newly formed, lengthily named concern the Associated Merchants of London and India Trading to the Northwest Coast of America. The Spanish claimed that the activities of these interloping fur traders violated the Treaty of Tordesillas, under which the pope had split the world in two between Spain and Portugal. Spain and Britain, however, came to terms in a series of three conventions that recognized the freedom of the seas and replaced a theoretical sovereignty with an effective sovereignty. In other words, henceforth territorial claims had to be backed up by real commercial or colonial interests—forts, ports, factories, depots, and settlements—not airy edicts issued by popes or misty claims of first discovery by windswept explorers for distant kings. Spain's agreement to accede (it had no other choice since France, its military ally, was consumed by revolutionary turmoil) and to provide compensation for losses resolved the Nootka Sound incident in Great Britain's favor and opened up Spain's *mare clausum* or closed ocean (the Pacific) to free navigation.[28]

The Nootka Sound Convention of 1790 also triggered an international space race, at least by eighteenth-century standards, for control of the west coast of North America, north of Alta California. Spain's role in this great competition came to an end with Napoleon's invasion, which reduced Spain's once-powerful monarch to little more than France's puppet. This left Great Britain, the United States, and Russia as the major rivals for control of western North America's resources. Following Cook's third voyage in 1778, as we have seen, George Vancouver conducted a careful survey of the Pacific Northwest coast above San Francisco from 1792 to 1794. These new lines on the maps of the admiralty aside, what made the difference on the ground was the activities of individual British traders, who developed a triangular transpacific trade between the Pacific Northwest; the Hawaiian Islands, which Cook had discovered; and China.

The key to this maritime trade was the fur of the sea otter, an animal that originally ranged from the Aleutian Islands to Baja California. Sea otters were especially plentiful along the Northwest Pacific coast, and their thick fur was highly desired in the markets of China. The British could trade their own industrial goods with Native peoples for sea otter pelts, and then sell the pelts to Chinese merchants in the trading ports of South China's Pearl River Delta in exchange for silk, tea, porcelain, and other valued articles. These Asian luxuries were then sold, in turn, in the Atlantic markets of Europe and North America. The emergence of this new Pacific commerce, which was dominated by private entrepreneurs rather than by large government monopolies, soon rivaled and then eclipsed the closed system of Spain's Manila galleons, which for centuries had tied the Philippine Islands to North America. And this more open, efficient, and competitive commerce formed the basis for the expansion of the British Empire into western Canada, in a classic instance of the flag following trade. As for Britain's Hudson's Bay Company and Canada's North West Company, their fierce rivalry became so expensive that they were forced to merge in 1821, leaving only the Hudson's Bay Company. (The bottom line was that the Hudson's Bay route to Europe was shorter than that of the North West Company.) By then Spain had withdrawn to California and the United States, and Britain had agreed to a joint occupation of the Oregon country, a rare thing in the history of diplomacy.[29]

The Corps of Discovery

No nation better represented this new era of fiercely competitive capitalism than did the young United States of America. And no national type more than the Yankee trader better epitomized this phase of global economic history. Although President Jefferson was an elite and a product of an older colonial order and slaveholding society, he was also an Enlightenment revolutionary who thought, and more significantly wrote, in universalist terms. Like Franklin and the other Founders, he was thus perfectly in tune with the views and aspirations of his fellow countrymen in the days of the Early Republic. These new Americans had cast off any sense of subordination to the mother country and saw themselves as independent of, and equal to, their British or European cousins. Above all, they were eager to take their rightful place in the world's markets now that, in the words of the contemporary historian David Ramsay, American ships "would no longer be confined by the selfish regulations of an avaricious stepdame."[30]

Well educated, brilliant, and intensely curious, Jefferson was fully aware of Cook's voyages and keenly grasped the commercial possibilities of an American transpacific trade. In fact, he had met John Ledyard in Paris in

1786. Ledyard was a Connecticut Yankee who had served on Cook's third voyage as a British marine and been an eyewitness to Cook's death at Kealakekua Bay on the Big Island.[31] Ledyard had planned to draw attention to the Pacific Northwest by walking there via Russia and Siberia, then returning home across the rest of North America. But he made it only as far as Irkutsk near Lake Baikal before he was arrested by the authorities. He later died in Cairo, Egypt, in a failed attempt to explore the source of the Niger River.

If Ledyard had failed to traverse North America, Alexander Mackenzie, as we have seen, had not. And as president, Jefferson was determined to press his country's interests in not only the Pacific Northwest but the lands in between—La Salle's Louisiana, which the United States purchased in 1803. To these ends, in Mackenzie redux he charged two of his fellow Virginians, Meriwether Lewis and William Clark, to make an east-west traverse of the continent—a mission part defensive in nature, and part commercial. And since this was the age of Cook and Humboldt, the exploration was also scientific in character. The next year Lewis and Clark led an expedition dubbed the Corps of Discovery. Thirty-three people—including the French Canadian Toussaint Charbonneau; his Shoshone wife, Sacagawea; her infant son, Jean-Baptiste Charbonneau; and York, Clark's Black slave—headed west from Mandan, North Dakota, where the expedition had wintered in 1804–5.[32] Lewis also brought along his dog, a Newfoundland named Seaman. The expedition ascended the Missouri River in six canoes and two pirogues, a "little fleet" that, Lewis allowed, was "not quite so rispectable as those of Columbus and Captain Cook" but was nevertheless "still viewed by us with as much pleasure as those deservedly famed adventurers ever beheld theirs; and I dare say with quite as much anxiety for their safety and preservation." Lewis then declared, "We were now about to penetrate a country at least two thousand miles in width, on which the foot of civilized man had never trodden; the good or evil it had in store for us was for experiment yet to determine, and these little vessels contained every article by which we were to expect to subsist or defend ourselves."[33]

The expedition was forced to make a portage around the Missouri River's Great Falls in what is now Montana. It then made its way through the "Stoney" or Rocky Mountains, at the time the western boundary of the United States, via Lemhi Pass on the border of the present-day Montana and Idaho. The corps then descended the Columbia River, on the western slope of the Continental Divide, before it finally reached the Pacific Ocean. The lower portion of the Columbia, whose headwaters lie in British Columbia, had already been explored and named by the Yankee trader Robert Gray in 1792 (Gray, captain of the *Columbia Rediviva*, was the first to circumnavigate the globe in a US ship). At the continent's terminus at the mouth of the Columbia River, on the Oregon side, across from Cape Disappointment, the Corps of Discovery built Fort Clatsop and spent the winter of 1805–6 there before making the long overland trip home.[34]

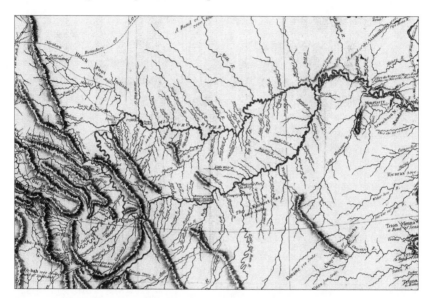

Figure 19. Samuel Lewis, William Clark, and Samuel Harrison, Detail of *A map of Lewis and Clark's track, across the western portion of North America from the Mississippi to the Pacific Ocean: by order of the executive of the United States in 1804, 5 & 6.* [Philadelphia: Bradford and Inskeep, 1814] Map. Prints and Photographs Division, Library of Congress, Washington, DC. https://www.loc.gov/item/79692907/.

In 1806 Lewis and Clark arrived back in St. Louis, originally a fur trading post founded by the French in 1764 and located below the confluence of the Missouri and Mississippi Rivers in the very heart of North America. The two explorers' diplomacy with Native peoples as well as their maps, notebooks, and natural history collections, some of which found their way into the nation's first museums, not only strengthened the US claim to the Pacific Northwest but also helped open up western North America to generations of European Americans, including the American fur trader John Jacob Astor, who in 1811 built Fort Astoria on the southern shore of the

Columbia River, near the Pacific Ocean. These men were hungry for new lands and opportunities. As with the journals Mackenzie kept on his epic trek, publication of the journals of Lewis and Clark was long delayed after the event, and not available to the public until 1814, eight years after the expedition's triumphal return to civilization. By then the War of 1812 had broken out, and Astor, who would go on to become one of North America's first millionaires, after Cortés, prudently sold his namesake fort to Canada's North West Company, which rechristened it Fort George.

Humboldt and the Rediscovery of America

On June 4, 1804, shortly after Lewis and Clark had begun their westward trek, Thomas Jefferson received the Prussian aristocrat, explorer, and naturalist Alexander von Humboldt as a dinner guest at the White House.[35] Over his long career and lifetime, Humboldt had made numerous contributions to science, principally to biogeography, and eventually became one of the most famous men in the Western world. As historian Stephen J. Pyne put it, "What Beethoven was to the music of the Romantic period, what Napoléon was to its politics, Humboldt was to its science."[36] Today Humboldt is probably best known as one of science's great popularizers. His ambitious multivolume *Kosmos* inspired the twentieth-century's most watched documentary series: Carl Sagan's *Cosmos*, which aired on PBS in 1980 and was remade and aired in 2014. Humboldt pioneered a new type: the scientist as society's moral conscience. Later Albert Einstein, Robert Oppenheimer, and Carl Sagan would all reprise this role. In Humboldt's day the great moral issue at hand was slavery. Humboldt was a great admirer of the United States. He shared the idealism of its founders, including Jefferson (they became lifelong correspondents). But he was also a strong critic of slavery in the Americas, while Jefferson was a slaveholder.

The Humboldt that Jefferson met in June 1804 was thirty-four years old (Jefferson was sixty-one). The young baron had just completed—at his own expense and with two Spanish passports, one issued by Madrid and the other by the Consejo de Indias—an epic five-year (1799–1804) journey through the Spanish colonies in Venezuela, Columbia, Ecuador, Peru, Cuba, and Mexico. Humboldt had made a very favorable impression on Spain's foreign minister, the science-minded Mariano Luis de Urquijo, who in Humboldt's case had broken with Spain's old policy of secrecy and insularity. Such a policy may have well served the security and mercantile interests of its American empire during the sixteenth and seventeenth centuries, but by the eighteenth century it had become a liability, as Urquijo realized. And by the dawn of the nineteenth century it was an invitation to disaster. The Spanish had become like the Aztecs, with a civilization at once brilliant and brittle. Humboldt's scholarship was rightly celebrated, but it arrived too late to be of any use to Madrid. By then Napoleon's actions in Spain had set the stage for the American wars of independence.

Before returning to Europe, Humboldt wanted to visit Philadelphia, the home of the American Philosophical Society, America's preeminent scientific organization, as well as Charles Willson Peale's museum.[37] Humboldt also wanted to go to the nation's capital to meet the nation's president, whom Humboldt called the *magistrat philosophe* (Humboldt also visited Jefferson at Monticello).[38] Humboldt was an admirer of Jefferson—not only as the author of the Declaration of Independence but also as that of *Notes on the State of Virginia* (1785).[39] Humboldt and Jefferson were men of the Enlightenment who believed that all of the universe was knowable through reason. Moreover, it was knowable, Humboldt thought, because the universe possessed an interconnected and interrelated unity, which could be determined through careful observation and precise measurement.[40] As Humboldt grandly put it, "The external world of phenomena has been delineated under the scientific form of a general picture of nature in her two great spheres, the uranological and the telluric or terrestrial. This delineation begins with the stars, which glimmer amidst nebulae in the remotest realms of space, and passing from our planetary system to the vegetable covering of the earth, descends to the minutest organisms which float in the atmosphere, and are invisible to the naked eye."[41] Humboldt gave to science and exploration a sense of wonder, a mood as much as a method.

It was in this Romantic spirit that Humboldt and his French companion, the botanist Aimé Bonpland, had explored the Orinoco River in Venezuela and Columbia, including its distributary the Casiquiare Canal, a natural waterway that linked the basins of the Orinoco and Amazon Rivers (alas, Lewis and Clark would discover that the river systems of the Missouri and the Columbia were not so joined but separated by the imposing Bitterroot Range).[42] In June of 1802 Humboldt and Bonpland (in the company of Carlos de Montúfar from Quito, a local nobleman whom the two had befriended and who would later distinguish himself in the struggle for the liberation of Ecuador) also climbed what was then believed to be the highest mountain in the world—Mount Chimborazo, an inactive stratovolcano located in the Cordillera Occidental range of the Andes. Altitude sickness and an insurmountable ravine, however, prevented the party from reaching the summit.

But of special interest to Jefferson was Humboldt's transcontinental journey across the Kingdom of New Spain, from Acapulco on the Pacific (the "Great Equinoctial Ocean") to Veracruz on the Gulf. Based in Mexico City, Humboldt explored the country from March of 1803 to February 1804. The baron had the knowledge, skills, and equipment—that is, sextants and chronometers—to correct or determine latitude and to fix longitude. He was thus able to bring an accuracy to his geography and cartography heretofore unknown. And as a former mining inspector in Prussia, he was uniquely qualified to observe and evaluate the extractive practices of Mexico's miners.

Jefferson was keenly interested in the lands and peoples of his Spanish neighbor. (The Louisiana Purchase Treaty had been signed in Paris, and Lewis and Clark had just set out on their long journey to the Pacific.) He could not have found a better and more reliable source of foreign intelligence than Humboldt. In fact, there was probably no one in the world outside Mexico or Spain more knowledgeable about New Spain than was the Prussian explorer and scientist—an aristocrat in every sense of the word. The Sage of Monticello learned from his distinguished and learned guest that Mexico was a country rich in natural resources, notably mineral wealth, and economic potential.[43] Humboldt did not visit the lands that now border the southwestern territory of the United States, specifically those between the Sabine River and the Rio Grande—that is, present-day Texas. But he did share with the president what he knew about them, including a new map of Mexico, designed with information provided by Don Antonio Alzate, Mexico's famous astronomer and naturalist. Humboldt reported that that these lands were largely deserted, containing "no more than at most 42,000 inhabitants, for the most part whites, descendants of European Spaniards who subsist on pastures and corn, which they cultivate in scattered tenant farms. The climate is hot; the earth is covered with secondary formations of limestone, very fertile however, especially in Nuevo Santander. The eastern part of the province of Texas, through which the present-day road passes from Potosi to Natchitotches, is savanna. The coast is poor, without a known port, full of shallow spots, and lined with little islands inhabited by independent Indians."[44] In other words, Spain's claims and later those made by Mexico to these lands were made more out of an inherited imperial conceit than based on settlers on the ground. And after the Nootka Convention of 1790, the guiding principle in international relations was now effective rather than a theoretical sovereignty.

Perhaps of even greater historical significance were Humboldt's reports, statistics, and maps relating to Mexico's fantastic mineral wealth. Jefferson's Swiss-born secretary of the treasury, Albert Gallatin, was so struck by Humboldt's staggering calculation that since the Conquest over five billion pesos' worth of gold and silver had been extracted from Mexico's mines that he checked Humboldt's math for himself. Gallatin found that Jefferson's distinguished guest had been indeed correct. It required little geopolitical imagination on the part of Jefferson or Gallatin (or Jefferson's secretary of state, James Madison, who also met Humboldt) to wonder if the mountains of the New Spanish provinces of Alta California or New Mexico might not be as rich in gold and silver as the Mexican cordillera.[45]

In 1811 Humboldt published in French his encyclopedic but engaging account of Mexico, *Essai politique sur le royaume de la Nouvelle-Espagne* (*Political Essay on the Kingdom of New Spain*). This multivolume work appeared one year after the parish priest Miguel Hidalgo y Costilla uttered the Cry of Dolores, starting Mexico's war of independence from Spain. Humboldt thus provided readers with a picture of the sunset years of the Spanish Empire. And on the basis of this work as well as his many other works on the Americas, statesmen and scholars such as Cuba's José Cipriano de la Luz y Caballero called him the New World's greatest discoverer after Columbus.

On the significance of Humboldt's work, Jefferson wrote to Humboldt, "It gives us a knowledge of that country more accurate than I believe we possess of Europe—the seat of science for a thousand years. It comes at a moment when those countries like Mexico are beginning to get interesting to the whole world. They are now becoming the scenes of political evolution to take their stations as integral members of the great family of nations."[46] That was in 1810. Three years later in another letter to Humboldt, Jefferson expanded upon his opinion, writing:

I think it most fortunate that your travels in those countries were so timed as to make them known to the world in the moment they were about to become actors on it's stage. that they will throw off their European dependance I have no doubt; but in what kind of government their revolution will end is not so certain. history, I believe furnishes no example of a priest-ridden people maintaining a free civil government.

Figure 20. Alexander Von Humboldt, *A Map of New Spain, from 16⁰ to 38⁰ North
Latitude Reduced from the Large Map* [London, Longman, Hurst, Rees, Orme and
Browne, Paternoster Row, 1804.] Map. Prints and Photographs Division, Library of
Congress, Washington, DC. https://www.loc.gov/item/2006626018/.

this marks the lowest grade of ignorance, of which their civil as well as religious leaders will always avail themselves for their own purposes. the vicinity of New Spain to the US. and their consequent intercourse may furnish schools for the higher, and example for the lower classes of their citizens. and Mexico, where we learn from you that men of science are not wanting, may revolutionise itself under better auspices than the Southern provinces...but of all this you can best judge, for in truth we have little knolege of them, to be depended on, but through you.[47]

Three centuries following the first Renaissance voyages, including Giovanni da Verrazzano's voyage up the Atlantic Coast in 1524, the Cook voyages, and the overland traverses of Mackenzie, Lewis and Clark, and Humboldt revealed to the Atlantic world the vast extent of the western North American continent.

But all this activity produced only the most preliminary of sketches, the roughest of outlines. The detail and interpretation would not be filled in for decades, work that in the United States, for instance, would involve a number of important military and civilian surveys—the precursors of the US Geological Survey.[48] Indeed, as late as 1904 the geographer Israel C. Russell complained that Canada's Labrador remained "in great part unexplored." And the discovery of Labrador—or the Labrador coast, anyway—dated back to the very beginnings of European exploration in the New World. Nevertheless, by the early decades of the nineteenth century—on maps in Montreal, Philadelphia, and Mexico City as well as in the great cities of Europe—Europeans and their Canadian, American, and Mexican contemporaries were only beginning to comprehend the immensity and variation of the North American continent. Still, a lot had been learned since 1507, when cartographer Martin Waldseemüller revealed the Island of Parias or the Cape of Good Fortune to the world.[49]

CHAPTER 11

The Thucydides Trap—and the Great Escape

English is the common root or stock from which our national language will be derived. All others will gradually waste away—and within a century and a half, North America will be peopled with a hundred millions of men, all speaking the same language.

Noah Webster, "An Essay on the Necessity,
Advantages and Practicality of Reforming the Mode of Spelling"

[The greatest political fact of modern times is] the inherited and permanent fact that North America speaks English.

Otto von Bismarck

HOW WEALTHY, HEALTHY, AND WISE—TO paraphrase Benjamin Franklin's proverb as well as to play upon Mahbub ul Haq's three traits of longevity, basic education, and per capita income—were the British and French populations of middle and upper North America by 1823? Not surprisingly, the answers vary considerably from region to region—north and south, east and west; from group to group—between Europeans and non-Europeans, that is, Natives and Africans or Blacks; and by sex—male and female. With this in mind, we can nevertheless make a number of generalizations, beginning with the fact that during the seventeenth century, Europeans who lived along the eastern seaboard and up the St. Lawrence Valley as far as the Lachine Rapids replaced the local and Indigenous hunting, gathering, and horticultural economies, which could support only a few, with an agricultural and trading economy that provided for many.

In 1600 the population of, and per capita GDP for, upper North America broke down as follows. Canada's population was 250,000; its per capita

GDP, $400 (for a hunting, gathering, and horticultural economy); and its GDP, $100 million. A century later, the population of Canada had fallen to 200,000—which is to say, there was a decline in the Native population. In contrast, the European population of Canada had increased from almost nobody, save for a few scattered fishermen and sailors, to 15,000 somebodies. During this century, Canada's GDP fell from $100 million to $86 million, but per capita GDP increased, from $400 to $430, which is a multicultural estimate. Another way to look at this change is that by 1700, the per capita GDP of Canada *as a whole* had overtaken Mexico's during the age of the Aztecs, which had stood at $425. Per capita GDP for Europeans in Canada, if separated out, was actually much higher, twice as high, in fact, at $800, while that for Natives or First Nations remained at $400, the ceiling of a hunting, gathering, and horticultural economy.[1]

The situation in the prefederal United States was very similar. In 1600, middle North America's population was 1.5 million. Over the course of the next century, the population had dropped from 1.5 million to 1 million—a loss of a third. The GDP of the seventeenth-century prefederal United States also dropped, from $600 million in 1600, to $527 million in 1700. The estimated multicultural per capita GDP, however, increased, just as in Canada but more significantly, rising from $400 to $527, which is to say $900 for Europeans and Africans, and $400 for Natives. In contrast, the per capita GDP of the mother country, the United Kingdom, was $1,250, higher than France's $910 or Sweden's $977 but well below that of the strikingly affluent Netherlands, with a per capita GDP of $2,130.[2]

For the first two centuries after Hernán Cortés, then, the Spanish North American economy, in terms of GDP, was ahead of the economies of what would become the United States and Canada. But as we have seen, by the early nineteenth century these positions dramatically reversed themselves. This story of shifting fortunes is crucial to understanding the broader contours of North American history. At the same time, it is interesting to note that as early as 1700 the per capita GDP of Europeans in the prefederal United States, at $900, had already surpassed Spain's per capita GDP of $853. In other words, English colonists in 1700 were already doing better than their contemporaries in Spain.[3] This remarkable fact says something important about the transatlantic world taking shape at the dawn of the eighteenth century.

To the question of wealth, we should add that John Q. Colonist, the common man, probably would have found the discussion of GDP here a little abstract, at least in the year 1700. And yet he would no doubt have appreciated the focus of future historians on the importance of land ownership, which was widespread and worth far more to the yeomen involved than its mere market value. Indeed, John Q. Colonist probably would have agreed with John Locke, the contemporary English philosopher who associated the natural right of estate or property with those of life and liberty. In British North America, this was not a remote theory. Property, and the security, liberty, and possibility for human flourishing, to say nothing of the peace of mind that came with it, was the very basis of day-to-day reality along the eastern seaboard and out on the western frontier. Indeed, it was precisely the promise of new lands—the resources of which were being seasonally exploited by relatively small bands of hunters, gatherers, and horticulturalists—that enticed European pastoralists and agriculturists into what they regarded as an American wilderness. And making this wilderness into a civilization was incredibly hard and dangerous work. Thomas Jefferson would later substitute for Locke's "property" the more felicitous phrase "the pursuit of happiness," but he was not simply replacing something separate and distinct that could be drawn on a map, recorded on a deed, or be bought and sold in the marketplace with an infinitely capacious idea or ideal. On the contrary, Jefferson's substitution was a substantive augmentation of what had become a central fact and promise of the American as well as the Canadian experience.[4]

The multicultural estimates (African, Native, and European) of the growth of population, GDP, and per capita GDP for the prefederal and federal United States from 1700 to 1820 reveal an impressive picture of social development. The population increased almost tenfold, from 1 million in 1700 to 9.98 million in 1820, despite the Native population's precipitous decline from 750,000 to 325,000. GDP rocketed up from $527 million in 1700 to 12.5 billion twelve decades later, a big reason why the fledgling United States was capable of successfully prosecuting two wars with the British Empire in 1776 and in 1812. And per capita GDP rose from $527 in 1700 to $1,257 in 1820, a fact that explains the strong attraction of America for Europe's immigrants.

Canada's story parallels that of America, except on a smaller scale. The multicultural estimate of the European and Indigenous population in 1700 was 200,000. By 1820, the population had expanded to 816,000. Over the same period, however, the number of Natives fell sharply from 185,000 to 75,000. Nevertheless, Canada's GDP rose from $86 million in 1700 to

$738 million in 1820, and its per capita GDP rose from $430 to $904. Thus the stage was set for a century of large-scale British immigration to, and national-identity making in, Canada.[5]

Unlike colonial New England, which received hundreds of thousands of immigrants, the population of New France (that is, Canada, or Quebec) was based almost solely on natural increase and had reached a population in excess of 70,000 by 1760—the start of the British regime (the Peace of Paris was signed later, in 1763). In respect to demography, Quebec and Mexico have similar population histories. Quebec's population was overwhelmingly French—in fact, 97 percent of its residents were descended from the loins of seventeenth-century French transplants. The British, it should be noted, already controlled Newfoundland, Britain's oldest colony outside of Ireland, and Nova Scotia. The pattern of Quebec's growth—an impressive 2.5 percent per annum; demographic evidence indicates that couples did not practice any form of birth control, the average age of women at last birth being forty)—remained unbroken after the conquest, except for the displaced elites. No fewer than two thousand of them would leave the country rather than suffer the indignity of living under a foreign flag.[6]

The rest of the European people of French Canada, however, stayed put and went about their lives pretty much as before, their world scarcely disturbed. This was not true, of course, of Nova Scotia's Acadians, a small French population. Since the Acadians had refused to swear an oath of loyalty to the British, they were deported, as a war measure, to other parts of the North American empire, although a number escaped the expulsion and fled to Quebec or to what became New Brunswick and Prince Edward Island. After the French and Indian War was over, these unfortunate people were eventually allowed to return to Nova Scotia, provided they swore an oath of loyalty and had the means to do so. The Acadians' plight was remembered in 1847 by the New England poet Henry Wadsworth Longfellow in his sympathetic *Evangeline*.

Canada's largest French population, three-quarters of whom were farmers, was in Quebec. The colony's only city worthy of the name was Quebec City, with a population of 8,000. Montreal, a small frontier town in 1760, was only half that size. The biggest advantage of an isolated, dispersed, and low-density population was the low incidence of infectious diseases, though these were not altogether absent; Canada experienced a serious outbreak of typhoid in 1687 and two deadly smallpox epidemics—one in 1703, the other in 1733. In sum, Quebec's birth rate was very high, and its mortality rate was relatively low. Life expectancy at birth for both sexes for the period from 1608 to 1760 was 35.5 years. Canada may have had long harsh winters and a short growing season, yet its forests teemed with wildlife and its freshwater lakes and rivers were pure and filled with fish. Even the Laurentian Shield, which Samuel de Champlain described as "a wilderness, being barren and uninhabited," full of "rocks and mountains and not ten arpents of arable land," a "frightful" and "abandoned" place, nevertheless possessed an abundance of sorts—a "grand quantity of blueberries" in "such plenty that it is marvelous."[7] In short, upper North America was a hard but healthy place to live.[8]

With America's independence from Britain, Canada's population would change, as thousands of English-speaking and Protestant American Loyalists fled, beginning in 1784, to the Maritimes or to Upper Canada (later Ontario). Few, however, chose to relocate in French Catholic Canada, outside Montreal (or Lower Canada, after 1791), and later Quebec. While residents of the former Thirteen Colonies dominated immigration to Canada until the failed US invasion of the War of 1812, there was also a notable influx of Scottish Highlanders—16,000 to 20,000—to Nova Scotia, Prince Edward Island, and eastern Upper Canada at the end of the eighteenth century. After the War of 1812 the flow of US immigrants slowed to a trickle and was replaced by largely British immigrants, who would profoundly shape Canada's national identity. As had been the case earlier with the Acadians, the British were concerned, and rightly so as events proved, about the Americans' reliability.[9]

On the eve of the War of 1812, Upper Canada's population consisted of about 60,000 people, mostly American in origin. It was an area that extended from the St. Lawrence River, southwest across the northern shores of Lakes Ontario and Erie, to what would become an international boundary and trade corridor, one linked by the St. Clair River, Lake St. Clair, and the Detroit River and one, a strait actually, that connects the upper Great Lakes with the lower. Canada's overall prewar population, which included Lower Canada and the Maritimes, came to a little over 500,000 souls. Following the wars with Madison and Napoleon, which ended in 1814 and 1815, respectively, the population of Canada increased to 722,000 by 1821; to 816,000, if we include Canada's tragically shrinking Native population, which had dropped from 185,000 in 1700 to 75,000 in 1820 and would continue to fall in the ensuing decades. The European population of Canada would finally pass the one million mark in 1831, eighty years after its neighbor to the south had done so.[10]

While historians have made much of the influx of British immigrants into Canada during the nineteenth century, one population historian, Marvin

McInnis, has drawn on Benjamin Franklin's well-known observation that the population of the American colonies was doubling every twenty-five years and applied it to Canada.[11] Land, after all, was just as plentiful, rich, and cheap in Canada as it was in America, the obdurate Laurentian Shield notwithstanding, facts that encouraged robust population growth, if not "superfecundity," in both countries. In McInnis's words, if "the rate of natural increase averaged 3% annum . . . the 511,000 people estimated to be living in Canada in 1811 would have increased through natural increase alone to 2,241,000 in 1861. That is 84% of the 3,175,000 enumerated in the census of that year." To put this another way, these figures match Thomas Robert Malthus's famous geometric progression in his 1798 *Essay on the Principle of Population*, an idea he derived from reading Benjamin Franklin's essay "Observations Concerning the Increase of Mankind." The idea of geometric progression and growing competition over available food sources later profoundly influenced Charles Darwin, evinced as a key basis of his theory of natural selection.[12] Natural increase, then, may actually have been the main driver of British Canada's population growth during the nineteenth century, as it had been of New France's during the eighteenth, suggesting more continuity in this regard than change. And we should add here that the cultural evolution of the eighteen century and the various theories of progress—or, in the case of Gibbon and Malthus, theories of decline—that thinkers and philosophes produced to explain it provided the groundwork and conceptual mindset for the nineteenth century's theories of organic evolution.[13]

In the prefederal and early federal United States, when it came to population growth, immigration was more important than natural increase in the seventeenth century; the reverse was true of the eighteenth and early nineteenth centuries. New England was the first region to experience rapid natural increase, followed by the Middle Colonies—the home of the major cities of New York and Philadelphia—and then the American South. Natural increase was also high among the slave population, a fact that distinguished the British North American colonies from other slave colonies in the Americas.[14] In broad strokes, the population in 1610 (that is, in Virginia), was 210 souls; by 1790, the year of the first US Census, this number had increased to 3.929 million. (The European population was 3.172 million, or 80.7 percent of the total; the African or Black population was 757,000.) The small community holed up inside a three-sided fort at Jamestown, the womb of the future United States, had ventured out to grow into a transcontinental polity that by 1806 stretched, at least on paper, from

North Carolina's Outer Banks to the Oregon Coast. By 1820 this number had grown to 9.639 million (the European population being 7.867 million, or 81.6 percent of the total; the African or Black population 1.772 million). Thus the United States had surpassed Mexico—at some point during the 1810s, while Mexico was distracted by the struggle for independence—to become the most populous country in North America.

What was the reason for the impressive population growth of the United States? The answer is that more Americans married—and married earlier and had larger families. In Benjamin Franklin's inestimable words, which have since been supported by empirical research, "With us in N. America, Marriages are generally in the Morning of life, — our Children are there-fore educated, and settled in the World by Noon, and thus our Business being done, we have an Afternoon and Evening of cheerful leisure to our-selves— . . . By these early Marriages, we are blest with more Children, and, from the Mode among us — founded in Nature — of every Mother suck-ling and nursing her own Child, more of them raised. The swift Progress of Population, —unparallel'd in Europe."[15] Americans were able to do these things because of the availability of good farmland, which produced good food, including Native corn—food that in turn produced strong bodies. By the middle of the eighteenth century, as a result of a better diet, American men literally towered over their British cousins by an average of 7 centime-ters or 2.7 inches, contemporary European theories of American degenera-cy, such as those propounded by George-Luis Leclerc, comte de Buffon, and Cornelius de Pauw, notwithstanding.[16]

With all of this landowning, farming, eating, marrying, sexual congress, and childbearing, although not necessarily in that order, the growth of the American population for the seventeenth and eighteenth centuries was brisk, averaging 5 percent per annum. (In comparison Mexico's growth rate, which was based largely on natural increase, did not reach 1.5 percent until the last quarter of the nineteenth century.) Natural increase was 2.5 percent during the eighteenth century, and slightly higher at 2.6 percent for the years between 1790 and 1820, as opposed to England's rate of natural increase for this latter period, which averaged 1.33 percent.[17] At the same time, beginning in the early nineteenth century, the United States began the demographic transition from high to low fertility and mortality lev-els, although in the United States, as opposed to other Western developed nations, the fertility rate in the European population declined before the mortality rate, which did not start to fall until the 1870s. Thus, in the early nineteenth century, the average woman of European descent bore seven to eight children, and life expectancy was between thirty-five and forty years of age.[18]

Throughout the mainland colonies, there were important regional, rural-urban, and racial or ethnic differences. That said, there were two basic demographic regimes: one in the North, which included New England and the Middle Colonies, and the other in the South, with its historically higher rate of mortality. In New England, where the sex ratio was relatively balanced, life expectancy from the time of birth was high but varied widely. During the seventeenth century the life expectancy for the Plymouth Colony was sixty-one to sixty-two years, while for eighteenth-century Salem, Massachusetts, it was between thirty-five and thirty-seven years.[19]

In marked contrast to New England, life expectancy in the southern colonies was tragically lower—perhaps by twenty years. In the South, White lives, especially those of immigrant White men—40 percent of whom died in the first decade after arrival—were short. Black lives were presumably even shorter, if not as short as those forced to work on the sugar islands in the Caribbean.[20] The longer-term survivors, European or African, were those who had managed to acclimate to North America's disease environment in a culling process called "seasoning." In addition to the notorious killers typhoid and dysentery, the tidewater lowlands in the Chesapeake region and elsewhere were ideal breeding grounds for mosquitoes, which in turn spread the malarial parasite *Plasmodium falciparum*—Africa's unwelcome contribution to the Columbian exchange, although there were many more positive ones as well.[21] Natural increase was not achieved in the region until after 1700, when the center of the population had moved inland, away from the deadly marshes. Also, it was then that women started marrying earlier, thereby increasing the number of childbearing years. As a result, the South's formerly lopsided sex ratio in favor of men was eventually brought into balance.[22]

The growth of the South's Black population during the course of the colonial era, which the economic historians John J. McCusker and Russell R. Menard have called "extraordinary," defies easy explanation. Evidently the rapid growth of the European and the African or Black populations paralleled one another, despite the fact that one lived in freedom and the other in slavery. What does seem to be clear is that the total number of Africans brought to the British islands in the Caribbean outnumbered the number of Africans brought to the British colonies on the mainland by five to one.

Nevertheless, by 1770 the total Black population on the North American continent was a little *larger* than that of the Caribbean.[23] Furthermore, from 1610 to 1810 an estimated 399,000 African slaves or enslaved Africans—4.5 percent of all African slaves brought to the Western Hemisphere, a small fraction of the total, according to the noted authority Philip Curtin—were brought to British North America, and another 28,000 to French and later Spanish Louisiana. (The African slave trade with the United States was abolished in 1807.) The cliometricians Robert Fogel and Stanley Engerman, however, estimate the number brought to British North America to be probably closer to 596,000.[24]

This transatlantic trade in human beings was conducted by a triangle of actors: first, by warring African kings who abducted their neighbors and rivals and traded these men, women, and children for "powder, musket, and shot"; second, by European merchants, traders, and other middlemen who conducted this nefarious business from slave forts along the West African coast, such as the Elmina Castle in Ghana and Goree Island in Senegal (diseases kept Europeans out of the interior of sub-Saharan Africa until late in the 1800s), as well as in the port cities of western Europe, North America, and the Caribbean; and third, by planter oligarchs and slaveholders in the American South and the West Indies.[25]

During the colonial era, slaves or bondspeople made up 95 percent of the African American population, which was concentrated in the South. In 1790 African Americans made up 1.7 percent of the population of New England and 6.2 percent of the Middle Colonies, but roughly one-third of the population in the South—37.6 percent of the Upper South and 32.6 percent of the Lower South. Most free Blacks, however, resided above the Mason-Dixon Line. Not everyone of African descent in the United States was a slave. But every slave in the United States was of African descent. It should be noted that Black slaves or enslaved Blacks were not the only form of bound labor in America. There were also sizable numbers of European indentured servants and prisoners of war as well as transported convicts.[26]

Apart from the ubiquity of the freehold farm, perhaps nothing distinguished British North America from Spanish North America more than the region's high rate of literacy. It was no accident that the famed Founding Father Benjamin Franklin got his start as a printer's apprentice and journalist at the *New England Courant*, a Boston newspaper founded by his brother James in 1721. There was a wide demand for reading matter in the English colonies—and money to be made by supplying it. Franklin's *Poor Richard's*

Almanac, which, beginning in 1733, was published every year for twenty-five years, sold ten thousand copies per annum. This enterprise made the former teenage runaway and now proud Philadelphian gentleman wealthy, if not healthy and wise.

Like land ownership, literacy or a basic education is a telling indicator of general well-being. It is therefore highly significant that historians Elisa Mariscal and Kenneth Sokoloff call the high rate of literacy in British North America "striking," because "virtually from the time of initial settlement, North Americans seem generally to have been convinced of the value of providing their children with a basic education, including the ability to read and write, and established schools to accomplish that goal."[27] Homeschooling was common in the rural areas. In the villages or towns, colonists funded their formal schools in any number of ways: charities, lotteries, licenses for dogs, taverns, marriages, slave trading, public land sales, and rate bills on parents with enrolled children. According to Kenneth Lockridge, as early as 1670 nearly 60 percent of White men in New England, where Bible-reading was a Puritan imperative, were literate, a figure that increased to close to 90 percent over a century later. The religious passions of the seventeenth century may have cooled over time, but the evidence shows that habits of literacy, once they had been acquired by the general population, persisted.

Literacy in New England and the Middle Colonies was higher than in the South, where formal education of the general population was met with hostility by at least some of the British authorities and where unlettered slaves or bondspeople made up a significant minority of the population. In 1671 Sir William Berkeley, the royal governor of Virginia, described formal schooling and the nonexistent state of printing in Virginia, exclaiming: "I thank God there are no free schools nor printing, and I hope we shall not have these hundred years; for learning has brought disobedience, and heresy, and sects into the world, and printing has divulged them, and libels against the best government. God keep us from both!"[28] Berkeley was not opposed to private education, however, and noted that, just as in rural England, homeschooling prevailed in the Old Dominion, where "every man" offers instruction "according to his ability." Like many in colonial America, he believed education was a private or family matter, not a public concern. This basic attitude did not change until the 1830s, when the spread of universal manhood suffrage, though led by northerners such as Horace Mann, was linked by Jacksonian reformers to the need for tax-supported public schools. In the United States the spread of suffrage and literacy went hand in hand.[29]

Throughout Britain's mainland colonies, schooling and the rate of literacy was higher among White men than White women, although White women would close the gap by the early nineteenth century. Schooling and the literacy rate were also higher in the English areas versus the French areas of Canada, and higher in the United States than in Canada as a whole. They were also higher in the cities than in the countryside, and by the end of the colonial era, remarkably enough, literacy was higher in British North America than in northwestern Europe, Scotland excepted.[30]

New Spain, as we have seen, lagged far behind its northern neighbors when it came to literacy. But New Spain's rate was also significantly lower than that of Argentina, Uruguay, Chile, Cuba, and Costa Rica. In fact, when it came to literacy in the Americas, Mexico ranked at the bottom, along with Brazil, Venezuela, Peru, Columbia, Bolivia, Guatemala, and Honduras.[31] Catholicism is often blamed for Latin America's low literacy rates. This is a fair criticism. Unlike Protestants, especially Calvinists, Catholics were not expected to read the scriptures for themselves. In the case of French Canada, where Catholicism prevailed, religion also correlates with low literacy. Following the rebellions for political reform of 1837–38, Lord Durham, Canada's governor-general and reformer, sent Sir Arthur William Buller to Lower Canada (Quebec) to investigate the state of education in the province, which was regarded as deplorable. Using Buller's statistics, along with census and other data, the social scientist Allan Greer estimates that in 1844, 31 percent of Quebec's rural French speakers were literate. This compared poorly with the 75 percent literacy rate of their rural English counterparts.[32] Greer goes on to place the history of literacy in Quebec in an international and continental context, which is worth quoting in full:

In the middle of the eighteenth century when three rural parishes in New France had signature rates close to 10%, seventeen country parishes of northern England had aggregate signature rates of 64% for men and 39% for women, while male farmers were 80% literate in New England. In a large sample favouring rural areas, the rates in France were 29% for men and 14% for women in 1686–90 and 47% and 27% respectively a century later. Based on Arthur Buller's statistics of 1838–39, it was estimated that 27% of adult Lower Canadians, 12% of rural francophones and 60% of rural anglophones could read and write. At about the same time, parish register signature rates—which probably exaggerate literacy slightly—were 70% for men and 54% for women in rural Yorkshire, while England as a whole had rates of 67% and 50% for men and women respectively. New England had long ago achieved virtual universal male literacy. Towards the middle of the nineteenth century French-Canadian illiteracy seems to have been more on a level with that prevailing in Italy, Spain and the Balkans. Cohort literacy rates derived from late nineteenth-century censuses show that progress was much more rapid in Quebec than it was in most countries in the second half of the century. The province probably advanced in this period to the level of European countries with medium illiteracy from the level of those with high illiteracy.[33]

In his seminal *Report on the Affairs of British North America* (1839), Lord Durham concluded that Quebec was "two nations warring in the bosom of a single state" and harshly condemned the French Canadians as a "people with no literature and no history." This criticism stung, and within a generation it led to real change. By 1861 the literacy rate in the French-majority and English-majority counties of Canada was 81.2 and 93 percent, respectively.[34] This was real progress. Still, the Catholic Church's hold over education was nearly complete. The Révolution tranquille (Quiet Revolution)—the secularization of Quebec—was still a good century away.

Mexico's social situation was similar to Quebec's, where the Catholic Church had a strong hand, but quite different from the rest of Anglo and mostly Protestant North America. The small minority of Spanish and Criollo elites saw little or no benefit—and some very real danger—in educating the Native and Mestizo masses. In addition to this profound inequality, the Catholic Church, which was largely responsible for Mexico's schools (and hospitals, it should be noted), had acted throughout the sixteenth and the seventeenth centuries as though ignorance would shield their American Indian flocks from the intellectual wolves of the Renaissance and the scientific revolution.[35] And during the eighteenth century the Church found the Enlightenment, with its overt anticlericalism, to say nothing of its secular explanations of the natural and human worlds, an even greater threat to their charges' innocence. It is very hard to assess the damage caused by three centuries of religious paternalism and social inequality, but it certainly helps explain Mexico's relative backwardness or lower social development vis-à-vis its two more religiously free and egalitarian northern neighbors.

John Bull and Brother Jonathan

The American Revolution turned Great Britain, the mother country, into an alien power. And while all men were created equal, nations, on the other hand, were decidedly not. In the years after the American Revolution, the United States found that in its relationship to Europe it operated very much from a position of weakness, if not helplessness. US social power—the nation's ability to get things done—was very limited during the Early Republic of 1780–1830. The Napoleonic Wars (1803–15) that followed the other Atlantic revolution of this period, the French Revolution of 1789, had reduced North America's other mother country, Spain, as a world power, but Spain would nevertheless commit itself to the reconquest of Mexico, leaving her former colony exhausted, isolated, and politically divided. Great Britain, on the other hand, emerged from these wars, including the War of 1812, triumphant in Europe and secure in Canada. And instead of trying to undermine and retake its former North American colonies, as Spain unwisely tried to do with Mexico, Great Britain pursued an enlightened policy of coexistence and coprosperity, which allowed the personifications of Great Britain and the United States—John Bull and Brother Jonathan, respectively—to pursue a number of accommodations with each other. In short, Great Britain, an established power, made way for the United States, a rising power, thus effecting a Thucydides escape from history—a rare achievement, according to the political scientist Graham T. Allison. Spain, on the other hand, both an established and a declining power, behaved more predictably when it endeavored to thwart Mexico's rise, thus falling squarely into a Thucydides trap.

In 1823 the United States served notice to Europe—above all to Spain—that the Americas now fell within its sphere of influence. This assertion of US hegemony was a brazen move, but it was done with Great Britain's tacit approval, to say nothing of its de facto naval support. The willingness of Great Britain and the United States to share rather than fight over the North American continent was a hugely significant development in world history. The decision explains much of the subsequent history of the nineteenth century and was the origin of the Special Relationship, which proved so important to the history of the twentieth. It also has an especial relevance to the twenty-first century, as the United States, an established power, contends with Communist China, a rising power, and the Sino-Russo autocratic axis. At the same time, the history of Anglo-American amity contrasts sharply with that of Spanish-Mexican hostility.

On October 21, 1804, in the Battle of Trafalgar, waged near Spain's Cape Trafalgar between Cádiz and the Strait of Gibraltar, Admiral Horatio Nelson and his British fleet decisively, indeed lopsidedly, defeated the combined and superior French and Spanish navies. The Spanish navy was destroyed, a development that had profound implications for New Spain. Nelson's smashing victory at sea ended Napoleon's plans of a cross-channel invasion of Britain and established British naval supremacy for the next century, a mighty shield that, in effect, provided North America with virtually free security. Without the Pax Britannica, North American development, in general, and US and Canadian development, in particular, would have proceeded along very different lines. This, however, is the long view. In the much shorter term Britain and France, following Nelson's victory at Trafalgar, erected dueling trade blocs to destroy each other's commerce. These were France's Continental System, a French-driven Brexit, and Britain's blockade of the continent of Europe, as provided under the Orders in Council of 1807.

These grand strategies, in particular the Rule of 1756, in which Great Britain cut off trade with nations that were trading with the enemy, ensnared neutrals, including the United States, that dared to trade with either France or Britain and their respective allies. Given Britain's naval supremacy and control of the Atlantic, America's merchant marine was far more impacted by Britain's wartime policy than France's. By 1807, in fact, 469 American ships had been captured by the British, or nearly half of America's entire merchant fleet. In addition, the British routinely violated US sovereignty by boarding American vessels to impress or coerce American sailors into British naval service. Between 1793 and 1812, thousands of US sailors found themselves forced to serve aboard His Majesty's ships. Matters came to a head when the HMS *Leopard* brazenly bombarded and boarded the frigate USS *Chesapeake* on June 22, 1807, off the coast of Norfolk, Virginia, to apprehend several British deserters.

The Greek historian Thucydides wrote that men go to war for one of three reasons: honor, fear, or self-interest. Clearly, British aggression or condescension put America's honor at stake and was therefore grounds for war, but the United States was woefully underprepared to defend its honor. And what naval forces it did possess were already deployed in the Mediterranean to protect American shipping from the state-sponsored piracy of the Barbary States (Morocco, Algiers, Tunis, and Tripoli). Jefferson and the Democratic-Republicans had earlier abandoned plans to build up an expensive frigate navy, and with it an offensive capability, in favor of building a fleet of small but relatively inexpensive shallow-draft gunboats, the use of which was strictly defensive. To clarify the difference: a frigate could carry up to forty-four guns and deliver a devastating and wood-splintering broadside, as opposed to a one-cannon gunboat. Frigates could also fight on the high seas, while Jefferson's gunboat navy was limited to the nation's harbors and home waters.[36]

Thus, since war was not a realistic option, Jefferson decided to place an embargo on all foreign trade and count on his country's self-reliance and native industry to make up for the lost European goods. But without a blue-water navy, Jefferson's embargo was impossible to enforce. He only succeeded in making himself unpopular in New England, whose economy was heavily dependent on trade with Britain. In 1809, with the Non-Intercourse Act, he modified the embargo by allowing trade with nations other than Britain and France. But since he still had no way to enforce the act without a blue-water navy, Non-Intercourse proved just as toothless as the embargo. In short, the nation's military capability poorly matched Jefferson's foreign policy. The means failed to agree with the president's ends—a predicament and weakness he passed on to his elected successor, fellow Virginian and friend James Madison (1809–17).[37]

Madison was undoubtedly one of America's keenest intellects and has rightly been called the Father of the Constitution for his contributions to that venerable document. But few men can be all things, as Madison's roles as statesman and commander-in-chief would prove. With Nathaniel Macon's Bill No. 2, which Madison signed into law on May 1, 1810, Congress came up with a replacement for the Non-Intercourse Act. Bill No. 2 was just as toothless, or perhaps more shipless, as was Jefferson's, but it did succeed in antagonizing Britain and setting the two nations on a road to war. Submissively, it stated that the United States would side with the trade bloc of whichever nation—France or Britain—agreed to stop attacking US shipping. Napoleon signaled his willingness to do so, and in response Madison reimposed non-intercourse against Britain. In other words, Madison tried to pressure Britain by injuring US interests, in particular New England's interests, an act of self-harm that impressed no one. And for all of that, the navies of Britain and France went right on preying on Yankee shipping, their war outweighing every other consideration. By 1810 the United States had lost a thousand ships to Britain and to British, New Brunswick, and Nova Scotia privateers, and five hundred to France. These numbers did not include ships lost to other flags, such as those of Denmark, Spain, Naples, and the Netherlands.

The War of 1812 between the United States and Great Britain has been called America's second war of independence. The Revolutionary War had more than secured US independence from Europe, as George Washington was able to use the Continental Army and America's immense geography, along with French naval support, to negate the advantages of British sea power. But the outcome of the War of 1812 was, in fact, one of the innumerable consequences of the turmoil caused by Napoleon's ambitions in Europe and on the Atlantic. Although the war's casus belli was the freedom of the seas, the Americans, whose navy was no match for Great Britain's (in 1812 the US Navy had seventeen ships versus the six hundred ships of the British fleet), elected to attack British Canada by land and waterway. Canada, which under Britain's Constitutional Act of 1791 had been divided into the two provinces of Upper Canada (Ontario) and Lower Canada (Quebec), proved less vulnerable, however, than the country might have appeared on a map. Thomas Jefferson thought acquiring Canada—and expelling the British from the continent, first from Quebec and then Halifax—would be simply a "mere matter of marching." For his generation, it should be pointed out, taking Canada was the Revolution's item of unfinished business.[38] It was an obsession much as reacquiring Taiwan remains—ever since the Chinese Revolution of 1949—an idée fixe of the Chinese Communist leadership.

Instead, the US invasions (there were multiple forays) of Canada were repulsed by British regulars, the Voltigeurs de Québec, fencibles, Canadian militia, and Native and Métis allies. The Canadians had the benefit of good leadership by men such as Sir Isaac Brock, Robert Ross, Alexander Cochrane, James Fitzgibbon, Charles-Michel d'Irumberry de Salaberry, and Tecumseh. And Canada had, of course, the backing of the Royal Navy, which by war's end had blockaded the entire American coast from New England to Georgia. There were also the many heroic acts of individual Canadians, notably Laura Secord, who trekked nearly twenty miles from Queenston to Beaver Dam to warn the British of an impending American attack. Like the American attacks on Canadian soil and waterways—the Battles of Queenston Heights, Châteauguay, Crysler's Farm, and Lundy's Lane, perhaps the bloodiest battle of the war—the British attacks on the republic to its south, such as at the Battles of Baltimore and New Orleans, were also repulsed. In fact, the former battle produced a national anthem, and the latter, which was actually fought after the Treaty of Ghent had officially concluded the war, a national hero and future president, the rags-to-riches Tennessean Andrew Jackson (whose men called him "Old Hickory").

In the Battle of Lake Erie on September 10, 1813, Oliver Hazard Perry, a US veteran of the Quasi-War and the Barbary Wars, led a naval force that prevailed over a British squadron. In a message to William Henry Harrison, another future president who vanquished the Prophet at Tippecanoe in 1811 and who would shortly defeat the Prophet's brother, Tecumseh, at the Battle of the Thames in 1813, Perry added the immortal lines to the nation's patriotic annals: "We have met the enemy and they are ours." He also stitched the defiant words "Don't Give Up the Ship" on his battle flag as a tribute to James Lawrence, the commander of the USS *Chesapeake*, which had been defeated by the frigate HMS *Shannon* in Boston Harbor. Lawrence was mortally wounded on June 1, 1813, and these words were reportedly the last he gave to his crew.

Perry's victory on Lake Erie and Commodore Thomas Macdonough's defeat of another British squadron on Lake Champlain in September of the next year improved America's bargaining position in the peace talks that had begun the month before Macdonough's victory, in August 1814, in the old canal-lined, cloth-producing neutral city of Ghent, in what is now Belgium. (The American delegation was led by John Quincy Adams—yet another future president—and included the war hawk and expansionist Henry Clay of Kentucky.) True, the British under the command of Robert Ross had burned down the public buildings of Washington on August 24, 1814. Sacking an enemy's capital is rightly considered a major blow, especially if carried out in retaliation, as this one was, for the American burning of York, Upper Canada's provincial capital, the year before. But the next month the Americans saved the port of Baltimore from attack, and Fort McHenry had survived a heavy bombardment from the sea (the future president James Buchanan had served as a private in Baltimore's defense). After Ross was killed by sniper fire at the Battle of North Point, the British withdrew.[39]

Still, the single most important military fact before the British and American delegations was that Napoleon had been defeated at the Battle of Leipzig in October 1813 and exiled to Elba, an island in the Mediterranean. (Napoleon would return to Paris in March 1815, resurrect the Grande Armée, and go on to be defeated at Waterloo by a coalition of armies led by the Duke of Wellington and Field Marshal Blücher.) The maritime issues

Figure 21. W. Ridgway and John Reuben Chapin, *Commodore Perry at the Battle of Lake Erie: "Ready! All ready your honor,"* ca. 1860. Steel engraving. New York: Virtue & Co. Photograph. Prints and Photographs Division, Library of Congress, Washington, DC. https://www.loc.gov/item/2012645270/.

that had divided the United States and Britain, neutral trading and impressment, were now moot, and with Napoleon, the greatest threat to Great Britain, unable to do any more harm—at least for the moment—the British were happy to put the American war behind them.

As for the Americans, although they had started the war, and their victories on land and sea had gone far to restore their honor, they otherwise had little to show for it. They found Britain and Canada united in purpose and more than ready, able, and willing to defend their territory. Indeed, the war gave Canada its first real sense of national identity. Worse, the US government was nearly bankrupt. The British blockade had strangled America's transatlantic trade and with it the government's major source of income—custom revenues. And worse than that, US casualties, killed and wounded, were nearly twice that of the British and Canadians, that is, 15,000 to 8,600. To put these figures into an Atlantic context, there were 47,000 killed and wounded in one day at the Battle of Waterloo on June 18, 1815. Americans would not learn to kill on a European scale until their own civil war. Nevertheless, the War of 1812 had become pointless and increasingly costly in both financial and human terms, especially so for the Americans. For the

British, peace with the Americans meant one less thing. For the Americans, it meant *everything*.

Since Native peoples kept few or no written records, it is difficult to ascertain Native casualty figures for the War of 1812. However, in 1890, with the closing of the American frontier, the US Bureau of Census offered these sweeping estimates:

> The Indian wars under the government of the United States have been more than 40 in number [since 1789]. They have cost the lives of about 19,000 white men, women and children, including those killed in individual combats, and the lives of about 30,000 Indians. The actual number of killed and wounded Indians must be very much greater than the number given, as they conceal, where possible, their actual loss in battle, and carry their killed and wounded off and secrete them. The number given above is of those found by the whites. Fifty percent additional would be a safe estimate to add to the numbers given [i.e., 60,000 Indians killed from 1789 to 1890].[40]

The Era of Good Feelings

The Treaty of Ghent was really the third act of a three-act play in which John Bull and Brother Jonathan learned how to share North America, and the Seven Seas, an experience that forged their oft-commented-on special, and seemingly lasting, relationship. The first act produced the Peace of Paris of 1783. The second act ended with Jay's Treaty in 1794. And the third and final act was the Treaty of Ghent—signed on Christmas Eve, 1814, and ratified the following year. All three dealt with more or less similar issues, which included maritime rights, commerce and trade, territorial control, Indian affairs, the abolition of the slave trade, and payment of individual debts owed and for property destroyed or confiscated. On the matter of territorial control and Indian affairs, the Treaty of Ghent reset the clock back to 1811—the *status quo ante bellum*—and relied on future arbitration to settle pretty much everything else. Since Jay's Treaty, the two sides had found, and after 1814 would continue to find, that arbitration was a far more productive way than annihilation to resolve conflicts. Of course, in theory arbitration could be used to settle international disputes all over the world. What made the relationship between the United Kingdom and the United States special was not just that they shared a civilization, one based on kindred ties as well as a shared culture—the King James Bible,

Shakespeare's sonnets and plays—but that they also held a continent in common.[41]

The shift from conflict to cooperation in Anglo-American relations occurred in Ghent and was based on two key cessions, one made on each side. Britain, for its part, would give up on the idea of an American Indian buffer state. The recent victories of William Henry Harrison and Andrew Jackson over Natives in the Old Northwest and Old Southwest closed a chapter in the Indian Wars (in 1814 Jackson defeated the Creeks at the Battle of Horseshoe Bend, on Alabama's Tallapoosa River, and forced them to cede 23 million acres of their homeland). The United States would henceforth contend with individual tribes largely on a one-on-one basis, and no longer with tribes in an alliance with, or support from, an interloping European power. This had been largely the situation in middle and upper North America since the 1600s. Indeed, what had distinguished Indigenous-White relations in this region from those in Mexico was the involvement in Native affairs of multiple European players. Europeans had long tried to play one tribe or First Nation against another, and Natives had tried to do the same thing in their dealings, commercial and military, with the European powers. And just as there would be now only one "Great Father" or president in the United States, there would be only one Great Father or, after 1837, one Queen Victoria in Canada (she reigned until 1901). Needless to say, these shifts and simplifications in North America's balance of power worked greatly to the advantage of the United States and to His (or Her) Britannic Majesty, just as they had long done with New Spain's viceroy and, after 1821, with Mexico's independence from Spain, Mexico's president. In fact, during the nineteenth century the Indian policies of Canada, the United States, and Mexico became virtually identical as all three sought to turn their former Native enemies into friends, and eventually citizens, by assimilating them in all respects into the dominant culture and converting their homelands into real estate. The 1800s was a time of intense nation-building and how to create one out of many, *e pluribus unum*, was the problem at hand.[42]

At Ghent the United States conceded its goal, which dated back to the Revolution, of evicting the British from the continent. Its once great rival would now be a powerful but friendly neighbor in the north, and a formidable naval presence at sea. With the final defeat of Napoleon in 1815 the Pax Britannica had dawned, and Europe would enjoy a century of relative peace, though this was later threatened by the rise of Germany and the decline of Turkey. It is against this changing background that the

United States and Great Britain agreed, in the Era of Good Feelings—these feelings being as much domestic, at the time, as they were transatlantic—to demilitarize the Great Lakes, under the Richard Rush–Charles Bagot Pact of 1817 and the Convention of 1818. The international border would now be defined as running west along the forty-ninth parallel, from the Lake of the Woods (apart from the Angle Inlet) to the Rocky Mountains. Furthermore, in what was a remarkable act of cooperation and goodwill, the two countries also agreed to jointly occupy the Oregon Country, where American settlers would soon outnumber British traders.

The British also agreed to look the other way when, in 1818, General Andrew Jackson tried and executed two British subjects after he invaded Florida and seized the Spanish forts of Pensacola and St. Marks. Jackson claimed that the two British Indian traders, Alexander Arbuthnot and Robert C. Ambrister, had incited the "Negroes & Indians in East Florida to war against the U States."[43] Since 1815, Ferdinand's Spain had sought to use negotiations over disputed territory between the United States and Spain to curtail US support for Latin America's independence movements. But Britain's determination to avoid conflict with the United States, or to be used by the Spanish to pressure the Americans, had the effect of isolating Spain's US ambassador, Don Luis de Onís. Bowing to reality, in 1819, under the Adams-Onís Treaty, the Spanish ambassador agreed to cede Florida (part of West Florida had already been annexed by the United States late in 1810 after American frontiersmen rebelled against Spanish rule, captured Fort San Carlos in Baton Rouge, and formed the short-lived "Republic of West Florida"). Spain also gave up its claims to lands in the Pacific Northwest, while the United States, in turn, agreed to a transcontinental border that was defined by the Red River, the Arkansas, and the forty-second parallel. The United States also recognized Spanish sovereignty over Texas. In other words, the United States conceded nothing, although it did agree to pay Spain up to $5 million in damages caused by American rebels. Two years later Spain lost all of the rest of North America to a war-ravaged, if independent, Mexico, with the Treaty of Córdoba.

Bellum Hispanicum

From the Cry of Dolores in 1810 to the March of the Army of the Three Guarantees (the new Mexican empire was to be independent, Catholic, and united) in 1821, Mexico had been in a state of war or turmoil. And after it won independence from Spain, it faced another fifty years of conflicting visions, pronunciamentos, civil strife, territorial secession and cession, and two major foreign invasions—one from North America, the other from Europe. The numbers encapsulate the sad tale. Mexico's GDP in 1820 was $5 billion. By 1870 the monetary value of all finished goods and services had barely climbed over $6 billion, while per capita GDP fell from $759 to $674 over the same period of time. Meanwhile, Mexico's population had increased from 6.5 million in 1820 to 9.2 million in 1870. In short, in this otherwise resource-rich country there was less and less money per capita, the scale at which the individual mattered, and more and more mouths to feed. If not for these troubles, all of which could be easily traced back to Napoleon's invasion of Spain and the catastrophic disruptions that it caused, life in Mexico might have continued on a steady upward trajectory, as it had done since the mid-seventeenth century. But that was not to be.[44]

After 1810 the Pax Hispanica, which Mexico had enjoyed for three centuries, came to a violent end with the insurgency. Mexico did inherit Spain's empire in North America but not Spain's navy, army, or power to influence events in Europe or North America. On the contrary, in the years after independence Mexico suffered Spain's enduring hostility as well as Spain's efforts to reconquer its former kingdom in the New World. This experience contrasted sharply with Britain's evolving relationship with its erstwhile colonies on the mainland of North America. Moreover, Mexico's social power, as measured by its war-making capacity, one of Morris's four critical traits (the others being energy capture, information technology, and social organization), was by definition but a small fraction of the Spanish Empire's former military might. Mexico was now merely one part of what had been formerly a much larger and more powerful whole.

In the coming and inevitable struggle over the control of the North American continent, the center of which had shifted from the capitals of Europe to those of North America, the United States found itself confronting Spain's imperial ghost, whose moans could be heard in Mexico's vaulted territorial claims and whose specter could be glimpsed in the vague and unmanned borders lining the maps of North America. In fact, in the region north of the Rio Grande Mexico's corporeality barely existed, apart from some forty thousand souls—less than 1 percent of its entire population. Moreover, these souls were thinly scattered over an enormous region, one stretching from the area west of the Indian trading post at Natchitoches in Louisiana's Red River Valley to the Mission San Carlos

Borromeo de Carmelo on California's Monterey Peninsula, two thousand miles away. The significance of these facts, as we have seen, was not lost on either Humboldt or Jefferson.

Epilogue

Peace is an armistice in a war that is continuously going on.

Thucydides

CHAPTER 12

The Clenched Fist and the Invisible Hand

BY 1823 THE DIE HAD been cast for the future of North America. Mexico was independent but isolated, poor, and weak. Canada enjoyed the protection of Great Britain, while Great Britain, the world's sole superpower, wisely chose to accommodate rather than challenge the rising power of the United States. The United States also found shade under Britain's protective parasol, which allowed the young nation the luxury of free security and with it the freedom to concentrate on its own development and westward expansion. Indeed, the Erie Canal—the first, after Mexico's *Desagüe de Huehuetoca,* of numerous continent-changing infrastructure projects—had been under construction since July 4, 1817, and would open for business in 1825. And with the Monroe Doctrine, the United States had boldly proclaimed its role in the geopolitical order. It would first dominate the continent and later the world, following the example of Great Britain, which had first secured the British Isles before becoming the first world power. There would be more warfare in North America, to be sure, as each national actor adjusted to the postcolonial order and reconciled its own internal contradictions. But the Monroe Doctrine, initially underwritten by the Royal Navy, was eventually enforced by the US military, thus providing Canada and Mexico with free security as well. And as a member of the British Empire, Canada was unique in that it enjoyed the double protection of Great Britain and the United States from threats abroad.

Of North America's troika of nations, Mexico, a brother of a different mother, would go its own way, as order and progress eluded the country until the establishment of the Porfiriato in 1876. And after the revolution of 1910–20, Mexico chose Latin America over Anglo America—at least on economic policy. Canada and the United States, on the other hand, children of a common mother, would share a common destiny. Both nations joined five others—Japan, France, Italy, Germany, and Great Britain—in the great metamorphosis of world politics that occurred over a few short, remarkable years between 1867 and 1871.[1]

This hinge of history began with the Confederation of Canada in 1867, when Canada united its colonies, without war or bloodshed, and made plans for a transcontinental railway and for the settlement of the western portions of upper North America. The following year, 1868, Japan restored the Meiji monarchy and embarked on a massive program of economic modernization, which included an ambitious naval buildup, coupled with an aggressive colonial policy. Japan would one day challenge North America's transpacific trading relationships. By 1869 the United States had broken the hold of the South's plantocracy by abolishing slavery and by terminating the special constitutional status of the slaveholding states. These things were accomplished by putting down an insurrection and by passing the Thirteenth, Fourteenth, and Fifteenth Amendments. The more radical efforts, by the standards of the time, to create from scratch a biracial democracy in the South met with much less success, however. No longer distracted by sectional issues and constitutional crises, the United States could now turn its enormous energies first westward and then outward. In France, the Second Empire collapsed and was replaced by the intensely nationalistic Third Republic in 1870, which lasted until Hitler's blitzkrieg in 1940. Also in 1870, Italy rose again after a long struggle of unification that ended with the triumphal annexation of Rome. And finally, in 1871, with the close of the Franco-Prussian War, Germany, under Otto von Bismarck—Germany's Lincoln—achieved national unification, an event that fundamentally altered the balance of power in Europe. Only Great Britain avoided a profound political change during this period, since the country had already committed itself to a long but steady program of social and electoral reform, with the Reform Acts of 1832, 1867, and 1884. To try to catch up with these seven industrial and capitalist countries, Russia and China, two large and lumbering rural economies, would adopt in 1917 and 1949, respectively, Marxist-Leninist programs of accelerated modernization and social development.

The emergence of these seven countries, including the democracies of the United States and Canada, would anchor what was now the modern international system—but not at first. Tensions among them would define the first half of the twentieth century and precipitate World Wars I and II, although notably Great Britain, the United States, and Canada—parent and siblings—all fought on the same side. Since World War II, however, the seven have opted to replace competition with cooperation, with all but one of them, Japan, joining NATO. Canada and the United States would go on to form the North American Air Defense Command. Founded in 1958, NORAD is the most important contiguous defense relationship in the world. Today these countries make up the Group of Seven, or G-7. And together they represent more than half of the globe's net wealth. Next to climate change, the greatest challenge facing the G-7 is the threat posed by the Gang of Two, or G-2, the revisionist powers Russia and China.

And whither Mexico? In the midst of *la década perdida*, the lost decade of the 1980s, when the economies of Mexico and the rest of Latin America fell far behind and deep into debt, the Mexican anthropologist Guillermo Bonfil Batalla offered perhaps the strongest rejection of Western development or the Eurocentric notion of progress. In 1987 he thundered bitterly:

> The recent history of Mexico, that of the last five hundred years, is the story of permanent confrontation between those attempting to direct the country toward the path of Western civilization and those, rooted in Mesoamerican ways of life, who resist. The first plan arrived with the European invaders but was not abandoned with independence. The new groups in power, first the Creoles and later the Mestizos, never renounced the westernization plan. They still have not renounced it. Their differences and the struggles that divide them express only disagreement over the best way of carrying out the same program. The adoption of that model has meant the creation within Mexican society of a minority country organized according to the norms, aspirations, and goals of Western civilization. They are not shared, or are shared from a different perspective, by the rest of the national population. To the sector that represents and gives impetus to our country's dominant civilizational program, I give the name "the imaginary Mexico." . . . Imaginary Mexico's westernization plan has been exclusionary and has denied the validity of Mesoamerican civilization.[2]

The leaders of Mexico rejected Batalla's argument, choosing the free market as the surest way out of the country's dire economic predicament. In 1992 Mexico signed the North American Free Trade Agreement (NAFTA), which was revised in 2020, and in 1994 it joined the elite Organization for Economic Co-operation and Development (OECD). Mexico, in short, reversed course and chose Anglo America over Latin America. Still, this progress may yet be undone by a resurgence of economic nationalism and dirigisme.[3]

In 1992 the United States issued the Defense Planning Guidance, commonly known as the Wolfowitz Doctrine, a globalized Monroe Doctrine 2.0 in which it proclaimed that it would no longer tolerate a rival anywhere else in the world. At the same time, in a rough transatlantic symmetry, Mexico joined NAFTA, and the European Union, the world's second united states, was formed. Thus, despite the passage of two centuries, world progress was still being driven by wars and markets—Ferguson's clenched fist and Adam Smith's invisible hand.

For the rest of the 1990s, the unipolarity of the United States would provide the global security and protection necessary for globalization and the spread of democracy, including the integration of Europe and the eastward expansion of the North Atlantic Treaty Organization (NATO), as countries that had been formerly oppressed by the Soviet Union, which now distrusted and feared Russia, eagerly sought the protection of the Western alliance. In this flourishing and creative period, the world became increasingly interdependent as peoples, goods, and ideas flowed more and more freely around the earth, aided by the World Wide Web and the Global Positioning System and less and less vexed by national border controls.

This heady time lasted nearly thirty years, from 1991 to 2022. The scholar Robert Kagan has aptly called it the "holiday from history." Adam Smith's wealthy world finally seemed close at hand. The Yugoslav Wars of the 1990s would test the Pax Americana, as would the global war on terrorism that started in 2001. But it was with Russia's overt and covert invasions of the South Caucasus in Georgia and the Donbas region of Ukraine, in 2008 and 2014, respectively, and especially the flagrantly illegal annexation of the Crimean Peninsula, that history and geography seemed to roar back with a vengeance. The ghosts of the geopolitical theorists Halford Mackinder, Nicholas J. Spykman, George Kennan, and Hans J. Morgenthau were once again seen haunting the "world island" of Eurasia, the most populous, richest, and strategically paramount landmass on earth, with a new sense of urgency.

Indeed, as much as the United States, an established power, has tried to avoid falling into a Thucydides trap with China, a rising power, it now finds itself in a second cold war as Communist China builds up its military and looks not only east, to dominate first Hong Kong (with the new and oppressive one-country, one-system policy) and later the South China Sea and Taiwan, but also west, to gain influence in Eurasia as well as Africa by means of the Belt and Road Initiative. At the same time the internet has been balkanizing into a "splinternet," while Russia, Turkey, Iran, India, and Sunni Islamic radicals all vie to reclaim past imperial glories.

With the end of the Cold War in 1991, which began with North Korea's invasion of South Korea in 1950 and ended with the implosion of the Soviet Union in 1991, Samuel Huntington foresaw a future "clash of civilizations." This realist idea, which was deeply rooted in history and geography, countered the prediction of Huntington's contemporary, the idealist and neo-Hegelian Francis Fukuyama, that with the triumph of democracy and free markets in the late 1980s and 1990s, the "end of history" was nigh. And with the start of the second cold war in 2022, marked by the alliance of autocracy announced between China and Russia in February 2022—against the ironic setting of the Winter Olympics, the point of which was to promote a more peaceful world—and Russia's subsequent full-scale armed invasion of Ukraine, the defense of the West as well as democracy itself have been once again at stake.

The outbreak of this new cold war has rejuvenated NATO and rekindled the special relationship between Great Britain and the United States, a relationship that can be dated back, as we have seen, to the original formulation of the Monroe Doctrine. In fact, no two nations in the world have provided more military and economic support to Ukraine in its war against Russian invaders than have the United States and the United Kingdom. And within the broader Anglosphere, support for NATO, NORAD, the "Five Eyes" (an informal intelligence alliance among the United States, Great Britain, Canada, Australia, and New Zealand, but notably not Ireland), and many other security arrangements has strengthened. Moreover, Joe Biden has promised that under his leadership America will reclaim its role as the leader of the democratic, rules-based world order. To this end, President Biden has reaffirmed US support for NATO, and with Canada's Justin Trudeau has agreed to modernize NORAD as well as begin a comprehensive dialogue on all things related to the US-Canadian Arctic. Moreover, Biden, Boris Johnson, and Scott Morrison, the prime minister of Australia, on September 15, 2021, announced a new security agreement, AUKUS. The purpose of the pact, which notably does not include New Zealand and was clumsily struck at France's expense, was designed to help contain China's growing ambitions in the Indo-Pacific region, which includes the Philippines. The special relationships among nations that makeup the global Anglosphere continue to be highly consequential in transatlantic and transpacific relations.

The Dustbin of History?

In late 2021, in response to Russia's military buildup on Ukraine's border and demand that the country forever be denied membership in NATO, President Biden's secretary of state, Antony J. Blinken, declared: "One country does not have the right to dictate the policies of another or to tell that country with whom it may associate; one country does not have the right to exert a sphere of influence. That notion should be relegated to the dustbin of history." This statement pointedly ignores the realities of geopolitics and would come as a great shock to America's continental and hemispheric neighbors Mexico and Canada, as well as Cuba and Venezuela, countries whose national histories have been—for good or ill, directly or indirectly— profoundly shaped by, and have unfolded entirely within, the sphere of influence of the United States. As Mexico's Porfirio Diaz once allegedly lamented, "Poor Mexico, so far from God, so close to the United States." This continues to be very much the case. And as for relegating the realities of social power (hard, soft, and otherwise) and claims of hegemony to the dustbin of history, Blinken's recent predecessors—President Trump's secretary of state, Rex Tillerson, in 2018, and his national security advisor, John Bolton, in 2019—have both explicitly reaffirmed the Monroe Doctrine (although, significantly, the 1823 rather than the 1992 version). Likewise, Russia and China have loudly reserved the right to interfere in their respective "near abroads." At the same time—and this point cannot be overemphasized—the United States remains committed to a world order based on democratic values, collective security, and a respect for national sovereignty, rather than to that described by Thucydides, where "the right . . . is only in question between equals in power, while the strong do what they can and the weak suffer what they must."

On the other hand, Russia's February 24, 2022, initiation of a wider war in Ukraine was a clarifying moment in the history of North America and, for that matter, the history of the world. For while Putin's war has united the West, it has also divided the world, as much of Latin America, Asia, and Africa has broken with the West. It has also divided North America. The United States and Canada, both members of NATO, have shown themselves in full support of the democracy and territory of Ukraine, while Mexico, so far at least, has adopted a more ambiguous, if not neutral, position—one seemingly at odds with Mexico's own history of repeated foreign invasions and loss of territory. But it is a position that invites comparison with the troubled history of Ireland, and Ireland's policy of neutrality in respect to

Ukraine. As a percentage of GDP, Mexico and Ireland spend on defense roughly 0.5 and 0.3 percent, respectively. These two countries enjoy, in effect, free security by virtue of the social power of others. In more than one respect, Mexico is the Ireland of North America.

The Closing of the Frontier and the Lifting of the Brandt Line

At the beginning of this book, I made the argument that, starting with the sixteenth century, the profound differences in levels of social development within North America and between North America and western Europe were key to understanding much of the history, deeply tragic and otherwise, that followed. What is the situation today? Notwithstanding the retreat from globalization and the advance of climate change—the latter a new fifth horseman of the apocalypse—the late Swedish statistician Hans Rosling declared:

> Poor developing countries no longer exist as a distinct group. That there is no gap. Today, most people, 75 percent, live in middle-income countries. Not poor, not rich, but somewhere in the middle and starting to live a reasonable life. At one end of the scale there are still countries with a majority living in extreme and unacceptable poverty; at the other is the wealthy world (of North America and Europe and a few others like Japan, South Korea, and Singapore). But the vast majority are already in the middle.

While overstating the case, Rosling points to the data when he argues that the terms "West and the rest," "developed and developing," "rich and poor," are now passé.[4] This point has obvious implications for the history of North America and the historic divide between the different levels of social development that existed above and below the waters of the Río Grande and between the two Mexicos—one rich and one poor.[5]

In 1894 in the article (and former paper) "The Significance of the Frontier in American History," Frederick Jackson Turner declared in the language of his day that the frontier line was the "outer edge of the wave—the meeting point between savagery and civilization," that is, between two different stages of social development. This wave moved steadily from east to west, with the westward expansion of the United States. Nearly a century later Willy Brandt, chancellor of the Federal Republic of Germany (West Germany), in effect globalized Turner's frontier of social development by visualizing the world as one divided into a more advanced and wealthy North and a poorer and less developed global South. The frontier line between the two, which separated Mexico from the rest of the continent of North America, was dubbed the Brandt Line. Turner's frontier, a line between two different developmental states, had closed in 1890. And by the end of the twenty-first century's second decade, the Brandt Line, as Rosling attests, which had moved, with economic liberalization and the spread of democracy, from North to South, can hardly be said to exist. Climate change, pandemics, bungling politicians, stupid policies, and the other horsemen of the apocalypse might very well derail or even reverse this progress. However, for now at least it is possible to glimpse a future North America defined more by social parity than by social disparity, as has been too long the case.

Notes

Chapter 1: On Method

1. Zoellick, *America in the World*, 12. See also Doshi, *The Long Game*.

2. Morris, *Why the West Rules*, 24.

3. See Allison, *Destined for War*, 2017.

4. I originally intended this book to be a big history of the American West or, to quote the Dutch historian Esther Quaedackers, a "little big history." Quaedackers, "A Case for Little Big Histories," 279. But try as I might, I could not make it work. There were simply too many geographical and cultural variables—and, frankly, too much arbitrariness. But I was able to resolve these difficulties, to find clarity, once I expanded my study of the region of the American West to include the entire continent of North America. This much larger region possessed an integrity and cohesiveness that the former lacked. In short, I was drawn to the whole, which was so much greater than the sum of its parts.

5. Historian Frank Roy Willis defines the West as "that civilization that developed in the continent of Europe and was carried to. . . areas in other parts of the world that were colonized by people from Europe." Frank Roy Willis, *Western Civilization* (New York: Macmillan, 1987), 1. See also Lawrence Birken, "What Is Western Civilization?" *History Teacher* 25 (1992): 451–61; and Meinig, *Atlantic America*, 64.

6. Kaplan, *Revenge of Geography*, 335; Nostrand, "Spanish Borderlands," 47–63; and Smith, "North America's Colonial European Roots," 30–37.

7. Harris, "France in North America," 65–88; Smith, "North America's Colonial European Roots," 37–40.

8. See Candiani, *Dreaming of Dry Land*. This drainage system fell into disrepair after Independence but was modernized during the Porfiriato.

9. John Wesley Powell's warning appeared in his *Report on the Lands of the Arid Region of the United States* (Washington, DC: Government Printing Office, 1878).

10. See Nash, *American West*; Carl Abbott, *The Metropolitan Frontier: Cities in the Modern American West* (Tucson: University of Arizona Press, 1993); and Pomeroy, *Pacific Slope*.

11. See Diamond, *Guns, Germs and Steel*; and Landes, *Wealth and Poverty of Nations.* For a more complicated argument, see Martinez, *Mexico's Uneven Development.*

12. Fuentes, *Buried Mirror*, 341.

13. Crosby, *Ecological Imperialism*; and Morris, *Why the West Rules.*

14. Fernlund, "American Exceptionalism or Atlantic Unity?," 359–99.

15. Snow, *Two Cultures*; and Rostow, *Stages of Economic Growth.*

16. Maddison, *World Economy*, is an essential reference.

17. See Elizabeth Stanton, "The Human Development Index: A History" (working paper, Political Economy Research Institute, University of Massachusetts at Amherst, 2007).

18. In his pioneering work "A Preliminary Index of Social Development," Raoul Naroll measured three traits: settlement size or urbanization, craft specialization, and organizational ramification or the communication of decisions from leaders to followers. The Aztecs or Mexica scored the highest on Naroll's index. They score highest on everyone's index.

19. Morris further elaborates on his methodology in Morris, *Measure of Civilization.* In fact, this book is the companion volume to his *Why the West Rules.*

20. Morris, *Why the West Rules*, 382.

21. Morris, 144. In four volumes, Michael Mann fleshes out the history of social power, using four categories of analysis: ideological, economic, military, and political. See Mann, *Sources of Social Power.*

22. Turner, "Significance of the Frontier," 207.

23. Margaret Mead, "The Role of Small South Sea Cultures in the Post War World," *American Anthropologist*, n.s., 45 (1943): 193–97.

24. Ruth Benedict, *The Chrysanthemum and the Sword: Patterns of Japanese Culture* (Boston: Houghton Mifflin, 1946), 15; A. L. Kroeber and Clyde Kluckhohn, *Culture: A Critical Review of Concepts and Definitions* (Cambridge, MA: Peabody Museum of American Archaeology and Ethnology, 1952), 145; and M. F. Ashley Montagu, *Man's Most Dangerous Myth: The Fallacy of Race* (New York: Columbia University, 1942), 47.

25. Crèvecoeur, "What Is an American?"

Chapter 2: On Asymmetry

1. Fernlund, "Great Battle of the Books," 6–30.

2. For an historical analysis of the antiquity question, see Fernlund, *William Henry Holmes*, 125–47.

3. J. D. Figgins, "The Antiquity of Man in America," *Natural History* 27 (1927): 229–39.

4. Fernlund, *William Henry Holmes*, 141–47. Unless indicated otherwise, the following account of Ice Age North America is based on David J. Meltzer's informative synthesis *First Peoples in a New World*, especially chapters 1, 2, 4, and 8.

5. See Willey and Phillips, *Method and Theory in American Archaeology.*

6. Anthony T. Boldurian and John L. Cotter, "Edgar B. Howard's Southwest Early Man Project," in Boldurian and Cotter, *Clovis Revisited*, 1–20.

7. Haynes, "Contributions of Radiocarbon Dating," 355–74.

8. Dillehay, *Settlement of the Americas*, xiii.

9. Erlandson et al., "Kelp Highway Hypothesis," 161–74.

10. William H. Holmes, "The Antiquity Phantom in American Archaeology," *Science* 62 (1925): 256–58.

11. Meltzer, *First Peoples in a New World*, 109.

12. Dillehay, *Settlement of the Americas*, 2–3.

13. Bennett et al., "Evidence of Humans in North America," 1528–31.

14. See Paul S. Martin, "Prehistoric Overkill: The Global Model," in Martin and Klein, *Quaternary Extinctions*, 354–403.

15. See Joseph. H. Greenberg, *Language in the Americas*; and Reich et al., "Reconstructing Native American Population History," 370–74.

16. Willey and Phillips, *Method and Theory in American Archaeology*, xii, 73. For a comprehensive discussion of cultural change and evolutionary development in North America, see Trigger and Washburn, *Cambridge History of the Native Peoples of the Americas*.

17. For an excellent overview of Native North America circa AD 1000, see McGhee, "Canada Y1K," 9–17. Native farming in North America has been well documented. See Nabhan, *Gathering the Desert*; Hurt, *Indian Agriculture in America*; and Miller, *From Colonization to Domestication*.

18. Willey and Phillips, *Method and Theory in American Archaeology*, 204.

19. Elliott, *Empires of the Atlantic World*, 12–13.

20. See Alfred Crosby's two seminal works, *The Columbian Exchange* and *Ecological Imperialism*.

21. Humboldt, *Political Essay*, 1:95; and Semo, *Capitalism in Mexico*, 9.

22. See McCaa, "Peopling of Mexico," 252.

23. Humboldt believed matlazáhuatl was a "mortal typhus" or "plague" that was "peculiar to the Indian race" and which "seldom appears more than once in a century." However, in the sixteenth century, he records that it was thought to have "raged in a particular manner" in 1545 and 1576. Humboldt, *Political Essay*, vol. 1, 117–18.

24. Dobyns, "Estimating Aboriginal American Population," 395–416; and Dobyns, *Their Number Become Thinned*, 35.

25. Humboldt, *Political Essay*, vol. 1, 95.

26. Fernandes et al., "Genetic History," 103–110.

27. Henige, "Contact Population of Hispaniola," 222–25.

28. See Cameron et al., *Beyond Germs*, introduction.

29. Las Casas, *Short Account*, 11, 43.

30. Coatsworth, "Structures, Endowments, and Institutions," 127–28.

31. Maddison, *World Economy*, 42, 114.

32. Crosby, "Summary on Population Size," 277–78.

33. Las Casas, *Short Account*, 43.

34. See Gibson, *Aztecs under Spanish Rule*, 381. By 1802, according to Alexander von Humboldt, there were 67,500 Whites in Mexico City.

35. Moreno-Estrada et al., "Genetics of Mexico," 1280–85.

36. Quoted in "Researchers Find Large Genetic Differences among Mexican Populations," *Stanford Daily*, July 5, 2014.

37. Moreno-Estrada et al., "Genetics of Mexico," 1280–85.

38. See Sherratt, "Plough and Pastoralism," 261–305.

39. Parry, *Discovery of the Sea*, xiv.

40. McCaa, "Peopling of Mexico," 246–47.

41. Harris, *Cannibals and Kings*, 166. See also Harner, "Ecological Basis for Aztec Sacrifice," 117–35; and Turner and Turner, *Man Corn*. For global perspectives, see Anawalt, "Understanding Aztec Human Sacrifice," 38–45; and Aldhouse-Green, *Dying for the Gods*.

42. Semo, *Capitalism in Mexico*, 6.

43. See Cohen and Armelagos, *Paleopathology at the Origins of Agriculture*. The papers here examine regions around the world, but the focus is on North America.

44. Steckel and Rose, *Backbone of History*, 587.

45. Steckel and Rose, 575, 578.

46. McCaa, "Peopling of Mexico," 246–47. See also Aufderheide, "Summary on Disease," 165–66.

47. Coatsworth, "Structures, Endowments, and Institutions," 129.

48. McCaa, "Paleodemography," 94–124.

49. Cook and Borah, *Essays in Population History*, 159.

50. Richard H. Steckel and Jerome C. Rose, "Patterns of Health in the Western Hemisphere," in Steckel and Rose, *Backbone of History*, 578.

51. Naroll, "Preliminary Index of Social Development," 687–715.

52. See Harari, *Sapiens*, 292–97.

53. Prescott, *History of the Conquest of Mexico*, 2:153.

54. McCaa, "Peopling of Mexico," 258.

55. In 1721, during a smallpox outbreak in Boston, local physician Zabdiel Boylston (1679–1766) introduced inoculation to North America with good results. His inoculation method involved directly exposing the patient to the smallpox virus; with Jenner's vaccination, the patient was also directly exposed but to cowpox, a less virulent virus related to smallpox. This method resulted in a milder infection and was thus less of a risk to the patient. Both methods conferred lifetime immunity.

56. McCaa, "Peopling of Mexico," 278.

57. Acuna-Soto et al., "When Half of the Population Died," 1–5.

58. Roberts, *History of the World*, 850.

59. Brading, *The First America*, 106.

60. Elliott, *Empires of the Atlantic World*, 52–53.

61. Maddison, *World Economy*, 113–15.

62. Semo, *Capitalism in Mexico*, 105.

63. Moreno-Estrada et al., "Genetics of Mexico," 1280–85.

64. See Elliott, *Empires of the Atlantic World*, 169–73; and Semo, *Capitalism in Mexico*, 105.

Chapter 3: The Renaissance Explores the East Coast

1. Parry, *Discovery of the Sea*, 29.

2. For "Erik the Red's Saga" and "The Saga of the Greenlanders," see Vidar Hreinsson, ed., *The Complete Sagas of the Icelanders, Including 49 Tales* (Reykjavik, Iceland: Leifur Eriksson, 1997), 1–18, 19–32.

3. "Saga of the Greenlanders," in Hreinsson, 22–23.

4. Marcus, *Conquest of the North Atlantic*, 59–78.

5. Kuitems et al., "Evidence for European Presence," 388–91.

6. The Norse could cross and recross the North Atlantic between Norway and East Greenland, along the sixty-first parallel. The naval historian G. J. Marcus calls this feat the "supreme achievement of Norse seamanship and navigation." Marcus, *Conquest of the North Atlantic*, 95–96. The establishment of the Greenland trade route was also the first transatlantic route in European history.

7. Greenland's southwest coast was once inhabited, probably by people of the Dorset culture, but it had been abandoned by the time the Vikings had arrived on the scene. Jones, *History of the Vikings*, 308.

8. "Erik the Red's Saga," in Hreinsson, *Complete Sagas*, 17; "Saga of the Greenlanders," in Hreinsson, *Complete Sagas*, 29. On the question of which name is appropriate, Inuit or Eskimo, the Alaska Native Language Center of the University of Alaska, Fairbanks, advises that the "people of Canada" prefer the name Inuit, whereas the Native people of Greenland refer to themselves as Greenlanders or Kalaallit. However, the term *Eskimo*, which means "netter of snowshoes," is still in use in Alaska. According to Jones, the Old Norse word *Skræling* was decidedly pejorative, meaning "screechers" or "uglies." Jones, *History of the Vikings*, 301.

9. Tomasson, *Iceland*, 15–16.

10. Tomasson, 57–58. See also Fagan, *Little Ice Age*; and White, *Cold Welcome*.

11. Jones, *History of the Vikings*, 306–11.

12. Parry, *Discovery of the Sea*, 44.

13. Jones, *History of the Vikings*, 306–11; Arneborg et al., "Human Diet and Subsistence Patterns," 119–33.

14. According to *The World Fact Book*, in 2021 Greenland's population stood at 57,799, and was 89.5 percent Greenlandic or Indigenous, and 7.5 percent European (largely Danes). It is the only country in North America where the Native population has remained in the majority, and the overwhelming majority at that.

15. Thomas Babington Macaulay, *The History of England*, vol. 4 (Philadelphia: E. H. Butler, 1856), 19. See Vernon Bogdanor, "The Monarchy and the Constitution," in *Parliamentary Affairs* 49 (1996): 407–22.

16. See Gleeson-White, *Double Entry*; and Wright, *Nonzero*, 149, 156, 335. According to Gleeson-White, the monk Luca Pacioli introduced double-entry bookkeeping in 1494 with the publication of the *Summa de Arthmetica, Geometrica, Proportioni et Proportionalita* ("Everything about Arithmetic, Geometry and Proportion").

17. On the history of Western exploration, I am very much in debt to the historians J. H. Parry, William H. Goetzmann, and Stephen J. Pyne, whose *Great Ages of Discovery* should serve as the new standard text in the field of exploration history.

18. Francesco Guidi-Bruscoli, "John Cabot," 392.

19. The circumference that Columbus calculated for the size of the world was 10 percent smaller than Ptolemy's, which in turn underestimated the real size of the world by 25 percent. Parry, *Discovery of the Sea*, 190.

20. See Hessler, *Naming of America*; Boorstin, *The Discoverers*, 244–54; and Fernández-Armesto, *Amerigo*, 199.

21. See Morison, *Great Explorers*, 77–78.

22. Kathleen Romoli, *Balboa of Darién: Discoverer of the Pacific*, 159–163.

23. Quoted in Morison, *European Discovery of America*, 471–73. For an illuminating sketch of this period and the transformative effect of the circumnavigation of Magellan's Armada de Molucca on it, see Manchester, *A World Lit Only by Fire*.

24. Parry, *Discovery of the Sea*, 258.

25. Quoted in Wroth, *Voyages of Giovanni da Verrazzano*, 133–43. I have relied closely on Wroth's illuminating commentary in "The Voyage of 1524: The Crossing; the Landfall; The New Land," 71–90.

26. In *Voyages of Delusion*, Glyn Williams focuses on the eighteenth-century explorations of North America. He juxtaposes these irrational endeavors with the rationalism of the Enlightenment.

27. Talese, *The Bridge*, 5.

28. Wroth, *Voyages of Giovanni da Verrazzano*, 133–43.

29. For the early Spanish and French colonization efforts, I am indebted to Weber, *Spanish Frontier in North America*; Fischer, *Champlain's Dream*; and Starr, *Continental Ambitions*.

30. Nevertheless, Newfoundland was more a fishery than a colony—until 1825, when it was finally granted official colonial status. Representative government followed in 1832, but union with Canada did not occur until 1949.

31. "Port-Royal, 1606: Humanism Inspires the Foundation of New France," chap. 11 in Starr, *Continental Ambitions*.

32. Fischer, *Champlain's Dream*, 145–46.

33. Fischer, 147.

34. Hallenbeck, *Land of the Conquistadors*, 17–21. Hallenbeck, a resident of Roswell, New Mexico, was a respected amateur historian and student of early New Mexican history who, in the Boltonian tradition, left his armchair for the field to test the claims of the past.

35. Chipman, *Nuño de Guzmán*, 141.

36. Cabeza de Vaca, *Adventures in the Unknown Interior of America*, translated and annotated by Cyclone Covey and with a new epilogue by William T. Pilkington (Albuquerque: University of New Mexico, 1983).

37. According to the Second Charter of Virginia, May 23, 1609, "We do also of our special Grace . . . grant . . . all those Lands, Countries, and Territories, situate, lying, and being in that Part of America, called Virginia . . . and all that Space and

Circuit of Land, lying from the Sea Coast of the Precinct aforesaid, up into the Land throughout from Sea to Sea, West and Northwest."

38. See Meinig, *Southwest*, 3–8.

39. See Haury, *The Hohokam*.

40. Lekson, "War in the Southwest," 607–24.

41. Hallenbeck, *Land of the Conquistadors*, 22.

42. Hammond and Rey, *Narratives of the Coronado Expedition*, 169.

43. Reed, "Transition to History," 594.

44. Hammond and Rey, *Narratives of the Coronado Expedition*, 177–78.

45. Hammond and Rey, 145.

46. Hammond and Rey, 178–79.

47. Weber, *Myth and the History of the Hispanic Southwest*, 19–32.

48. Hallenbeck, *Land of the Conquistadors*, 26; Sauer, *Road to Cíbola*, 28.

49. See Fernlund, *William Henry Holmes*, 102–24; and Pyne, *How the Grand Canyon Became Grand*, 5–8.

50. In July 2017 a metal detection survey—led by Dr. Clay Mathers—of the Coronado State Monument found artifacts that have been definitely linked to the site with Coronado's expedition. Recovered objects include copper crossbow boltheads, chain mail armor, caret-headed nails, and lead shot.

51. Bolton, *Coronado*, 281.

52. Albornoz, *Hernando De Soto*, 236.

53. Wright, "Naming of the Mississippi River," 529–30; and Hastings, *Lakes of Pontchartrain*, 21–29.

54. Unless otherwise indicated, this section is based on John Leddy Phelan's excellent study *The Hispanization of the Philippines*, 3–14.

55. Bjork, "Link That Kept the Philippines Spanish," 28.

56. Schurz, *Manila Galleon*, 216–229.

57. For a balanced treatment of this controversial figure in New Mexico's history, see Simmons, *The Last Conquistador*.

58. Peter H. Wood, "La Salle: Discovery of a Lost Explorer," *American Historical Review* 89 (1984): 294–323.

59. Francis Parkman, *La Salle*, 472–73; Melinda Marie Jetté, " 'At the Hearth of the Crossed Races': Intercultural Relations and Social Change in French Prairie, Oregon, 1812–1843," PhD diss., University of British Columbia, 2004.

Chapter 4: The Enlightenment Explores the West Coast

1. Golder, *Bering's Voyages*, 6.

2. For good general accounts of a region where east meets west, see Chevigny, *Russian America*; Gibson, *Imperial Russia in Frontier America*; Smith and Barnett, *Russian America*; and Fitzhugh and Crowell, *Crossroads of Continents*.

3. For a balanced account of this controversial figure, see Beebe and Senkewicz, *Junípero Serra*.

4. On the Spanish reconnaissance of the western coast of North America, I am again indebted to Weber, *Spanish Frontier in North America*, 249–53; and also to

Engstrand, "Seekers of the 'Northern Mystery,' " 78–110. See also Engstrand, *Spanish Scientists in the New World*.

5. Parkman, *Montcalm and Wolfe*, 5.

6. Quoted in Beaglehole, *Life and Times of Cook*, 89–90. Unless indicated otherwise, my account of Cook's voyages is based on Beaglehole's biography.

7. Sheehan and Westfall, *Transits of Venus*, 125–30, 161–83.

8. Beaglehole, *Life and Times of Cook*, 107.

9. Quoted in Beaglehole, 182.

10. Howse, *Greenwich Time*, 71–72.

11. Beaglehole, *Life and Times of Cook*, 506–7.

12. Porter, *Gibbon*, 101.

13. Drake, *The World Encompassed*, 64, 80. This book was edited by Drake's nephew and was based on the notes of Francis Fletcher, the ship chaplain. Drake died in 1596.

14. Schurz, *Manila Galleon*, 229.

15. Quoted in Beaglehole, *Voyage of the Resolution and Discovery*, 293–94.

16. Quoted in Beaglehole, 316.

17. Quoted in Beaglehole, 296–97.

18. Quoted in Beaglehole, 297.

19. In 1867 the US Coast and Geodetic Survey named the island group in honor of the Russian czar Alexander II.

20. Quoted in Beaglehole, *Voyage of the Resolution and Discovery*, 349–51.

21. In 1926 Roald Amundsen of Norway technically found a northwest passage by flying over the polar ice cap between Europe and North America in the Italian-built airship the *Norge*. Similarly, in 1958, a year after the successful launch of the Soviet satellite Sputnik, the Tennessee-born William Robertson Anderson cruised under the geographic North Pole on board a nuclear submarine, the Jules Verne namesake the USS *Nautilus*. With climate change, the old dream of an ice-free shipping lane might finally become a reality.

22. Rousseau blamed the existence of inequality on the emergence of private property. "The first Man," Rousseau thundered, "who, after enclosing a Piece of Ground, took it into his Head to say, *This is mine*, and found People simple enough to believe him, was the true Founder of civil society. How many Crimes, how many Wars, How many Murders, how many Misfortunes and Horrors, would that Man have saved the Human Species, who pulling up the Stakes or filling up the Ditches should have cried to his Fellows: Be sure not to listen to the Imposter; you are lost, if you forget that the Fruits of the Earth belong equally to us all, and the Earth itself to nobody!" Jean-Jacques Rousseau, *A Discourse Upon the Origin and the Foundation of the Inequality among Mankind* (1754; repr., London: R. and J. Dodsley, 1761), 97.

23. *The Pacific Journal of Louis-Antoine de Bougainville, 1767–1768*, trans. and ed. John Dunmore (London: Hakluyt Society, 2002), 73–74. See Jean Fornasiero and John West-Sooby, "The Acquisitive Eye? French Observations in the Pacific from Bougainville to Baudin," in *Discovery and Empire: The French in the South Seas*, ed.

John West-Sooby, 69–98 (Adelaide, South Australia: University of Adelaide Press, 2013), 69–98.

24. Beaglehole, *Voyage of the Resolution and Adventure*, 174–75.

Chapter 5: A Short History of Cultural Evolution

1. For a fuller and more extended discussion of the idea of cultural evolution, see Fernlund, "Great Battle of the Books," 6–30.

2. David Hume produced *The History of England* (1754–61); William Robertson, *The History of Scotland, 1542–1603* (1759) and *The History of America* (1777–96); and Edward Gibbon, *The History of the Fall and Decline of the Roman Empire* (1776–88).

3. Bacon, *New Organon*, 100.

4. Matthew Arnold, *Culture and Anarchy: An Essay in Political and Social Criticism* (1869), viii, Internet Archive, https://archive.org/details/dli.granth.72045/page/n3/mode/2up.

5. Deutsch, *Beginning of Infinity*, 385.

6. Deutsch, 387.

7. See Hans Rosling, Ola Rosling, and Anna Rosling Rönnlund, *Factfulness: Ten Reasons We're Wrong about the World—and Why Things Are Better than You Think*, 27–28.

8. See Rosling, Rosling, and Rosling Rönnlund, 23.

9. Swift, *Battle of the Books*, 13–50. The original title was "A Full and True Account of the Battle Fought Last Friday between the Ancient and Modern Books in Saint James's Library."

10. Duncan Forbes, introduction to Ferguson, *History of Civil Society*, xiii–xiv.

11. Porter, *Gibbon*, 15–41.

12. Hobbes, *Leviathan*, 96–97.

13. See Morris, *War!*, 18.

14. Ferguson, *History of Civil Society*, 232.

15. Bronowski's point was that just as there was a national dimension to the contemporary American and French Revolutions, as their names make clear, so too was there a specific national character to the Industrial Revolution. This crucial change in the modes of production did indeed start in England, actually in the countryside of the Midlands, and was largely driven, at least initially, by common men. Bronowski, *Ascent of Man*, 259.

16. Adam Smith proposed his own four-stage theory of socioeconomic development, his stages being hunting, pastoralism, agriculture, and commerce. The "cake of custom" was an expression coined by the Victorian Walter Bagehot, an influential journalist, editor of the *Economist*, and a keen political observer. His *Physics and Politics: Or, Thoughts on the Application of the Principles of "Natural Selection" and "Inheritance" to Political Society* was published in 1872.

17. Francis Parkman chose as his topic the fall of New France, while for William H. Prescott it was the rise of New Spain.

18. The theme of decline was ubiquitous in Romantic art and literature. See the sonnet "Ozymandias" by Percy Bysshe Shelley in *Rosalind and Helen*, 72, or Frank Dillon's 1856 painting *The Colossal Pair, Thebes* at the St. Louis Museum of Art in Missouri.

19. Sarmiento, *Facundo*, 59. See Crowley, *Domingo Faustino Sarmiento*, 61.

20. Turner, "Significance of the Frontier," 199–227.

21. Fernlund, "American Exceptionalism or Atlantic Unity?," 359–99.

22. For more on "Old Hickory in the Americas," see Langley, *America and the Americas*, 54–55. In the United States the franchise was extended to Black men in 1869 with the passage of the Fifteenth Amendment, and to all women in 1919 with the enactment of the Nineteenth Amendment. However, the Black franchise had to be resecured with the Voting Rights Act in 1965.

23. For biographies of Sarmiento and Turner, see Crowley, *Domingo Faustino Sarmiento*; and Bogue, *Frederick Jackson Turner*.

24. Rhodes, "History," 49–50.

25. Tylor, *Primitive Culture*, 1.

26. Morgan, *Ancient Society*, 19.

27. Morgan, 553; Ferguson, *History of Civil Society*, 105.

28. Arthur de Gobineau's enormously influential Essai sur l'inégalité des races humaines ("Essay on the Inequality of Human Races") was published in four volumes between 1853 and 1855.

29. Morgan, *Ancient Society*, 553.

30. See Engels, *Origin of the Family*, 9.

31. Harris, *Rise of Anthropological Theory*, 29.

32. In Mexico, the leading positivists were Gabino Barreda (1818–1881) and Justo Sierra (1848–1912).

33. Fernlund, "American Exceptionalism or Atlantic Unity?," 362–67.

34. Sarmiento had also been drawn to the idea of types. To Crowley, "Herein lies the key to the whole Sarmiento narrative, the very goal and dimension of his writing. People are not primarily characters in their own right, but rather national prototypes. These are either exemplary personages to be emulated, such as Lincoln, Franklin, and Horace Mann, or they are undesirables." Crowley, *Sarmiento*, 62.

35. In 1946 Carlton J. H. Hayes, president of the American Historical Association and former US ambassador to Spain, would challenge the ethnocentric history of his colleagues, imploring them to speak to the issues confronting Western civilization—of which the United States forms an integral part. Hayes, "American Frontier," 199–216.

36. Snow, *Two Cultures*, 23.

37. Ruskin, *Stones of Venice*, 1:15 and 3:35, 60, 95, 170.

38. The old Palace of Westminster burned down in 1834. The new palace, which stands today, was rebuilt from 1840 to 1876. The architects were Charles Barry and Augustus Pugin—the latter a noted Gothic Revivalist who stressed functionalism over style. As such, he was a target of Ruskin's criticism. Canada's Parliament buildings, which opened in 1866, were influenced by both of these Gothic Revivalists.

39. See Hewison, *Ruskin and His Contemporaries*, which was published as part of the bicentennial of Ruskin's birth in 1819.

40. Morris, *Why the West Rules*, xx.

Chapter 6: The Two Mexicos

1. Phelan, *Millennial Kingdom*, 14–16. This was not to happen all at once. The seeds of this coming change were believed to have been planted long ago amid the ruins of the Roman Empire by Benedict of Norcia (AD 480–547), the founder of Western monasticism.

2. Phelan, *Millennial Kingdom*, 17, 23; Parry, *Discovery of the Sea*, 234–60.

3. Greenleaf, "Mexican Inquisition," 315–44.

4. Cortés and the conquistadors Francisco Pizarro, Vasco Núñez de Balboa, and Hernando de Soto escaped the poverty-stricken region of Extremadura for the promise of riches in the New World.

5. According to an exhibit label in Mexico's National Museum of Anthropology, which the author has been unable to improve upon, Cortés was a "skilled soldier and cunning expert in human psychology."

6. Cortés's burn-the-ships order had historical precedent. After landing in Persia in 334 BC, Alexander the Great burned his boats to commit his troops to a conquer-or-die policy. Closer to home, in AD 711, after landing at Gibraltar, the Berber and Muslim general Tāriq ibn Ziyād, "Taric el Tuerto," gave the same order. He went on to conquer Visigothic Spain.

7. Paz, *Labyrinth of Solitude*, 93. For the Aztec perspective, see León-Portilla, *The Broken Spears*; Austin, *Myth of Quetzalcoatl*; Clendinnen, *Aztecs*; and Townsend, *Fifth Sun*.

8. Velázquez celebrated the tercio in his painting *The Surrender of Breda* (c. 1625), depicting the Dutch surrendering to the Spanish. This masterpiece hangs in the Museo Nacional del Prado, Madrid.

9. Daniel, "Tactical Factors," 188.

10. For a classic description of Aztec society, see Katz, "Evolution of Aztec Society," 14–25.

11. Daniel, "Tactical Factors," 188; Hassig, *Aztec Warfare*, 88.

12. Carrasco, *Tenochca*, 29–30.

13. Semo, *Capitalism in Mexico*, 23–24.

14. Harner, "Ecological Basis for Aztec Sacrifice," 119. Marvin Harris notes that "if an occasional finger or toe was all anyone could expect, the system would probably not have worked. But if the meat was supplied in concentrated packages to the nobility, soldiers, and their retainers, and if the supply was synchronized to compensate for deficits in the agricultural cycle, the payoff for Moctezuma and the ruling class might have been sufficient to stave off political collapse." Harris, *Cannibals and Kings*, 165–66.

15. The Templo Mayor was excavated in the 1970s. The Huey Tzompantli was not discovered until 2015, when a team of archaeologists from the National Institute of Anthropology and History (INAH) in Mexico began excavations of a

site underneath a colonial-era home near Mexico City's great cathedral. See Wade, "Feeding the Gods."

16. Watts et al., "Ritual Human Sacrifice," 228–31. The authors conclude, "Religion has long been proposed to play a functional role in society, and is commonly claimed to underpin morality. . . . Our findings suggest that religious rituals also played a darker role in the evolution of modern complex societies. In traditional Austronesian cultures there was substantial religious and political overlap, and ritualised human sacrifice may have been co-opted by elites as a divinely sanctioned means of social control. . . . Unpalatable as it might be, our results suggest that ritual killing helped humans transition from the small egalitarian groups of our ancestors, to the large stratified societies we live in today."

17. The exhibit on the Siege of Tenochtitlán at the Museo Histórico Naval in Puerto Vallarta, Jalisco, with its accompanying animation, brilliantly captures the military drama of this crucial moment in North American history.

18. Paz, *Labyrinth of Solitude*, 96.

19. Semo, *Capitalism in Mexico*, 2.

20. Semo, 25.

21. Semo, 121.

22. Martínez, "Encomenderos españoles." Martínez compares the indirect rule of the British in India with what he argues occurred in New Spain under the Spanish. See also Fisher, "Indirect Rule in the British Empire." In short, the nobles or *pipiltin* parted company with the commoners or *macehualtin* in order to become part of the upper social strata, occupied by the conquistadors, and to increase their holdings. Semo, *Capitalism in Mexico*, 35.

23. Himmerich, *Encomenderos of New Spain*, 3–17.

24. Charles Gibson believes that Cortés may have made private promises to individual Tlaxcalan leaders. By 1585, however, these expedient promises had evolved into a "general agreement involving extraordinary favors for the whole province of Tlaxcala." That this occurred, and that it was recognized by the Audiencia and accepted by the king, was a testament to the mastery of Spanish law and politics by Tlaxcalan officials. Gibson, *Tlaxcala in the Sixteenth Century*, 160–61.

25. Rodríguez O., "Emancipation of America."

26. New Spain's mint, which turned bars of silver into coins, was located in Mexico City. See Brading, *Miners and Merchants*, 6n4; Semo, *Capitalism in Mexico*, 21–22, 85–89; and Terra, *Humboldt*, 166.

27. Semo, *Capitalism in Mexico*, 79.

28. The *alcabala* duty was introduced in 1575 and was initially 2 percent on all merchandise exchanged or sold beyond the local market. It was gradually increased and by 1770 it had reached eight percent. There were no fewer than eighty *alcabala* areas in New Spain. The tax provided the viceroy with a major source of revenue. It also retarded the development of a national market. Semo, *Capitalism in Mexico*, 85.

29. Semo, 32.

30. Parry, *Discovery of the Sea*, 238.

31. Parry, "Audiencia of New Galicia," 267.

32. The first of these missions, the Mission San Diego de Alcalá, was built in 1769. The Mission San Francisco de Asís or the Mission Dolores was built in 1776, the same year that the English colonists, on the other side of the continent, declared their independence from Great Britain. The last and northernmost of these missions, the Mission San Francisco Solano, was founded in 1823, after Mexico had broken away from Spain and President Monroe proclaimed hemispheric hegemony. The missions were made of whitewashed adobe, covered in red clay tile, and graced with courtyards, patios, and gardens.

33. Semo, *Capitalism in Mexico*, 106–7.

34. Gibson, *Aztecs under Spanish Rule*, 231–32. Under the repartimiento, Native communities were compelled to provide Spanish enterprises up to 4 percent of their workers. A gang would leave its village on Monday and work at a particular enterprise from Tuesday to the following Monday, at which point they were paid and allowed to return home. As they left, another gang from another community arrived to replace them. And so on. An Indian could not be forced to work more than two or three times a year. See Semo, *Capitalism in Mexico*, 129–30.

35. On the Zócalo, in the heart of Mexico City, a prominent monument was erected to honor Martínez in 1878.

36. Hoberman, "Technological Change in a Traditional Society," 386–407.

37. The Spanish were cognizant of England's activities in North America in almost real time, by seventeenth-century standards. The Zúñiga chart, which was named after Don Pedro de Zúñiga, the Spanish ambassador to England, depicts a rough outline of Fort James. This intelligence was communicated to King Philip III of Spain in September 1608, a mere fifteen months after the establishment of the English colony.

38. Humboldt, *Political Essay*, 2:126.

39. Quoted in Terra, *Humboldt*, 164.

40. See Candiani, *Dreaming of Dry Land*, 3–4. In the nineteenth century a second drainage system was built, which included the Grand Canal, a twenty-nine-mile drainage ditch. It was considered Mexico's Brooklyn Bridge—a major feat of engineering and point of civic pride. This project, the Sistema de Desagüe del Valle de México, was started under the empire of Maximilian and was completed by the Porfiriato in 1900.

41. Karl Wittfogel, an anti-Communist Marxist, was the author of the classic study *Oriental Despotism: A Comparative Study of Total Power*. Wittfogel linked water control with social power.

42. Candiani, in *Dreaming of Dry Land*, projects Wittfogel's hydraulic thesis onto Mexico's colonial era; and Worster, in *Rivers of Empire*, modifies and applies the idea to the modern American West.

43. The Spanish were not miners and for expertise turned to German and Italian sources, namely the woodcut-illustrated *De re metallica* (1556) by Georg Bauer ("Georgius Agricola") and Vannoccio Biringuccio's *De la pirotechnia (1540)*. Semo, *Capitalism in Mexico*, 12.

44. See Richard L. Garner, *Mining Trends in the New World, 1500–1810* (2007), 56, https://www.insidemydesk.com/lapubs/miningtrends.pdf. According to Garner,

"The silver-tax accounts usually distinguished between *plata de azogue* (silver from mercury) and *plata de fuego* (silver by smelting)," 56–57.

45. In 1554 at Pachuca, Hidalgo, Bartolomé de Medina (a merchant from Seville), using mercury and salt, succeeded in extracting silver from ore in what came to be known as the "patio process." Boyer, "Mexico in the Seventeenth Century," 455–78.

46. Dobado and Marrero, "Role of the Spanish Imperial State," 864. This is an important paper. The authors argue that the Mexican economy, driven by the growth of silver mining, benefited from Spanish colonialism. They take issue with the dependency theorists (*dependistas*) who argue that Latin America's underdevelopment is a legacy of colonial-era exploitation, and with the "resource curse hypothesis" or "Dutch disease" school of thought, which blames the malformation of the Mexican economy on the emphasis on silver extraction for the benefit of the mother country. There is a contrary school of thought that holds that the rise in tax revenues on silver under the Bourbons was due more to the practices of a predatory state than to the generation of greater and more efficient mining activity as a result of sound government policies, as Dobado and Marrero suggest.

47. Brading and Cross, "Colonial Silver Mining"; Bakewell, *Silver Mining and Society*. In *Capitalism in Mexico* Semo argues that the growth of silver mining turned Mexico's feudal economy into one that "displayed significant manifestations of embryonic capitalism" (72–78). For the Native perspective, see Haskett, " 'Our Suffering with the Taxco Tribute.' "

48. While free labor existed in the silver mines of Mexico, the labor in the *obrajes*, in contrast, was coerced. Indeed, the *obraje* was more like a prison than a proto-factory. Salvucci, "Capitalism and Dependency," 414.

49. Semo, *Capitalism in Mexico*, xx.

50. De Soto in *The Mystery of Capital* argues that the failure of Latin America to secure property rights inhibited the growth of capitalism.

51. Dobado and Marrero, "Role of the Spanish Imperial State," 862–70.

52. Dobado and Marrero, 862–70.

53. Jamie E. Rodríguez O. prefers the term Spanish Monarchy instead of Spanish Empire because "first, monarchy is a form of government in the same manner that a republic is. Second, the term empire implies a degree of subordination that did not exist at the time and that the people of those monarchies, whether in Europe or America, did not accept. That sort of subordinate relationship was characteristic of the later European empires of the nineteenth century. Third, the term empire suggests a degree of centralization and control that did not exist at the time." Rodríguez O., "Emancipation of America," 131, 138.

54. The College of San Francisco de Sales, which taught grammar, rhetoric, philosophy, and theology, was established in 1734 by royal decree of the Bourbon king, Philip V of Spain. San Miguel's future namesake, Ignacio Allende, studied there. The exhibits in the Casa de Ignacio Allende museum in San Miguel del Allende proudly and richly document the city's rich heritage and history.

55. David and Wright, in "Increasing Returns," use these terms to describe the US mining economy during the late nineteenth century.

56. Gott, *Cuba*, 41–42.

Chapter 7: Mexico's Axial Age

1. On the Axial Age, several of the key works are: Jaspers, *Origin and Goal of History*; Bellah, *Religion in Human Evolution*; Donald, *Origins of the Modern Mind*; and Armstrong, *The Great Transformation*.

2. Nicolas Baumard, Alexandre Hyafil, and Pascal Boyer, "What Changed during the Axial Age: Cognitive Styles or Reward Systems?," *Communicative and Integrative Biology* 8, no. 5 (2015): e1046657.

3. Ong, *Orality and Literacy*, 14; Kaestle, "History of Literacy," 16.

4. See Fletcher, *Conversion of Europe*.

5. Since the 1700s, Greenland has remained Lutheran, and the island is today an independent diocese in the Danish Evangelical Lutheran Church.

6. From 1525 to 1810 the mendicants and the Jesuits founded 1,145 missions throughout the country, many of which were established before there was effective Spanish control. See Waldinger, "Long-Run Effects of Missionary Orders." Waldinger's findings "show higher present-day educational outcomes (literacy and school completion rates) in regions that had historical Mendicant orders, which were committed to alleviating poverty and sought to reduce social inequality in colonial Mexico by educating the native population. These outcomes are not evidenced in regions that had historical missions associated with the Jesuits, whose focus in Mexico lay on providing high-quality education to the colony's elite in urban centers, and less on missionary work in rural areas." She notes that scholars have studied the long-term effects of missionary work carried out in colonial Africa and have reached similar conclusions.

7. Cushner, *Why Have You Come Here?* Cushner looks at the big picture: the Jesuits in the Americas, including Mexico. The Jesuits were also active in Canada and Maryland.

8. In Kino's own words: "California no es isla, sino penisla." Bolton, *Padre on Horseback*, 56.

9. Ricard, *Spiritual Conquest of Mexico*, 291.

10. Pardo, *Origins of Mexican Catholicism*, 7.

11. Díaz, *History of the Conquest of New Spain*, 355. Díaz was an eyewitness to the Conquest, and his account is written from the soldier's perspective.

12. Given the "pigmentocracy" the Spanish would erect in New Spain, one cannot overstate the significance of the skin color of Our Lady of Guadalupe, especially after the Mexican Revolution.

13. Just how complete was revealed in the late 1920s by the ferocious reaction, known as the Cristero Rebellion, to the anticlericalism of the Mexican constitution of 1917.

14. Serge Gurzinski suggests that after the arrival of Christian missionaries, traditional native hallucinogenic visions induced by peyote, mushroom, or *oloiuqui* incorporated Christian figures—Christ, the Virgin Mary, angels—and were viewed by the Christian conquerors as "miraculous." See Gurzinski, *Conquest of Mexico*.

15. The historical details of the miracle at Tepeyac are in dispute. Nevertheless, Juan Diego was beatified in 1990 and canonized in 2002. Canada, it should be noted, would produce the "Lily of the Mohawks." A Native convert, Saint Kateri Tekakwitha, baptized Catherine, died in 1680 at the age of twenty-four. Her shrine at Kahnawake on the St. Lawrence River, opposite Montreal, like that of Our Lady of Guadalupe, inspires pilgrims from all over the world. She was canonized by Pope Benedict XVI on October 21, 2012.

16. For an important interpretation of this period, see Palmer, *Age of the Democratic Revolution*.

17. Weckmann, *Medieval Heritage of Mexico*, 212.

18. From the preface to Starr, *Continental Ambitions*.

19. By literacy, I refer to Carl F. Kaestle's definition: "The ability to decode and comprehend written language at a rudimentary level, that is, the ability to look at written words corresponding to ordinary oral discourse, to say them, and to understand them." Kaestle, "History of Literacy," 13, 23. The historian Henry Bamford Parkes counted only ten primary schools in the entire country. Parkes, *A History of Mexico*, 109–15.

20. These calculations of the church's immense wealth are based on Lucas Alamán (1792–1853), an intellectual and, as Parkes points out, a defender of the church. Parkes, *A History of Mexico*, 109–15; Semo, *Capitalism in Mexico*, 95–96.

21. Gerónimo de Mendieta, *Historia eclesiástica indiana* (1870; reprint, Mexico City: Salvador Chávez Hayhoe, 1945), 70, quoted in Robert T. Jiménez, *The History of Reading and the Uses of Literacy in Colonial Mexico*," technical report no. 494 (Urbana-Champaign: Center for the Study of Reading, University of Illinois, 1990), 10, https://www.ideals.illinois.edu/bitstream/handle/2142/17965/ctrstread-techrepv01990i00494_opt.pdf.

22. The press was acquired by the reforming priest of Taos, Antonio José Martínez (1793–1867).

23. Elliott, *Empires of the Atlantic World*, 369–402.

24. Parkes, *A History of Mexico*, 109–15.

25. Cipolla, *Literacy and Development in the West*, 26–32; Frago, "History of Literacy in Spain," 574.

26. Ricard, *Spiritual Conquest of Mexico*, 289.

27. Rodriguez, *Charting the Future of Translation History*, 267.

28. Morales, "The Native Encounter with Christianity," 146.

29. The practice of separating Native students from their parents and local communities dates back to the establishment of the very first Indian schools. This particular means of assimilation would continue for five centuries and occurred throughout North America.

30. Rodriguez, *Charting the Future of Translation History*, 263–264.

31. Estarellas, "College of Tlatelolco." In 1572, the first Indian to be ordained as a priest was Don Pablo Caltzontzin, son of the last king of Michoacán. Incidentally, the oldest university in the United States is Harvard College, founded in 1636; the

oldest in Canada, the Séminaire de Québec (which later evolved into the Université Laval), officially dates back to 1663. Tlateloco was eventually eclipsed by the Royal and Pontifical University of Mexico, which was established in 1551.

32. Semo, *Capitalism in Mexico*, 20.

33. In Europe, chickens provided a measure of the barest minimum of material well-being. As Henry IV (1589–1610), the king of France, once stated: "I want there to be no peasant in my realm so poor that he will not have a chicken in his pot." Over three hundred years later, the king's standard was expanded to include not only a chicken in every pot but also "a car in every garage," a slogan associated with President Herbert Hoover.

34. Semo, *Capitalism in Mexico*, 80.

35. Olko and Sullivan, "Nahuatl Language Research and Revitalization."

36. Ricard, *Spiritual Conquest of Mexico*, 292.

37. The theorists included the "Renaissance man" *Leone Battista Alberti (1404–1472)*.

38. George Kubler, "Mexican Urbanism," 169 and 171.

39. Dobado and Marrero, "Role of the Spanish Imperial State," 857. As a point of comparison, London's population was 960,000 in 1801. Wells, "Population of England's Colonies in America," 100–101.

40. It is an interesting North American fact that New York City (specifically Manhattan), Montréal, and Mexico City were built on islands, although Mexico City lost its insular character after the Spanish drained the surrounding Lake Texcoco. Edward L. Glaeser has suggested that the "success of finance and business services on the island of Manhattan hinges critically on the advantage that the island has in bringing people together and speeding the flow of knowledge." This same geographical advantage might also help explain the historical significance of Montréal and Mexico City. See Glaeser, "Urban Colossus."

41. Per capita GDP is determined by dividing GDP (the total output of goods and services produced in a year) by the total number of people in a given country or nation. So that these numbers are comparable across time and space, they are converted into constant 1990 international or Geary-Khamis dollars (a fictional unit with the same purchasing power parity as the US dollar in 1990). Before 1700, the economies of China and India had the largest gross domestic products in the world. Unless otherwise indicated, the dollars referred to in this study are Geary-Khamis dollars.

42. Maddison, *World Economy*, 42, 71, 76, 81, 84, 113–14.

43. Coatsworth, "Structures, Endowments, and Institutions," 127–28.

44. Colin A. MacLachlan and Jaime E. Rodríguez O. believe that "colonial Mexico constituted a special case in Latin American history. The Viceroyalty of New Spain was the largest, wealthiest, and most populous political entity on the continent. It developed a richer and more complex society that the rest of Iberian America. In many ways, the northern viceroyalty functioned as a metropolis of the Spanish Empire in the New World. Indeed, by the eighteenth century, New Spain with

its prosperous economy and complex social structure seemed to rival the mother country." MacLachlan and Rodríguez O., *Forging of the Cosmic Race*, xvii.

45. Maddison, *World Economy*, 81.

46. Foner, *Free Soil, Free Labor, and Free Men*. The classic studies or hypotheses on the relationship of land and people in North American history are Borah, *New Spain's Century of Depression*; and Turner, "Significance of the Frontier."

47. Since the spread of diseases seemed to go largely from the Old World to the New, rather than the other way around, William H. McNeill found himself asking, "Why did the Amerindians not have diseases of their own with which to mow down invading Spaniards?" McNeill, *Plagues and Peoples*, 21.

48. McCaa, "Peopling of Mexico," 246–47.

49. Moreno-Estrada, "Genetics of Mexico"; and Fernandes et al., "Genetic History."

50. Maddison, *World Economy*, 121–23.

51. This is admittedly a modern and very secular perspective. No doubt contemporary imperial apologists would cite the introduction of Christianity and European lifeways, technology, plants, and animals as well as the suppression of war and human sacrifice and ritual cannibalism as Spain's outstanding contributions to the New World.

52. Stephen Bergen, "Exhibition [at the *Archivo General de Indias* in Seville] Tells Story of Spanish Children Used as Vaccine 'Fridges' in 1803," *Guardian*, July 27, 2021.

53. Maddison, *World Economy*, 121–23.

54. "The first great swell of population growth in the Mexican subcontinent began almost ten thousand years ago with the domestication of gourds, squash, corn and beans. The last started less than three-quarters of a century ago—thanks to advances in public health, food production, and mass education." McCaa, "Peopling of Mexico," 241.

55. According to McCaa (294–95), the decrease in birth rates was "due, at least prior to the twentieth-century fertility transition, to changing marriage ways—not to birth control within marriage. With women marrying 'later,' although still relatively early compared to rural folk of Western Europe or colonial British America, and widows confined to a secondary marriage market, sexual activity languished for a measurable fraction of the female population. Birth rates declined accordingly, although they remained much higher than anything seen in Western Europe since the Middle Ages."

56. See Nesvig, *Ideology and Inquisition*.

57. Spain's per capita GDP in 1500 was $661 dollars. By comparison, Spain's was lower than France's at $727, dollars and that of the United Kingdom at $714 dollars.

58. Maddison, *World Economy*, 81, 84, 114.

59. Humboldt, *Political Essay*, 1:110, 184.

60. The figures for the United States and Canada are multicultural averages (European, African, and Indigenous). See Maddison, *World Economy*, 42, 46–47, 87, 113–15, 142.

61. It would take the United States much longer to overtake the UK. In 1820, the UK's population was 21,239,000, its GDP was $36.2 billion, and its per capita income was $1,706.

Chapter 8: The Two Spains

1. Maddison, *World Economy*, 114.

2. Briggs, "Le Pays des Illinois," 33.

3. See Rodríguez O., "Emancipation of America," 138–39.

4. Woodward, "Spanish Army," 586–607.

5. For analysis of the Cortes of Cádiz, I am indebted to Rodríguez O., "Hispanic Revolution," and Elliott, *Empires of the Atlantic World*, 369–402.

6. In 1924 some two-thirds of the American Indians in the United States were citizens. The Citizenship Act of 1924 extended citizenship to the remaining third. Elliott, *Empires of the Atlantic World*, 369–402.

7. In North America, Mexico led the way on universal manhood suffrage. However, Mexico was dilatory on expanding the franchise to include women, which did not occur until October 17, 1953, decades after women won the right to vote in the United States and Canada.

8. Elliott, *Empires of the Atlantic World*, 369–402.

9. Rodríguez O., "Emancipation of America," 131.

10. Alamán, "Siege of Guanajuato," 172.

11. Robert L. *Scheina, Latin America's Wars, vol. 1, The Age of Caudillo, 1791–1899* (*Washington, DC: Brassey's, 2003*), 84.

12. France has had no fewer than five republics: the First Republic (1792–1804); the Second Republic (1848–52); the Third Republic (1870–1940); the Fourth Republic (1946–58); and the Fifth Republic (1958 to the present).

13. See Reed, *Caste War of Yucatán*.

14. I am indebted to the standards in American diplomatic history: May, *Making of the Monroe Doctrine* (1975); Bemis, *John Quincy Adams* (1949); and Perkins, *Monroe Doctrine* (1927), as well as to more recent scholarship such as Sexton, *Monroe Doctrine*; and Zoellick, *America in the World*.

15. Morris, *Measure of Civilization*, 53–62.

16. Morris, 56.

17. Morris, 61.

18. Morris, 61. See also Rosling, Rosling, and Rosling Rönnlund, *Factfulness*, 27–28.

19. Morris, *Measure of Civilization*, 144.

20. Bouchette, *British Dominions in North America*, 350–51.

21. There would not be another official census in Mexico until 1895, after the creation of the Civil Registry. In the meantime, population statistics were indirectly maintained by the church, since Mexicans had to pay fees to parish priests for documents related to birth, baptism, marriage, and death. Since it is likely that the poor avoided paying at least some of these fees, it can be assumed that church records for the nineteenth century were less than reliable.

22. Today Mexico City is still larger than any other city on the continent—but not by much. Its population is 8.85 million, slightly higher than New York City's at 8.62 million. Each city has another 10 million in its environs. In the 1970s Toronto surpassed Montreal as Canada's largest city. Today its population is 2.93 million, while the Greater Toronto Area is closer to 6.5 million, as of 2016. Montréal's population is 1.78 million, while the broader metropolitan area exceeds 4 million.

23. Humboldt, *Political Essay*, 1:99.

24. Some scholars wonder if the spread of printing was not the great turning point in cultural history. Kaestle, "History of Literacy," 19. See Elizabeth L. Eisenstein, *Printing Press as an Agent of Change*.

25. Spence, *Memory Palace of Matteo Ricci*, 22.

26. Seville lost its trade monopoly to Cádiz after the Guadalquivir River silted up, making navigation upriver difficult.

27. Kaestle, "History of Literacy," 35.

28. Morris, *Measure of Civilization*, 175.

29. See Wallace and Hoebel, *Comanches*. For a revisionist account of the Comanches, see Hämäläinen, *Comanche Empire*.

30. In 1775 the US Congress voted to create an army of twenty-eight regiments, or 20,000 men. The following year it voted to expand the army to eighty-eight regiments, or 75,000 men. In actuality, the army was less than one-half to one-third of its paper strength. Millet, Maslowski, and Feis, *For the Common Defense*, 53.

31. Archer, *Army in Bourbon Mexico*, 299–301.

32. Quoted in Parker, *Military Revolution*, 10. However, Ansani, " 'French Artillery,' " concludes that at "the beginning of the sixteenth century. . . these transformations were only incompletely carried out," 378.

33. The objections in the Early Republic to standing armies, a distrust that can be traced back to England's Civil Wars (1642–51), which had produced the New Model Army that Oliver Cromwell subsequently used to impose a military dictatorship on the country, did not extend to stationary defenses.

34. A key essay is McNeill, "Age of Gunpowder Empires." For the concept of free security, see Woodward, "Age of Reinterpretation."

Chapter 9: Neo-Europes and Middle Grounds

1. Bridenbaugh and Bridenbaugh, *No Peace Beyond the Line*, 3.

2. See Harris, *Reluctant Land*. Quebec was defensible providing it was properly manned; with only eighteen men at his disposal, Governor Champlain was obliged to surrender it to a superior English force in 1629 (the Kirke expedition). The English also captured Port Royal. These settlements were returned to France's Louis XIII in 1632, under the Treaty of Saint-Germain-en-Laye.

3. McInnis, "Population of Canada," 374; and Charbonneau, Desjardins, Légaré, and Denis, "Population of the St. Lawrence Valley," 100.

4. Moogk, "Reluctant Exiles," 463–64.

5. Charbonneau, Desjardins, Légaré, and Denis, "Population of the St. Lawrence Valley," 104–6. Unlike the population records for British and Spanish North

America, which are discontinuous, incomplete, or nonexistent, the records for New France are superb because the clergy kept excellent parish registers of births, marriages, and deaths. There were also censuses in 1666, 1667, 1681, and 1765—the last taken at the beginning of the British regime. In addition, there were two censuses for Quebec City, one in 1716 and one in 1744. With so much rich documentation, the University of Montreal in 1966 initiated its Research Program in Historical Demography to conduct an exhaustive reconstruction of Quebec's Catholic population from the beginnings of French colonization, including lists of the *filles du roi*. The result was a computerized population register, the Population Register of Historical Quebec, composed of biographical files of every individual of European ancestry who lived in the Laurentian Valley during the French regime.

6. Maddison, *World Economy*, 76.

7. Moogk, "Reluctant Exiles," 464; McInnis, "Population of Canada," 373.

8. Charbonneau, Desjardins, Légaré, and Denis, "Population of the St. Lawrence Valley," 118–19.

9. Charbonneau, Desjardins, Légaré, and Denis, 118–19. The French military presence or the stationing of troops in Canada was small. However, on three separate occasions—the 1660s, the 1690s, and the 1750s—arriving troops made up half the number of the colony's immigrants.

10. In strong contrast to the British Isles, France was miserly when it came to emigration. And for those French who did emigrate, the major points of destination were the sugar islands and Guyana, not the St. Lawrence Valley, which received only about 7 to 8 percent of the total. Charbonneau, Desjardins, Légaré, and Denis, "Population of the St. Lawrence Valley," 106. In France, Canada had a reputation for being a land of mosquitoes, long winters, rattlesnakes, and "the Iroquois our enemies." For all but the most stout of heart, these inconveniences would have discouraged most immigrants. Moogk, "Reluctant Exiles," 465.

11. Altman, "Economic Growth in Canada," 694; Maddison, *World Economy*, 76. The lives and lifeways of the descendants of these hardy *ancien régime* French settlers, the habitants, were later captured in the paintings of the Dutch Canadian artist Cornelius Krieghoff (1815–1872).

12. Hudson was English, but on this expedition he sailed for the Dutch. In 1610 he would discover Hudson Bay for the English. Fischer, *Champlain's Dream*, 270–71.

13. In one of the first accounts of the Dutch settlements in North America, Adriaen van der Donck called the land "fine, acceptable, healthy, extensive, and agreeable." See Van der Donck, *Description of the New Netherlands*, 2.

14. While both were Christians, Protestants believed in salvation through faith alone; Catholics, however, believed in salvation through faith *and* deeds. In the sixteenth and seventeenth centuries, much blood was spilled over the seemingly trivial question of what divided the two: the efficacy of good works.

15. Later known as the Minerva of the North, Christina was only six when her father was killed.

16. Finland was then part of the eastern frontier of the Swedish imperial realm.

17. See Hoffecker, Waldron, and Williams, eds. *New Sweden in America*; and Thompson, *Contest for the Delaware Valley*. The "forest Finns" were used by the Swedish to turn Sweden's forests and later New Sweden's forests, by slash-and-burn methods, into farmland.

18. After the Peace of Westphalia in 1648, which ended the Eighty Years' War and the Thirty Years' War, the Spanish abandoned St. Martin, and it was subsequently divided and shared by the Dutch and the French.

19. White, *Middle Ground*, argues that Europeans and Natives found a middle ground (in the region of the Great Lakes or the *pays d'en haut*) where each side was able to accommodate the other. The expiration dates of this and other middle grounds, however, were relatively short.

20. In 1650 Peter Stuyvesant negotiated a treaty in Hartford with Edward Hopkins, the English governor of Connecticut. The two men arrived at a north-south boundary line between Dutch and English North America, which in Long Island today separates Nassau and Suffolk Counties.

21. Rensselaerswyck was a bona fide European manor, made up of lords and tenants, a feudal relic that somehow survived into the republican, capitalist, and industrial nineteenth century, before the democratic forces stirring in Jacksonian America finally swept it away in the Anti-Rent War of 1839–45. The seigneurial system in Quebec, another feudal relic, was not abolished until 1854.

22. Shorto, *Island at the Center of the World*, argues that Anglocentric scholars have failed to appreciate the significance of the liberal inheritance of the Dutch to American history. More superficially, the Dutch in North America also left a bevy of place names, such as Coney Island, Harlem, the Catskills, and the Schuylkill River. Americans also replaced the English *master*, which was associated with slavery, with the Dutch word *boss*.

23. Briggs, "Le Pays des Illinois," 30–31.

24. North America's Indian Wars continued for three centuries. They finally ended in a violent cluster of events, a coda, toward the end of the nineteenth century. These were the Battle of Loon Lake in Saskatchewan, stopping the North-West Rebellion (of Métis and First Nations peoples against the Confederation of Canada) in 1885; the surrender of the warrior and medicine man Geronimo and his band of Chiricahua Apache to US troops at Skeleton Canyon, Arizona, in 1886; and the tragic Battle of Wounded Knee on the Lakota Pine Ridge Reservation in South Dakota in 1890. The elimination of the Apache threat brought security to both sides of the US-Mexican border. In Mexico, the Indian Wars also terminated at roughly the same time. In 1898 the Yaqui Rebellion was suppressed in the state of Sonora, and in 1901 the Caste War of Yucatán came to a close after decades of conflict between the Native and majority Maya and the minority of European-descended Yucatecos.

25. The French did retain two small islands, Saint Pierre and Miquelon, which lay to the south of Newfoundland, as well as fishing rights.

26. Maddison, *World Economy*, 71, 76, 114.

27. See Kulikoff, *British Peasants to Colonial American Farmers*, 113.

28. Benjamin Franklin, "Observations Concerning the Increase of Mankind, Peopling of Countries, &c," 1751, Founders Online, https://founders.archives.gov/documents/Franklin/01-04-02-0080#BNFN-01-04-02-0080-fn-0013.

29. Taxes consumed a "few percentage points" of a colonist's income. Higher taxes, however, were tolerated during wartime. See Rabushka, "Colonial Roots of American Taxation." According to the economist Richard T. Ely, whose economic history influenced Frederick Jackson Turner, there is "reason to believe that one of the things against which our forefathers in England and the American colonies contended was not against oppressive taxation but against the payment of any taxes at all. It required a long struggle to bring about a complete and ready acknowledgment of the right of taxation." Ely, *Taxation*, 108.

30. To obtain revenue, the Spanish crown devised a system of customs and monopolies. These included the *quinto real* (the royal fifth on silver), which in 1548 was lowered to a tithe and to 5 percent on gold; the *alcabala*, an indirect tax on all sales; the *estancio del mercurio* (quicksilver monopoly); tribute; and the sale of positions and offices at public auctions, as well as forced loans on merchants, landowners, and bureaucrats. It took Mexican independence to break Spain's fiscal control over the colony.

31. Rabushka, "Colonial Roots of American Taxation."

32. This was not true of all Natives everywhere. Native involvement in the French fur trade was significant.

33. Maddison, *World Economy*, 71, 76, 114.

34. Semo, *Capitalism in Mexico*, 48.

35. Trudel, *Canada's Forgotten Slaves*, catalogs the existence of about 4,200 slaves—a relatively small number in comparison to the American South, the Caribbean, or Brazil—two-thirds of whom were Native and one-third Black. Slavery was abolished throughout the British Empire, including Canada, in 1833 and in what had been formerly French Louisiana in 1865, with the end of the American Civil War.

36. To what extent the Industrial Revolution was financed by the production of cotton by American slaves has become a matter of intense scholarly debate. See Olmstead and Rhode, *Creating Abundance*. Prominent revisionist works from the "new history of capitalism" are Beckert, *Empire of Cotton*; Baptist, *The Half Has Never Been Told*; and Johnson, *River of Dark Dreams*.

37. See Ettinger, *James Edward*; and Phinizy Spalding, *Oglethorpe in Perspective*.

38. For good and ill and long into the future, abolition, temperance, and anti-Catholicism would all drive American politics.

39. Patrick Tailfer and William Stephens soon led a movement to overturn Georgia's ban on slavery.

40. See Wilson, *The Oglethorpe Plan*.

41. See Kohn, "South to Freedom."

42. Kaufmann and Pape, "Explaining Costly International Moral Action," 631.

43. "IV. Jefferson's Observations on DéMeunier's Manuscript, 22 June 1786," Founders Online, https://founders.archives.gov/documents/Jefferson/01-10-02-0001-0005.

44. The scholarship on North American slavery is indeed vast and includes David Brion Davis's magisterial *Problem of Slavery* trilogy. Perhaps the seminal work remains Edmund Morgan's masterfully written and ironic *American Slavery, American Freedom: The Ordeal of Colonial Virginia*, in which he explains the nexus or seeming paradox of White freedom and Black slavery.

45. See Merkel, "Jefferson's Failed Anti-Slavery Proviso."

Chapter 10: Transatlantic Wars and Transcontinental Treks

1. Semo, *Capitalism in Mexico*, 157. Unless otherwise indicated, the diplomatic history that follows is based on Robert B. Zoellick's fresh synthesis in *America in the World*, 1–68.

2. In *The Dead March*, Peter Guardino argues that the outcome of the war was decided by the superior resources that the United States could command.

3. As a counterpoint to this Atlantic focus, see Mapp, *Elusive West*.

4. US Bureau of the Census, *Historical Statistics of the United States: Colonial Times to 1970*, bicentennial ed., pt. 2 (Government Printing Office: Washington, DC, 1975), 1168.

5. See Anderson, *Battle for the Fourteenth Colony*.

6. McInnis, "Population of Canada," 371–78.

7. McInnis, 371–78.

8. George Washington to Marie-Joseph-Paul-Yves-Roch-Gilbert du Motier, Marquis de Lafayette, November 15, 1781, Founders Online, https://founders.archives.gov/documents/Washington/99-01-02-07408.

9. Americans would not act to export their democratic ideals until 1898, when they fought to liberate Cuba, Puerto Rico, and the Philippines from the recent and reputed outrages of Spanish rule. By then, like the French a century before, Americans had abandoned the tradition of caution well expressed by John Quincy Adams, the secretary of state, who on July 4, 1821, declared of America: "She goes not abroad, in search of monsters to destroy." See Risen, *Crowded Hour*.

10. See Toll, *Six Frigates*, 19.

11. "The Jay Treaty 1794 and Associated Documents," Avalon Project: Documents in Law, History, and Diplomacy, https://avalon.law.yale.edu/18th_century/jay.asp.

12. For a good recent, if traditional, account, of the settlement of the Old Northwest, see McCullough, *The Pioneers*.

13. Oster, " 'To Extirpate the Indians,' " 587–622.

14. Knight, "Haitian Revolution," 107–8.

15. The colony's Europeans and the *affranchis* or Mulattos made up a small minority of the population.

16. After securing a large indemnity, France recognized Haiti's independence in 1825.

17. For the changing views on Dessalines's historical reputation, see Girard, "Jean-Jacques Dessalines," 549–82.

18. Quoted in Gayarré, *History of Louisiana*, 525.

19. For the essential study of the Louisiana Purchase and its aftermath, see Kastor, *The Nation's Crucible*.

20. Quoted in Lamb, *Sir Alexander Mackenzie*, 16.

21. Lamb, 4–10.

22. Lamb, 163.

23. The Slavey were Athabaskan-speaking, like the Navajo and Apache, and called themselves the Dene Tha'. They were attacked and enslaved by the much more powerful Algonquian-speaking Cree, hence the name Slavey, which is what the Europeans called these people. The Cree, in turn, became powerful by becoming rich in guns as a result of the horse-and-gun revolution introduced by French and English fur traders, which between 1730 and 1779 transformed the northwestern plains in terms of interethnic relations and the distribution of resources. See Binnema, *Common and Contested Ground*.

24. Lamb, *Sir Alexander Mackenzie*, 16.

25. Peter Pond (1739/40–1807) was a partner in the North West Company. In 1789 he knew the Canadian West as well as anyone. Lamb, 7–14, 17.

26. The site, located near Elcho Harbour on the Dean Channel, is now the Sir Alexander Mackenzie Provincial Park in British Columbia. Lamb, 343, 378.

27. Among the book's many buyers were France's emperor Napoleon Bonaparte and the US president Thomas Jefferson. Lamb, 34–36.

28. Gough, *Northwest Coast*, 95.

29. See Van Dyke, *Merchants of Canton and Macao*.

30. Quoted in Toll, *Six Frigates*, 19.

31. Ledyard, *Captain Cook's Last Voyage*, 146.

32. There are many proposals for where the American West begins. In his *Travels with Charley in Search of America*, published in 1962, the celebrated writer John Steinbeck, in the company of his French poodle, Charley, marked the beginning of the American West at Mandan, North Dakota, a small town off what is today Interstate 94. Mandan lies on the western side of the Missouri River, across from the state capital of Bismarck.

33. Meriwether Lewis, William Clark, et al., journal entry, April 7, 1805, *The Journals of the Lewis and Clark Expedition*, ed. Gary Moulton (Lincoln: University of Nebraska Press, 2005), https://lewisandclarkjournals.unl.edu/item/lc.jrn.1805-04-07#lc.jrn.1805-04-07.01.

34. In 1788 the English captain and maritime fur trader John Meares gave Cape Disappointment its discouraging name after he failed to find the mouth of the Columbia River, which was blocked by a river bar. The Spanish later seized Mears and his partners' ships, precipitating the Nootka Sound crisis.

35. As a student at Göttingen University, Humboldt had befriended the naturalist Georg Forster, the author of *A Voyage towards the South Pole and Round the World* (1777). Forster and his father had accompanied Captain James Cook on Cook's second voyage (1772–75) to the Pacific.

36. Pyne, *Dutton's Point*, 11.

37. Benjamin Franklin founded the American Philosophical Society in 1743. The former Yankee printer believed the colonies had reached the stage in their development where they could now "improve upon the common stock of knowledge."

38. Quoted in Gasper, "Young Man from 'Ultima Thule,' " 250.

39. Humboldt admired George Washington as well and visited Mount Vernon.

40. See Aaron Sachs, *The Humboldt Current: Nineteenth-Century Exploration and the Roots of American Environmentalism*; Laura Dassow Walls, *The Passage to Cosmos: Alexander von Humboldt and the Shaping of America*. There has been a renaissance of interest in Humboldt among American intellectuals. The author is grateful to Dr. Sachs for his comments on the paper, "The Changing Cosmos: From Alexander von Humboldt to Edwin P. Hubble," which the author delivered in 2010 at Lake Tahoe during the annual meeting of the Western History Association.

41. Humboldt, *Cosmos*.

42. The Casiquiare, a natural canal, connected the Upper Orinoco with the Río Negro, a tributary of the Amazon. Thus, two of South America's great rivers were connected. The economic potential of this fact seemed enormous.

43. Famous for its silver mines during the colonial era, modern Mexico remains rich not only in silver but in other minerals as well, such as gold, lead, copper, iron, zinc, molybdenum, manganese, fluorite, titanium, coal, salt, and sulfur.

44. Ulrike Moheit, ed., *Alexander von Humboldt: Briefe aus Amerika, 1799–1804* (Berlin: Akademie Verlag, 1993), 307–308.

45. Quoted in Gasper, "Young Man from 'Ultima Thule,' " 257.

46. Quoted in Terra, *Humboldt*, 186.

47. Thomas Jefferson to Alexander von Humboldt, December 6, 1813, Founders Online, https://founders.archives.gov/documents/Jefferson/03-07-02-0011.

48. The first director of the USGS was Clarence King, who soon stepped down to enter private practice as a mining consultant. King was succeeded in 1881 by the no less capable John Wesley Powell. The Geological Survey of Canada (GSC) was founded in 1842; its first director was William Edmond Logan. Despite the fact that the mining of silver in Mexico dates back to the sixteenth century, the Servicio Geológico Mexicano (SGM), headquartered in Pachuca, Hidalgo, was not established until 1944 (the SGM evolved out of the "Directing Committee for Mexican Mineral Resource Research"). With the work of the USGS, the GSC, and the SGM, North America's vast mineral and water resources have been the subject of an ongoing comprehensive, systematic, and scientific study.

49. Russell, *North America*, 72.

Chapter 11: The Thucydides Trap—and the Great Escape

1. Maddison, *World Economy*, 71, 76, 81, 84, 87. That Maddison combines the GDP of Europeans and Africans, whose plight was strikingly different from that of their European overseers, points out a major weakness of his otherwise useful approach.

2. Maddison, 59, 71, 76, 81, 84, 87.

3. Maddison, 58, 59 66. Lynch, *Spain under the Hapsburgs*, makes the case that Mexico became more economically independent during the seventeenth century.

See also Salvucci, *Textiles and Capitalism in Mexico*; and Richard J. Salvucci, "An Obscure Century in a Backward Country: Woodrow Borah and New Spain's Century of Depression," Projects 2001: Significant Works in Economic History, EH.net, https://eh.net/book_reviews/new-spains-century-of-depression/.

4. Thomas Jefferson regarded John Locke, along with Isaac Newton and Francis Bacon, as one of the three greatest men the world had ever produced, his "trinity." Conklin, *Pursuit of Happiness*, argues that Jefferson's phrase had a "distinct meaning" that "included a belief in first principles by which the created world is governed, the idea that these first principles were discoverable by man, and the belief that to pursue a life lived in accordance with those principles was to pursue a life of virtue, with the end result of happiness, best defined in the Greek sense of *eudaimonia*, or human flourishing" (101). It was a call for a life of rigor, discipline, and reason—of jurisprudence.

5. Buckner, "Presidential Address."

6. According to Charbonneau, Desjardins, Légaré, and Denis, "Population of the St. Lawrence Valley," the "1,500 men and 1,100 women who immigrated before 1680 can be said to be responsible for two-thirds of the genetic makeup of today's Québecers," making this group a true founding population (119–31).

7. Fischer, *Champlain's Dream*, 324.

8. Fischer, 126.

9. McInnis, "Population of Canada," 371–84.

10. Maddison, *World Economy*, 76.

11. And given this rate, Franklin advised the mother country to take heed of how they treated their colonial children because in a century's time "the greatest Number of Englishmen will be on this Side the Water." Benjamin Franklin, "Observations Concerning the Increase of Mankind, Peopling of Countries, &c," 1751, Founders Online, https://founders.archives.gov/documents/Franklin/01-04-02-0080.

12. Critics accused Malthus of overemphasizing natural increase and downplaying immigration as relative factors in the growth of the American colonial population. This is known as the "superfecundity" thesis. However, modern scholarship largely supports the contention of Franklin and Malthus, at least for the eighteenth century. See Gemery, "White Population," 144. It is interesting to note that in the genealogy of ideas the social development of British North America served, in part, as an inspiration for the biological theory of evolution.

13. McInnis, "Population of Canada," 379.

14. Walsh, "African American Colonial Population," 198.

15. Quoted in Gemery, "White Population," 151–52.

16. Quoted in Gemery, 174–75.

17. Quoted in Gemery, 177–79.

18. Gemery, 307.

19. Gemery, table 5.6, 163.

20. The documentary record for African Americans in colonial America is as poor as it rich for French Catholics in colonial Canada. However, despite scholarly arguments about slave agency, resistance, etc., the skeletal evidence that has been

unearthed to date is incontrovertible: beginning in adolescence, male and female slaves were overworked and physically stressed—and no doubt mentally taxed as well. There may have been some agency and resistance, but in any event their lot was still extremely hard and cruel. Walsh, "African American Colonial Population," 218–19.

21. See Carney, "African Rice," 377–96.

22. Gemery, "White Population," 163–65; Smith, "Mortality and Family," 403–27.

23. McCusker and Menard, *Economy of British America*, 231.

24. Walsh, "African American Colonial Population," 195.

25. Morris, *War!*, 196, 202.

26. Walsh, "African American Colonial Population," 192–93.

27. Mariscal and Sokoloff, "Schooling," 160–61.

28. Quoted in Monroe, *American Public School System*, 53.

29. Monroe, 16.

30. Mariscal and Sokoloff, "Schooling," 168, 173; Grubb, "Growth of Literacy," 451–82.

31. Mariscal and Sokoloff, "Schooling," 175.

32. Greer, "Pattern of Literacy in Québec," 315.

33. Greer, 331.

34. Mariscal and Sokoloff, "Schooling," table 1, 173.

35. Perhaps Mexico's most impressive hospital was the Hospicio Cabañas in Guadalajara. It was founded in 1791, late in the colonial era, and was designed by the Spaniard Manual Tolsá, a neoclassical architect and sculptor.

36. The Barbary Wars, America's first conflict with the Arab world, were essentially a commercial struggle, not a religious or cultural one.

37. For a sympathetic treatment of Jefferson's foreign policy, see Tucker and Hendrickson, *Empire of Liberty*.

38. The passage in its entirety was: "I see, as you do, the difficulties & defects we have to encounter in war, and should expect disasters, if we had an enemy on land capable of inflicting them. but the weakness of our enemy there will make our first errors innocent, & the seeds of genius which nature sows with even hand through every age & country, & which need only soil & season to germinate, will develope themselves among our military men. some of them will become prominent, and, seconded by the native energy of our citizens, will soon, I hope, to our force, add the benefits of skill. the acquisition of Canada this year, as far as the neighborhood of Québec, will be a mere matter of marching; & will give us experience for the attack of Halifax the next, & the final expulsion of England from the American continent." Thomas Jefferson to American journalist William Duane, August 4, 1812, Founders Online, https://founders.archives.gov/documents/Jefferson/03-05-02-0231.

39. For a series of nicely crafted vignettes, see Langguth, *Union 1812*, 237–56. For the Canadian perspective, see also Stanley, *War of 1812*. Incidentally, Stanley helped design Canada's maple-leaf flag, which was adopted in 1965, replacing the Red Ensign of 1868–1965.

40. US Bureau of the Census, *Report on Indians Taxed and Indians Not Taxed in the United States, (except Alaska) at the Eleventh U.S. Census: 1890* (Washington, DC: Government Printing Office, 1894), 673–78.

41. Hickey, *War of 1812*, 286–301. Hickey argues that the Americans won the war at the bargaining table in Ghent rather than on a battlefield in North America. It was a triumph of diplomacy.

42. Three key pieces of North American legislation were Mexico's Ley Lerdo (1856), Canada's Indian Act (1876), and the United States' Dawes Act (1887). In the nineteenth century, it was widely believed in North America and Europe that the twin bases of bourgeois civilization were private property and the sanctity of contract. With this in mind, these three classically liberal and reformist laws all sought to do the essentially the same things, if in different ways: namely, to break up the lands held in common by Indians and to turn them eventually into individual, title-holding, God-fearing Christian landowners. In the words of Canada's John A. Macdonald: "The great aim of our legislation has been to do away with the tribal system and assimilate the Indian people in all respects with the other inhabitants of the Dominion as speedily as they are fit to change" (1887). Throughout much of world history, needless to say, pluralism was a value little appreciated by nations and empires.

43. Quoted in Anderson and Cayton, *Dominion of War, 240–41*.

44. Maddison, *World Economy*, 121, 132, 142.

Chapter 12: The Clenched Fist and the Invisible Hand

1. I am indebted to Conrad Black for this important insight. See Black, *Rise to Greatness*, 332–33.

2. Batalla, *México Profundo*, xv–xvi.

3. Mexico joined the OECD in 1994, having narrowly met the three criteria for membership: 1)first, it was a democracy with a defensible record on human rights; 2)second, it had made the transition from a protected to an open economy (it was a member of NAFTA); and 3)third, Mexico had a GDP at least as high as the poorest member, i.e., Turkey.

4. See Rosling, *Factfulness*, 27–28.

5. As previously noted, nearly half (44 percent) of Mexico's population lives below the poverty line.

Bibliography

Note on Sources

The literature on the history of North America from the reign of Montezuma to the presidency of Monroe is a veritable ocean of immensity. However, this book in no way tries to provide an encyclopedic coverage of the subject. Rather, it offers the reader a single narrative—one based largely on the twin ideas of social development and social power—that encompasses the stories of three emerging nations. The following list of books and articles is, therefore, hardly exhaustive.

Acemoglu, Daron, and James A. Robinson. *The Narrow Corridor: States, Societies, and the Fate of Liberty.* New York: Penguin, 2019.

Acemoglu, Daron, Simon Johnson, and James Robinson. "Reversal of Fortune: Geography and Institutions in the Making of the Modern World Income Distribution." *Quarterly Journal of Economics* 118 (2002): 1231–94.

Acuna-Soto, Rodolfo, David W. Stahle, Matthew D. Therrell, Richard D. Griffin, and Malcolm K. Cleaveland. "When Half of the Population Died: The Epidemic of Hemorrhagic Fevers of 1576 in Mexico." *FEMS Microbiology Letters* 240, no. 1 (2004): 1–5.

Adams, Richard E. W., and Murdo J. McLeod, eds. *Mesoamerica.* Vol. 2 of *The Cambridge History of the Native Peoples of the Americas.* Cambridge, UK: Cambridge University Press, 2000.

Aiton, Arthur S. *Antonio de Mendoza: First Viceroy of New Spain.* Durham, NC: Duke University Press, 1927.

Alamán, Lucas. "The Siege of Guanajuato." In *The Mexico Reader: History, Culture, Politics,* edited by Gilbert M. Joseph and Timothy J. Henderson, 171–88. Durham, NC: Duke University Press, 2002.

Albornoz, Miguel. *Hernando De Soto: Knight of the Americas.* Translated by Bruce Boeglin. New York: Franklin Watts, 1986.

Alchon, Suzanne Austin. *A Pest in the Land: New World Epidemics in a Global Perspective.* Albuquerque: University of New Mexico Press, 2003.

Aldhouse-Green, Miranda. *Dying for the Gods: Human Sacrifice in Iron Age and Roman Europe.* Stroud, UK: Tempus, 2001.

Aldrich, Robert. *Greater France: A History of French Overseas Expansion*. New York: St. Martin's Press, 1996.

Allen, Robert, Tommy Bengtsson, and Martin Dribe, eds. *Living Standards in the Past: New Perspectives on Well-Being in Asia and Europe*. Oxford, UK: Oxford University Press, 2005.

Allison, Graham T. *Destined for War: Can America Escape the Thucydides Trap?* Boston: Houghton Mifflin Harcourt, 2017.

Altman, Ida, and James Horn, eds. *"To Make America": European Emigration in the Early Modern Period*. Berkeley: University of California Press, 1991.

Altman, Morris. "Economic Growth in Canada, 1695–1739: Estimates and Analysis." *William and Mary Quarterly* 45 (1988): 684–711.

Ambrose, Stephen. *Undaunted Courage: Meriwether Lewis, Thomas Jefferson, and the Opening of the American West*. New York: Simon and Schuster, 1996.

Anawalt, Patricia R. "Understanding Aztec Human Sacrifice." *Archaeology* 35 (1982): 38–45.

Anderson, Fred. *Crucible of War: The Seven Years' War and the Fate of Empire in British North America, 1754–1766*. New York: Alfred A. Knopf, 2001.

———. *A People's Army: Massachusetts Soldier's and Society in the Seven Years' War*. Chapel Hill: University of North Carolina Press, 1984.

Anderson, Fred, and Andrew Cayton. *The Dominion of War: Empire and Liberty in North America, 1500–2000*. New York: Penguin, 2005.

Anderson, Mark R. *The Battle for the Fourteenth Colony: America's War of Liberation in Canada, 1774–1776*. Lebanon, NH: University Press of New England, 2013.

Andrews, Kenneth R. *Trade, Plunder, and Settlement: Maritime Enterprise and the Genesis of the British Empire, 1480–1630*. New York: Cambridge University Press, 1984.

Andrews, Kenneth R., Nicholas P. Canny, and Paul Edward Hedley Hair, eds. *The Westward Enterprise: English Activities in Ireland, the Atlantic, and America, 1480–1650*. Detroit: Wayne State University Press, 1979.

Anna, Timothy E. *Forging Mexico, 1821–1835*. Lincoln: University of Nebraska Press, 1998.

———. *The Mexican Empire of Iturbide*. Lincoln: University of Nebraska Press, 1999.

Ansani, Fabrizio. " 'The French Artillery Is Very Good and Very Effective': Hypotheses on the Diffusion of a New Military Technology in Renaissance Italy." *Journal of Military History* 83 (2019): 347–78.

Archer, Christian I. *The Army in Bourbon Mexico, 1760–1810*. Albuquerque: University of New Mexico Press, 1977.

Archer, Richard. "New England Mosaic: A Demographic Analysis for the Seventeenth Century." *William and Mary Quarterly* 47, no. 4 (1990): 477–502.

Armstrong, Karen. *The Great Transformation: The Beginning of Our Religious Traditions*. New York: Alfred A. Knopf, 2006.

Arneborg, Jette, Niels Lynnerup, and Jan Heinemeier. "Human Diet and Subsistence Patterns in Norse Greenland, AD c. 980–AD c. 1450: Archaeological Interpretations." *Journal of the North Atlantic* 3 (2012): 119–33.

Aufderheide, Arthur C. "Summary on Disease before and after Contact." In *Disease and Demography in the Americas*, edited by John W. Verano and Douglas H. Ubelaker, 165–66. Washington, DC: Smithsonian Institution Press, 1992.

Austin, Alfredo López. *The Myth of Quetzalcoatl: Religion, Rulership, and History in the Nahua World*. Translated by Russ Davidson. 1973. Reprint, Boulder: University Press of Colorado, 2015.

Axtell, James. *After Columbus: Essays in the Ethnohistory of Colonial North America*. New York: Oxford University Press, 1988.

———. *Before 1492: Encounters in Colonial North America*. New York: Cambridge University Press, 1992.

———. *The Invasion Within: The Contest of Cultures in Colonial North America*. New York: Oxford University Press, 1985.

Bacon, Francis. *The New Organon*. Edited by Lisa Jardine and Michael Silverthorne. 1620. Reprint, Cambridge, UK: Cambridge University Press, 2000.

Bailyn, Bernard. *Atlantic History: Concept and Contours*. Cambridge, MA: Harvard University Press, 2005.

———. *The Ideological Origins of the American Revolution*. Cambridge: Harvard University Press, 1967.

———. *Voyagers to the West: A Passage in the Peopling of America on the Eve of the Revolution*. New York: Knopf, 1986.

Baker, Keith, ed. *The Old Regime and the French Revolution*. Chicago: University of Chicago Press, 1987.

Bakewell, Peter J. *Silver Mining and Society in Colonial Mexico: Zacatecas, 1546–1700*. Cambridge, UK: Cambridge University Press, 1971.

Balmer, Randall H. *A Perfect Babel of Confusion: Dutch Religion and English Culture in the Middle Colonies*. New York: Oxford University Press, 1989.

Bannon, John Francis. *The Spanish Borderlands Frontier, 1513–1821*. New York: Holt, Rinehart and Winston, 1970.

Baptist, Edward E. *The Half Has Never Been Told: Slavery and the Making of American Capitalism*. New York: Basic Books, 2014.

Barker, Graeme. *The Agricultural Revolution in Prehistory: Why Did Foragers Become Farmers?* Oxford, UK: Oxford University Press, 2006.

Barratt, Glynn. *Russia in Pacific Waters, 1715–1825*. Vancouver: University of British Columbia Press, 1981.

Baseler, Marilyn C. *"Asylum for Mankind": America, 1607–1800*. Ithaca, NY: Cornell University Press, 1998.

Baskerville, Peter. *Ontario: Image, Identity, and Power*. Don Mills, ON: Oxford University Press, 2002.

Batalla, Guillermo Bonfil. *México Profundo: Reclaiming a Civilization*. Translated by Philip A. Dennis. 1987. Reprint, Austin: University of Texas Press, 1996.

Baumard, Nicolas, Alexandre Hyafil, and Pascal Boyer. "What Changed during the Axial Age: Cognitive Styles or Reward Systems?" *Communicative and Integrative Biology* 8, no. 5 (2015): e1046657.

Beaglehole, J. C., ed. *The Voyage of the Resolution and Adventure, 1772–1775.* Vol. 2 of *The Journals of Captain James Cook on His Voyages of Discovery.* Cambridge, UK: Cambridge University Press, 1969.

———, ed. *The Voyage of the Resolution and Discovery, 1776–1780.* Vol. 3, pt. 1, of *The Journals of Captain James Cook on His Voyages of Discovery.* Cambridge, UK: Cambridge University Press, 1967.

———. *The Life and Times of Captain James Cook.* Stanford, CA: Stanford University Press, 1974.

Becker, Carl. *The Declaration of Independence: A Study in the History of Political Ideas.* New York: Harcourt Brace, 1922.

Beckert, Sven. *Empire of Cotton: A Global History.* New York: Vintage, 2014.

Beddard, Robert, ed. *The Revolutions of 1688.* Oxford: Clarendon Press, 1991.

Beebe, Rose Marie, and Robert M. Senkewicz. *Junípero Serra: California, Indians, and the Transformation of a Missionary.* Norman: University of Oklahoma Press, 2015.

Belich, James. *Replenishing the Earth: The Settler Revolution and the Rise of the Anglo-World, 1783–1939.* Oxford: Oxford University Press, 2009.

Bell, David A. *The First Total War: Napoleon's Europe and the Birth of Warfare as We Know It.* Boston: Houghton Mifflin, 2007.

Bellah, Robert N. *Religion in Human Evolution: From the Paleolithic to the Axial Age.* Cambridge: Harvard University Press, 2011.

Bellwood, Peter. *First Farmers: The Origins of Agricultural Societies.* Oxford: Blackwell, 2005.

Bemis, Samuel Flagg. *John Quincy Adams and the Foundations of American Foreign Policy.* New York: Knopf, 1949.

Bender, Thomas. *A Nation among Nations: America's Place in World History.* New York: Hill and Wang, 2006.

Benedictow, Ole. *The Black Death, 1346–1353: The Complete History.* Rochester, NY: Boydell, 2004.

Benjamin, Craig, Esther Quaedackers, and David Baker, eds. *The Routledge Companion to Big History.* Abingdon, UK: Routledge, 2020.

Bennett, Matthew R., David Bustos, Jeffrey S. Pigati, Kathleen B. Springer, Thomas M. Urban, Vance T. Holliday, Sally C. Reynolds, et al. "Evidence of Humans in North America during the Last Glacial Maximum." *Science* 373 (2021): 1528–31.

Berger, Henry. *St. Louis and Empire: 250 Years of Imperial Quest and Urban Crisis.* Carbondale: Southern Illinois University Press, 2015.

Berlin, Ira. *Many Thousands Gone: The First Two Centuries of Slavery in North America.* Cambridge, MA: Harvard University Press, 1998.

Berton, Pierre. *Flames across the Border: The Canadian-American Tragedy, 1813–1814.* Boston: Little, Brown. 1981.

———. *The Invasion of Canada, 1812–1813.* Boston: Little, Brown. 1980.

Biggar, Nigel. *In Defence of War.* Oxford: Oxford University Press, 2013.

Billington, Ray Allen. *Frederick Jackson Turner: Historian, Scholar, Teacher.* New York: Oxford University Press, 1973.

Binnema, Theodore. *Common and Contested Ground: A Human and Environmental History of the Northwestern Plains.* Norman: University of Oklahoma Press, 2001.

Bitterli, Urs. *Cultures in Conflict: Encounters between European and Non-European Cultures, 1492–1800.* Translated by Ritchie Robertson. Stanford, CA: Stanford University Press, 1989.

Bjork, Katherine. "The Link That Kept the Philippines Spanish: Mexican Merchant Interests and the Manila Trade, 1751–1815." *Journal of World History* 9 (1998): 25–50.

Black, Conrad. *Rise to Greatness: The History of Canada from the Vikings to the Present.* Toronto: McClelland and Stewart, 2014.

Black, Jeremy. *Britain as a Military Power, 1688–1815.* London: University College London Press, 1999.

———. *Warfare in the Eighteenth Century.* London, Cassell, 2006.

Black, Jeremy, and Philip Woodfine, eds., *The British Navy and the Use of Naval Power in the Eighteenth Century.* Leicester, UK: Leicester University Press, 1988.

Blackburn, Robin. *The Making of New World Slavery: From the Baroque to the Modern, 1492–1800.* New York: Verso, 1997.

Blanning, Timothy. *The French Revolutionary Wars, 1787–1802.* London: Hodder and Stoughton, 1996.

Bliss, Michael. *Northern Enterprise: Five Centuries of Canadian Business.* Toronto: McClelland and Stewart, 1987.

Bliss, Robert M. *Revolution and Empire: English Politics and the American Colonies in the Seventeenth Century.* New York: Manchester University Press, 1990.

Bogue, Allan G. *Frederick Jackson Turner: Strange Roads Going Down.* Norman: University of Oklahoma Press, 1998.

Bolton, Herbert E. *Coronado: Knight of Pueblos and Plains.* 1949. Reprint, Albuquerque: University of New Mexico Press, 1990.

———. "The Epic of Greater America." *American Historical Review* 38 (1933): 448–474.

———. "The Mission as a Frontier Institution in the Spanish-American Colonies." *American Historical Review* 23 (1917): 42–61.

———. *The Padre on Horseback: A Sketch of Eusebio Francisco Kino, S.J., Apostle to the Pimas.* 1932. Reprint, Chicago: Loyola University Press, 1986.

Bonney, Richard, ed. *The Rise of the Fiscal State in Europe, c. 1200–1815.* Oxford, UK: Oxford University Press, 1999.

Boorstin, Daniel J. *The Discoverers: A History of Man's Search to Know His World and Himself.* New York: Vintage, 1985.

Borah, Woodrow Wilson. *New Spain's Century of Depression.* Berkeley: University of California Press, 1951.

Borneman, Walter R. *The French and Indian War: Deciding the Fate of North America.* New York: HarperCollins, 2006.

Bothwell, Robert. *The Penguin History of Canada.* Toronto: Penguin, 2006.

Boldurian, Anthony T., and John L. Cotter. *Clovis Revisited: New Perspectives on Paleoindian Adaptations from Blackwater Draw, New Mexico.* Philadelphia: University of Pennsylvania Press, 1999.

Bough, Barry M. *First Across the Continent: Sir Alexander Mackenzie.* Norman: University of Oklahoma Press, 1997.

Bouchette, Joseph. *The British Dominions in North America, or a Topographical Description of the Provinces of Lower and Upper Canada.* London: Longman, Rees, Orme, Brown, and Green, 1831.

Boyer, Paul, and Stephen Nissenbaum. *Salem Possessed: The Social Origins of Witchcraft.* Cambridge, MA: Harvard University Press, 1974.

Boyer, Richard. "Mexico in the Seventeenth Century: Transition to a Colonial Society." *Hispanic American Historical Review* 57 (1977): 455–78.

Boxer, Charles R. *The Portuguese Seaborne Empire.* New York: Knopf, 1969.

Brading, D. A. *The First America: The Spanish Monarchy, Creole Patriots, and the Liberal State, 1492–1867.* Cambridge, UK: Cambridge University Press, 1991.

———. *Miners and Merchants in Bourbon Mexico, 1763–1810.* Cambridge, UK: Cambridge University Press, 1971.

Brading, D. A., and Harry E. Cross. "Colonial Silver Mining: Mexico and Peru." *Hispanic Historical Review* 52 (1972): 545–79.

Bragdon, Kathleen J. *Native People of Southern New England, 1500–1650.* Norman: University of Oklahoma Press, 1996.

Brando, José Antonio. *"Your Fyre Shall Burn No More": Iroquois Policy toward New France and Its Native Allies to 1701.* Lincoln: University of Nebraska Press, 1997.

Braudel, Fernand. *The Mediterranean and the Mediterranean World in the Age of Philip II.* 2 vols. Translated by Siân Reynolds. London: Fontana, 1972.

Brescia, Michael M., and John C. Super. *North America: An Introduction.* Toronto: University of Toronto Press, 2009.

Brewer, John. *The Sinews of Power: War, Money, and the English State, 1688–1783.* New York: Alfred A. Knopf, 1989.

Bridenbaugh, Carl, and Roberta Bridenbaugh. *No Peace beyond the Line: The English in the Caribbean, 1624–1690.* New York: Oxford University Press, 1972.

Briggs, Winstanley. "Le Pays des Illinois." *William and Mary Quarterly* 47 (1990): 30–56.

Bronowski, Jacob. *The Ascent of Man.* Boston: Little, Brown, 1973.

Brooks, James F. *Captives and Cousins: Slavery, Kinship, and Community in the Southwest Borderlands.* Chapel Hill: University of North Carolina Press, 2002.

Buckner, Phillip. "Presidential Address: Whatever Happened to the British Empire?" *Journal of the Canadian Historical Association* 4 (1994): 3–32.

Buckner, Phillip, and John G. Reid, eds. *The Atlantic Region to Confederation: A History.* Toronto and Fredericton: University of Toronto Press and Acadiensis Press, 1984.

Bumsted, J. M. *Fur Trade Wars: The Founding of Western Canada.* Winnipeg: Great Plains Publications, 1999.

———. *Lord Selkirk: A Life.* Winnipeg: University of Manitoba Press, 2008.

———. *Pre-Confederation.* Vol. 1 of *Interpreting Canada's Past.* Toronto: Oxford University Press, 1993.

Burkhart, Louise M. *The Slippery Earth: Nahua-Christian Moral Dialogue in Sixteenth-Century Mexico.* Tucson: University of Arizona Press, 1989.

Cadigan, Sean T. *Newfoundland and Labrador: A History.* Toronto: University of Toronto Press, 2009.

Calloway, Colin G., ed. *Dawnland Encounters: Indians and Europeans in Northern New England.* Hanover, NH: University Press of New England, 1991.

———. *One Vast Winter Count: The Native American West before Lewis and Clark.* Lincoln: University of Nebraska Press, 2003.

Campbell, Randolph B. *An Empire for Slavery: The Peculiar Institution in Texas.* Baton Rouge: Louisiana State University Press, 1989.

Cameron, Catherine M., Paul Kelton, and Alan C. Swedlund, eds. *Beyond Germs: Native Depopulation in North America.* Tucson: University of Arizona Press, 2015.

Candiani, Vera S. *Dreaming of Dry Land: Environmental Transformation in Colonial Mexico City.* Stanford, CA: Stanford University Press, 2014.

Canny, Nicholas, ed. *Europeans on the Move: Studies on European Migration, 1500–1800.* New York: Oxford University Press, 1994.

———. "The Ideology of English Colonization: From Ireland to America." *William and Mary Quarterly* 30 (1973): 575–98.

Carneiro, Robert. "Scale Analysis as an Instrument for the Study of Cultural Evolution." *Southwestern Journal of Anthropology* 18 (1962): 149–69.

Carney, Judith A. "African Rice in the Columbian Exchange." *Journal of African History* 42 (2001): 377–96.

Carrasco, Davíd. *City of Sacrifice: The Aztec Empire and the Role of Violence in Civilization.* Boston: Beacon, 1999.

Carrasco, Pedro. *The Tenochca Empire of Ancient Mexico: The Triple Alliance of Tenochtitlan, Tetzcoco, and Tlacopan.* Norman: University of Oklahoma, 1999.

Caruso, John Anthony. *The Mississippi Valley Frontier: The Age of French Exploration and Settlement.* Indianapolis: Bobbs–Merrill, 1966.

Cayton, Andrew R. L., and Fredrika J. Teute, eds. *Contact Points: American Frontiers from the Mohawk Valley to the Mississippi, 1750–1830.* Chapel Hill: University of North Carolina Press, 1998.

Cervantes, Fernando. *The Devil in the New World: The Impact of Diabolism in New Spain.* New Haven, CT: Yale University Press, 1994.

Charbonneau, Hubert, Bertrand Desjardins, Jacques Légaré, and Hubert Denis. "The Population of the St. Lawrence Valley, 1608–1760." In *A Population History of North America,* edited by Michael Haines and Richard Steckel, 99–142. Cambridge, UK: Cambridge University Press, 2000.

Chase, Kenneth. *Firearms: A Global History to 1700.* Cambridge, UK: Cambridge University Press, 2003.

Chavéz, Alicia Hernádez. *Mexico: A Brief History.* Translated by Andy Klatt. Berkeley: University of California Press, 2006.

Chevigny, Hector. *Russian America: The Great Alaskan Adventure, 1741–1867.* New York: Viking, 1965.

Chipman, Donald E. *Nuño de Guzmán and the Province of Pánuco in New Spain, 1518–1533*. Glendale, CA: A. H. Clark, 1967.

Christian, David. *Maps of Time: An Introduction to Big History*. 2nd ed. Berkeley: University of California Press, 2011.

Christiansen, Eric. *Norsemen in the Viking Age*. Oxford: Blackwell, 2006.

Christian, William A., Jr. *Local Religion in Sixteenth-Century Spain*. Princeton, NJ: Princeton University Press, 1981.

Chodos, Robert, and Eric Hamovitch, *Quebec and the American Dream*. Toronto: Between the Lines, 1991.

Choquette, Leslie. *Frenchmen into Peasants: Modernity and Tradition in the Peopling of French Canada*. Cambridge, MA: Harvard University Press, 1997.

Cipolla, Carlo. *Guns, Sails, and Empires: Technological Innovation and the Early Phases of European Expansion, 1400–1700*. New York: Random House, 1965.

———. *Literacy and Development in the West*. Harmondsworth, UK: Penguin, 1969.

Cleary, Patricia. *The World, the Flesh, and the Devil: A History of Colonial St. Louis*. Columbia: University of Missouri Press, 2011.

Clendinnen, Inga. *Aztecs: An Interpretation*. Cambridge, UK: Cambridge University Press, 1991.

Coatsworth, John H. "Structures, Endowments, and Institutions in the Economic History of Latin America." *Latin American Research Review* 40 (2005): 127–28.

Cobbe, Hugh. *Cook's Voyages and the Peoples of the Pacific*. London: British Museum, 1979.

Coe, Michael. *Breaking the Maya Code*. 3rd ed. London: Thames & Hudson, 2012.

Cohen, Mark Nathan, and George J. Armelagos, eds. *Paleopathology at the Origins of Agriculture*. New York: Academic Press, 1984.

Cordell, Linda, and Maxine McBrinn. *Archaeology of the Southwest*. 3rd ed. Walnut Creek, Calif.: Left Coast, 2012.

Corkran, David H. *The Carolina Indian Frontier*. Columbia, SC: University of South Carolina Press, 1970.

Collinson, Patrick. *The Birthpangs of Protestant England: Religious and Cultural Change in the Sixteenth and Seventeenth Centuries*. London: Macmillan, 1988.

Colten, Craig E., and Geoffrey L. Buckley, eds., *North American Odyssey: Historical Geographies for the Twenty-First Century*. Lanham, MD: Rowman and Littlefield, 2014.

Conklin, Carli N. *The Pursuit of Happiness in the Founding Era: An Intellectual History*. Columbia: University of Missouri Press, 2019.

Conrad, Geoffrey W. *Religion and Empire: The Dynamics of Aztec and Inca Expansionism*. Cambridge, UK: Cambridge University Press, 1984.

Conrad, Margaret R. *A Concise History of Canada*. Cambridge, UK: Cambridge University Press, 2012.

Conrad, Margaret R., and James K. Hiller. *Atlantic Canada: A History*. Don Mills, ON: Oxford University Press, 2010.

Cook, Noble David, and W. George Lovell, eds. *"Secret Judgments of God": Old World Disease in Colonia, Spanish America*. Norman: University of Oklahoma Press, 1991.

Cook, Sherburne F., and Woodrow Borah. *Essays in Population History: Mexico and California.* Berkeley: University of California Press, 1979.

Cook, Warren L. *Flood Tide of Empire: Spain and the Pacific Northwest, 1543–1819.* New Haven, CT: Yale University Press, 1973.

Cooper Alarcón, Daniel. *The Aztec Palimpsest: Mexico and the Modern Imagination.* Tucson: University of Arizona Press, 1997.

Cordell, Linda S. *Archaeology of the Southwest.* New York: Academic Press, 1997.

———. *Prehistory of the Southwest.* New York: Academic Press, 1984.

Cortés, Hernando. *Letters from Mexico.* New Haven, CT: Yale University Press, 1986.

Crane, Verner W. *The Southern Frontier, 1670–1732.* New York: W. W. Norton, 1981.

Craven, Avery. "The 'Turner Theories' and the South." *Journal of Southern History* 5 (1939): 291–314.

Craven, Wesley Frank. *The Colonies in Transition, 1660–1713.* New York: Harper and Row, 1968.

Creighton, Donald Grant. *The Empire of the St. Lawrence.* Toronto: Macmillan, 1956.

Crèvecoeur, J. Hector St. John de. "What Is an American?" In *Letters from an American Farmer and Other Essays: J. Hector St. John de Crèvecoeur,* edited by Dennis D. Moore. Cambridge: Harvard University Press, 2012.

Cronon, William. *Changes in the Land: Indians, Colonists, and the Ecology of New England.* New York: Hill and Wang, 1983.

Crosby, Alfred. *The Columbian Exchange: Biological and Cultural Consequences of 1492.* Westport, CT: Greenwood Press, 1972.

———. *Ecological Imperialism: The Biological Expansion of Europe, 900–1000.* New York: Cambridge University Press, 1986.

———. "Summary on Population Size before and after Contact." In *Disease and Demography in the Americas,* edited by John W. Verano and Douglas H. Ubelaker, 165–66. Washington, DC: Smithsonian Institution Press, 1992.

Crowley, Frances G. *Domingo Faustino Sarmiento.* New York: Twayne, 1972.

Curtin, Philip D. *The Rise and Fall of the Plantation Complex: Essays in Atlantic History.* 2nd ed. New York: Cambridge University Press, 2012.

Cushner, Nicholas P. *Why Have You Come Here? The Jesuits and the First Evangelization of Native America.* New York: Oxford University Press, 2006.

Daniel, Douglas A. "Tactical Factors in the Spanish Conquest of the Aztecs." *Anthropological Quarterly* 65 (1992): 187–94.

Daniels, John D. "The Indian Population of North America in 1492." *William and Mary Quarterly* 49, no. 2 (1992): 298–320.

Dauenhauer, Nora Marks, Richard Dauenhauer, and Lydia T. Black, eds. *Anóoshi Lingít Aaní Ká / Russians in Tlingit America: The Battles of Sitka, 1802 and 1804.* Classics of Tlingit Oral Literature. Seattle: University of Washington Press, 2008.

David, A. Paul, and Gavin Wright. "Increasing Returns and the Genesis of American Resource Abundance." *Industrial and Corporate Change* 6 (1997): 203–45.

Davies, K. G. *The North Atlantic World in the Seventeenth Century.* Minneapolis: University of Minnesota Press, 1974.

Davies, Paul. *Europe: A History*. Oxford: Oxford University Press, 1994.

Davis, David Brion. *The Problem of Slavery in the Age of Emancipation*. New York: Knopf, 2014.

———. *The Problem of Slavery in the Age of Revolution, 1770–1823*. Ithaca, NY: Cornell University Press, 1975.

———. *The Problem of Slavery in Western Culture*. Ithaca, NY: Cornell University Press, 1966.

Daws, Gavan. *Shoal of Time: A History of the Hawaiian Islands*. New York: Macmillan, 1968.

Debo, Angie. *And Still the Waters Run*. Princeton, NJ: University of Princeton Press, 1940.

de Glete, Jan. *Warfare at Sea, 1500–1650: Maritime Conflicts and the Transformation of Europe*. London: Routledge, 1999.

Delage, Denys. *Bitter Feast: Amerindians and Europeans in Northeastern North America, 1600–1664*. Translated by Jane Brierly. Vancouver: University of British Columbia, 1993.

De La Teja, Jesús F. *San Antonio de Bexar: A Community on New Spain's Northern Frontier*. Albuquerque: University of New Mexico Press, 1995.

Demos, John P. *A Little Commonwealth: Family Life in Plymouth Colony*. New York: Oxford University Press, 1970.

Dennis, Matthew. *Cultivating a Landscape of Peace: Iroquois-European Encounters in Seventeenth-Century America*. Ithaca, NY: Cornell University Press, 1993.

DePalma, Anthony. *Here: A Biography of the New American Continent*. New York: Public Affairs, 2001.

DePalo, William A. *The Mexican National Army, 1822–1852*. College Station: Texas A and M University Press, 1997.

De Soto, Hernando. *The Mystery of Capital: Why Capitalism Triumphs in the West and Fails Everywhere Else*. New York: Basic Books, 2000.

de Terra, Helmut. *Humboldt: The Life and Times of Alexander von Humboldt, 1769–1859*. New York: Alfred A. Knopf, 1955.

Deutsch, David. *The Beginning of Infinity: Explanations that Transform the World*. New York: Viking, 2011.

Devine, T. M. *Scotland's Empire, 1600–1815*. London: Allan Lane, 2003.

Devoto, Bernard. *The Course of Empire*. Boston: Houghton Mifflin, 1952.

Diamond, Jared. *Guns, Germs and Steel: The Fate of Human Societies*. New York: W. W. Norton, 1997.

———. *The World Until Yesterday: What Can We Learn from Traditional Societies?* New York: Viking, 2012.

Díaz del Castillo, Bernal. *The History of the Conquest of New Spain*. Edited by Davíd Lee Carrasco. 1632. Albuquerque: University of New Mexico Press, 2008.

Dickason, Olive Patricia, with David T. McNab. *Canada's First Nations: A History of the Founding Peoples from Earliest Times*. 4th ed. Don Mills, ON: Oxford University Press, 2008.

Dickinson, John, and Brian Young. *A Short History of Quebec*. 3rd ed. Montreal: McGill–Queen's University Press, 2008.

Diehl, Richard. *Tula: The Toltec Capital of Ancient Mexico*. London: Thames and Hudson, 1983.

Dillehay, Thomas D. *The Settlement of the Americas: A New Prehistory*. New York: Basic Books, 2000.

Dobado, Rafael, and Gustavo A. Marrero. "The Role of the Spanish Imperial State in the Mining-Led Growth of Bourbon Mexico's Economy." *Economic History Review* 64 (2011): 855–84.

Dobyns, Henry F. "Estimating Aboriginal American Population: An Appraisal of Techniques with a New Hemispheric Estimate." *Current Anthropology* 7 (1966): 395–416.

——. *Their Number Become Thinned: Native American Population Dynamics in Eastern North America*. Knoxville: University of Tennessee Press, 1983.

Donald, Merlin. *Origins of the Modern Mind: Three Stages in the Evolution of Culture and Cognition*. Cambridge, MA: Harvard University Press, 1991.

Donck, Adriaen van der. *Description of the New Netherlands*. Translated by Jeremiah Johnson. 1655. New York: Cosimo Classics, 2010.

Doshi, Rush. *The Long Game: China's Grand Strategy to Displace the American Order*. New York: Oxford University Press, 2021.

Dowd, Gregory Evans. *A Spirited Resistance: The North American Indian Struggle for Unity, 1745–1815*. Baltimore: Johns Hopkins University Press, 1992.

Drake, Sir Francis. *The World Encompassed*. 1628. Reprint, New York: Da Capo Press, 1969.

Draper, Theodore. *A Struggle for Power: The American Revolution*. New York: Random House, 1996.

Duffy, Christopher. *Military Experience in the Age of Reason*. London: Routledge, 1987.

Dunn, Richard S. *Sugar and Slaves: The Rise of the Planter Class in the English West Indies, 1624–1713*. Chapel Hill: University of North Carolina Press, 1972.

Dunn, Richard S., and Mary Maples Dunn, eds., *The World of William Penn*. Philadelphia: University of Pennsylvania Press, 1986.

Dunnell, Robert C. "Evolutionary Theory and Archaeology." *Advances in Archaeological Method and Theory* 3 (1980): 35–99.

Dye, David H., and Cheryl Anne Cox, eds. *Towns and Temples along the Mississippi*. Tuscaloosa: University of Alabama Press, 1990.

Dyke, Paul A. Van. *Merchants of Canton and Macao: Politics and Strategies in Eighteenth-Century Chinese Trade*. Hong Kong: Hong Kong University Press, 2011.

Earle, Peter. *The Pirate Wars*. New York: St. Martin's Griffin, 2006.

Eccles, W. J. *The Canadian Frontier, 1534–1760*. Albuquerque: University of New Mexico Press, 1983.

——. *France in America*. Rev. ed. Markham, ON: Fitzhenry and Whiteside, 1990.

Echenberg, Myron. *Humboldt's Mexico: In the Footsteps of the Illustrious German Scientific Traveller*. Montreal: McGill–Queen's University Press, 2017.

Edmunds, R. David, and Joseph L. Peyser. *The Fox Wars: The Mesquakie Challenge to New France*. Norman: University of Oklahoma Press, 1993.

Eeckhout, Peter, and Geneviève Le Fort, eds. *Wars and Conflicts in Prehispanic Mesoamerica and the Andes*. Oxford, UK: John and Erica Hedges, 2005.

Egerton, Douglas R., Alison Games, Jane G. Landers, Kris Lane, and Donald R. Wright. *The Atlantic World: A History, 1400–1888*. Hoboken, NJ: Wiley-Blackwell, 2007.

Eisenhower, John S. D. *So Far from God: The U.S. War with Mexico, 1846–1848*. New York: Random House, 1989.

Eisenstein, Elizabeth L. *The Printing Press as an Agent of Change: Communications and Cultural Transformations in Early-Modern Europe*. Cambridge, UK: Cambridge University Press, 1980.

Ekberg, Carl. *French Roots in the Illinois Country: The Mississippi Frontier in Colonial Times*. Urbana: University of Illinois Press, 1998.

———. *Stealing Indian Women: Native Slavery in the Illinois Country*. Urbana: University of Illinois Press, 2007.

Ekberg, Carl, and Sharon Person. *St. Louis Rising: The French Regime of Louis St. Ange de Bellerive*. Urbana: University of Illinois Press, 2015.

Elias, Norbert. *The Civilizing Process: Sociogenetic and Psychogenetic Investigations*. Translated by Edmund Jephcott. 1939. Reprint, Oxford, UK: Basil Blackwell, 1982.

Elliott, Sir John H. *Empires of the Atlantic World: Britain and Spain in America, 1492–1830*. New Haven, CT: Yale University Press, 2006.

Eltis, David. *The Rise of African Slavery in the Americas*. Cambridge, UK: Cambridge University Press, 2000.

Elton, Geoffrey. *Reformation Europe, 1517–1559*. London: Fontana, 1963.

Ely, Richard T. *Taxation in American States and Cities*. New York: Thomas Y. Crowell, 1888.

Engstrand, Iris H. W. "Seekers of the 'Northern Mystery': European Exploration of California and the Pacific." In *Contested Eden: California Before the Gold Rush*, edited by Ramón A. Gutiérrez and Richard J. Orsi, 78–110. Berkeley: University of California Press, 1998.

———. *Spanish Scientists in the New World: The Eighteenth-Century Expeditions*. Seattle: University of Washington Press, 1981.

Engelbert, Robert, and Andrew N. Wegmann, eds. *French Connections: Cultural Mobility in North America and the Atlantic World, 1600–1875*. Baton Rouge: Louisiana State University Press, 2020.

Engels, Frederick. *The Origin of the Family, Private Property and the State*. Translated by Ernest Untermann. 1884. Reprint, Chicago: Charles H. Kerr, 1908.

Erlandson, Jon M., Michael H. Graham, Bruce J. Bourque, Debra Corbett, James E. Estes, and Robert S. Steneck. "The Kelp Highway Hypothesis: Marine Ecology, the Coastal Migration Theory, and the Peopling of the Americas." *Journal of Island and Coastal Archaeology* 2 (2007): 161–74.

Esdaile, Charles. *Napoleon's Wars: An International History, 1803–1815*. London: Allen Lane, 2007.

Estarellas, Juan. "The College of Tlatelolco and the Problem of Higher Education for Indians in 16th Century Mexico." *History of Education Quarterly* 2 (1962): 234–43.

Ettinger, Amos Aschbach. *James Edward Oglethorpe: Imperial Idealist.* Hamden, CT: Archon, 1968.

Etulain, Richard. *Beyond the Missouri: The Story of the American West.* Albuquerque: University of New Mexico Press, 2006.

Ewers, John C. *Plains Indian History and Culture: Essays on Continuity and Change.* Norman: University of Oklahoma Press, 1997.

Fagan, Brian. *The First North Americans: An Archaeological Journey.* London: Thames and Hudson, 2012.

——. *The Little Ice Age: How Climate Made History, 1300–1850.* New York: Basic Books, 2000.

Fausz, J. Frederick. *Founding St. Louis: First City of the New West.* Charleston, SC: History Press, 2011.

Fernandes, Daniel M., Kendra A. Sirak, Harald Ringbauer, Jakob Sedig, Nadin Rohland, Matthew Mah, Swapan Mallick, et al. "A Genetic History of the Pre-Contact Caribbean." *Nature* 590 (2021): 103–10.

Fernández-Armesto, Felipe. *Straits: Beyond the Myth of Magellan.* London: Bloomsbury, 2022.

Ferguson, Adam. *An Essay on the History of Civil Society.* 1767. Edited by Duncan Forbes. 1767. Reprint, Edinburgh: Edinburgh University Press, 1966.

Ferguson, Brian, and Neil Whitehead, eds. *War in the Tribal Zone: Expanding States and Indigenous Warfare.* Santa Fe, NM: School of American Research, 1992.

Ferling, John. *Almost a Miracle: The American Victory in the War of Independence.* New York: Oxford University Press, 2007.

Fernandes, Daniel M., Kendra A. Sirak, Harold Ringbauer, Jakob Sedig, Nadin Rohland, Olivia Cheronet, Matthew Mah, et al. "A Genetic History of the Precontact Caribbean." *Nature* 590 (2020): 103–10.

Fernández-Armesto, Felipe. *The Americas: A Hemispheric History.* New York: Modern Library, 2003.

——. *Amerigo: The Man Who Gave His Name to America.* New York: Random House, 2007.

——. *Pathfinders: A Global History of Exploration.* New York: W. W. Norton, 2006.

——. *Straits: Beyond the Myth of Magellan.* London: Bloomsbury, 2022.

Fernlund, Kevin Jon. "American Exceptionalism or Atlantic Unity? Frederick Jackson Turner and the Enduring Problem of American Historiography." *New Mexico Historical Review* 89 (2014): 359–99.

——. "The Great Battle of the Books between the Cultural Evolutionists and the Cultural Relativists: From the Beginning of Infinity to the End of History." *Journal of Big History* 4 (2020): 6–30.

——. "To Think Like a Star: The American West, Modern Cosmology, and Big History." *Montana The Magazine of Western History* 59 (Summer 2009): 23–44.

——. *William Henry Holmes and the Rediscovery of the American West.* Albuquerque: University of New Mexico Press, 2000.

Fieldel, Stuart J. *Prehistory of the Americas.* New York: Cambridge University Press, 1992.

Fierlbeck, Katherine. *Political Thought in Canada: An Intellectual History*. Peterborough, ON: Broadview Press, 2006.

Findlay, Ronald, and Kevin O'Rourke. *Power and Plenty: Trade, War, and the World Economy in the Second Millennium*. Princeton, NJ: Princeton University Press, 2007.

Fischer, David Hackett. *Albion's Seed: Four British Folkways in America*. New York: Oxford University Press, 1989.

———. *Champlain's Dream: The European Founding of North America*. New York: Simon and Schuster, 2008.

Fisher, Michael H. "Indirect Rule in the British Empire: The Foundations of the Residency System in India, 1764–1858." *Modern Asian Studies* 18 (1984): 393–428.

Fisher, Raymond H. *Bering's Voyages: Whither and Why*. Seattle: University of Washington Press, 1977.

Fisher, Robin, and Hugh Johnston, eds. *Captain James Cook and His Times*. Seattle: University of Washington Press, 1979.

Fitzhugh, William W. Fitzhugh, and Aron Crowwell, eds. *Crossroads of Continents: Cultures of Siberia and Alaska*. Washington, DC: Smithsonian Institution Press, 1988.

Flannery, Tim. *The Eternal Frontier: An Ecological History of North America and Its Peoples*. New York: Atlantic Monthly Press, 2011.

Fleming, Patricia Lockhart, and Yvan Lamonde, eds. *A History of the Book in Canada*. 3 vols. Toronto: Toronto University Press, 2004, 2005, 2007.

Fletcher, Richard. *The Conversion of Europe: From Paganism to Christianity, 371–1386 AD*. New York: HarperCollins, 1997.

Flores, Dan. *Horizontal Yellow: Nature and History in the Near Southwest*. Albuquerque: University of New Mexico, 1999.

Fogel, Robert William, and Stanley L. Engerman. *Time on the Cross: The Economics of American Negro Slavery*. 2 vols. Boston: Little, Brown, 1974.

Foley, Robert, and M. Mirazón Lahr. "The Evolution of the Diversity of Cultures." *Philosophical Transactions of the Royal Society B: Biological Sciences* 366 (2011): 1080–89.

Foner, Eric. *Free Soil, Free Labor, and Free Men: The Ideology of the Republican Party before the Civil War, with a New Introductory Essay*. 1970. Reprint, Oxford University Press, 1995.

Forbes, Jack D. *Apache, Navaho, and Spaniard*. Norman: University of Oklahoma Press, 1994.

Foster, Stephen, ed. *British North America in the Seventeenth and Eighteenth Centuries*. Oxford, UK: Oxford University Press, 2014.

———. *The Long Argument: English Puritanism and the Shaping of New England Culture, 1570–1700*. Chapel Hill: University of North Carolina Press, 1991.

Ford, Corey. *Where the Sea Breaks Its Back: The Epic Story of Early Naturalist Georg Steller and the Russian Exploration of Alaska*. 2nd ed. Portland, OR: Alaska Northwest, 2003.

Frago, Antonio Viñao. "The History of Literacy in Spain: Evolution, Traits, and Questions." *History of Education Quarterly* 30 (1990): 573–99.

Francis, Mark. *Herbert Spencer and the Invention of Modern Life.* Ithaca, NY: Cornell University Press, 2007.

Francis, R. Douglas, Richard Johns, and Donald B. Smith. *Origins: Canadian History to Confederation.* 6th ed. Toronto: Nelson Education, 2010.

Fried, Morton. *The Evolution of Political Society.* New York: Random House, 1967.

Friesen, Gerald. *Canadian Prairies: A History.* Toronto: University of Toronto Press, 1987.

Frost, Orcutt William. *Bering: The Russian Discovery of America.* New Haven, CT: Yale University Press, 2003.

Fuentes, Carlos. *The Buried Mirror: Reflections on Spain in the New World.* 1992. Reprint, Boston: Mariner, 1999.

Fussell, Betty. *The Story of Corn.* Albuquerque: University of New Mexico Press, 2004.

Gad, Finn. *The History of Greenland.* 3 vols. Vol. 1, *Earliest Times to 1700*; vol. 2, *1700–1782*; vol. 3, *1782–1808.* Montreal: McGill–Queen's University Press, 1971–83.

Gaddis, John Lewis. *The Landscape of History: How Historians Map the Past.* Oxford, UK: Oxford University Press, 2002.

Gagnon, Serge. *Quebec and its Historians, 1840–1920.* Montreal: Harvest House, 1982.

———. *Quebec and its Historians: The Twentieth Century.* Montreal: Harvest House, 1985.

Galloway, Patricia K., ed. *La Salle and His Legacy: Frenchmen and Indians in the Lower Mississippi Valley.* Jackson: University Press of Mississippi, 1982.

Gallay, Alan. *The Indian Slave Trade: The Rise of the English Empire in the American South, 1670–1717.* New Haven, CT: Yale University Press, 2003.

Ganshof, François Louis. *Feudalism.* Translated by Philip Grierson. 1947. Reprint, London: Longmans, Green, 1952.

Gardiner, Robert, and Richard Unger, eds. *Cogs, Caravels, and Galleons: The Sailing Ship, 1000–1650.* London: Chartwell, 2000.

Garner, Richard L., and Spiro E. Stefanou, *Economic Growth and Change in Bourbon Mexico.* Gainesville: University Press of Florida, 1993.

Garreau, Joel. *The Nine Nations of North America.* New York: Avon, 1981.

Gasper, Gerhard. "A Young Man from 'Ultima Thule' Visits Jefferson: Alexander von Humboldt in Philadelphia and Washington." *Proceedings of the American Philosophical Society* 155 (2011): 247–62.

Gat, Azar. *War in Human Civilization.* Oxford, UK: Oxford University Press, 2006.

Gay, Peter. *The Enlightenment.* 2 vols. Vol. 1, *The Rise of Paganism.*; vol. 2, *The Science of Freedom.* 1969. Reprint, New York: W. W. Norton, 1995–96.

Gayarré, Charles. *History of Louisiana: The Spanish Domination.* New York: Redfield, 1854.

Gemery, Henry A. "The White Population of the Colonial United States, 1607–1790." In *The Population History of North America*, edited by Michael R. Haines and Richard H. Steckel, 143–90. Cambridge, UK: Cambridge University Press, 2000.

Gemery, Henry A., and Jan S. Hogendorn, eds. *The Uncommon Market: Essays in the Economic History of the Atlantic Slave Trade*. New York: Academic Press, 1979.

Genovese, Eugene D. *Roll, Jordan, Roll: The World the Slaves Made*. New York: Vintage, 1972.

Gerhard, Peter. *A Guide to the Historical Geography of New Spain*. Rev. ed. Norman: University of Oklahoma, 1993.

———. *The North Frontier of New Spain*. Rev. ed. Norman: University of Oklahoma Press, 1993.

———. *The Southeast Frontier of New Spain*. Rev. ed. Norman: University of Oklahoma Press, 1993.

Gerschrenkon, Alexander. *Economic Backwardness in Historical Perspective*. Cambridge: Harvard University Press, 1962.

Gibson, Charles. *The Aztecs under Spanish Rule: A History of the Indians of the Valley of Mexico, 1519–1810*. Stanford, CA: Stanford University Press, 1964.

———. *Spain in America*. New York: Harper and Row, 1966.

———. *Tlaxcala in the Sixteenth Century*. Stanford, CA: Stanford University Press, 1967.

Gibson, James R. *Imperial Russia in Frontier America: The Changing Geography of Supply of Russian America, 1784–1867*. New York: Oxford University Press, 1976.

Gilderhus, Mark T. "The Monroe Doctrine: Meanings and Implications." *Presidential Studies Quarterly* 36 (2006): 5–16.

Gipson, Lawrence Henry. "The American Revolution as an Aftermath of the Great War for Empire, 1754–1763." *Political Science Quarterly* 65 (1950): 86–104.

Giraldez, Arturo. *The Age of Trade: The Manila Galleons and the Dawn of the Global Economy*. Lanham, MD: Rowman and Littlefield, 2015.

Girard, Philippe R. "Jean-Jacques Dessalines and the Atlantic System: A Reappraisal." *William and Mary Quarterly* 69 (July 2012): 549–82.

Gitlin, Jay. *The Bourgeois Frontier: French Towns, French Traders, and American Expansion*. New Haven, CT: Yale University Press, 2010.

Gitlin, Jay, Barbara Berglund, and Adam Arenson, eds. *Frontier Cities: Encounters at the Crossroads of Empire*. Philadelphia: University of Pennsylvania Press, 2012.

Gitlin, Jay, Robert Michael Morrissey, and Peter J. Kastor, eds. *French St. Louis: Landscape, Contexts, and Legacy*. Lincoln: University of Nebraska Press, 2021.

Glaeser, Edward L. "Urban Colossus: Why New York Is America's Largest City." *Federal Reserve Bank of New York Economic Policy Review* 11 (2005): 7–24.

Gleeson-White, Jane. *Double Entry: How the Merchants of Venice Created Modern Finance*. New York: Norton, 2012.

Goetzmann, William H. *Exploration and Empire: The Explorer and the Scientist in the Winning of the American West*. New York: Knopf, 1967.

Goetzmann, William H., and Glyndwr Williams. *The Atlas of North American Exploration: From the Norse Voyages to the Race to the Pole*. New York: W. W. Norton, 1992.

Golder, F. A. *Bering's Voyages: An Account of the Efforts of the Russians to Determine the Relation of Asia and America*. New York: American Geographical Society, 1922.

Gott, Richard. *Cuba: A New History.* New Haven, CT: Yale University Press, 2005.

Gough, Barry M. *The Northwest Coast: British Navigation, Trade, and Discoveries to 1812.* Vancouver: University of British Columbia Press, 1992.

Graeber, David, and David Wengrow. *The Dawn of Everything: A New History of Humanity.* New York: Farrar, Straus and Giroux, 2021.

Granatstein, J. L. *Canada's Army: Waging War and Keeping the Peace.* 2nd ed. Toronto: University of Toronto Press, 2011.

Greenberg, Joseph. H. *Language in the Americas.* Stanford, CA: Stanford University Press, 1987.

Greenblatt, Stephen. *Marvelous Possessions: The Wonder of the New World.* Chicago: University of Chicago Press, 1991.

Greene, Jack P., and Philip D. Morgan, eds. *Atlantic History: A Critical Appraisal.* New York: Oxford University Press, 2009.

Greene, Jack P., and J. R. Pole, eds. *Colonial British America: Essays in the New History of the Early Modern Era.* Baltimore: Johns Hopkins University Press, 1984.

Greenleaf, Richard E. "The Mexican Inquisition and the Indians: Sources for the Ethnohistorian." *Americas* 34 (1978): 315–44.

———. *The Mexican Inquisition of the Sixteenth Century.* Albuquerque: University of Oklahoma Press, 1969.

Greer, Allan. "The Pattern of Literacy in Quebec, 1745–1899." *Histoire Sociale* 44 (1978): 295–325.

———. *The People of New France.* Toronto: University of Toronto Press, 1997.

Guardino, Peter. *The Dead March: A History of the Mexican-American War.* Cambridge: Harvard University Press, 2017.

Griffin, Patrick, ed. *Experiencing Empire: Power, People, and Revolution in Early America.* Charlottesville: University of Virginia Press, 2017.

Grubb, F. W. "Growth of Literacy in Colonial America: Longitudinal Patterns, Economic Models, and the Direction of Future Research." *Social Science History* 14 (1990): 451–82.

Guidi-Bruscoli, Francesco. "John Cabot and His Italian Financiers." *Historical Research* 85 (2012): 392.

Gurzinski, Serge. *The Conquest of Mexico: The Incorporation of Indian Societies into the Western World, 16th–18th Centuries.* Translated by Eileen Corrigan. 1988. Cambridge, UK: Polity Press, 1993.

Gutiérrez, Ramón A. *When Jesus Came, the Corn Mothers Went Away: Marriage, Sexuality, and Power in New Mexico, 1500–1846.* Stanford, CA: Stanford University Press, 1991.

Gutiérrez, Ramón A., and Richard J. Orsi, eds. *Contested Eden: California before the Gold Rush.* Berkeley: University of California Press, 1998.

Haber, Stephen, ed. *Political Institutions and Economic Growth in Latin America: Essays in Policy, History, and Political Economy.* Stanford, CA: Hoover Institution Press, 2000.

Hahn, Steven C. *The Invention of the Creek Nation, 1670–1763.* Lincoln: University of Nebraska Press, 2004.

Haines, Michael R. "The White Population of the United States, 1790–1920." In *A Population History of North America*, edited by Michael R. Haines and Richard H. Steckel, 305–70. Cambridge, UK: Cambridge University Press, 2000.

Haines, Michael R., and Richard H. Steckel, eds. *A Population History of North America*. Cambridge, UK: Cambridge University Press, 2000.

Hainsworth, Roger, and Christine Churches. *The Anglo-Dutch Naval Wars, 1652–1674*. Stroud, UK: Sutton, 1998.

Hall, Bert. *Weapons and Warfare in Renaissance Europe: Gunpowder, Technology, and Tactics*. Baltimore: Johns Hopkins University Press, 1997.

Hallenbeck, Cleve. *Land of the Conquistadors*. Caldwell, ID: Caxton, 1950.

Hallowell, Gerald, ed. *The Oxford Companion to Canadian History*. Don Mills, ON: Oxford University Press, 2004.

Hämäläinen, Pekka. *The Comanche Empire*. New Haven, CT: Yale University Press, 2008.

Hammond, George P., and Agapito Rey, eds. *Narratives of the Coronado Expedition, 1540–1542*. Albuquerque: University of New Mexico Press, 1940.

Handlin, Oscar. "The Significance of the Seventeenth Century." In *Seventeenth-Century America: Essays in Colonial History*, edited by James Morton Smith, 3–12. Chapel Hill: University of North Carolina Press, 1959.

Handlin, Oscar, and Mary F. Handlin. "Origins of the Southern Labor System." *William and Mary Quarterly* 7 (1950): 199–222.

Hanke, Lewis, ed. *Do the Americas have a Common History? A Critique of the Bolton Theory*. New York: Knopf, 1964.

Harari, Yuval Noah, *Sapiens: A Brief History of Humankind*. New York: Harper Perennial, 2015.

Harding, Richard. *The Evolution of the Sailing Navy, 1509–1815*. London: St. Martin's Press, 1995.

—— *Seapower and Naval Warfare, 1650–1830*. London: University College London Press, 1999.

Harner, Michael. "The Ecological Basis for Aztec Sacrifice." *American Ethnologist* 4 (1977): 117–35.

Harris, Marvin. *Cannibals and Kings: Origins of Cultures*. New York: Random House, 1977.

——. *The Rise of Anthropological Theory: A History of Theories of Culture*. 1968. Reprint, Walnut Creek, CA: Altamira Press, 2001.

Harris, R. Cole. "The Colonists of Seventeenth-Century Canada." In *Interpreting Canada's Past*, vol. 1, *Pre-Confederation*, edited by J. M. Bumsted, 108–20. Toronto: Oxford University Press, 1993.

——. "France in North America." In *North America: The Historical Geography of a Changing Continent*, edited by Thomas F. McIlwraith and Edward K. Muller, 65–88. Lanham, MD: Rowman and Littlefield, 2001.

——. *The Reluctant Land: Society, Space, and Environment in Canada before Confederation*. Vancouver: University of British Columbia Press, 2008.

Harris, William V. *Ancient Literacy*. Cambridge: Harvard University Press, 1989.

Haskett, Robert S. "'Our Suffering with the Taxco Tribute': Involuntary Mine Labor and Indigenous Society in Central New Spain." *Hispanic American Historical Review* 71 (1991): 447–75.

Hassig, Ross. *Aztec Warfare: Imperial Expansion and Political Control.* Norman: University of Oklahoma Press, 1988.

———. *Time, History, and Belief in Aztec and Colonial Mexico.* Austin: University of Texas Press, 2001.

———. *War and Society in Ancient Mesoamerica.* Berkeley: University of California Press, 1992.

Hastings, Robert W. *The Lakes of Pontchartrain: Their Histories and Environments.* Jackson: University Press of Mississippi, 2009.

Haury, Emil W. *The Hohokam: Desert Farmers and Craftsmen.* Tucson: University of Arizona Press, 1978.

Haycox, Stephen, James K. Barnett, and Caedmon A. Liburd, eds. *Enlightenment and Exploration in the North Pacific, 1741–1805.* Seattle: University of Washington Press, 1997.

Hayes, Carlton J. H. "The American Frontier–Frontier of What?" *American Historical Review* 50 (1946): 199–216.

Hayes, Derek. *Historical Atlas of the Pacific Northwest: Maps of Exploration and Discovery; British Columbia, Washington, Oregon, Alaska, Yukon.* Seattle: Sasquatch, 1999.

Haynes, Gary, ed. *American Megafaunal Extinctions at the End of the Pleistocene.* Amsterdam: Springer, 2009.

Haynes, C. Vance, Jr. "Contributions of Radiocarbon Dating to the Geochronology of the Peopling of the New World." In *Radiocarbon Dating after Four Decades,* edited by R. E. Taylor, A. Long, and R. Kra, 355–74. Tucson: University of Arizona Press, 1992.

Henige, David. *Numbers from Nowhere: The American Indian Population Contact Debate.* Norman: University of Oklahoma Press, 1998.

———. "On the Contact Population of Hispaniola: History as Higher Mathematics." *Hispanic American Historical Review* 58 (1978): 217–37.

Herlihy, David, ed. *The History of Feudalism.* Atlantic Highlands, NJ: Humanities Press, 1970.

Herman, Arthur. *The Scottish Enlightenment: The Scots' Invention of the Modern World.* London: Harper Perennial, 2001.

Herring, George. *From Colony to Superpower: American Foreign Relations since 1776.* Oxford, UK: Oxford University Press, 2011.

Hessler, John W. *The Naming of America: Martin Waldseemüller's 1507 World Map and the Cosmographiae Introductio.* London: D. Giles, 2008.

Hewison, Robert. *Ruskin and His Contemporaries.* London: Pallas Athene, 2018.

Heyrman, Christine Leigh. *Southern Cross: The Beginnings of the Bible Belt.* New York: Knopf, 1997.

Himmerich y Valencia, Robert. *The Encomenderos of New Spain, 1521–1555.* Austin: University of Texas Press, 1991.

Hickey, Donald R. *The War of 1812: The Forgotten Conflict*. Urbana: University of Illinois, 2012.

Hill, Christopher. *The Century of Revolution, 1603–1714*. New York: W. W. Norton, 1961.

Hill, Peter P. *Napoleon's Troublesome Americans: Franco-American Relations*. Washington, DC: Potomac, 2005.

Hijiya, James A. "Why the West Is Lost." *William and Mary Quarterly* 51 (1994): 276–92.

Hinderaker, Eric. *Elusive Empires: Constructing Colonialism in the Ohio Valley, 1673–1800*. New York: Cambridge University Press, 1997.

Hinderaker, Eric, and Peter C. Mancall. *At the Edge of Empire: The Backcountry in British North America*. Baltimore, MD: Johns Hopkins University Press, 2003.

Hoak, Dale, and Mordechai Feingold, eds. *The World of William and Mary: Anglo-Dutch Perspectives on the Revolution of 1688–89*. Stanford, CA: Stanford University Press, 1996.

Hobbes, Thomas. *Leviathan*. 1651. Oxford, UK: Clarendon, 1909.

Hoberman, Louisa Schell. "Technological Change in a Traditional Society: The Case of the *Desagüe* in Colonial Mexico." *Technology and Culture* 21 (1980): 386–407.

Hobsbawm, Eric. *The Age of Revolution, 1789–1848*. New York: Vintage, 1964.

Hodder, Ian, Glynn Issac, and Norman Hammond, eds. *Pattern of the Past: Studies in Honour of David Clarke*. Cambridge: University Press, 1981.

Hodson, Christopher. *The Acadian Diaspora: An Eighteenth-Century History*. New York: Oxford University Press, 2012.

Hoffecker, Carol E., Richard Waldron, and Lorraine E. Williams, eds. *New Sweden in America*. Newark: University of Delaware Press, 1995.

Hoffman, Philip. "Prices, the Military Revolution, and Western Europe's Comparative Advantage in Violence." *Economic History Review* 64, supp. 1 (2011), 39–59.

Holder, Preston. *The Hoe and the Horse on the Plains: A Study of Cultural Development among North American Indians*. Lincoln: University of Nebraska Press, 1970.

Horn, James, William Kelso, Douglas Owsley, and Beverly Straube. *Jane: Starvation, Cannibalism, and Endurance at Jamestown*. Jamestown, VA: Jamestown Rediscovery Project, 2013.

Howse, Derek, ed. *Background to Discovery: Pacific Exploration from Dampier to Cook*. Berkeley: University of California Press, 1990.

———. *Greenwich Time and the Discovery of the Longitude*. Oxford: Oxford University Press, 1980.

Howard, David A. *Conquistador in Chains: Cabeza de Vaca and the Indians of the Americas*. Tuscaloosa: University of Alabama Press, 1997.

Howard, Michael. *War in European History*. Rev. ed. Oxford: Oxford University Press, 2009.

Hu-DeHart, Evelyn. *Missionaries, Miners, and Indians: Spanish Contact with the Yaqui Indians of Northwestern New Spain, 1533–1820*. Tucson: University of Arizona Press, 1981.

Hudson, Charles, and Carmen Chaves Tesser, eds. *The Forgotten Centuries: Indians and Europeans in the American South, 1521–1704.* Athens: University of Georgia Press, 1994.

Humboldt, Alexander von. *Cosmos: A Sketch of a Physical Description of the Universe.* 5 vols. Translated by E. C. Otté. New York: Harper and Brothers, 1852.

———. *Political Essay on the Kingdom of New Spain.* 4 vols. Translated by John Black. London: Longman, Hurst, Rees, Orme, Brown, and Colburn, 1811.

Hunt, William R. *Arctic Passage: The Turbulent History of the Land and People of the Bering Sea, 1697–1975.* New York: Charles Scribner's Sons, 1975.

Hunter, Douglas. *The Race to the New World: Christopher Columbus, John Cabot, and a Lost History of Discovery.* New York: Palgrave MacMillan, 2012.

Huntington, Samuel P. *Who Are We? The Challenges to America's National Identity.* New York: Simon and Schuster, 2004.

Huppert, George. *After the Black Death: A Social History of Early Modern Europe.* Bloomington: Indiana University Press, 1998.

Hurt, R. Douglass. *Indian Agriculture in America.* Lawrence: University of Kansas Press, 1987.

Hutton, Andrew Paul. *The Apache Wars: The Hunt for Geronimo, the Apache Kid, and the Captive Boy Who Started the Longest War in American History.* New York: Crown, 2016.

Hyde, Anne. *Empires, Nations, and Families: A New History of the North American West, 1800–1860.* New York: Ecco, 2012.

Imber, Colin. *The Ottoman Empire, 1300–1650: The Structure of Power.* London: Palgrave, 2002.

Inalcik, Halil. *The Ottoman Empire: The Classical Age, 1300–1600.* New York: Praeger, 1973.

Inikori, Joseph, and Stanley Engermann, eds. *The Atlantic Slave Trade: Effects on Economies, Societies, and Peoples in Africa, the Americas, and Europe.* Durham, NC: Duke University Press, 1992.

Innes, Stephen. *Creating the Commonwealth: The Economic Culture of Puritan New England.* New York: W. W. Norton, 1995.

Innes, Stephen, ed. *Work and Labor in Early America.* Chapel Hill: University of North Carolina Press, 1988.

Innis, Harold A. *The Cod Fisheries: The History of an International Economy.* Toronto: University of Toronto Press, 1954.

———. *The Fur Trade in Canada: An Introduction to Canadian Economic History.* Rev. ed. Toronto: University of Toronto Press, 1956.

Insh, George Pratt. *Scottish Colonial Schemes, 1620–1686.* Glasgow: Maclehose, Jackson, 1922.

Israel, Jonathan I. *The Dutch Republic: Its Rise, Greatness, and Fall, 1477–1806.* Oxford, UK: Oxford University Press, 1995.

———. *Radical Enlightenment: Philosophy and the Making of Modernity, 1650–1750.* Oxford, UK: Oxford University Press, 2002.

Jackson, Clare. *Devil-Land: England Under Siege, 1588–1688.* London: Allen Lane, 2021.

Jaenen, Cornelius J. *Friend and Foe: Aspects of French-Amerindian Cultural Contact in the Sixteenth and Seventeenth Centuries*. Toronto: University of Toronto Press, 1976.

James, Lawrence. *Raj: The Making and Unmaking of British India*. New York: St. Martin's Griffin, 1997.

Jaspers, Karl. *The Origin and Goal of History*. New Haven, CT: Yale University Press, 1953.

John, Elizabeth A. H. *Storms Brewed in Other Men's Worlds: The Confrontation of Indians, Spanish, and French in the Southwest, 1540–1795*. Norman: University of Oklahoma Press, 1996.

Johnson, Walter. *River of Dark Dreams: Slavery and Empire in the Cotton Kingdom*. Cambridge, MA: Belknap Press, 2013.

Jones, Dan. *Powers and Thrones: A New History of the Middle Ages*. New York: Viking, 2021.

Jones, David. "Virgin Soils Revisited". *William and Mary Quarterly* 60 (2003): 703–42.

Jones, Gwyn. *A History of the Vikings*. Oxford, UK: Oxford University Press, 2001.

———. *The Norse Atlantic Saga: Being the Norse Voyages of Discovery and Settlement to Iceland, Greenland, and North America*. 2nd ed. Oxford, UK: Oxford University Press, 1986.

Jones, Howard Mumford. *The Pursuit of Happiness*. Cambridge, MA: Harvard University Press, 1953.

Jones, Oakah. *Nueva Vizcaya: Heartland of the Spanish Empire*. Albuquerque: University of New Mexico Press, 1988.

Jordan, Winthrop D. *White over Black: American Attitudes toward the Negro, 1550–1812*. New York: W. W. Norton, 1977.

Jorgensen, Joseph G. *Western Indians: Comparative Environments, Languages, and Cultures of the 172 Western American Indian Tribes*. San Francisco: Freeman, 1980.

Joseph, Gilbert M., and Timothy J. Henderson, eds. *The Mexico Reader: History, Culture, Politics*. Durham, NC: Duke University Press, 2002.

Josephy, Alvin M. Jr., *The Patriot Chiefs: A Chronicle of American Indian Resistance*. New York: Penguin, 1976.

Juana Inés de la Cruz, Sister. *A Sor Juana Anthology*. Translated by Alan S. Trueblood. Cambridge, MA: Harvard University Press, 1988.

Kaestle, Carl F. "The History of Literacy and the History of Readers." *Review of Research in Education* 12 (1985): 11–53.

Kagan, Robert. *The Jungle Grows Back: America and Our Imperiled World*. New York: Knopf, 2018.

Kamen, Stanley. *Empire: How Spain Became a World Power, 1492–1763*. New York: Harper, 2003.

———. *Philip of Spain*. New Haven, CT: Yale University Press, 1999.

Kaplan, Robert D. *The Revenge of Geography: What the Map Tells Us about the Coming Conflicts and the Battle against Fate*. New York: Random House, 2012.

Katz, Friedrich. "The Evolution of Aztec Society." *Past and Present*, no. 13 (1958): 14–25.

Katz, Stanley N., John M. Murrin, and Douglas Greenberg, eds. *Colonial America: Essays in Politics and Social Development*. 4th ed. New York: McGraw-Hill, 1993.

Kastor, Peter. *The Nation's Crucible: The Louisiana Purchase and the Creation of America*. New Haven, CT: Yale University Press, 2004.

Kaufmann, Chaim D., and Robert A. Pape. "Explaining Costly International Moral Action: Britain's Sixty-Year Campaign against the Atlantic Slave Trade." *International Organization* 53 (1999): 631–68.

Kearns, Gerard. *Geopolitics and Empire: The Legacy of Halford Mackinder*. New York: Oxford University Press, 2009.

Keegan, John. *Fields of Battle: The Wars of North America*. New York: Knopf, 1997.

———. *A History of Warfare*. New York: Vintage, 1993.

Keeley, Lawrence. *War before Civilization: The Myth of the Peaceful Savage*. New York: Oxford University Press, 1996.

Kelly, Sean M. *Los Brazos de Dios: A Plantation Society in the Texas Borderlands, 1821–1865*. Baton Rouge: Louisiana State University Press, 2010.

Kessell, John L. *Spain in the Southwest: A Narrative History of Colonial New Mexico, Arizona, Texas, and California*. Norman: University of Oklahoma Press, 2003.

Kessell, John L., and Rick Hendricks, eds. *By Force of Arms: The Journals of Don Diego de Vargas*. Albuquerque: University of New Mexico Press, 1992.

Khlebnikov, Kyrill T. *Colonial Russian America: Kyrill T. Khlebnikov's Reports, 1817–1832*. Translated by Basil Dmytryshyn and E. A. P. Crownhart-Vaughan. Portland: Oregon Historical Society, 1976.

Kicza, John E. *Colonial Entrepreneurs: Families and Business in Bourbon Mexico City*. Albuquerque: University of New Mexico Press, 1983.

———. *Resilient Cultures: America's Native Peoples Confront European Colonization, 1500–1800*. Upper Saddle River, NJ: Prentice-Hall, 2003.

Kiple, Kenneth F., ed. *The Cambridge World History of Human Disease*. New York: Cambridge University Press, 1993.

Kiple, Kenneth F., and Stephen V. Beck, eds. *Biological Consequences of the European Expansion, 1450–1800*. Brookfield, VT: Ashgate, 1997.

Kirk, Sylvia Van. *Many Tender Ties: Women in Fur-Trade Society, 1670–1870*. Norman: University of Oklahoma Press, 1980.

Kishlansky, Mark. *A Monarchy Transformed: Britain, 1603–1714*. New York: Penguin, 1996.

Klein, Herbert S. *The Atlantic Slave Trade*. New York: Cambridge University Press, 1999.

Knaut, Andrew L. *The Pueblo Revolt of 1680: Conquest and Resistance in Seventeenth-Century New Mexico*. Norman: University of Oklahoma Press, 1997.

Knight, Franklin W. "The Haitian Revolution." *American Historical Review* 105 (2000): 103–15.

Kristiansen, Kristian, and Thomas Larsson. *The Rise of Bronze Age Society: Travels, Transmissions, and Transformations*. Cambridge, UK: Cambridge University Press, 2005.

Kohn, Martin. "South to Freedom: The Underground Railroad Also Led to Mexico." *Humanities* 34, no. 2 (March/April 2013), https://www.neh.gov/humanities/2013/marchapril/statement/south-freedom.

Kubler, George. "Mexican Urbanism in the Sixteenth Century." *Art Bulletin* 24 (1942): 160–71.

Kuitems, Wallace M., Birgitta L. Wallace, Charles Lindsay, Andrea Scifo, Petra Doeve, Kevin Jenkins, Susanne Lindauer, Pınar Erdil, et al. "Evidence for European Presence in the Americas in AD 1021." *Nature* 601 (2021): 388–91.

Kulikoff, Allan. *From British Peasants to Colonial American Farmers*. Chapel Hill: University of North Carolina Press, 2000.

———. *Tobacco and Slaves: The Development of Southern Cultures in the Chesapeake, 1680–1800*. Chapel Hill: University of North Carolina Press, 1986.

Lamb, H. H. "The Early Medieval Warm Epoch and Its Sequel." *Palaeogeography, Palaeoclimatology, Palaeoecology* 1 (1965): 13–37.

Lamb, W. Kaye, ed. *The Journals and Letters of Sir Alexander Mackenzie*. Cambridge, UK: Cambridge University Press, 1970.

Lambert, Frank. *The Barbary Wars: American Independence in the Atlantic World*. New York: Hill and Wang, 2005.

Landes, David. *The Wealth and Poverty of Nations: Why Some Are So Rich and Some So Poor*. New York: W. W. Norton, 1998.

Landsman, Ned C. *Scotland and Its First American Colony, 1683–1765*. Princeton, NJ: Princeton University Press, 1985.

Langguth, A. J. *Union 1812: The Americans Who Fought the Second War of Independence*. New York: Simon and Schuster, 2006.

Langley, Lester D. *America and the Americas: The United States in the Western Hemisphere*. Athens: University of Georgia Press, 1989.

Larsen, Laurence M. "The Church in North America (Greenland) in the Middle Ages." *Catholic Historical Review* 5 (1919): 175–94.

Las Casas, Bartolomé de. *A Short Account of the Destruction of the Indies*. Translated and edited by Nigel Griffin. 1552. Reprint, London: Penguin Classics, 2004.

Leach, Douglas Edward. *Arms for Empire: A Military History of the British Colonies in North America, 1607–1763*. New York: Macmillan, 1973.

———. *Flintlock and Tomahawk: New England in King Philip's War*. New York: Macmillan, 1958.

LeBlanc, Steven. *Prehistoric Warfare in the American Southwest*. Salt Lake City: University of Utah Press, 1999.

Ledyard, John. *A Journal of Captain Cook's Last Voyage to the Pacific Ocean, and in Quest of a North-West Passage, between Asia and America*. Hartford, CT: Nathaniel Patten, 1783.

Lee, Wayne, ed. *Warfare and Culture in World History*. New York: New York University Press, 2011.

Lekson, Stephen H. "War in the Southwest, War in the World." *American Antiquity* 67 (October 2002): 607–24.

León-Portilla, Miguel. *Aztec Thought and Culture*. Norman: University of Oklahoma Press, 1990.

———. *The Broken Spears: The Aztec Account of the Conquest of Mexico*. Translated by Lysander Kemp. 1959. Boston: Beacon Press, 1962.

Lepore, Jill Lepore. *The Name of War: King Philip's War and the Origins of American Identity*. New York: Knopf, 1998.

Livi-Bacci, Massimo. *Conquest: The Destruction of the American Indios*. Translated by Carl Ipsen. Malden, MA: Polity Press, 2008.

———. *The Population of Europe: A History*. Translated by Cynthia De Nardi Ipsen and Carl Ipsen. Oxford: Blackwell, 2000.

Lockhart, James. *The Nahuas after the Conquest: A Social and Cultural History of the Indians of Central Mexico, Sixteenth through Eighteenth-Centuries*. Stanford, CA: Stanford University Press, 1992.

Lockridge, Kenneth A. *Literacy in Colonial New England: An Inquiry into the Social Context of Literacy in the Early Modern West*. New York: W. W. Norton, 1974.

Lloyd, Trevor O. *The British Empire, 1558–1983*. New York: Oxford University Press, 1984.

Lovejoy, David S. *The Glorious Revolution in America*. New York: Harper and Row, 1972.

Lovejoy, Paul. *Transformations in Slavery: A History of Slavery in Africa*. 2nd ed. Cambridge, UK: Cambridge University Press, 2000.

Lynch, John. *Spain, 1516–1598: From Nation State to World Empire*. Oxford, UK: Basil Blackwell, 1992.

———. *Spain under the Hapsburgs*. Vol. 2., *Spain and America, 1598–1700*. Oxford, UK: Basil Blackwell, 1969.

McCaa, Robert. "Paleodemography: From Ancient Times to Colonialism and Beyond." In *The Backbone of History: Health and Nutrition in the Western Hemisphere*, edited by Richard H. Steckel and Jerome C. Rose, 94–124. Cambridge, UK: University of Cambridge, 2002.

———. "The Peopling of Mexico from Origins to Revolution." In *The Population History of North America*, edited by Michael R. Haines and Richard H. Steckel, 241–304. Cambridge, UK: University of Cambridge, 2002.

McCoy, Drew. *The Elusive Republic: Political Economy in Jeffersonian America*. Chapel Hill: University of North Carolina Press, 1980.

McCullough, David. *The Pioneers: The Heroic Story of the Settlers Who Brought the American Ideal West*. New York: Simon and Schuster, 2019.

McCusker, John J., and Russell R. Menard. *The Economy of British America, 1607–1789*. Chapel Hill: University of North Carolina Press, 1985.

McDermott, John Francis. *The Spanish in the Mississippi Valley, 1762–1804*. Urbana: University of Illinois Press, 1974.

MacDonald, David. *The Lives of Fort de Chartres: Commandants, Soldiers, and Civilians in French Illinois, 1720–1770*. Carbondale: Southern Illinois University Press, 2016.

McGhee, Robert. "Canada Y1K: The First Millennium." *Beaver*, 1999–2000, 9–17.

McIlwraith, Thomas F., and Edward K. Muller, eds. *North America: The Historical Geography of a Changing Continent*. 2nd ed. Lanham, MD: Rowman and Littlefield, 2001.

MacLachlan, Colin A., and Jaime E. Rodríguez O., eds. *The Forging of the Cosmic Race: A Reinterpretation of Colonial Mexico*. Berkeley: University of California Press, 1980.

McInnis, Marvin. "The Population of Canada in the Nineteenth Century." In *A Population History of North America*, edited by Michael Haines and Richard Steckel, 371–432. Cambridge, UK: Cambridge University Press, 2000.

McNeill, John Robert. *Atlantic Empires of France and Spain: Louisbourg and Havana, 1700–1763*. Chapel Hill: University of North Carolina Press, 1985.

McNeill, William H. "The Age of Gunpowder Empires, 1450–1800." Washington, DC: American Historical Association, 1989.

———. *Plagues and Peoples*. New York: Doubleday, 1977.

Maddison, Angus. *The World Economy: Historical Statistics*. Paris: Organization of Economic Co-operation and Development, 2003.

Malone, Dumas. *American Origins to 1789*. New York: Appleton-Century-Crofts, 1960.

Malone, Patrick M. *The Skulking Way of War: Technology and Tactics among the New England Indians*. New York: Madison, 1991.

Malotki, Ekkehart, and Ellen Dissanayake. *Early Rock Art of the American West*. Seattle: University of Washington Press, 2018.

Makarova, Raisa V. *Russians on the Pacific, 1743–1799*. Translated by Richard A. Pierce and Alton S. Donnelly. Kingston, ON: Limestone Press, 1975.

Manchester, William. *A World Lit Only by Fire: The Medieval Mind and the Renaissance; Portrait of an Age*. New York: Back Bay , 1992.

Mann, Charles. *1491: New Revelations of the Americas before Columbus*. New York: Knopf, 2005.

———. *1493: Uncovering the New World Columbus Created*. New York: Knopf, 2011.

Mann, Michael. *The Sources of Social Power*. 6 vols. Vol. 1, *A History of Power from the Beginning to AD 1760*; vol. 2, *The Rise of Classes and Nation States, 1760–1914*; vol. 3, *Global Empires and Revolution, 1890–1945*; vol. 4, *Globalizations, 1945–2011*. Cambridge, UK: Cambridge University Press, 1986–2012.

Manning, Richard. *Against the Grain: How Agriculture Hijacked Civilization*. New York: North Point Press, 2005.

Mapp, Paul W. *The Elusive West and the Contest for Empire, 1713–1763*. Chapel Hill: University of North Carolina Press, 2011.

Marcus, Geoffrey J. *The Conquest of the North Atlantic*. New York: Oxford University Press, 1981.

Mariscal, Elisa, and Kenneth Sokoloff. "Schooling, Suffrage, and the Persistence of Inequality in the Americas, 1800–1945." In *Political Institutions and Economic Growth in Latin America: Essays in Policy, History, and Political Economy*, edited by Stephen Haber, 159–218. Stanford, CA: Hoover Institution Press, 2000.

Martel, Heather. *Deadly Virtue: Fort Caroline and the Early Protestant Roots of American Whiteness.* Gainesville: University Press of Florida. 2019.

Martin, Paul S., and Richard G. Klein, eds. *Quaternary Extinctions: A Prehistoric Revolution.* Tucson: University of Arizona Press, 1984.

Martínez, Bernardo García. "Encomenderos españoles y *British residents:* El sistema de dominio indirecto desde la perspectiva Novohispana." *Historia Mexicana* 60 (2011): 1915–78.

Martinez, Oscar J. *Mexico's Uneven Development: The Geographical and Historical Context of Inequality.* New York: Routledge, 2015.

Marshall, P. J., ed. *The Oxford History of the British Empire.* Vol. 2, *The Eighteenth Century.* New York: Oxford University Press, 1998.

May, Ernest R. *The Making of the Monroe Doctrine.* Cambridge, MA: Belknap Press, 1975.

May, Henry F. *The Enlightenment in America.* New York: Oxford University Press, 1976.

Meinig, D. W. *Atlantic America, 1492–1800.* Vol. 1 of *The Shaping of America: A Geographical Perspective on 500 Years of History.* New Haven, CT: Yale University Press, 1986–98.

———. *Southwest: Three Peoples in Geographical Change, 1600–1970.* New York: Oxford University Press, 1971.

Meltzer, David J. *First Peoples in a New World: Colonizing Ice Age America.* Berkeley: University of California Press, 2009.

Melville, Elinor G. K. *A Plague of Sheep: Environmental Consequences of the Conquest of Mexico.* New York: Cambridge University Press, 1994.

Melvoin, Richard I. *New England Outpost: War and Society in Colonial Deerfield.* New York: W. W. Norton, 1989.

Merkel, William G. "Jefferson's Failed Anti-Slavery Proviso of 1784 and the Nascence of Free Soil Constitutionalism." *Seton Hall Law Review* 38, no. 2 (2008): 555–603, https://ssrn.com/abstract=1123973.

Merrell, James H. *The Indians' New World: Catawbas and Their Neighbors from European Contact Through the Era of Removal.* Chapel Hill: University of North Carolina Press, 1989.

———. "Some Thoughts on Colonial Historians and American Indians." *William and Mary Quarterly* 46 (1989): 94–119.

Meyer, Roy W. *The Village Indians of the Upper Missouri: The Mandans, Hidatsas, and Arikaras.* Lincoln: University of Nebraska Press, 1977.

Middleton, Richard. *Cornwallis: Soldier and Statesman in a Revolutionary World.* New Haven, CT: Yale University Press, 2022.

Miller, D. Shane. *From Colonization to Domestication: Population, Environment, and the Origins of Agriculture in Eastern North America.* Salt Lake City: University of Utah Press, 2018.

Miller, John Chester. *The Wolf by the Ears: Thomas Jefferson and Slavery.* New York: Free Press, 1977.

Miller, J. R. *Skyscrapers Hide the Heavens: A History of Indian White Relations in Canada.* Rev. ed. Toronto: University of Toronto Press, 1991.

Miller, Shawn William. *An Environmental History of Latin America*. New York: Cambridge University Press, 2007.

Millet, Allen R., Peter Maslowski, and William B. Feis. *For the Common Defense: A Military History of the United States from 1607 to 2012*. New York: Free Press, 2012

Milner, Marc. *Canada's Navy: The First Century*. 2nd ed. Toronto: University of Toronto Press, 2010.

Moheit, Ulrike, ed. *Alexander von Humboldt: Briefe aus Amerika, 1799–1804*. Berlin: Akademie, 1993.

Monaghan, E. Jennifer. *Learning to Read and Write in Colonial America*. Amherst: University of Massachusetts Press, 2005.

Monroe, Paul. *Founding of the American Public-School System: A History of Education in the United States, from the Early Settlements to the Close of the Civil War Period*. New York: Macmillan, 1943.

Moogk, Peter N. "Reluctant Exiles: Emigrants from France in Canada before 1760." *William and Mary Quarterly* 46 (1989): 463–505.

Moore, Dennis D., ed. *Letters from an American Farmer and Other Essays: J. Hector St. John de Crèvecoeur*. Cambridge: Harvard University Press, 2012.

Mooney, James. "The Aboriginal Population of America North of Mexico." *Smithsonian Miscellaneous Collections* 80, no. 7 (1928): 1–40.

Morales, Francisco. "The Native Encounter with Christianity: Franciscans and Nahuas In Sixteenth-Century Mexico." *Americas* 65 (2008): 137–59.

Moreno-Estrada, Andrés, Christopher R. Gignoux, Juan Carlos Fernández-López, Fouad Zakharia, Martin Sikora, Alejandra V. Contreras, Victor Acuña-Alonzo, Karla Sandoval, et al. "The Genetics of Mexico Recapitulates Native American Substructure and Affects Biomedical Traits." *Science* 344 (2014): 1280–85.

Morgan, Edmund S. *American Slavery, American Freedom: The Ordeal of Colonial Virginia*. New York: W. W. Norton, 1975.

———. *Inventing the People: The Rise of Popular Sovereignty in England and America*. New York: W. W. Norton, 1988.

———. *The Puritan Dilemma: The Story of John Winthrop*. Boston: Little, Brown, 1958.

Morgan, Lewis Henry. *Ancient Society, or Researchers in the Lines of Human Progress from Savagery through Barbarism to Civilization*. New York: Henry Holt, 1877.

Morton, Desmond. *A Military History of Canada*. Toronto: McClelland and Stewart, 2007.

Morison, Samuel Eliot. *The European Discovery of America: The Southern Voyages*. New York: Oxford University Press, 1974.

———. *The Great Explorers: The European Discovery of America*. New York: Oxford University Press, 1978.

Morris, Ian. *The Measure of Civilization: How Social Development Decides the Fate of Nations*. Princeton, NJ: University of Princeton Press, 2013.

———. *War! What Is It Good For?: Conflict and the Progress of Civilization, from Primates to Robots*. New York: Farrar, Straus and Giroux, 2014.

———. *Why the West Rules—For Now: The Patterns of History, and What They Reveal about the Future.* New York: Farrar, Straus, and Giroux, 2010.

Munroe, John A. *Colonial Delaware: A History.* Millwood, NY: KTO, 1978.

Murrin, John M. "Beneficiaries of Catastrophe: The English Colonies in America." In *The New American History,* edited by Eric Foner, 3–23. Philadelphia: Temple University Press, 1997.

Murphy, Terrence, and Roberto Perrin, eds. *A Concise History of Religion in Canada.* Don Mills, ON: Oxford University Press, 1996.

Nabhan, Gary Paul. *Gathering the Desert.* Tucson: University of Arizona Press, 1985.

Nadeau, Kathleen. *The History of the Philippines.* Westport, CT: Greenwood Press, 2008.

Naroll, Raoul. "A Preliminary Index of Social Development." *American Anthropologist* 58 (1956): 687–715.

Nash, Gary B. *Red, White, and Black: The Peoples of Early America.* Englewood Cliffs, NJ: Prentice-Hall, 1982.

Nash, Gerald D. *The American West in the Twentieth Century: A Short History of an Urban Oasis.* Englewood Cliffs, NJ: Prentice-Hall, 1973.

Nabokov, Peter, and Dean Snow. "Farmers of the Woodlands." In *America in 1492: The World of the Indian Peoples before the Arrival of Columbus,* edited by Alvin M. Josephy Jr., 119–46. New York: Knopf, 1992.

Nesvig, Martin Austin. *Ideology and Inquisition: The World of the Censors in Early Mexico.* New Haven, CT: Yale University Press, 2009.

Noll, Mark A., David W. Bebbington, and George A. Rawlyk, eds. *Evangelicalism: Comparative Studies of Popular Protestantism in North America, the British Isles, and Beyond, 1700–1990.* New York: Oxford University Press, 1994.

Norrie, Kenneth, and Douglas Owram. *A History of the Canadian Economy.* Toronto: Harcourt Brace Jovanovich, 1991.

Norwich, John Julius. *A History of Venice.* New York: Knopf, 1982.

Nostrand, Richard L. "The Spanish Borderlands." In *North America: The Historical Geography of a Changing Continent,* edited by Thomas F. McIlwraith and Edward K. Muller, 47–63. Lanham, MD: Rowman and Littlefield, 2001.

Novick, Peter. *That Noble Dream: The "Objectivity Question" and the American Historical Association.* Cambridge, UK: Cambridge University Press, 1988.

Obeyesekere, Gananath. *The Apotheosis of Captain Cook: European Mythmaking in the Pacific.* Princeton, NJ: Princeton University Press, 1997.

O'Brien, Michael J., and R. Lee Lyman. "Evolutionary Archaeology: Current Status and Future Prospects." *Evolutionary Archaeology* 11 (2002): 26–36.

Offner, Jerome A. "On the Inapplicability of 'Oriental Despotism' and the 'Asiatic Mode of Production' to the Aztecs of Texcoco." *American Antiquity* 46 (1981): 43–61.

Okie, William Thomas. *Georgia Peach: Culture, Agriculture, and Environment in the American South.* New York: Cambridge University Press, 2016.

Olko, Justyna, and John Sullivan. "Toward a Comprehensive Model for Nahuatl Language Research and Revitalization." *Proceedings of the Fortieth Annual Meeting of the Berkeley Linguistics Society* 40 (2014): 369–97.

Olmstead, Alan L., and Paul W. Rhode. *Creating Abundance: Biological Innovation and American Agricultural Development.* Cambridge, UK: Cambridge University Press, 2008.

Ong, Walter J. *Orality and Literacy: The Technologizing of the Word.* 1982. London: Routledge, 2002.

Onuf, Peter S. *The Mind of Thomas Jefferson.* Charlottesville: University of Virginia Press, 2007.

Onuf, Peter S., and Nicholas P. Cole, eds. *Thomas Jefferson, the Classical World, and Early America.* Charlottesville: University of Virginia Press, 2011.

Oster, Jerry." 'To Extirpate the Indians': An Indigenous Consciousness of Genocide in the Ohio Valley and Lower Great Lakes, 1750s–1810." *William and Mary Quarterly* 72 (2015): 587–622.

Otis, Delos Sacket. *The Dawes Act and the Allotment of Indian Lands.* Norman: University of Oklahoma Press, 1973.

Pardo, Osvaldo F. *The Origins of Mexican Catholicism: Nahua Rituals and Christian Sacraments in Sixteenth-Century Mexico.* Ann Arbor: University of Michigan, 2004.

Paré, Madeline Ferrin, with Bert M. Fireman. *Arizona Pageant: A Short History of the 48th State.* Tempe: Arizona Historical Foundation, 1970.

Parker, Geoffrey. *The Military Revolution: Military Innovation and the Rise of the West.* 1988. Reprint, Cambridge, UK: Cambridge University Press, 1996.

Parkes, Henry Bamford. *A History of Mexico.* 1938. Reprint, Boston: Houghton Mifflin, 1969.

Parkin, Jon. *Taming the Leviathan: The Reception of the Political and Religious Ideas of Thomas Hobbes in England, 1640–1700.* Cambridge, UK: Cambridge University Press, 2007.

Parkman, Francis. *La Salle and the Discovery of the Great West.* 1879. Reprint, Boston: Little, Brown, 1907.

——— . *Montcalm and Wolfe: France and England in North America.* 2 vols. Boston: Little, Brown, 1910.

Parry, J. H. *The Age of Reconnaissance: Discovery, Exploration and Settlement, 1450–1650.* Berkeley: University of California Press, 1981.

——— . "The Audiencia of New Galicia in the Sixteenth Century." *Cambridge Historical Journal* 6 (1940): 267.

——— . *The Discovery of the Sea.* Berkeley: University of California Press, 1974.

——— . *The Spanish Seaborne Empire.* New York: Knopf, 1966.

Paz, Octavio. *The Labyrinth of Solitude; The Other Mexico; Return to the Labyrinth of Solitude; Mexico and the United States; The Philanthropic Ogre.* Translated by Lysander Kemp, Yara Milos, and Rachel Phillips Belash. New York: Grove Press, 1985.

Palmer, R. R. *The Age of the Democratic Revolution: A Political History of Europe and America, 1760–1800, Vol. 1: The Challenge.* Princeton, NJ: Princeton University Press, 1959.

Pauketat, Timothy R., and Thomas E. Emerson. *Cahokia: Domination and Ideology in the Mississippian World.* Lincoln: University of Nebraska Press, 1997.

Pencak, William, and Conrad Edick Wright, eds. *Authority and Resistance in Early New York*. New York: New-York Historical Society, 1988.

Perkins, Dexter. *The Monroe Doctrine, 1823–1826*. Cambridge, MA: Harvard University Press, 1927.

———. *The Monroe Doctrine, 1826–1867*. Baltimore, MD: John Hopkins Press, 1933.

Perry, Mary Elizabeth, and Anne J. Cruz, eds. *Cultural Encounters: The Impact of the Inquisition in Spain and the New World*. Berkeley: University of California Press, 1991.

Phelan, John Leddy. *The Hispanization of the Philippines: Spanish Aims and Filipino Responses, 1565–1700*. Madison: University of Wisconsin Press, 1959.

———. *The Millennial Kingdom of the Franciscans in the New World*, 2nd rev. ed. Berkeley: University of California Press, 1970.

Phillips, William D., Jr., and Cara R. Phillips. *The Worlds of Christopher Columbus*. Cambridge, UK: Cambridge University Press, 1992.

Phillipson, Nicholas. *Adam Smith: An Enlightened Life*. New Haven, CT: Yale University Press, 2010.

Pike, Ruth. *Enterprise and Adventure: The Genoese in Seville and the Opening of the New World*. Ithaca, NY: Cornell University Press, 1966.

Pincus, Steve. *1688: The First Modern Revolution*. New Haven, CT: Yale University Press, 2010.

Pinker, Steven. *Enlightenment Now: The Case for Reason, Science, Humanism, and Progress*. New York: Viking Penguin, 2018.

Pletcher, David. *The Diplomacy of Annexation: Texas, Oregon, and the Mexican War*. New York: Columbia University Press, 1973.

Pohl, John. *Aztec Warrior, AD 1325–1521*. Oxford: Osprey, 2001.

Pomeroy, Earl S. *The Pacific Slope: A History of California, Oregon, Washington, Idaho, Utah, and Nevada*. New York: Knopf, 1965.

Poole, Stafford. *Our Lady of Guadalupe: The Origins and Sources of a Mexican National Symbol, 1531–1797*. Tucson: University of Arizona Press, 1995.

Porter, John. *The Vertical Mosaic: An Analysis of Social Class and Power in Canada*. 1965. Reprint, Toronto: University of Toronto Press, 2015.

Porter, Roy. *Gibbon: Making History*. New York: St. Martin's Press, 1988.

Prebble, John. *The Darien Disaster: A Scots Colony in the New World, 1698–1700*. New York: Holt, Rinehart, and Winston, 1969.

Prescott, William H. *History of the Conquest of Mexico, with a Preliminary View of the Ancient Mexican Civilization, and the Life of the Conqueror, Hernando Cortes*. 2 vols. 6th ed. London: Richard Bentley, 1850.

Prince, J. L. *The Dutch Republic in the Seventeenth Century*. New York: St. Martin's Press, 1998.

Prucha, Francis Paul. *The Great Father: The United States and the American Indians*. Lincoln: University of Nebraska Press, 1984.

———. *The Sword of the Republic: The United States Army on the Frontier, 1783–1846*. Bloomington: Indian University Press, 1977.

Pyne, Stephen J. *Dutton's Point: An Intellectual History of the Grand Canyon*. Grand Canyon, AZ: Grand Canyon Natural History Association, 1982.

———. *The Great Ages of Discovery: How Western Civilization Learned about a Wider World*. Tucson: University of Arizona Press, 2021.

Quaedackers, Esther. "A Case for Little Big Histories." In *The Routledge Companion to Big History*, edited by Craig Benjamin, Esther Quaedackers, and David Baker, 279–99. Abingdon, UK: Routledge, 2020.

Quinn, David B. *North America from Earliest Discovery to First Settlements: The Norse Voyages to 1612*. New York: Harper and Row, 1977.

Rabushka, Alvin. "The Colonial Roots of American Taxation, 1607–1700." *Policy Review*, August and September 2002, Hoover Institution. https://www.hoover.org/research/colonial-roots-american-taxation-1607-1700.

———. *Taxation in Colonial America*. Princeton, NJ: University of Princeton Press, 2008.

Raff, Jennifer. *Origin: A Genetic History of the Americas*. New York: Grand Central, 2022.

Ray, Arthur J. *Indians in the Fur Trade: Their Role as Trappers, Hunters, and Middlemen in the Lands Southwest of Hudson Bay, 1660–1870*. Toronto: University of Toronto Press, 1974.

Rebok, Sandra. *Humboldt and Jefferson: A Transatlantic Friendship of the Enlightenment*. Charlottesville: University of Virginia Press, 2014.

Rediker, Marcus. *Between the Devil and the Deep Blue Sea: Merchant Seamen, Pirates, and the Anglo-American Maritime World, 1700–1750*. New York: Cambridge University Press, 1987.

Reed, Erik K. "Transition to History in the Pueblo Southwest." *American Anthropologist* 56, no. 4 (1954): 592–97.

Reed, Nelson A. *The Caste War of Yucatán*. Rev. ed. Stanford, CA: Stanford University Press, 2001.

Reich, David, Nick Patterson, Desmond Campbell, Arti Tandon, Stéphane Mazières, Nicolas Ray, Maria V. Parra, et al. "Reconstructing Native American Population History." *Nature* 488 (2013): 370–74.

Reid, John G. *Acadia, Maine, and New Scotland: Marginal Colonies in the Seventeenth Century*. Toronto: University of Toronto Press, 1981.

Remini, Robert V. *The Legacy of Andrew Jackson: Essays on Democracy, Indian Removal, and Slavery*. Baton Rouge: Louisiana University Press, 1988.

Restall, Matthew. *The Maya World: Yucatec Culture and Society, 1550–1850*. Stanford, CA: Stanford University Press, 1997.

Rhodes, James Ford. "History." In *Annual Report of the American Historical Association*, 43–63. Washington, DC: Government Printing Office, 1899.

Ricard, Robert. *The Spiritual Conquest of Mexico: An Essay on the Apostolate and the Evangelizing Methods of the Mendicant Orders in New Spain, 1523–1572*. Translated by Lesley Byrd Simpson. 1933. Reprint, Berkeley: University of California Press, 1966.

Richards, John. *Unending Frontier: An Environmental History of the Early Modern World*. Berkeley: University of California Press, 2003.

Richter, Daniel K. *The Ordeal of the Longhouse: The Peoples of the Iroquois League in the Era of European Colonization*. Chapel Hill: University of North Carolina Press, 1992.

———. "War and Culture: The Iroquois Experience." *William and Mary Quarterly* 40 (1983): 528–59.

Riding, Alan. *Distant Neighbors: A Portrait of the Mexicans*. New York: Vintage, 1986.

Rink, Oliver A. *Holland on the Hudson: An Economic and Social History of Dutch New York*. Ithaca, NY: Cornell University Press, 1986.

Risen, Clay. *The Crowded Hour: Theodore Roosevelt, the Rough Riders, and the Dawn of the American Century*. New York: Scribner, 2019.

Roberts, Andrew. *The Last King of America: The Misunderstood Reign of George III*. New York: Viking, 2021.

Roberts, J. M. *The History of the World*. 6th ed. Oxford, UK: Oxford University Press, 2013.

Rodney, Walter. *How Europe Underdeveloped Africa*. London: Bogle-L'Ouverture, 1972.

Rodriguez, Lourdes Arencibia. *Charting the Future of Translation History*. Ottawa, ON: University of Ottawa Press, 2006.

Rodríguez O., Jaime E. "The Emancipation of America." *American Historical Review* 105 (2000): 131–52.

———. *The Evolution of the Mexican Political System*. Wilmington, DE: Scholarly Resources, 1993.

———. "The Hispanic Revolution: Spain and America, 1808–1826." *Ler Historia* 57 (2009): 73–92.

———. *The Independence of Spanish America*. Cambridge, UK: Cambridge University Press, 1998.

Rogers, Clifford, ed. *The Military Revolution Debate*. Boulder, CO: Westview Press, 1995.

Romoli, Kathleen. *Balboa of Darién: Discoverer of the Pacific*. New York: Doubleday, 1953.

Ronda, James P. *Astoria and Empire*. Lincoln: University of Nebraska Press, 1990.

Rosling, Hans, Ola Rosling, and Anna Rosling Rönnlund. *Factfulness: Ten Reasons We're Wrong about the World——and Why Things Are Better than You Think*. New York: Flatiron, 2018.

Rothenberg, Gunther. *The Napoleonic Wars*. London: Cassell, 2000.

Rostow, W. W. *The Stages of Economic Growth: A Non-Communist Manifesto*. Cambridge, UK: Cambridge University Press, 1960.

Rudd, Kevin. *The Avoidable War: The Dangers of a Catastrophic Conflict between the US and Xi Jinping's China*. New York: Public Affairs, 2022.

Ruskin, John. *The Stones of Venice*. 3 vols. 2nd ed. London: Smith, Elder, 1858–67.

Russell, Israel C. *North America*. New York: D. Appleton, 1904.

Russell, Peter. *Prince Henry "The Navigator": A Life*. New Haven, CT: Yale University Press, 2000.

Sachs, Aaron. *The Humboldt Current: Nineteenth-Century Exploration and the Roots of American Environmentalism*. New York: Viking, 2006.

Sahlins, Marshall. *Apologies to Thucydides: Understanding History as Culture and Vice Versa.* Chicago: University of Chicago Press, 2004.

———. *Historical Metaphors and Mythical Realities: Structure in the Early History of the Sandwich Islands Kingdom.* Ann Arbor: University of Michigan Press, 1981.

———. *Stone Age Economics.* Chicago: Aldine, 1972.

Salisbury, Neal. "The Indians' Old World: Native Americans and the Coming of Europeans." *William and Mary Quarterly* 53 (1996): 435–58.

———. *Manitou and Providence: Indians, Europeans, and the Making of New England, 1500–1643.* New York: Oxford University Press, 1982.

Salvucci, Richard J. "Capitalism and Dependency in Latin America." In *The Cambridge History of Capitalism,* edited by Larry Neal and Jeffrey G. Williamson, 1:1403–30. New York: Cambridge University Press, 2014.

———. *Textiles and Capitalism in Mexico: An Economic History of the Obrajes, 1539–1840.* Princeton, NJ: Princeton University Press, 1987.

Sanders, William, Jeffrey R. Parsons, and Robert S. Santley. *The Basin of Mexico: Ecological Processes in the Evolution of a Civilization.* New York: Academic Press, 1979.

Sarmiento, Domingo Faustino. *Facundo: Civilization and Barbarism.* Translated by Kathleen Ross. Berkeley: University of California Press, 2003.

Sauer, Carl O. *The Road to Cíbola.* Berkeley: University of California, 1932.

———. *Seventeenth Century North America.* Berkeley: Turtle Island, 1980.

———. *Sixteenth Century North America.* Berkeley: University of California Press, 1971.

Scarry, C. Margaret, and John F. Scarry. "Native American 'Garden Agriculture' in Southeastern North America." *World Archaeology* 37 (2005): 259–74.

Schroeder, Susan, ed. *Native Resistance and the Pax Colonial in New Spain.* Lincoln: University of Nebraska Press, 1997.

Schurz, William Lytle. *The Manila Galleon: The Romantic History of the Spanish Galleons Trading between Manila and Acapulco.* New York: E. P. Dutton, 1939.

Schwantes, Carlos A. *Columbia River: Gateway to the West.* Moscow, Idaho: University of Idaho Press, 2000.

Schwartz, Stuart, ed. *Implicit Understandings: Observing, Reporting, and Reflecting on the Encounters between Europeans and Other Peoples in the Early Modern Era.* New York: Cambridge University Press, 1994.

Scott, James C. *Against the Grain: A Deep History of the Earliest States.* New Haven, CT: Yale University Press, 2017.

Semo, Enrique. *The History of Capitalism in Mexico: Its Origins, 1521–1763.* Translated by Lidia Lozano. 1973. Reprint, Austin: University of Texas Press, 1993.

Service, Elman R. *Cultural Evolutionism: Theory in Practice.* New York: Holt, Rinehart and Winston, 1971.

Sexton, Jay. *The Monroe Doctrine: Empire and Nation in Nineteenth-Century America.* New York: Hill and Wang, 2011.

Shaffer, Lynda Norene. *Native Americans before 1492: The Moundbuilding Centers of the Eastern Woodlands.* Armonk, NY: M. E. Sharpe, 1992.

Sheehan, William, and John Westfall. *The Transits of Venus*. Amherst, MA: Prometheus, 2004.

Shelley, Percy Bysshe. *Rosalind and Helen, a Modern Eclogue; with Other Poems*. London: C. and J. Ollier, 1819.

Sheriff, Carol. *The Artificial River: The Erie Canal and the Paradox of Progress*. New York: Hill and Wang, 1996.

Sheridan, Richard B. *Sugar and Slavery: An Economic History of the British West Indies, 1623–1775*. Baltimore: Johns Hopkins University Press, 1973.

Sherratt, Andrew. "Plough and Pastoralism: Aspects of the Secondary Products Revolution." In *Pattern of the Past: Studies in Honour of David Clarke*, edited by Ian Hodder, Glynn Issac, and Norman Hammond, 261–305. Cambridge, UK: Cambridge University Press, 1981.

Shorto, Russell. *The Island at the Center of the World: The Epic Story of Dutch Manhattan and the Forgotten Colony That Shaped America*. New York: Vintage, 2005.

Silver, Timothy. *A New Face on the Countryside: Indians, Colonists, and Slaves in South Atlantic Forests, 1500–1800*. New York: Cambridge University Press, 1990.

Simmons, Marc. *The Last Conquistador: Juan de Oñate and the Settling of the Far Southwest*. Norman: University of Oklahoma Press, 1991.

Smith, Adam. *An Inquiry into the Nature and Causes of the Wealth of Nations*. Edited by Edwin Cannan. 1776. Reprint, New York: Modern Library, 1937.

Smith, Barbara Sweetland, and Redmond J. Barnett, eds. *Russian America: The Forgotten Frontier*. Tacoma: Washington State Historical Society, 1990.

Smith, Daniel Blake. "Mortality and Family in the Colonial Chesapeake." *Journal of Interdisciplinary History* 8 (1978): 403–27.

Smith, G. Hubert, and W. Raymond Wood, eds. *The Explorations of the La Vérendryes in the Northern Plains, 1738–43*. Lincoln: University of Nebraska Press, 1980.

Smith, Jeffrey S. "North America's Colonial European Roots, 1492 to 1867." In *North American Odyssey: Historical Geographies for the Twenty-First Century*, edited by Craig E. Colten and Geoffrey L. Buckley, 30–37. Lanham, MD: Rowman and Littlefield, 2014.

Smith, Michael. *The Aztecs*. 3rd ed. Oxford: Blackwell, 2011.

Snow, C. P. *The Two Cultures and the Scientific Revolution*. 1959. Reprint, Cambridge, UK: Cambridge University Press, 1998.

Snow, Dean R. *The Iroquois*. Cambridge, MA: Blackwell, 1994.

Spalding, Phinizy. *Oglethorpe in Perspective: Georgia's Founder after Two Hundred Years*. Tuscaloosa: University of Alabama Press, 2009.

Sobel, Mechal. *The World They Made Together: Black and White Values in Eighteenth-Century Virginia*. Princeton, NJ: Princeton University Press, 1987.

Sosin, Jack M. *English America and the Revolution of 1688*. Lincoln: University of Nebraska Press, 1982.

Spence, Jonathan D. *The Memory Palace of Matteo Ricci.* New York: Viking, 1984.

Spicer, Edward H. *Cycles of Conquest: The Impact of Spain, Mexico, and the United States on the Indians of the Southwest, 1533–1960.* Tucson: University of Arizona Press, 1962.

Springborg, Patricia, ed. *The Cambridge Companion to Hobbes's "Leviathan."* Cambridge, UK: Cambridge University Press, 2007.

Stanley, George F. G. *New France: The Last Phase, 1744–1760.* Toronto: McClelland and Stewart, 1968.

———. *The War of 1812: Land Operations.* Toronto: Macmillan, 1983.

Stannard, David. *American Holocaust: The Conquest of the New World.* New York: Oxford University Press, 1993.

Starr, Kevin. *Continental Ambitions: Roman Catholics in North America–The Colonial Experience.* San Francisco: Ignatius, 2016.

Steckel, Richard H., and Jerome C. Rose, eds. *The Backbone of History: Health and Nutrition in the Western Hemisphere.* Cambridge, UK: University of Cambridge, 2002.

Steele, Ian K. *Warpaths: Invasions of North America.* New York: Oxford University Press, 1994.

Stegner, Wallace. *Beyond the Hundredth Meridian: John Wesley Powell and the Second Opening of the West.* Boston: Houghton, Mifflin, 1954.

Steller, Georg Wilhelm. *Journal of a Voyage with Bering, 1741–1742.* Edited by O. W. Frost. Translated by Margritt A. Engel and O. W. Frost. Stanford, CA: Stanford University Press, 1988.

Stern, Steve J. "Latin America's Colonial History: Invitation to an Agenda." *Latin American Perspectives* 12 (1985): 3–16.

———. "The Rise and Fall of Indian-White Alliances: A Regional View of 'Conquest' History." *Hispanic American Historical Review* 61 (1981): 461–91.

Stewart, Gordon T. *The Origins of Canadian Politics: A Comparative Approach.* Vancouver: University of British Columbia Press, 1986.

Stone, Lawrence, ed. *An Imperial State at War: Britain from 1689 to 1815.* New York: Routledge, 1994.

St-Onge, Nicole, Carolyn Podruchny, and Brenda Macdougall, eds. *Contours of a People: Metis Family, Mobility, and History.* Norman: University of Oklahoma Press, 2014.

Stout, Harry S., and D. G. Hart, eds. *New Directions in American Religious History.* New York: Oxford University Press, 1997.

Swift, Jonathan. *The Battle of the Books and Other Short Pieces.* 1704. Reprint, London: Cassell, 1891.

Sugden, John. *For God, Country and Booty: Sir Francis Drake.* New York: Henry Holt, 1991.

Sugiyama, Saburo. *Human Sacrifice, Militarism, and Rulership: Materialization of State Ideology at the Feathered Serpent Pyramid, Teotihuacán.* Cambridge, UK: Cambridge University Press, 2005.

Szasz, Ferenc Morton. *Scots in the North American West, 1709–1917.* Norman: University of Oklahoma Press, 2000.

Talese, Gay. *The Bridge.* New York: Harper and Row, 1964.

Taylor, Alan. *American Colonies: The Settling of North America.* New York: Penguin, 2001.

Taylor, R. E., A. Long, and R. Kra, eds. *Radiocarbon Dating after Four Decades.* Tucson: University of Arizona Press, 1992.

Taylor, William B., and Franklin Pease, eds. *Violence, Resistance, and Survival in the Americas: Native Americans and the Legacy of Conquest.* Washington, DC: Smithsonian Institution Press, 1994.

Teja, Jesús F. de la. *San Antonio de Bexar: A Community on New Spain's Northern Frontier.* Albuquerque: University of New Mexico Press, 1995.

Thomas, Evan. *John Paul Jones: Sailor, Hero, Father of the American Navy.* New York: Simon and Schuster, 2003.

Thomas, Hugh. *Conquest: Cortés, Montezuma, and the Fall of Old Mexico.* New York: Simon and Schuster, 1993.

Thompson, Mark L. *The Contest for the Delaware Valley: Allegiance, Identity, and Empire in the Seventeenth Century.* Baton Rouge: Louisiana State University Press, 2013.

Thornton, John. *Africa and Africans in the Making of the Atlantic World, 1400–1680.* New York: Cambridge University Press, 1992.

Tilly, Charles, ed. *The Formation of National States in Western Europe.* Princeton, NJ: Princeton University Press, 1975.

Toll, Ian W. *Six Frigates: The Epic History of the Founding of the U.S. Navy.* New York: W. W. Norton, 2006.

Tomasson, Richard F. *Iceland: The First New Society.* Minneapolis: University of Minnesota Press, 1980.

Tovell, Freeman M. *At the Far Reaches of Empire: The Life of Juan Francisco de la Bodega y Quadra.* Vancouver: University of British Columbia Press, 2008.

Townsend, Camilla. *Fifth Sun: A New History of the Aztecs.* Oxford, UK: Oxford University Press, 2019.

Trigger, Bruce G. "Early Native North American Responses to European Contact." *Journal of American History* 77 (1991): 1195–1215.

——. *Natives and Newcomers: Canada's "Heroic Age" Reconsidered.* Montreal: McGill–Queen's University Press, 1986.

Trigger, Bruce G., and Wilcomb E. Washburn, eds. *The Cambridge History of the Native Peoples of the Americas.* Vol. 1, *North America*, pt. 1. New York: Cambridge University Press, 1996.

Trudel, Marcel. *Canada's Forgotten Slaves: Two Hundred Years of Bondage.* Translated by George Tombs. Montreal: Véhicule, 2013.

Turchin, Peter. *Historical Dynamics: Why States Rise and Fall.* Princeton, NJ: Princeton University Press, 2003.

Tucker, Robert W., and David C. Hendrickson. *Empire of Liberty: The Statecraft of Thomas Jefferson.* New York: Oxford University Press, 1992.

Turner, Christy G., and Jacqueline A. Turner, *Man Corn: Cannibalism and Violence in the Prehistoric Southwest.* Salt Lake City: University of Utah Press, 1999.

Turner, Frederick Jackson. "The Significance of the Frontier in American History."
In *Annual Report of the American Historical Association for 1893*, 197–227.
Washington, DC: Government Printing Office, 1894.

Tylor, Edward B. *Primitive Culture: Researchers into the Development of Mythology,
Philosophy, Religion, Art, and Custom.* Vol 1. 1871. Reprint, New York: Harper
and Row, 1958.

Ubelaker, Douglas H. "Population Size: Contact to Nadir." In *Handbook of North
American Indians,* edited by Douglas H. Ubelaker, 3:694–701. Washington,
DC: Smithsonian Institution, 2006.

Uglow, Jenny. *The Lunar Men: Five Friends whose Curiosity Changed the World.* New
York: Farrar, Straus and Giroux, 2002.

Usner, Daniel H., Jr. *Indians, Settlers, and Slaves in a Frontier Exchange Economy:
The Lower Mississippi Valley before 1783.* Chapel Hill: University of North Carolina Press, 1992.

Utley, Robert M., and Wilcomb E. Washburn. *The American Heritage History of the
Indian Wars.* New York: Simon and Schuster, 1977.

Vassberg, David E. *The Village and the Outside World in Golden Age Castile: Mobility
and Migration in Everyday Life.* Cambridge, UK: Cambridge University Press,
1996.

Vaughan, Alden T. *American Genesis: Captain John Smith and the Founding of Virginia.* Boston: Little, Brown, 1975.

Vaughan, Mary Kay. *Cultural Politics in Revolution: Teachers, Peasants, and Schools
in Mexico, 1930–1940.* Tucson: University of Arizona Press, 1997.

———. *The State, Education and Social Class in Mexico, 1880–1928.* Dekalb: Northern Illinois University Press, 1982.

Verano, John W., and Douglas H. Ubelaker. *Disease and Demography in the Americas.* Washington, DC: Smithsonian Institution Press, 1992.

Vigneras, Louis-André. *The Discovery of South America and the Andalusian Voyages.* Chicago: University of Chicago Press, 1976.

Villegas, Daniel Cosío, Ignacio Bernal, Alejandra Moreno Toscano, Luis González,
and Eduardo Blanquel. *A Compact History of Mexico.* Mexico City: El Colegio
de México, 1974.

Vincent, Theodore G. *The Legacy of Vincent Guerrero, Mexico's First Black President.*
Gainesville: University Press of Florida, 2001.

Wade, Lizzie. "Feeding the Gods: Hundreds of Skulls Reveal Massive Scale of Human Sacrifice in Aztec Capital." *Science* (American Association for the Advancement of Science), June 20, 2018.

Waldinger, Maria. "The Long-Run Effects of Missionary Orders in Mexico." *Journal
of Development Economics* 127 (July 2017): 355–78.

Waldram, James B., D. Ann Herring, and T. Kue Young, eds. *Aboriginal Health in
Canada: Historical, Cultural, and Epidemiological Perspectives.* 2nd ed. Toronto: University of Toronto Press, 2006.

Wallace, Anthony F. C. *The Death and Rebirth of the Seneca.* New York: Knopf, 1969.

Wallace, Ernest, and E. Adamson Hoebel. *The Commanches: Lords of the South
Plains.* Norman: University of Oklahoma Press, 1987.

Walls, Laura Dassow. *The Passage to Cosmos: Alexander von Humboldt and the Shaping of America.* Chicago: University of Chicago Press, 2009.

Walsh, Lorena S. "African American Colonial Population." In *A Population History of North America*, edited by Michael Haines and Richard Steckel, 191–240. Cambridge, UK: Cambridge University Press, 2000.

Walvin, James. *Black Ivory: A History of British Slavery.* London: HarperCollins, 1992.

Watts, Joseph, Oliver Sheehan, Quentin D. Atkinson, Joseph Bulbulia, and Russell D. Gray. "Ritual Human Sacrifice Promoted and Sustained the Evolution of Stratified Societies." *Nature* 532 (2016): 228–31.

Weber, David. *Myth and the History of the Hispanic Southwest.* Albuquerque: University of New Mexico Press, 1987.

———. *The Spanish Frontier in North America.* New Haven, CT: Yale University Press, 1992.

Weber, William. *Neither Victor nor Vanquished: America in the War of 1812.* Washington, DC: Potomac, 2013.

Webb, Walter Prescott. *The Great Plains.* 1931. Reprint, Lincoln: University of Nebraska Press, 1981.

Weckmann, Luis. *The Medieval Heritage of Mexico.* Translated by Frances M. Lopéz-Morillas. New York: Fordham University Press, 1992.

Weeks, William Earl. *John Quincy Adams and American Global Empire.* Lexington: University Press of Kentucky, 1992.

Wells, Peter. *The Barbarians Speak: How the Conquered Peoples Shaped Roman Europe.* Princeton, NJ: Princeton University Press, 1999.

Wells, Robert V. "The Population of England's Colonies in America: Old English or New Americans." *Population Studies* 46 (1992): 85–102

Weslager, C. A. *Dutch Explorers, Traders, and Settlers in the Delaware Valley, 1609–1664.* Philadelphia: University of Pennsylvania Press, 1961.

White, Richard. *The Middle Ground: Indians, Empires, and Republics in the Great Lakes Region, 1650–1815.* Cambridge, UK: Cambridge University Press, 1991.

———. *The Roots of Dependency: Subsistence, Environment, and Social Change among the Choctaws, Pawnees, and Navajos.* Lincoln: University of Nebraska Press, 1983.

White, Sam. *A Cold Welcome: The Little Ice Age and Europe's Encounter with North America.* Cambridge, MA: Harvard University Press, 2017.

Whiten, Andrew, Robert A. Hinde, Kevin Laland, and Christopher Brian Stringer. "Culture Evolves." *Philosophical Transactions of the Royal Society B: Biological Sciences* 366 (2011): 938–48.

Wilkie, James W., and Rebecca Horn. "An Interview with Woodrow Borah." *Hispanic American Historical Review* 65 (1985): 401–41.

Willey, Gordon R., and Philip Phillips, *Method and Theory in American Archaeology.* 1958. Reprint, Tuscaloosa: University of Alabama Press, 2016.

Williams, Eric. *Capitalism and Slavery.* Chapel Hill: University of North Carolina Press, 1944.

Williams, Glyn. *Voyages of Delusion: The Quest for the Northwest Passage.* New Haven, CT: Yale University Press, 2002.

Williams, Glyndwr. "The Pacific: Exploration and Exploitation." In *The Oxford History of the British Empire*, vol. 2, *The Eighteenth Century*, edited by P. J. Marshal, 552–75. New York: Oxford University Press, 1998.

Wills, Garry. *Inventing America: Jefferson's Declaration of Independence.* Garden City, NY: Doubleday, 1978.

Wilson, Gilbert L. *Buffalo Bird Woman's Garden: Agriculture of the Hidatsa Indians.* 1917. Reprint, St. Paul: Minnesota Historical Society Press, 1987.

Wilson, Thomas D. *The Oglethorpe Plan: Enlightenment Design in Savannah and Beyond.* Charlottesville: University of Virginia Press, 2012.

Withey, Lynne. *Voyages of Discovery: Captain Cook and the Exploration of the Pacific.* New York: William Morrow, 1987.

Wittfogel, Karl. *Oriental Despotism: A Comparative Study of Total Power.* New Haven, CT: Yale University Press, 1957.

Woodward, Colin. *American Nations: A History of the Eleven Rival Regional Cultures of North America.* New York: Penguin, 2011.

Wolf, Eric R. *Europe and the People without History.* Berkeley: University of California Press, 1969.

Wood, Gordon S. *Empire of Liberty: A History of the Early Republic, 1789–1815.* New York: Oxford University Press, 2009.

Wood, Peter H. *Black Majority: Negroes in Colonial South Carolina from 1670 through the Stono Rebellion.* New York: Knopf, 1974.

———. "La Salle: Discovery of a Lost Explorer." *American Historical Review* 89 (April 1984): 294–323.

Woods, Patricia Dillon. *French-Indian Relations on the Southern Frontier, 1699–1762.* Ann Arbor: UMI Research Press, 1980.

Woodward, C. Vann. "The Age of Reinterpretation." *American Historical Review* 66 (1960): 1–19.

Woodward, Margaret L. "The Spanish Army and the Loss of America, 1810–1824." *Hispanic American Historical Review*, 48 (1968): 586–607.

Worster, Donald. *Rivers of Empire: Water, Aridity, and the Growth of the American West.* New York: Pantheon, 1985.

Wright, Muriel H. "The Naming of the Mississippi River." *Chronicles of Oklahoma* 6 (1928): 529–30.

Wright, Robert. *Nonzero: The Logic of Human Destiny.* New York: Pantheon, 2000.

Wright, Ronald. *Stolen Continents: Conquest and Resistance in the Americas.* Toronto: Penguin, 2003.

Wroth, Lawrence C., ed. *The Voyages of Giovanni da Verrazzano, 1524–1528.* New Haven, CT: Yale University Press, 1970.

Yazawa, Melvin. *Representative Government and the Revolution: The Maryland Constitutional Crisis of 1787.* Baltimore: Johns Hopkins University Press, 1975.

Zoellick, Robert B. *America in the World: A History of U.S. Diplomacy and Foreign Policy.* New York: Twelve, 2020.

Index

About the Author

Kevin Jon Fernlund is Professor of History at the University of Missouri–St. Louis, where he teaches undergraduate and graduate courses in North American, Military, and Big History. A Fulbright Scholar (in Vietnam, 2001–2) and former director of the Western History Association (2006–12), he is the author of *Lyndon Johnson and Modern America* and *William Henry Holmes and the Rediscovery of the American West*.

CPSIA information can be obtained
at www.ICGtesting.com
Printed in the USA
FSHW011255140421
80343FS